HISTORY OF IMPERIAL CHINA

Timothy Brook, General Editor

The Early Chinese Empires: Qin and Han
Mark Edward Lewis

China between Empires: The Northern and Southern Dynasties
Mark Edward Lewis

China's Cosmopolitan Empire: The Tang Dynasty
Mark Edward Lewis

The Age of Confucian Rule: The Song Transformation of China
Dieter Kuhn

The Troubled Empire: China in the Yuan and Ming Dynasties
Timothy Brook

China's Last Empire: The Great Qing
William T. Rowe

D1211286

THE AGE OF CONFUCIAN RULE

THE SONG TRANSFORMATION
OF CHINA

Dieter Kuhn

THE BELKNAP PRESS OF
HARVARD UNIVERSITY PRESS
Cambridge, Massachusetts
London, England

Copyright © 2009 by the President and Fellows of Harvard College
All rights reserved
Printed in the United States of America

First Harvard University Press paperback edition, 2011

Library of Congress Cataloging-in-Publication Data
Kuhn, Dieter, 1946–
The age of Confucian rule: the Song transformation of China / Dieter Kuhn.
p.   cm.—(History of Imperial China)
Includes bibliographical references and index.
ISBN 978-0-674-03146-3 (hardcover)
ISBN 978-0-674-06202-3 (pbk.)
1. China—History—Song dynasty, 960-1279.
2. China—Intellectual life—221 B.C.–960 A.D.
3. Confucianism and state—China.   I. Title.
DS748.55.K84 2009
951'.024—dc22   2008006910

CONTENTS

	Introduction	I
1	A Time of Turmoil	10
2	Model Rulers	29
3	Reforming into Collapse	49
4	The Song in the South	71
5	Three Doctrines	99
6	Education and Examination	120
7	Life Cycle Rituals	138
8	Exploring the World Within and Without	160
9	Transforming the Capitals	187
10	A Changing World of Production	213
11	Money and Taxes	233
12	Private Lives in the Public Sphere	251
	Conclusion	276
	Dynastic Rulers	283
	Measures	286
	Pronunciation Guide	287
	Notes	289
	Bibliography	313
	Acknowledgments	341
	Index	343

MAPS

1. Landscape of Contemporary China   6
2. Provinces of Contemporary China   7
3. The Later Liang Empire and Its Neighbors   21
4. Provinces of the Northern Song Dynasty   60
5. Kaifeng and Its River Connections   73
6. Southern Song and Jin Dynasties   79
7. Tang Capital Chang'an   188
8. Northern Song Capital Kaifeng   193
9. Southern Song Capital Hangzhou   206
10. Road and Canal Network of the Northern Song   225

FIGURES

1. *Emperor Taizu Visits His Advisor on a Snowy Winter Night*   35
2. The Liao Pavilion of Guanyin in Jixian   116
3. The Coffin of Madame Sun Siniangzi   154
4. The Tomb of the Princess of Chen and Her Husband   158
5. *A Solitary Temple amidst Clearing Peaks*   170
6. *Sketches of Precious Creatures*   172
7. Emperor Huizong's *Cranes of Good Omen*   174
8. *Han Xizai's Night Revelry*   175
9. *Travelers along the River in Early Snow*   176
10. Ceiling Painting in a Liao Dynasty Tomb   178
11. Tomb Mural of Mr. Zhao and His Wife   180
12. Tomb Mural of Women Softening Silk Fabrics   181
13. Water-Power-Driven Astronomical Clockwork   185
14. Kaifeng City Gate, Street Life, and Wine Restaurant   198
15. Bulky Transport Barge on the Bian River   201
16. The Northern Silk-Reeling Frame   221
17. Water-Powered Bast-Fiber Thread-Twisting Frame   222
18. *Water Mill*   223
19. Relief Plate for Printing Paper Money   235
20. *Madame Zhou Doing Her Morning Toilet*   258
21. Portrait of Empress Liu   259
22. Translucent Sleeveless Vest with Peonies, in Leno Weave   266
23. Loom for Weaving Leno Fabrics   267

THE AGE OF CONFUCIAN RULE

The Song Transformation of China

INTRODUCTION

THE tenth-century transition from the late Tang to the early Song empire marks the most decisive rupture in the history of imperial China. The "old world" of the northern hereditary aristocratic families, with genealogies going back hundreds of years, finally vanished in the turmoil and civil wars between 880 and 960, and with their fall the old statecraft was forgotten or lost. A newly emerging class of scholar-officials, trained in Confucian doctrine and graduated in a competitive civil service examination system, was willing and well-prepared to take on responsibility for reshaping Chinese tradition. Their political, ideological, philosophical, cultural, literary, artistic, technological, and scientific achievements, combined with powerful economic forces that reconfigured daily life, have come to define our understanding of the Song as a transformative dynasty. Few periods in Chinese history are as rewarding as this in demonstrating the willingness of the Chinese to restructure and reform their society as a whole. Some historians have gone so far as to call the Song transformation a Chinese "renaissance" that heralded the dawn of modernity.

Previous dynasties had relied on the great families, aristocratic officials, scholars, and military men. It was only during the Song empire that thinking and writing, government and administrative action, were brought down to a common denominator, one which Peter K. Bol encapsulated in his translation of Confucius's term *siwen* as "this culture of ours." During the Song dynasty, a new self-consciousness and self-esteem took shape among the people who identified themselves as descendants of the Han Chinese. The social system they invented during the Song empire became the paradigm for what Chinese and Westerners of the twentieth century would refer to as "traditional China."

The Han empire (206 B.C.–A.D. 220) was built on a foundation of territorial and administrative unification laid by the Qin dynasty (221 B.C.– 206 B.C.). The Tang empire (618–907) profited from the consolidating achievements of the Sui dynasty (581–618). But the Song rulers faced a different and more difficult situation. The dynasty's founder, Emperor Taizu (r. 960–976), did not find the same sort of well-prepared ground for his empire that the Sui had bequeathed to the Tang. He and his brother-successor, Emperor Taizong (r. 976–997), still had to conquer the kingdoms in Sichuan, central, and south China as well as in Shanxi province in order to unify the realm. The third emperor, Zhenzong (r. 997– 1022), in an exemplary consolidation effort, took steps to enforce and stabilize the centralized state authority, and at the same time devised a foreign policy of coexistence that set the standard for centuries to come.

Aspiring to establish a long-lasting dynasty, these three model emperors understood that they must create precedents suitable not just for themselves but for their successors. They began by defining the "inner nature" of the dynasty and the centrality of Confucian ideology and cultural values. They then devised new policies of statecraft rooted in those precepts and specified the role of government officials in carrying them out. Like their predecessors in the Han and Tang, the new rulers consulted Confucian scholars in fashioning their reforms. But they added to this sage counsel the pragmatism of their own experience as military men and rulers. This time around, the recycling of Confucianism produced a surprisingly different result—a militocracy of a new make.

Hailing from a military background and aware of the disastrous consequences of military force during the past eighty years, Emperor Taizu realized the need for a powerful civil government. Following his lead, the Song emperors deliberately strengthened the civil principle (*wen*) over the military principle (*wu*). They negotiated bilateral agreements and peace treaties in response to the military challenges of the alien Liao, Xi Xia, and Jin regimes on their borders. To strengthen civil society, the Song emperors imposed economic, tax, and monetary reforms. Song scholars were encouraged to investigate nature, conduct experiments, and invent new technologies in agriculture, textile and ceramic production, iron refining, ship building, armaments manufacture, and many other fields. Merchants who carried those innovations to market were able to commercialize the remotest corners of the empire.

In architecture and urban planning, more open designs for cities in the Northern and Southern Song led to a twenty-four-hour lifestyle, and this in turn spurred the growth of local markets and national commerce. Innovative forms of entertainment appeared on the stage, and a new sophistication in the pictorial arts emerged. Philosophers throughout the realm widened their intellectual views to include concepts of rationality and broadened their categories for systemizing ideas and achievements. In the field of law, Confucian precepts led to a reduction in capital punishment. In almost all of these areas the Song outshone China's earlier model dynasty, the Tang.

This new order was sustained by the rise of a class of elite civil servants who were chosen on the basis of a nationwide examination in the Confucian classics. Getting a classical education became the key to a career of influence, privilege, wealth, power, and sometimes fame. New officials were recruited from the children of the scholar-official elite, the land-owning gentry, and wealthy mercantile families. Instead of handwritten scrolls, printed and bound books produced by a booming publishing industry helped families from modest backgrounds secure the education they desired for their children in private and state-run schools. Zhao Ruyu declared in 1194, when he held the position of chief examiner: "A scholar should congratulate himself that he has been born in such a time." In this heady atmosphere, the political, moral, and behavioral ideology of Confucianism came to regulate not just the public behavior but the private lives of the upper class. Passing the civil service examination would become the aspiration of tens of thousands of ambitious educated men in every dynasty until the abolition of the exam system in 1905.

Despite this new ladder to social status and comfort, most Song Chinese would never belong to the official class. The Song was a multilayered society, consisting at the bottom of the deprived and underprivileged who struggled for survival and at the top of a tiny class who lived in unimaginable luxury, in households numbering more than one hundred family members, relatives, and servants. In between were low-ranking officials, merchants, and farmers who tilled their own land. Living conditions for agricultural workers were better than in previous dynasties, but the majority still devoted their energies to solving the simple but critical problems of everyday life: how to obtain enough food for themselves and their families while avoiding oppression, exploitation, and misfortune. The taxes paid in cash, kind, and labor service by the anonymous and voiceless mass of self-managing farmers near the bottom of the social pyramid underwrote the economic prosperity and domestic security of more prosperous classes above them and made the new urban lifestyle possible.

The rich prose and poetry of the period bear witness to the living and working conditions of the common people as well as the affluent. Song poets felt sympathy for laborers and accused high-handed and self-enriching officials of oppressing them. But in the end the poets accepted the destiny of the masses as a natural state. Luo Ye, of whose life during Song times almost nothing is known, observed in his *Newly Compiled Tales of an Old Drunkard* (*Xinbian cuiweng tanlu*): "From ancient times until today, mankind has been divided into two categories of people: the clever and cultured, and the unlearned and coarse. The first kind knows the true value of life and respects the Five Virtues. The coarse fall into the worst iniquities." Only a few percent of all people in the history of China have escaped the designation of "coarse." Those among the Song who had to struggle against the eternal cycle of hard physical labor, erratic weather, the bad moods of landlords and superiors, the corruption of officials, and the trap of debt did not concern themselves with the aesthetic or philosophical preferences of intellectuals. The fashionable and insightful question-and-answer games of the privileged minority of scholars and officials held no meaning for them at all. When flood, drought, or plagues of locusts prevented them from delivering their tax crops, they faced the prospect of life in debt bondage. Those who abandoned the soil to earn their subsistence in handicraft lived on "wages determined by the current rate of room and board," as Han Yu observed in his biography of Wang Chengfu, the mason.[1]

If the Song dynasty reaped unprecedented benefits from the flowering of civil society, it also paid a price for its military shortcomings. The agricultural and sedentary Han Chinese had coexisted with nonsedentary nomadic people of the north and west for hundreds of years, gathering experience of their demands and menace, military invasions and warfare. But from the start, and more than any other previous Chinese empire, the Song had to share the former Tang territory with regimes of non-Chinese ethnic origin. At the dissolution of the Tang empire, the north and northeast regions of China (former Manchuria) belonged to alien dynasties that would hold on to this territory for more than 450 years, while the central plain, central, and south China were divided among the Five Dynasties (907–960) and the Ten Kingdoms (902–979). The viselike enclosure of Han Chinese territory during the tumultuous period of the Tang disintegration imposed an irredeemable mortgage on the Song empire.

This was the most difficult heritage bequeathed to one of the longest-lasting dynasties in Chinese history. Song emperors and their officials feared their neighbors as a formidable threat to their dynastic dominance and ethnic superiority. Even after the consolidation of Song territorial power in 979, the Song elites could not invent a remedy for the psychological disadvantage of being unable to equate the Song empire with the territorial achievements of the glorious Han and Tang dynasties. At its height, the Song empire comprised just over 2.6 million square kilometers, a territory much smaller than the Tang empire or the People's Republic of China, which today covers about 9.5 million square kilometers (Maps 1 and 2). During the 319 years of Song rule, no "China" as it was understood before or since existed, but rather a territory divided among different nations (peoples whose members share a distinct ethnic or cultural identity) and states (polities with centralized, bureaucratic governments), no single one of which held primacy. From a geopolitical vantage-point, a Song history is a study in regionalism.[2] Ultimately the dynasty would be unable to defend even this reduced realm.

In the view of many Song intellectuals, the barbarians on their borders differed greatly from the Han Chinese. They did not speak the same language or share the same cultural values. Their clothes were of a different cut, and their strangely shaved heads did not conform with Chinese practice. Especially important, they lacked the rituals of status differentiation that were so important to the Chinese—between prince and subject, father and son, man and woman. In short, from the Chinese perspective, they did not live at the center of world civilization but at the periphery. While these alien tribes may have been politically on a par with the Song and militarily superior, they were despised as the cultural inferiors of the Han Chinese.

Although many texts, from Han Yu early in the ninth century to later Confucians, can be read today as xenophobic, their main arguments were cultural, not racial. For Confucius, a person's degree of cultural assimilation determined whether he was regarded as Chinese or barbarian. About two hundred fifty years after Han Yu, Shao Yong described his understanding of himself and his place in the world in a single sentence: "I am happy because I am a human and not an animal, a male and not a female, a Chinese and not a barbarian, and because I live in Luoyang, the most wonderful city in the world." But after another hundred years had

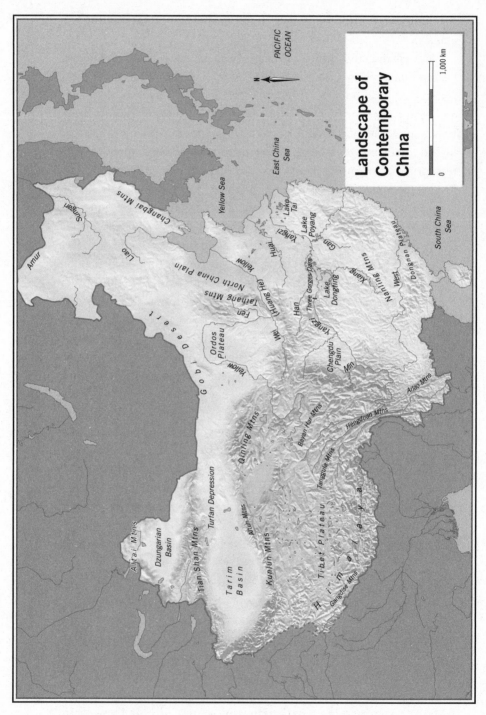

Map I

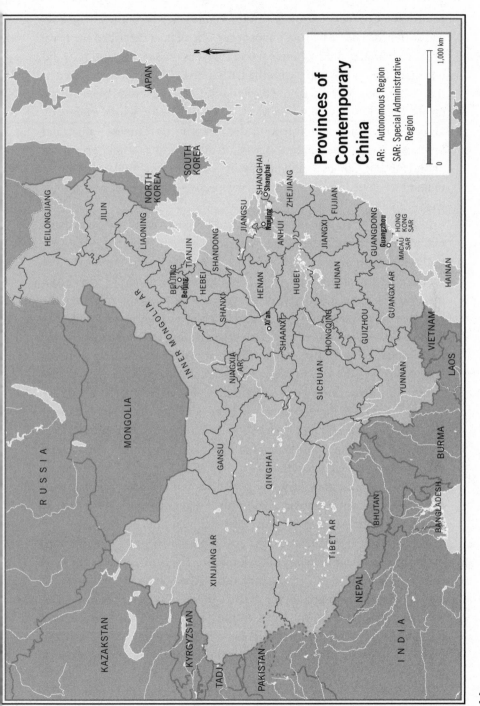

Provinces of Contemporary China

AR: Autonomous Region

SAR: Special Administrative Region

0   1,000 km

Map 2

passed, the Confucian attitude toward China's northern alien neighbors had stiffened. The utilitarian philosopher Chen Liang described the place of the barbarians in the Chinese world: "Just as the sages of antiquity did not share the central plain with the barbarians, 'China should share neither culture nor rituals with the barbarians.'"[3] Of the several alien groups on the Song borders, only the Mongol Yuan dynasty, which eventually absorbed the Song, would leave a deep imprint on Chinese values and practices. Today, the Chinese speak of their various ethnic groups as "non-Han but Chinese" and so pay lip service to the modern idea of a multiethnic state. This was not the perspective of the Song, nor of their less sedentary neighbors.

In 1126–27, facing an invasion by the alien Jin dynasty, the Song court was forced to abandon Kaifeng, its capital city on the central plain—the traditional Chinese heartland—and flee to remote, exotic territory in the south, where it held onto power for another 152 years, until 1279. Given the overwhelming military skill of its enemies, it is amazing that the Northern and Southern Song dynasties lasted as long as they did. The weaknesses of the empire in the face of aggression were many. In theory, Confucians denounced war as a matter of principle. The way of peace was regarded as the way of kings; war was condemned as the way of dictators. This orthodox view had its critics, and in practice the military strategists and moralist thinkers (who were all Confucians by education) spent a lot of time and energy debating issues of peace, war, and defense. Even Zhu Xi, the moralist champion of Neo-Confucianism, condemned the Jurchens as enemies with whom the Chinese cannot live under the same sky, "because they have murdered our fathers." But officials who advocated military initiatives against alien regimes faced a hard time at court, because most court officials favored a policy of coexistence.

Even when war was unavoidable, the Song's offensive strategies were outmoded and their defenses not a lot better. Four times before the final collapse—in 1005, 1123, 1142, and 1208—the Song accepted humiliating treaties that downgraded the dynasty to vassal status, thus sacrificing the principle of one world and one ruler in favor of *realpolitik* and a peace agreement with militant neighbors. Pragmatic chief councilors, experienced in financial matters affecting the national economy, convinced the emperors that paying annual subsidies to the alien regimes was far more economical than financing long-lasting war campaigns with uncertain outcomes.

Measured by military prowess, strategic innovation, and state hegemony, the Song was a weak dynasty, and eventually it was overrun. Its lingering death cannot be attributed to just one cause, but its emphasis on civil administration over military efficiency may have contributed to the weakening of the state and the decline of public morale. In the end, the desperate efforts of the Song to withstand foreign aggression failed. But at the height of its prosperity the Song was one of the most humane, cultured, and intellectual societies in Chinese history, and perhaps in all of world history. During the three centuries of Song rule, Confucian ideology became a powerful force in both public and private life, and government policy was framed by the ethical and educational precepts of this ancient philosophy. The revival and especially the reworking of Confucian values and patterns of thinking by the creative rulers, scholar-officials, and artists of the Song empire laid the foundations of education, government, and civil society for every succeeding dynasty, and strengthened a sense of chineseness among the descendants of the Han that would endure for centuries.

I

A TIME OF TURMOIL

HE IS called "emperor" in English, but the Chinese called him *huangdi,* meaning "celestial magnificence." As the Son of Heaven, the supreme ruler of the realm, the ritual head of state, and the chief of a dynastic clan, the emperor acted as the mediator between Heaven and the people. Heaven, variously interpreted as an ethical principle and also as a person-ified deity, was the authority through which the emperor ruled; yet the destiny of a dynasty was not Heaven-sent but man-made. And among men, the most important was the emperor. Heaven could not and did not make decisions: governing was the emperor's responsibility, and deci-sions were his to make.

This was the Confucian view, and in a memorial of 1085, Lü Gongzhu—a close companion of the Song chief councilor Sima Guang and sometime tutor of the heir apparent—explained its implications for the survival of a dynasty: "Although Heaven is high and far away, Heaven inspects the empire daily. Heaven responds to the deeds of the ruler. If he continuously cultivates himself and treats his people justly . . . then Heaven sends prosperity, and the Son of Heaven receives the realm for all times. There will be no misfortune and nobody will create trouble. If he, however, neglects the deities, ill-treats his people, and does not fear the Mandate of Heaven, there will be misfortune."[1]

Lü placed responsibility for dynastic decline squarely on the shoul-ders of the emperor, but this was far too simple. For more than 130 years, the Tang empire's system of government and administration had been solidly grounded in the loyalty and self-understanding of an aristocratic class and of educated officials who believed in the cultural and political achievements and superiority of the dynasty. The backbone of Tang society could not be easily broken within a few years or even decades by the incompetence of one ruler. The final disintegration of the Tang between 820 and 907 required several unqualified emperors and the most adverse conditions at court to drive the dynasty to ruin. Many officials and historians in the Song dynasty (despite their own Confucian education) understood this, and explained the downfall of their predecessors in the rational terms of failed statecraft.

When Li Chun, better known as Emperor Xianzong, ascended the "dragon throne" on September 5, 805, as the eleventh emperor of the Tang dynasty, the chances for the empire's survival improved considerably. Fifty years earlier, in 755, the Sogdian warlord An Lushan had led a rebellion that took control of the Tang capitals and forced the emperor to flee to the southwest. An Lushan was murdered by his own son just two years after the uprising, and in 763 the insurrection was finally crushed. But the next four decades were a time of turmoil for the Tang.

The prominent court official and Confucian scholar Han Yu received the news of Xianzong's ascent to the throne during his exile in Hunan province, where he had been reduced to the position of a petty police officer. Han was miserable in this post. He suffered from the humid climate, was alarmed by the strangeness of the natural environment in the south, and feared that he would be poisoned. When he heard the beat of the big drums in front of the county office announcing a new Tang emperor, Han knew that exiled and demoted officials like himself would be allowed to return to the capital.[2] As he wrote two years later in the introduction to the poem *The Sagacious Virtue of the Emperor of the Yuanhe Period* (*Yuanhe shengde shi*), he was convinced as he prepared for his journey home that a period of great peace had begun and that the Tang court would be restored to its former splendor. An amnesty was announced, and the people, old and young, were joyful. "Heaven has made you emperor to rule over all under Heaven," he told Xianzong, "and for one hundred thousand years happiness will prevail and nobody will be in want."[3]

And indeed, from the start of his rule, the emperor known to history as "the Restorer" forcefully tried to stem the tide of dynastic decline. An autocratic ruler and a man possessed with the rightness of his ideas, Xianzong (r. 805–820) not only invested his energy in trying to turn the power game with provincial governors in his favor but also deployed all of the administrative, financial, and military means available to him to recover control over the rebellious northeastern provinces and re-establish central authority. He and his competent officials were seriously committed to warding off territorial fragmentation and renewing the glory of the early Tang emperors.

Despite several setbacks, the relentless Xianzong achieved some of his goals. He restored the ruler's reputation and the dynasty's authority, and he regained control of some of the renegade northeastern provinces and the taxes they yielded. But Xianzong's highest ambition—to restore the Tang empire throughout its former territory—would not be fulfilled. He died on February 14, 820, allegedly at the hands of two eunuchs. The only successful emperor during the Tang dynasty's attempt at restoration thus met a violent death before seeing his reforms completed. After him, not a single candidate for the throne was powerful enough to hold the complicated system of officials, governors, and eunuchs in a productive balance. At several points in Chinese history the disintegration of a dynasty seemed to develop a momentum of its own, and that appears to have been the case with the Tang. During its last century, one able ruler was not enough to steer the damaged ship of state to safety. With Xianzong's death, the last hope for a recovery of the Tang was gambled away by ignorant court assassins who did not understand what was at stake.

The Tang decline accelerated under the four emperors who immediately followed Xianzong—immature and incompetent men who possessed neither the stature nor the stamina for the job. A contemporary, Du Mu, asked in a poem written in 825 why in the past seventy years so much shameful disgrace was brought on the dynasty. Emperor Xianzong had excelled in wisdom, but now, he wrote, trying to wipe out the rebels and insurgents is as difficult as climbing up to Heaven. Yet the personal deficiencies of Xianzong's successors were not the only causes of the dynasty's decline. The faltering empire was stalked by other dangers.

After Xianzong, the number of eunuchs increased to probably as many as six thousand, and many of them were promoted to high-ranking positions in the elite Palace Army. Their ability to manipulate succession to the throne made future emperors dependent on their services and their networks. Second, conflicts broke out within the ranks of government officials and paralyzed the government. Factional strife had been swiftly crushed in the past by powerful emperors, but there were no powerful emperors after Xianzong. And third, the weakness at the center of the empire gave strength to the military governors at the periphery and encouraged their aspirations for autonomy.

Emperor Muzong was just twenty-five years old when he ascended the throne in 820, following Xianzong's death. A product of the inner palace, he was inexperienced in matters of government, preferring to hold banquets, go hunting, and indulge his sexual appetites. In 823 while playing a game of polo—a rugged sport favored by the aristocracy—he suffered injuries to which he succumbed in 824. The men who followed him on the throne were at the mercy of their eunuchs. They were either murdered or inadvertently poisoned by them in a search for drugs that would extend their natural life. Muzong's son and successor, Emperor Jingzong, who, like his father, spent much time among a clique of eunuch polo-players, acquired notoriety for behaving in ways that even they considered unbearable. In 827, after a night of boozing with his fellow sportsmen, the nineteen-year-old emperor was murdered at their hands. His younger brother and successor, Emperor Wenzong, devoted himself to more studious pursuits, but he was neither quick-witted nor strong enough to emancipate himself from dependence on the eunuchs. He undertook two bloody, abortive attempts to get rid of them and then died, disillusioned, at the age of thirty, probably from an overdose.

Emperor Wuzong ascended the throne in 840 and promptly had his former competitors and their supporters executed. He became famous in Chinese history for his persecution of Buddhists. After Wuzong died six years later at the age of thirty-two—again, from drug poisoning—he was succeeded by Emperor Xuanzong (r. 846–859), a difficult and cranky man endowed with an excellent memory and a penchant for obsessively investigating court affairs. Although more than twenty-five years had passed since the suspicious death of his father (Emperor Xianzong) in 820, Xuanzong reopened the unsolved case and relentlessly persecuted all he suspected of involvement in this misdeed. In 859 Emperor Xuanzong too died from poisoning. The reigns of his successors—Emperor Yizong (r. 859–873) and Emperor Xizong (r. 873–888)—were characterized by even more intense eunuch power, official strife, and growing disorder in the northern provinces. The last two emperors, Zhaozong (r. 888–904) and Jingzong (r. 904–907), witnessed the final conquest of the dynasty by alien powers.

The Persecution of Buddhists

Once every thirty years during the Tang dynasty, with crowds of tens of thousands in attendance, a bone relic of the Buddha was ceremoniously transferred to the capital and displayed in Buddhist temples. In 818 Emperor Xianzong observed the grand spectacle from a tower and ordered the eunuchs to bring the relic to the palace so that he could examine it himself. The official Han Yu, perhaps driven by his concern for the popular welfare as well as by personal political motives, reacted passionately and even xenophobically to this news. In his 819 *Memorial on the Bone of the Buddha* (*Lun Fogu biao*) he described the Buddha as "a man of the barbarians who did not speak the language of China and wore clothes of a different fashion."[4] Han contended that Buddhism had shortened the life spans of previous emperors, and he questioned the emperor's involvement in Buddhist affairs. Regarded as a milestone in the relation of Confucian intellectuals to the "foreign" religion of Buddhism, Han's memorial expressed an anti-foreignism that would flourish during the Neo-Confucian revival of the Song dynasty.

But in the 840s, when systematic persecution of Buddhists suddenly intensified, the fundamental cause lay not in anti-foreignism or even in religious disputes. The crisis arose because of a tax system that favored the aristocratic clans, big landowners, and the Buddhist church, which had amassed large monastic estates over the centuries. During Emperor Xianzong's rule, officials had discussed the urgent need for tax reform to stabilize the national economy and the state treasury, but all proposals met with stiff opposition by the profiteers of the system. After his death, as the tax yield dwindled away, poverty and famine caused despair in the countryside, and ruthless assaults by bandits in the villages from Henan province to the Huai River forced many farmers and tenants to take up their belongings and migrate to safer areas. To address the crisis, the government needed to tap new financial resources.

Seizing the assets of Buddhist monks seemed to offer a simple and, in Chinese history, a well-established solution to the financial shortfall—it had already been successfully practiced in 446, 486, 574, and 577.[5] In 842 Emperor Wuzong started a campaign to secularize the Buddhist church by expropriating more than 4,600 monasteries, temples, and estates, melting down Buddhist sculptures of gold, silver, and bronze, and converting the precious metals into coins and ingots. In the process he compelled 265,000 Buddhist priests, monks, and nuns to return to the secular world as common taxpayers. In addition to abolishing the tax-exempt privileges of the clergy, he registered as taxpayers more than 150,000 slaves who had served in Buddhist monasteries.

The secularizationists destroyed more than 40,000 religious buildings of various types, innumerable scriptures, and other precious religious objects. Emperor Wuzong used strong words in his proclamation against Buddhism, describing the campaign as an effort to get rid of the Buddhist pest and to root out evil. He proudly declared his persecution of Buddhism a political success, but the Japanese monk Ennin, an eyewitness to Emperor Wuzong's campaign, considered these acts a disaster for Chinese Buddhism.[6]

In 847 Emperor Xuanzong reversed course and allowed Buddhist monasteries to reopen and religious activities to resume, and his successor, Yizong, became a fervent promoter of Buddhism. In 955, however, the Later Zhou Emperor Shizong once again looked to Buddhist monasteries for a solution to the dynasty's cash-flow problem. Citing deplorable conditions and low morale, he dissolved most of the monasteries and confiscated their metal and other valuable objects. By the time the Song came to power in 960, only 2,694 monasteries out of 30,336 had survived this purge.

Shizong went further by issuing an edict prohibiting self-mutilation and other acts of religious devotion that had been practiced by Buddhists for centuries. In a state of ecstasy and frenzy, some fanatics sacrificed pieces of their own flesh on the altar, cut off limbs, or immolated themselves. Shizong's edict was designed to bring such ecstatic acts of "Buddhist fervor" to an end, along with the religious charisma they generated.[7]

Three and a half centuries after Emperor Wuzong's persecution of Buddhism began, a poet voicing public opinion against the religion would ask the rhetorical question, "Until there is an end to huge halls, giant Buddha statues, how can the weary people ever escape hunger and death?"[8] This remained a persuasive opinion among elites and state officials in the Song dynasty, though the majority of the Chinese people certainly did not agree.

Banditry in the Countryside

Proceeds from Buddhist estates replenished the coffers of the privileged classes and the emperor, but they did not stabilize the weakened Tang economy or relieve the state's ongoing financial crisis. Due to a heavy tax and labor service burden in the 850s, the economic situation of farmers in the countryside became desperate, even in the agriculturally well-developed southeastern regions. As the living conditions of farmers slid below subsistence level, they looked for other sources of income to survive. Rather than abandon their small farms, some of those who had tilled the soil for generations sold their children into slavery or rented out their wives. But many were still unable to cover their tax debts, and eventually their property was seized. Displaced and landless, former owners and tenant-farmers who had lost their families and homes viewed banditry as a way to secure a livelihood and escape the landlord's bullies, the claws of usurers, and the local police force.[9]

In January 860 the robber chief Qiu Fu gathered approximately 30,000 followers in eastern Zhejiang. In 868 a mutiny of Tang troops at the southwestern frontier in Yunnan province paved the way for a large-scale rebellion under the command of the supply officer Pang Xun.[10] When Pang Xun reached Xuzhou in the same year, his so-called Righteous Army, composed of deserters, vagrants, peasants, beggars, robbers, and river pirates, numbered more than 200,000 men. The Tang army reluctantly called the alien Shatuo Turkish cavalry into action to put down the insurrection, but still it took a year of fighting to defeat the rebels.

Political order was restored on the surface, but for ordinary people, especially the rural population, living conditions continued to deteriorate. During the 870s bandit gangs grew large enough to attack small fortified towns and pose a danger to the prefectures, whose administration was hampered by military border conflicts, crop failures, and famine. The most infamous bandit leader was the unsuccessful examination candidate Huang Chao—"the mad bandit" as he was sworn at by the poet and official Wei Zhuang. Huang hailed from an affluent family that had managed a profitable salt trade, and at first he operated with his gang in western Shandong and eastern Henan.[11] In 878, calling himself the "heaven-storming generalissimo," Huang became the leader of all the bandit troops. When government forces put pressure on him, he marched his army southward across the Yangzi, plundering affluent cities in his path in order to fill his war chest. In May 879 he sacked Guangzhou and massacred 120,000 people, including Indian, Arabic, and Persian merchants and their families, along with Chinese.

By July 880 his band had grown to 600,000 men, and for the first time he attempted to topple the Tang dynasty. In December he conquered Luoyang and immediately marched westward to take the capital city of Chang'an. The young Tang emperor Xizong—having lost faith in the once-elite Palace Army, which by this time had deteriorated to ranks of mostly untrained and elderly soldiers—followed the example of Emperor Xuanzong, who in 756 had fled from the troops of An Lushan to the safety of Sichuan province. While there, Xizong received the message that Huang Chao had entered the capital in January 881, proclaimed himself emperor of the Qi dynasty, and made himself and his bandit entourage at home in the Imperial City.

Though Huang Chao held the capital in an iron grip, he was unable to obtain urgently needed supplies to feed his huge army, and for the next two years his men resorted to cannibalism.[12] In 883 Huang's army killed more than a thousand people every day for food. Cannibalism had been known in Chinese history for a long time as a desperate response to starvation, but under certain circumstances it was also an act of piety, vengeance, bravery, punishment, or torture. On many occasions when rebels ran out of food, they captured people and ate them; sometimes they salted or pickled the corpses to preserve them for later consumption. In years of famine, humans were slaughtered like livestock, chopped to pieces, and cooked for food. Human flesh was often more plentiful and cheaper than dog meat. In 1366 Tao Zongyi wrote in his *Talks While the Plough Is Resting (Chuogeng lu)* that "in the past and present rebellious soldiers have eaten human flesh. They called it 'flesh of thought' or 'two-legged mutton'. These are unnatural practices of bandits which cannot be eradicated."[13]

With its capital overrun by the heaven-storming generalissimo's army, the Tang court in far away Sichuan called the young Shatuo Turk Li Keyong (856–908), leader of the dominant military power at the northern border, for help. When Li approached the capital city in 883, Huang Chao hastily retreated to Henan and shortly thereafter returned to his native Shandong province, where he and his family were beheaded by members of his own clan in the summer of 884. The following spring the young Tang emperor Xizong returned to a capital city in ruins.

By then the Tang dynastic house had lost control of its former empire.[14] Too many areas were in rebellion, and too many warlords contended for local authority. The poet Wei Zhuang, who was in Chang'an during the depressing years when Huang's bandits overran the capital, described the situation in his narrative poem *The Lament of the Lady of Qin (Qinfu yin)*:

> Chang'an lies in silence: what's there now?
> In ruined markets and desolate streets, ears of wheat sprout . . .
> The Hanyuan Hall is the haunt of foxes and hares . . .
> Along the Avenue of Heaven one walks on the bones of high
> officials.[15]

Military governors acting as independent warlords treated the emperors Xizong and Zhaozong as their vassals. Zhu Wen (852–912), born into the family of a poor teacher of the Confucian classics, became one of the most willful, pugnacious, and brutish of these men. In 903 he solved his problems at the Chinese court by rounding up the eunuchs in the emperor's residence and murdering them. On February 15, 904, he ordered his men to pull down all the buildings in the city and transport the construction materials to Luoyang. That same year, he ordered Emperor Zhaozong to be killed, and in 907 he forced the last Tang emperor, Jingzong, to abdicate. Proclaiming himself founder and ruler of the Later Liang, he declared his dynasty the successor of the Tang and elevated his military stronghold, the city of Kaifeng, to the position of Eastern Capital.

The demolition of Chang'an in 904 and its reduction to a military prefecture in 907 meant far more than just the physical loss of the Tang metropolis and a capital that had served China for more than a thousand years. It traumatized the Chinese people and brought to an end the age of dynasties dominated by aristocratic families, with their now-antiquated values and out-dated notions of statecraft.

Five Dynasties, Ten Kingdoms

Zhu Wen was the most successful of the warlords, but he was not the only man who participated in the dismemberment of the Tang imperial territory.[16] By 907 the empire was split up among at least ten political newcomers—most of them landless peasants, robbers, and smugglers, but at least one a former slave—whose military and political careers began with bloody campaigns to establish regional strongholds. Their territories were collectively known as the Ten Kingdoms, named after old regional states in the Zhou dynasty of the first millennium B.C. As political powers, most of these kingdoms were much weaker than the Five Dynasties that would rule over the former Tang territory comprising the heartland of north and northern central China in quick succession. But by promoting commerce and creating a favorable climate for the flourishing of the arts, some of these kingdoms made cultural contributions that would later be credited to the Song.

The Five Dynasties are known today as the Later Liang (907–923), Later Tang (923–936), Later Jin (936–947), Later Han (947–951), and Later Zhou (951–960). In 912 Zhu Wen, founder of the Later Liang, met the same fate he had so mercilessly delivered to his many enemies. One of his sons killed him, and shortly thereafter the assassin himself fell victim to his brother, Zhu Youzhen.[17] The first of the Five Dynasties, like the four that would follow, was ruined not by its founder but by the incompetent rulers who succeeded him.[18]

In January 923 Li Cunxu, son of Li Keyong—the Shatuo Turk who had helped the Tang dynasty drive Huang Chao and his band from Chang'an—proclaimed the Later Tang dynasty, with Luoyang as its new capital. The dynasty's name revealed the founder's program: to restore the Tang to power. Eunuchs and aristocratic officials who had escaped the previous slaughter and been in hiding for years returned to the court. But the clock could not be turned back: Li Cunxu was killed in 926 by mutinying troops. His successor, Li Siyuan (r. 926–933), realized the dynasty's administrative shortcomings and chose to begin his rule with a frightening demonstration of his political determination: he liquidated the eunuchs at his court. He also made an effort to revitalize the official bureaucracy, which had suffered decades of neglect, and he built the Imperial Bodyguard, an army that served the emperor exclusively. After his death, the throne changed hands twice, but the dynasty survived only another four years before it was succeeded by the Later Jin dynasty.

The Later Jin developed the Imperial Bodyguards into an effective instrument for keeping the governors and their troops under control. But in 938 the Khitan empire to the northeast forced the Later Jin to cede sixteen northern prefectures to them, and in 947 the dynasty collapsed. Its successor, the Later Han dynasty, tried to counteract the Khitan influence, but in 951, after its second emperor, Yindi, got involved in the murder of a great number of prominent officials, the commander of the Imperial Bodyguards—a Han Chinese by the name of Guo Wei—rebelled and proclaimed himself emperor of the Later Zhou dynasty. Having understood and profited from the dangerous potential of the Imperial Bodyguards, he replaced it with a new Palace Army under his personal command. When Guo Wei died in 954, he was succeeded by his adopted son, Chai Rong, who was in turn succeeded by his six-year-old son. In February 960 the commander of the Palace Army, Zhao Kuangyin, orchestrated a coup d'état that deposed the child emperor and founded his own dynasty, the Song. He became the first Song emperor, Taizu. Looking back at the history of the Five Dynasties about one hundred years later, Ouyang Xiu characterized this period of Chinese history: "The Five Dynasties lasted only fifty years. Five times changed the state and there were thirteen rulers from eight [different] families. Of the scholars who were unfortunate enough to emerge in this period, few could keep their integrity intact when they attained their complete restraint."[19]

When the Song dynasty came into power in 960, it had to accept a geopolitical system in which no state dominated all its neighbors.[20] The Song continually had to negotiate power with the alien states on its borders. In the northeast was the Khitan (Great Liao) empire and in the northwest was the Tangut (Xi Xia) kingdom. In the southwest, the Nanzhao (and later the Dali kingdom) and in the south the kingdom of Annan (Vietnam) had established themselves as political powers long before the Song dynasty was founded. Along the western border were the Tibetans and the Tuyuhuns. Even in China proper, the ruling families in three of the successive Five Dynasties had been Shatuo Turks.

Their fear of alien regimes, particularly of the Liao and Xi Xia to the north, impeded the ability of the Han Chinese to recognize the regional achievements of these peoples. The "barbarians" were viewed as uncivilized intruders who disturbed the proper course of history, which meant Chinese history exclusively—the only history considered worthy of being investigated and recorded. The Liao emperors were well aware of the Chinese cultural arrogance. But the Song Chinese, for the duration of their dynasty, were always surrounded by these uncultivated peoples, with their unknown origins, strange appearance, uncivilized customs, disconcerting behavior, and unimaginable nomadic way of life. They had no choice but to deal with their unpredictable chieftains and rulers, who often commanded ferocious military forces that challenged the ethnic, cultural, and political, as well as military, hegemony of the Han Chinese.[21]

The Khitan Empire (Great Liao Dynasty)

The tenth century was the century of alien regimes. In 907, the year that the Tang fell to the Later Liang dynasty, the leader of the Khitan tribe to the northeast, Abaoji (872–926), established the Khitan khanate. Later known as the Great Liao dynasty, it would become the dominant military power of the tenth century (Map 3).

The Khitans belonged to the Eastern Xianbei tribes, who in the first half of the first millennium lived in today's southeastern Inner Mongolia.[22] Most of the Khitan people were pastoral. Moving from place to place to find water and grass, they made a living from herding, fishing,

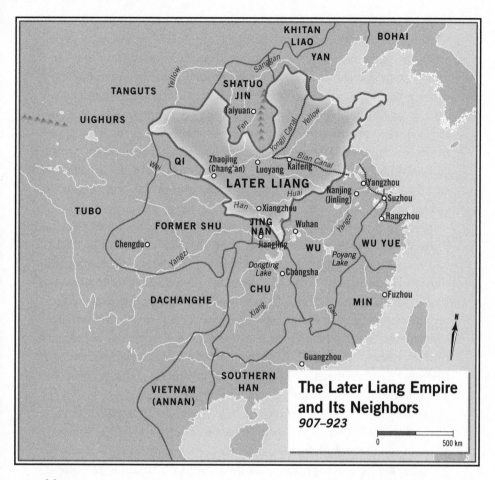

Map 3

and hunting. They raised sheep, horses, and cattle, and with their ox-drawn carts they covered long distances between the northwestern steppes of the camel breeders and the southeastern agricultural lowlands of the pig breeders. Some Khitans may have tilled the soil, but most farmers who lived within the Liao territory were Han Chinese or members of other non-Khitan ethnic groups. Like most nomadic people, for whom garments made of leather, wool, felt, and fur were indispensable, the Khitan also bartered for textiles, especially silks, which were regarded as a valuable commodity.

When the great Khitan leader Abaoji, of the Yila tribe, assumed the title of *kaghan* (supreme ruler), or khan, in 907, the office was elective, though only members of the leading family of the ruling clan were eligible for election. If the family failed in its responsibilities, it was quickly replaced by another competitor for power. In 916, when Abaoji was re-elected a fourth time to the position of khan, he decided to follow Chinese custom and assume the title of emperor in a formal ceremony. His dynasty was named Khitan. Some years after Abaoji's death, his clan—once more in the Chinese manner, and contrary to the tribal custom of the Khitan—adopted Yelü as the family surname.[23] In 947 the Khitan emperor—yet again following the Chinese model—changed the dynasty's name to Liao, and then Great Liao. Thus was the Yelü family, which had once headed a confederation of Khitan clans, transformed into an imperial household.[24]

In 983, one year into the reign of Emperor Shengzong, the dynastic name Khitan was restored. Then in 1066 the name was changed back to Liao. During Mongol rule over Central Asia in the first half of the thirteenth century, the ethnic designation "Khitan" was transmitted as Kitaia, Cathaia, and Cathay into the Slavonic world and southern and central Europe and became a synonym for China, especially northern China. Marco Polo (1254–1324), the famous Venetian merchant-traveler, referred to China as Cathay.[25] Only in the sixteenth century did Europeans realize that Cathay and Manzi (southern China) formed the geographical unity that today makes up China.[26]

The founder of the Khitan empire, Yelü Abaoji, set the model for rule in his dynasty. To secure his leadership, he ordered the killing of thousands of opponents, whom he regarded as rebels. In 916 he pronounced his eldest son, Bei, as his heir apparent—a cultural adaptation to Chinese hereditary succession. The Yelü clan felt uneasy about this, but Abaoji's adoption of Chinese customs continued unabated. He founded a Confucian temple and preferred the great Confucius over Buddha because the Han Chinese had followed this philosopher throughout most of their history. Also in the Chinese manner, he built a Supreme Capital (Shangjing), though he and the Khitan nobles continued their nomadic practice of touring their territory, living in yurts, and ruling from temporary residences according to the season. "During the autumn and winter they shunned the cold; during the spring and summer they avoided the heat . . . For each of the four seasons [the emperor] had a temporary place as residence."[27]

In 920 Abaoji ordered the creation of an ideographic script, based on Chinese characters, in which each large character represented a single word (logogram).[28] Five years later, Abaoji's younger brother, Tiela, the most talented language expert among the Khitans, created an additional script of small characters representing sounds (phonograms) which, taken together, formed a word.[29] With the invention of these two scripts, the hitherto illiterate Khitans were able to communicate in writing, and this achievement sent a political signal of their determination to create an ethnic and cultural identity of their own. It took several years and the exchange of a number of official documents before Chinese scholars at the court of the Later Tang dynasty were able to decipher Khitan script. To date, approximately 370 small characters have been identified and partially decoded.[30]

Abaoji's reign was marked by a series of aggressive military campaigns. In 924 and 925 he subdued the tribes of northern Mongolia and pressed far west to the Orkhon River and into the western Gansu corridor. His second son, Deguang (902–947), occupied the northeastern Ordos region, where the Tuyuhun and Tangut tribes had settled. One year later, Abaoji conquered the wealthy Bohai kingdom in eastern Manchuria and made his son Bei ruler of the newly created vassal kingdom Dongdan, situated at the border of present-day North Korea.

Abaoji died in September 926, and his elder son—a cultivated scholar well-versed in Chinese art and literature and an expert in music and medicine—was not, to the other chieftains' taste, a Khitan leader. Rejecting Bei as the heir apparent, they preferred Deguang, who also had received a proper education but in addition excelled as an experienced warrior. Furthermore, Deguang had the support of his mother, Empress Chunqin, who later bore the title Empress Dowager Yingtian. Known as the "blood and iron empress," she was in command of her own strong force of horsemen.[31] After her husband, Abaoji, died, she showed strong determination to participate in ruling the Liao empire. In accordance with Khitan custom, she should have followed him into his grave, but instead of sacrificing herself, she cut off her hand and had it placed in his tomb.

As Emperor Taizong (r. 926–947), Abaoji's second son continued the military policy of his father. In 938, when he forced the Later Jin dynasty to cede sixteen bordering prefectures in present Beijing, Hebei, and Shanxi—including the prefectures of Youzhou (Beijing) and Yunzhou (Datong)—to the Liao, the Khitans gained control of two major entrances into China. After intense fighting, Taizong in early 947 triumphantly marched into the Later Jin capital, Kaifeng, pillaged the palace and the residences, took the Emperor Chudi (meaning "the emperor who went away") prisoner, along with his family, and humiliated him by deposing him as ruler and mocking him with the title "duke of infidelity." While occupying the capital of Kaifeng, Emperor Taizong must have taken note of its cultured urban lifestyle and the political significance of Chinese architecture.

The year 947 was a busy time for Taizong. He ordered the deportation of Chudi, his family, the ladies of the harem, eunuchs, and artists—175 persons in all—to his Supreme Capital in Manchuria. He changed the name of his dynasty from Khitan to the Great Liao dynasty, and in the same year he founded the Southern Capital of the Liao dynasty near Beijing, which copied the ward model of the former Tang capital Chang'an. The southward extension of the Liao state called for a reorganization of its political structure.[32] The territory was divided into a northern and southern region, a division that took into account long-existing cultural and ethnic divisions. This administrative system worked on the principle of dual administration, but the central offices of both administrations (the governments or chancelleries) were based in the Supreme Capital.

The administration of the Northern Region was called the "national system." The region included the Supreme and Central Capitals and was home to the tribal Khitan people. The administration of the Southern Region was known as the "Han-Chinese system." That region, which included the Southern, Eastern, and Western Capitals, was home to the Han Chinese, the Bohai, and other sedentary people whose government was deliberately modeled after the Tang government. The northern administration employed only Khitan officials and wielded more power; the Xiao clan, which supplied all of the female consorts for the Yelü clan, had the political say there. The imperial Yelü clan dominated in the south. This model of government, for the first time in Chinese history, paid tribute to the specific features and demands of a multiethnic society.

When the Khitan troops started to plunder the villages of Hebei in 947, they met fierce resistance from various quarters. Emperor Taizong decided to withdraw to the north and abandoned the idea of proclaiming himself emperor of north China. His successors followed his example and refrained from strategies of conquest but devised a less strenuous way to benefit from the wealth of their industrious Chinese neighbors. By the tenth century the Khitans no longer behaved as nomadic peoples had done in previous centuries—by attacking one another when they were in need of essentials for their own survival. By the early eleventh century they had learned how to seize fortified towns in order to expand the state's territory. These new and more efficient techniques of warfare helped secure a reliable subsistence and strengthened the unity of the clans.

When the eleven-year-old Yelü Longxu (posthumously named Shengzong) was selected to become the sixth Liao emperor on October 14, 982, one of the few competent, well-balanced, and just rulers of the Liao empire ascended the throne. During the first half of his long reign, the Empress Dowager Chengtian (942–1009) controlled the court and the dynasty.[33] She even commanded her own troops on the battlefield against the Song. The *Dynastic History of the Liao* (*Liao shi*) characterizes the rule of her son this way: "Shengzong may be viewed the most successful Liao emperor; most [of his success, however, must be attributed] to his mother's instruction."[34] In several wars he finally succeeded in pacifying much of northern Asia. By 997 he ruled over Manchuria. The Jurchens and the Tanguts depended on him as vassals, and in China he held the region of Beijing and Datong.

In two decades, with an empire extending from eastern Manchuria to the Tianshan Mountains in the west, Emperor Shengzong had created the preconditions for a balance of power in Inner Asia that lasted for almost one hundred years.[35] He could decide whose envoys he wanted to receive, who he would consider a worthy vassal, with which nations of Central Asia he would exchange presents and establish relations. He entertained connections with Japan and the Arabic Abbasids, who asked for a marriage arrangement with a Khitan princess. With his oath agreement of 1005 at Shanyuan, which established peace with the Song, his historical reputation was guaranteed.

The Liao emperors now had enough silver ingots in their coffers to reward loyal vassals. The much sought-after silk products they received as tribute from the Chinese, along with the presents of the Song's annual envoys, enabled them to make a profit while satisfying the demands of the barter trade in the markets of Central and West Asia.[36] Shengzong also constructed roads and bridges and reclaimed wasteland for farmers. In 988 he made a serious attempt to win the sympathy of the Chinese elite within his territory by establishing the *jinshi* civil service examination on a regular basis for his Chinese subjects exclusively.[37] Shortly afterward, twenty to forty candidates graduated annually. In total, the *jinshi* examination, which was held in the Southern Capital fifty-four times, produced about two thousand Han Chinese graduates. In 994 a Liao calendar was introduced which followed the Chinese model.[38]

After a reign of almost half a century, Emperor Shengzong died on June 26, 1031. Yelü Zongzhen (1016–1055), later canonized as Emperor Xingzong, succeeded him to the throne. Once again, the boy's mother, Noujin, assumed the regency and ruled the empire, and even after she was banished in 1034 she was able to reappear at court and exert some political influence. Emperor Xingzong favored Chinese methods of governance and promulgated a Chinese-based code of laws, which was revised in 1051. His positive attitude toward Chinese culture, combined with the heavy burden of military service, caused tensions within Khitan society. The pro-Khitan opposition managed to keep the Han Chinese within Khitan borders under control, not allowing them to buy slaves or own bows and arrows.[39]

In 1044 a border rebellion led to a war between the Khitans and the Tanguts that lasted until 1053. By the time Emperor Xingzong died on August 28, 1055, the most prosperous period of the Liao dynasty had come to an end.

The Tangut (Xi Xia) Kingdom

As in the case of the Khitan, most information that has come down to us about the history of the Tanguts is from biased sources written in Chinese.[40] We do not know how the Tanguts perceived their own history. Even the dynastic histories of China refused this regime the legitimate status of a Chinese dynasty by excluding it. Chinese scholars hold the opinion that the ruling house of the Tanguts can be identified with the Dangxiang, a Qiang tribe inhabiting the steppes of Qinghai and parts of northwestern Sichuan from Han times onward.[41] By ethno-linguistic criteria, the Tanguts are related to the Tibetans. The origin of the name Tangut, which appears in inscriptions in 735, is not known. It was later used and propagated by the Khitans.[42] The Tanguts called themselves Mi or Mi-nyag, in Chinese Miyao or Mianyao.

The essentials of what we know about this kingdom can be briefly described. In the late eighth century the Tanguts—under pressure from Tibetans and other peoples—obtained permission from the Tang court to settle in Xia prefecture, at the inhospitable borderland of the Ordos Desert, a region that supported hunting, herding, and raising livestock but little agriculture. In exchange, the Tanguts helped the struggling Tang dynasty in the 870s and 880s, especially against Huang Chao. One of the Tangut leaders adopted the Tang dynastic family name Li and was enfeoffed by the Tang as the duke of Xia. The Tanguts enjoyed an autonomous status and political independence as long as they remained subservient to the Tang.

The early Song emperors were fully aware of the military power of the Tanguts, who, under the leadership of Li Yixing (d. 967) for thirty-two years, had solidified their position in the northwest. The Song's founding emperor, Taizu, looking for an ally against the far more dangerous Khitans, showed a keen interest in continuing peaceful relations with them. Thus, the prestigious title of king of Xia was posthumously conferred upon Li Yixing. Though this gesture of friendship appeared to recognize the Tangut state's autonomy—provided it remained a peaceful and subservient vassal to the Chinese state—in fact the Song as well as the Liao emperors were intent upon forcing the Tanguts to accept a subsidiary status.

A period of difficult relations followed. In 982 Tangut envoys under the leadership of Li Jipeng (d. 1004), who was very fond of Chinese urban life, surrendered to the Song and offered the court the four central Tangut prefectures in present-day Shanxi province in exchange for titles and subsidies which would allow them a Chinese lifestyle. But the majority of Tanguts, who for more than three hundred years had put down roots in this land, did not agree with this humiliating and selfish act of treason. Li Jiqian (963–1004), a cousin of Li Jipeng with a reputation for martial skill, raised a military force of 20,000 warriors to stir up tribal unrest and provoke, not very successfully, the Song forces along the border. The year 982 is often designated as the beginning of the Sino-Tangut war, which lasted with interruptions until 1004.[43]

In 986 when the second Song emperor, Taizong, unsuccessfully invaded Liao territory, Li Jiqian offered his submission to the Liao dynasty. This act did not hinder another branch of the Tanguts from continuing peace negotiations with the Song. The new, rather uneasy Tangut-Khitan relationship turned out to be a constant source of friction, despite Li Jiqian's marriage to a Liao princess in 989 and the conferring of the title king of Xia on him by the Liao emperor.[44] He extended the Tangut territory to the west and north, into the Gansu corridor and neighboring Inner Mongolia.

By the last two decades of the tenth century, the various branches of the Tanguts, including the Liao vassal Li Jiqian and the Song dependent Li Jipeng, formed the third side of a power triangle with the Song and the Liao. Li Jiqian's son, Li Deming (983–1032), continued to maintain the

tribe's difficult dual relations into the next millennium. He was acknowledged by the Liao ruler in 1004, yet in 1006 acted as military governor of
Dingnan with a Chinese title given by Emperor Zhenzong, who provided
him with cash, tea, silk, and a donation of winter clothing. In 1028 he extended the Tangut territory to the important trade centers of Ganzhou,
Liangzhou (Wuwei), and Zhangye. The economic preconditions for an
independent Xia dynasty as it was founded in 1038 were thus put in
place.[45]

The relations between the Xi Xia and Liao in the tenth century were as
tense as between the Song and its northern neighbors. The Song government of Emperor Zhenzong realized that its military forces were not able
to defeat the Liao and the Xi Xia forces nor recover the northern territories formerly belonging to the Tang empire. Thus the Song pragmatically
decided to negotiate affordable peace terms with their belligerent northern neighbors. These efforts resulted in bilateral peace treaties with the
Liao dynasty in 1005, renegotiated in 1042, and with the Xi Xia in 1044.
Aside from the Xi Xia wars in the early 1080s, the keyword characteriz-
ing Song foreign policy toward the northern regimes was, in modern
terms, "coexistence." The Song paid annual subsidies in silk and silver
and thus saved a lot of money that would have been squandered on futile
war campaigns. The Liao and Xi Xia courts used these revenues to sus-
tain their clansmen and allies, secure their loyalty, and stay in political
power. Coexistence secured by subsidies was the Song strategy to solve
problems at the northern border until the Mongols arrived on the historical stage.

2

MODEL RULERS

BETWEEN 960 and 1022, the early emperors of the Song and their councilors set high standards of governmental practice, intellectual activity,
and personal conduct that would serve as a model for their successors.
The first two emperors, Zhao Kuangyin (Emperor Taizu) and his brother
Zhao Kuangyi (Emperor Taizong), were regarded during Song times, and
still today, as exemplary rulers—the most vigorous and politically astute
emperors of the dynasty.[1] The third emperor, Zhenzong, in the early part
of his reign, completed the consolidation of the realm that his uncle and
father had started and developed an innovative foreign diplomacy that
kept peace with the Song's powerful neighbors to the north. Under the
leadership of these three men—all lovers of learning—Song China came
closer to the ideal of Confucian rule than any other dynasty in Chinese
history. "This dynasty," a memorial submitted shortly after 1169 by the
utilitarian philosopher and state theorist Chen Liang confirmed, "bases
the state on Confucianism; the strengthening of Confucianism [in this
way] is unique among the previous dynasties."[2]

The term "Confucian state" does not denote anything abstract, theoretical, or utopian and should not be confused with idealized constructs
of Confucian rule borrowed from antiquity. Rather, it points to the "his-
torically close association of the leading intellectual tradition with the
dominant bureaucracy."[3] Confucianism rooted in the classics offered an
ethic based on humaneness, righteousness, appropriateness, filial piety,
loyalty, the civil principle over the military, and the performance of rites.
It was taken as a guide to action designed for a cultivated upper class—an

educational elite that relied on the service of all the other classes in a hierarchically organized society.

Although Confucianism incorporated religious elements from pre-Confucius times such as ancestor worship and state sacrifices (both dressed in strict and much-debated ritualism), the Confucian state cannot be compared with medieval Christian kingdoms or Islamic caliphates—political structures inseparably linked to monotheistic creeds that claimed sole rights. Song emperors could live and perform rituals according to Confucian rules but still be devoted followers of Daoism and Buddhism. It was only in the thirteenth century that the formerly pragmatic Confucian ideology started to be transformed into state orthodoxy.[4]

The Confucian state of Song times had no chance of surviving in subsequent dynasties. But contrary to critics of the nineteenth and twentieth centuries who viewed Confucianism only as a rigid corset inhibiting Chinese development, many rules and values that grew out of the Song's Confucian ideology helped a rapidly changing Chinese society after Song times to maintain some of the defining cultural particularities that are still considered valid even today.

Founding the Dynasty

The fall of the Later Zhou dynasty and the rise of the Song began shortly after July 27, 959, when the sudden death of the Emperor Shizong put a six-year-old boy on the dragon throne. Early the next year, Zhao Kuangyin, confidential advisor to the late emperor and inspection commander of the Palace Army, marched with his troops northward to fight the Khitans and their ally, the Northern Han. Zhao seized this opportunity to stage a well-prepared coup d'état.[5]

Out of personal loyalty to their commander, Zhao's troops—following an established procedure for usurpation—proclaimed him Son of Heaven at the courier relay station near Chen Bridge, about 20 kilometers northeast of Kaifeng.[6] After being asked three times to accept the throne (these requests were part of the ritual), Zhao agreed, but under two conditions: that the generals would obey his orders and that they would not harm the child emperor or the population of the capital. A short time later, Zhao Kuangyin officially took control of the empire, the child emperor was forced to abdicate, and the Song dynasty commenced on February 3, 960.

The new Emperor Taizu (meaning Supreme Progenitor) named his dynasty "Song" after the ancient name of the place in Henan province to which he was assigned before seizing power. Taizu took control of 111 prefectures divided into 638 counties.[7] He established his Eastern Capital in Kaifeng (formerly Bianzhou), which had served that function for the preceding Later Liang, Later Jin, and Later Zhou dynasties. And as with all the previous major dynasties, he established a secondary capital (the Western Capital) in present-day Luoyang.[8]

During his seventeen years on the throne, Emperor Taizu laid the foundations for a dynasty that would continue for over three centuries and produce eighteen rulers. In every Chinese dynasty, the founding emperor —entrusted with the Mandate of Heaven—set the indisputable and idealized model of rule and behavior for the successive reigns of his descendants. He was the person who provided, pronounced, and lived the political—and in many cases the cultural and intellectual—pattern of the dynasty that all his successors and their subjects would abide by.

The *Dynastic History of the Song* (*Song shi*), written in the fourteenth century, explains the exemplary role of the founder this way: "From antiquity one could predict the pattern of a dynasty from the founding and unifying ruler and what was esteemed [by him] in his times. When the Cultivated [and Virtuous] Progenitor [Emperor Taizu] changed the mandate, he first employed civil officials and took power away from the military officials. Esteeming the *wen* [civil principle] by the Song had its origin in this."[9] Around 1060 the philosopher Shao Yong praised the Song rule as an extraordinary feat in Chinese history because, among other reasons, the pacification of the empire was accomplished after the establishment of the throne, and for a hundred years there has been no threat of insurrection.[10] More than one hundred years later the philosopher Zhu Xi unemotionally summed up this view: "Our dynasty looked into [the policy of] the Five Dynasties and brought the warlordism to an end."[11] The priority of the civil principle over the military principle—a fundamental ideal of Confucianism—became the creed of the Song dynasty.[12]

A northerner whose native home was in Zhuo county in today's Hebei province, Emperor Taizu was born in the Jiema garrison of Luoyang as the second of five brothers. According to legend, at his birth "a rosy glow filled the chamber and purple mist wafted to the rooftops."[13] He excelled as a military leader, horseman, and archer, but he was also a remarkable civil administrator. He refused to sentence his officials to death for simply disagreeing with him, preferring forfeiture of rank or salary, exile or banishment, as the typical punishments for official misconduct—an example adopted by his successors. Though dangerous or treacherous officials were sometimes assassinated, as reported from Southern Song times, officials critical of imperial policy made wide use of their relative freedom to engage in often heated debates.

Emperor Taizu was idealized by Chinese historians as a protector of the people who aspired to live by the humanitarian and benevolent standards of Confucian teachings. A modest man who detested luxury and splendid residences, he sympathized with the common people in the countryside and concerned himself with the economic well-being of the nation. As characterized by the famous scholar and reformer Fan Zhongyan, Emperor Taizu was a noble man: first in worrying about the world's troubles and last in enjoying its pleasures.[14]

Unifying the Realm

Emperor Taizu's ascent to the dragon throne ended more than eight decades of treason, warfare, raids, bloodshed, and slaughter, but he still faced a host of problems. A number of local power-holders who styled themselves as kings of independent states had to be eliminated in order to unite Chinese territory under his rule. New governmental and administrative structures were required to support an efficient civil service bureaucracy, and an elite class of loyal, committed, well-trained, and educated officials had to be appointed. Furthermore, foreign relations with the Khitan empire demanded more efficient military and diplomatic strategies. The new ruler approached these many tasks with alacrity, though he did not live long enough to see them all accomplished.

Having risen to power in the military ranks and being well acquainted with the political ambitions of his brothers in arms, Emperor Taizu must have felt a strain in his relations with the other commanders. This may explain why—at the occasion when his troops proclaimed him Son of Heaven—he demanded that the generals swear to obey his orders. He wanted to end the warlordism that had developed over the past eighty years once and for all. From his time in active service, he understood the danger that powerful commanders posed to a young dynasty. But he also knew that he had to rely on these very forces at least until the Song empire could be unified.

On the one hand, Zhao's aspirations were directed at giving the nation a period of peace and security unknown for many decades, and this could be achieved only by consolidating a civil system of government and strengthening civil order at the expense of military rule. But on the other hand, any social reforms that the high military ranks construed as weakening their position could easily lead to an unwanted confrontation with his commanders, who would fear losing face, status, political influence, and financial advantages.

According to the Chinese history books (though whether all of this happened in the way the history books describe remains open to debate), Emperor Taizu asked his advisor Zhao Pu how to handle this difficult balancing act. The loyal official recommended that he first regain military power over the regional commanders. The emperor took this advice.[15] He masterminded a cunning act of social engineering without parallel in Chinese history. On August 20, 961, he gathered the former conspirators who had helped elevate him to the throne, along with other senior commanders, for a drinking party. This episode later became famous as "dissolving military power over a cup of wine," an expression meaning to remove people from power in an easy and discreet way.[16] He subtly and diplomatically suggested to the senior commanders that they should relinquish their military authority, leave the court, and serve as governors in the prefectures. There, they would be furnished with a mansion and a large estate where they could enjoy life until the natural end of their days. Emperor Taizu must have explained his position most convincingly, for the next day—or so the story goes—all of the commanders accepted his offer.

In the years to come, the old commanders were replaced by younger generals who were subordinate and loyal to the emperor and who conducted warfare in keeping with his humane principles: do not loot the countryside, do not abuse the civilian population, avoid loss of life whenever possible.[17] This model of rule, unique in Chinese history, could not be ignored by his contemporaries or successors throughout the empire.

But Emperor Taizu's emphasis on the civil principle was not designed to reduce the manpower of the dynasty's military forces. On the contrary, the number of career soldiers in the Palace Army and in provincial forces increased steadily.[18] By the early 970s the emperor personally commanded an army estimated at 220,000 men.[19] At the end of his rule it totaled 378,000. This inflationary growth may have occurred because Emperor Taizu had to defeat the kingdoms of the south, in addition to policing the northern territory he had inherited from the Later Zhou. During the reign of his brother and successor, Zhao Kuangyi (Emperor Taizong, Supreme Ancestor, r. 976–997), the army increased to 666,000

men, and by 1018, when the third emperor, Zhenzong, suggested a reduction of the empire's military forces, their number had reached astronomical proportions: 912,000 men.

The unification of China and the annexation of the six remaining kingdoms of the Ten Kingdoms represented not only a political but also an
economic necessity. The emperor urgently needed money to underwrite
his border war against the Liao dynasty in the north, and a critical element in obtaining these funds was the submission of the kingdoms in central and south China to taxation. On the challenge of reunifying all Chinese territories under his rule, Taizu remarked to his brother: "From the
time of the Five Dynasties the evil of war pervades and the state treasury
is empty. We should first get hold of Shu [Sichuan], thereafter of
Guangnan and Jiangnan [the south and southeast]. Only then we are able
to satisfy the needs of the nation."[20]

In several campaigns over a period of almost twenty years, conducted
by both Taizu and Taizong, the remaining independent kingdoms were
conquered. The strategy started in 963 with Southern Ping at the middle
Yangzi, followed by Later Shu in Sichuan province in 965. But in 968
Emperor Taizu was not sure what to do next. As a general, he knew that
the submission of the Northern Han kingdom that bordered the powerful
Khitan empire should take military priority, but victory there would not
be easy to achieve. Perhaps it would be best to solidify the south first.
During one of his many sleepless nights he decided to consult his advisor,
Zhao Pu.[21]

As he had done so often before, the emperor sneaked out of the palace
in disguise so that he could talk with his counselor in private. The scene
was depicted by Liu Jin in a painting captioned *Emperor Taizu Visits His
Advisor Zhao Pu on a Snowy Winter Night* (*Xueye fang Pu tu*). Zhao Pu
had returned home, though he was still dressed in his official robe and
hat, when he heard someone knocking at the front gate. Opening it, he
was shocked to see the emperor standing there, snow swirling all around.
They seated themselves on mats in the hall, and the charcoal fire was lit
to roast meat (Fig. 1). As soon as Zhao Pu's wife had served wine, the
two men started to talk about the emperor's urgent concern. Zhao Pu
convinced him that "the south first, the north later" was the strategy to
follow.[22] So the emperor decided to unify the remaining southern states
before tackling the thornier problems in the north, following Zhao's advice of "the easy first, the difficult later."[23]

The Southern Han in Guangdong and Guangxi fell in 971, and the

Fig. 1   *Emperor Taizu Visits His Advisor Zhao Pu on a Snowy Winter Night.*
Liu Jun, fifteenth century. Section of a hanging scroll, ink on silk. Palace
Museum, Beijing.

Southern Tang with its capital Nanjing in Jiangsu followed in 975, along
with Jiangxi. Shortly after ascending to the throne in 976, Emperor
Taizong completed the unification of the Song territory with the submission of the southeastern Wu Yue kingdom in Zhejiang in 978, and the
Shatuo Turkish Northern Han in Shanxi in the first month of 979.

    In the north, the unification process was hampered several times by
Liao interference, especially in the 960s and early 970s. And even after unification was completed in 979, the Song army suffered a terrible
defeat that July on the banks of the River Gaoliang (situated outside
the present Xizhimen Gate of Beijing).[24] Emperor Taizong, who led the
troops, barely avoided being taken prisoner by escaping in a mule cart.
Two months later the Song army was defeated at Mancheng, and other
military setbacks followed until the reign of the third emperor, Zhenzong.

    Emperor Taizu died suddenly under suspicious circumstances on No-
vember 14, 976, at the age of forty-nine.[25] With heavy snow falling outside, the emperor summoned his younger brother to his deathbed, to give

him instructions about succession to the throne. Nobody else was present to overhear their conversation. Popular speculation had it that Zhao Kuangyi murdered his brother Emperor Taizu, "the sound of the axe in the shadow of the flickering candle." However, it is more probable that Emperor Taizu fulfilled the promise he had given to Empress Dowager Du on her deathbed that he would be succeeded by his younger brother, even though he had two adult sons by the time of his death. Elevating a brother rather than a son to the throne, as the succession procedure required, was unprecedented, but it may have helped to prevent a dynastic crisis.[26] Fulfilling the prophesy of a Daoist god mediated by a Daoist priest—a prophesy that amounted "to nothing less than a divine justification"—the younger brother succeeded Taizu as emperor.[27] Emperor Taizu's sons did not live to grow old. The elder cut his own throat in 979, and the younger one died an unspecified death soon afterward.

Centralizing State Authority

Emperor Taizong was a military man like his brother (though less likable), and by 979 he ruled over the largest territory in Song history. In 984 he officially acknowledged the decades of the Five Dynasties as a historical period and adopted the symbolic element of fire and the corresponding color red for the Song, thus legitimizing the dynasty in the cosmic order. Red had been the color of the ancient Zhou dynasty, whose Confucian philosophy influenced Song scholar-officials so deeply and with such lasting effect.

In addition to adopting his brother's mission of unification, Taizong committed himself to Taizu's program of civil reform. Centuries later, Xu Du (c. 1156) would describe the dynasty's early governance this way: "From the founding of the dynasty there were many reforms in many areas of politics. All officials were asked to join the discussion about the reforms envisaged."[28] There may have been consultations in the early days, but exchanges of opinions did not take place in a relaxed atmosphere of tea drinking, as had been the case between the early Tang emperors and their councilors.[29] Taizu and Taizong probably entertained their senior officials at banquets and other sorts of gatherings, and no doubt they asked for comments on the advantages and disadvantages of various courses of action. But the first two Song emperors ultimately decided important questions by themselves. More than half a century later, in his essay *On the Difficulty of Being a Ruler* (*Wei jun nan lun*), Ouyang Xiu commented: "Alas, the difficulty of selecting [suitable] men is great indeed! But it is not as difficult as judging advice."[30]

Song officials could only envy their Tang predecessors, who merely had to get an imperial "okay" before issuing the relevant edict. The Song court felt overawed and stifled by the emperor's authority and presence. Thus, they asked to be allowed to submit written summaries on all matters of concern, for the emperor's preliminary consideration before meetings took place. The emperor granted this formal procedure and thus created a new bureaucratic standard of court behavior. Although these written memoranda strengthened the position of the emperor and enhanced the authority of the dynasty, this form of direct governing could function only as long as a workaholic emperor ruled China. During the reign of Emperor Zhenzong, senior officials gained influence at court, and informal discussions and decision-making became the norm.

After founding his dynasty and particularly while unifying its territory, Emperor Taizu needed a loyal and competent class of civil officials to staff his palace bureaucracy, the provincial administrations, the ministries, and the numerous agencies and bureaus throughout the realm. The population's support of his dynasty, which Taizu enjoyed, was no substitute for officials who could function as reliable intermediaries between the emperor and the people. China during this period had no institutionalized authorities comparable to medieval Europe's Catholic Church, nobility, and merchant organizations, which kept cities running and balanced the power of the king. The Song empire needed a system that would reliably supply these much-needed civil servants. The system of governance that Emperor Taizu finally chose was similar to that of the Tang dynasty, but with some basic differences.

First, the Song emperor could no longer rely on members of aristocratic lineages, whose power had been based on birth and landholding, to fill his offices. During the previous eighty years of turmoil, the various wars and factional conflicts had considerably reduced the number and influence of these elites. A new class of scholar-officials, drawn from a wider social background, would have to step into the vacancy.

Second, the Song adopted the Tang system of government, which consisted of many obsolete offices, titles, and functions. It cried out for restructuring, and the first three Song emperors made attempts to eliminate discrepancies and redundancies and streamline the system. But over time the result was an even more complicated overlay of bureaucracy.

Third, Emperor Taizu designed the structure of his government with one primary goal in mind: to strengthen and centralize power in his own hands. The bureaucracy was designed to serve the interests of his dynasty exclusively. He appointed qualified officials who were responsible to him directly, and the efficiency of this centralized system of authority depended on the energy and commitment of the emperor himself. When less able rulers came to the throne, the defects of centralization became more apparent, especially during the period of disruption when the Northern Song collapsed and the Southern Song was unable to find ways to consolidate its power.

According to the *Dynastic History of the Song,* the government consisted of the traditional Three Departments: the Central Secretariat, the Chancellery (an advisory agency), and the Department of State Affairs. Each department was headed by a chief councilor whose official duty was "to assist the emperor, to manage the hundred offices and to regulate the numerous affairs of state, and to have all matters controlled."[31] The chief councilors could have been equal in rank, but internal differences in their official designation were evident from the additional official titles they held as well as from the principles of seniority they followed.[32] Only the Central Secretariat was placed inside the palace precinct, where it played a powerful role in decision-making. The other two departments were situated outside the palace and functioned as the executive core of the central government. Their charge was to handle all sorts of paperwork and implement the decisions, edicts, commands, and orders of the emperor. The Department of State Affairs comprised six ministries: Personnel, Revenue, Rites, War, Justice, and Works.[33] In 1129 the Central Secretariat and the Chancellery were fused into one Secretariat.

Fiscal affairs were under control of the State Finance Commission, an independent branch of the government that had been under the authority of the chief councilors during the Tang dynasty. Another powerful and independent unit, the Bureau of Military Affairs, served as a counterpart to the Central Secretariat. These two ministries held most of the power and were able to exert influence on the emperor.[34] The whole structure of the various governing bodies, however, leaves no doubt that it was tailored to fit the early emperors' concept of direct rule, and that putting this elaborate bureaucratic routine into effect day after day could work efficiently only so long as the control-obsessed rulers who established the system were on the throne.

Throughout its long history, the Song government provided many examples of the growing influence of the chief councilors and of competing political constituencies among officials, at court, and within the imperial family. Yet these complicated networks of power did not relieve successive emperors of their responsibilities as the Son of Heaven. They must have felt the system's focus on one man at the center, in charge of and responsible for everything, as a heavy burden. Physically and psychologically weak emperors found themselves at the mercy of empress dowagers and court officials.

Emperor Taizu wanted the upper echelons of officials, particularly the chief councilors who were in close contact with him, to be men of learning. Therefore as early as 973 he initiated "a palace examination under his own personal supervision" that allowed him to get a direct impression of his potential appointees.[35] The palace examination was not a Song invention: it had already been practiced by the Tang empress Wu Zetian in 689. During Emperor Taizu's entire rule, no more than 350 degrees were awarded.[36] It was Emperor Taizong, realizing the need for loyal men throughout his large empire, who prepared the ground for a nationwide civil service recruitment system. In 977 he proclaimed his wish to search broadly for superior men, and shortly thereafter five hundred candidates received a variety of degrees—more degrees in one year than his brother had awarded during his entire reign. Throughout Taizong's tenure, 5,816 candidates, many of them from humble backgrounds, became degree-holders.[37]

Emperor Zhenzong emulated his father by topping his predecessor's examination results. In the third year of his reign (1000 A.D.), the number of degree-holders who passed the final examinations in the capital reached 1,538—the largest number of successful candidates in the entire history of the Chinese civil service examination system, before or since.

An elaborate system of written examinations led some candidates to the most highly esteemed degree of *jinshi* (presented scholar, very often translated in Western languages as "doctor of letters"). In 983 it became the custom to honor the graduates of the *jinshi* examination with a banquet in the Imperial Garden of Magnificent Trees situated in the western part of the capital. New scholar-officials no longer derived their worldview from their family background and genealogy but from their knowledge of the Confucian canon, from their understanding of Confucian ethics, and from their ability to function as administrative generalists. The result was a new career path for scholars—as professional civil servants—and a new class of scholar-officials drawn from a broad range of backgrounds. The social identity of these officials as a nationwide elite endured for almost a millennium.

Printing and Politics

The tenth century holds a key position in the history of Chinese printing and book publication.[38] Following in the footsteps of several officials and scholars who had commissioned the printing of books, Emperor Taizong promoted and administered a number of extensive publication projects, garnering a reputation as a cultivated and erudite ruler in the process.[39] In addition to continuing to publish the Confucian classics in the 980s and 990s, Taizong initiated the collation of official historical works.[40] His successors, the emperors Zhenzong and Renzong, carried on this newly invented "tradition," which led to twenty-one historical collations, not to mention compilations in other fields of endeavor.

The creation of these compilations no doubt nurtured the working relationship between the emperor and his scholar-officials and led to a mutual understanding of Chinese cultural and intellectual history. But there was also a political side to Taizong's book projects that should not be underestimated. His employment of scholars who had served under Emperor Taizu allowed Taizong to put to rest questions about the legitimacy of his rule, after having followed his brother to the throne under questionable circumstances. Furthermore, Taizong's employment of scholars from conquered or pacified kingdoms must have relieved some of the stresses these officials felt after the deaths of those rulers. Eight hundred years later, the Qianlong emperor would observe that the main purpose of the publication activities of Song Emperor Taizong was to legitimize the rule and restore the virtue of an emperor who had "usurped" the throne.

Emperor Taizong could call on a tradition of book printing that went back more than half a century. In 925 Wu Zhaoyi, minister in the state of Later Shu in Sichuan, commissioned a printing of the *Anthology of Rhyme Prose* (*Wenxuan*), a work originally compiled between 526 and 531. Impressed by these activities in Sichuan, in 932 Feng Dao, who served as a minister to eleven rulers in five different dynasties between 907 and 954—a career unprecedented in Chinese history—undertook a printing of the Confucian classics from woodblocks; it was completed in 953 in 130 volumes. As if trying to keep ahead in a competition with

Feng Dao, Wu Zhaoyi published another edition of the Confucian classics in 951 in Sichuan. Private persons could purchase the books.

After his conquest of the Later Shu in 965, Emperor Taizu came across Wu Zhaoyi's name in one of the confiscated publications. Because the emperor was fond of his work, Wu Zhaoyi was the only high official of the Later Shu court who was not punished and whose property was not expropriated. As for Feng Dao, Song officials (unsurprisingly) made him the scapegoat for all the ills of the Five Dynasties. The chief councilor and historian Sima Guang criticized him about one hundred years later as "an inn to many travelers," that is, a man lacking loyalty.[41]

These publication initiatives document the fact that by the middle of the tenth century—with a delay of more than two hundred years, compared with the mass publications of the Buddhists—print had become an accepted medium of communication in Confucian circles. Taizong's appointees were assigned to institutes and archives, where they compiled a wide range of materials. Among the first publications was the *Finest Flowers of the Preserve of Letters* (*Wenyuan yinghua*) of 982, an anthology of literature in one thousand chapters that was the gigantic successor to the *Anthology of Rhyme Prose* (*Wenxuan*). Three major publications bear the programmatic title of his reign period, Taiping xingguo (Ascended Nation in Grand Tranquility), which lasted from 976 to 984. The first, *Extensive Records of the Grand Tranquility Reign* (*Taiping guangji*) of 978, edited by Li Fang (925–996) and others, was an anthology of sociological and mythological items that included tales, feats of magic, omens, strange talents, dreams and ghost stories, oddities and novelettes, and much more in the form of quotations from 485 original titles composed during the Han and Tang dynasties.

A few years later, in 984, the same editor and his group of more than ten scholars finished compiling the *Imperially Reviewed Encyclopedia of the Grand Tranquility Reign* (*Taiping yulan*), the largest encyclopedia of Chinese knowledge available in print at the time. Items were selected from 1,690 sources and arranged in one thousand chapters with 5,363 subsections in chronological order. Among the main sections are heaven, earth, rulers, literature, rituals, military matters, diseases, anatomy, barbarians, flora, and fauna. It took Emperor Taizong an entire year to read the compilation and make suggestions for corrections.

Around 980 Yue Shi completed the third publication bearing the reign title: the *Record of the World during the Grand Tranquility Reign* (*Taiping huanyu ji*). Like the other works, it was based on Tang publications, but at two hundred chapters, including biographies and various types of literature, it replaced a shorter national geography of 813 written by Li Jifu. This geography greatly influenced the composition of local gazetteers in later dynasties.

The great compilation projects carried out primarily under Emperor Taizong publicly demonstrated that the Song dynasty embraced the cultural traditions of the Han Chinese and intended to preserve them for future generations.[42] To cap off his achievements, in 996, the year before his death, Taizong ordered a commission of scholar-officials headed by Xing Bing "to prepare an authoritative edition of the classical texts."[43] His son and successor, Emperor Zhenzong, who also cherished written works, saw to the completion of the publication of the *Seven Classics* (*Qijing*), comprising 165 chapters, in October 1001. In 1011 an edition of the *Thirteen Classics* (*Shisanjing*) as we have them today was finished—an indispensable set of books for all candidates taking the civil examinations and for future historians of Chinese culture.[44]

Now it was possible for civil service candidates to obtain copies of literary and historical works and study them in preparation for their examinations. Printing technology also helped the state gain control over the proliferation of knowledge during the Song "renaissance." By deciding what did and did not rise to the level of book publication, scholar-officials helped to define both knowledge and education. Equally important, the emperor's participation in these publishing projects allowed the dynasty to set standards and conventions—for authorship and title, paper and ink, format and binding—that would be influential far beyond Song times. Without the economic success and the general acceptance of printing in Song society, the revival of Confucian learning on a nationwide basis, at a price within reach of most who aspired to become civil servants, could not have happened in such a short period of time.

As so often happens, this new technology provoked opposition in some quarters, particularly from scholars whose hand-written manuscripts were being replaced. The versatile writer Su Shi (1037–1101) feared that the quality of scholarship would suffer. Ye Mengde (1077–1148) complained that the quality of texts would deteriorate and that printed texts would be considered perfect, even when they were riddled with errors. And Zhu Xi, whose Neo-Confucian philosophy profited most from the new medium, grumbled that people read books carelessly and inattentively, that they no longer learned texts by heart, and that they considered copying a text by hand as too much to ask.

Despite these complaints, the eleventh century saw the invention of movable type, which replaced carved woodblocks. The scholar-official Shen Gua attributed the invention of this new printing technology to Bi Sheng in the 1040s, but it was the scholar-official Wang Zhen, an expert in many fields, who overcame the technical problems of the new printing technology with publication of a local gazetteer in 1298.[45]

All of these great compilation projects publicly demonstrated not only that the Song emperors viewed themselves as responsible for the up-keep of the cultural tradition but also that they were prepared to exploit a new technology to popularize the Confucian message. The cultural and economic consequences that resulted from the popularization of printing in Song times cannot be overrated. As paper production increased, printing centers mushroomed in the southeastern provinces and in Sichuan, and they invented standards of all sorts for their products—ranging from layout, font, and color of ink to the size and quality of paper and methods of binding. With these improvements came a change in the upper class's attitude toward reading, writing, and collecting texts. Once individual handwritten manuscripts no longer had to be copied by hand but could be endlessly reproduced for a mass market, the value of products and their price changed as well. Handwritten manuscripts, now rare, became precious, legitimately printed books became affordable, and pirated copies became cheap. Scholars were able to set up book collections, even libraries. The invention of movable-type printing may well be compared with the revolution that took place in writing and composing texts a few decades ago, when the typewriter was replaced by the personal computer.

The Rule of the Civil Principle

Emperor Zhenzong, who reigned for almost twenty-five years, lacked experience in warfare and did not enjoy a reputation as a warrior. Compared with his autocratic uncle and father, he was regarded as a bookish, indecisive, weak emperor easily swayed by argument.[46] He made good use of his abilities in the early years of his tenure, however, by expanding the civil examination system and establishing an administrative structure on all levels. The Central Secretariat became the most important place for regular consultations between the emperor with his chief councilors and for decision-making.

Zhenzong tried to rule in conformity with the civil principle propagated by his father, and he came close to the ideal of a Confucian ruler.

He opened his morning audience at dawn in the front hall of the palace. As a rule, audiences took place on the fifth and tenth days of every ten-day cycle. The emperor received his chief councilors and senior officials from the Bureau of Military Affairs, the State Finance Commission, the capital city of Kaifeng, and other government agencies. He listened to the lengthy reports submitted to the throne, which afterward had to be discussed and decided. This work dealing with reports and memoranda continued after breakfast. Only in the afternoon was the emperor released from his duties and allowed to retire to his private quarters.

The evenings could well involve another meeting with his ministers. We learn from a petition to Emperor Shenzong by Lü Gongzhu, filed in 1085, that at every moment the emperor had to conform to a strict code of conduct and virtue: "Each single action and each word of a ruler has to be written down by the historian. If you [the ruler] display a lack of virtue, it is not only to the disadvantage of the people but its recording in the histories will serve as a source of ridicule for countless generations. Therefore you should rise early and go to bed late, work hard and refine your self-cultivation, rule righteously and just and control your heart in agreement with the rites. The most minute goodness should be practiced, the smallest evil should be eliminated."[47]

Generally, Zhenzong's rule was in line with the examples set by his predecessors. And after his reign, governing followed a fairly uniform pattern, until a major reorganization took place between 1078 and 1085.[48] If his reign had come to an end in early 1004, Zhenzong's decisions and actions would have secured him a prominent place in the history of the Song dynasty. But his rule was far from finished on January 25, 1004, when the reign period Xianping (Total Tranquility) was replaced by the reign period Jingde (Manifest Virtue).

The reign period Total Tranquility was not in fact totally tranquil. It was overshadowed by a problem that Emperor Taizong, at the time of his death, had left unresolved: the dangerous military encounters with the belligerent Khitans of the Liao dynasty. As early as 999 Emperor Zhenzong attempted to come to peace terms with the Khitans, whose forces were raiding north China, but his efforts were a diplomatic failure. His determination, however, was commented on favorably even two hundred years later by Hong Mai.[49]

In those years the Liao empire was ruled by the Empress Dowager Xiao, and the Khitan horsemen served under her command. In autumn

1004 the self-confident and awe-inspiring chief councilor Kou Zhun persuaded Emperor Zhenzong to follow the example of his predecessors and establish his military reputation by taking personal command of the Song army on the battlefield. Emperor Zhenzong emphatically rejected the advice of Wang Qinruo to move the court to the safety of Nanjing in central China or even Sichuan, as the Tang emperors had done. Instead, he decided to give evidence of his military determination.[50]

Negotiations between the Khitan and the Song took place even as military conflict continued. Emperor Zhenzong wanted to stop the bloodshed, and the Khitans had stretched so far from their home base that they risked having their supply lines cut off. Fearing an escalation of the war on both sides, the emperors of the Song and Liao finally agreed on two oath documents (shishu) dating from January 19 and 24, 1005, which were exchanged on January 28, 1005. These oaths became widely identified with Shanyuan, a small town north of Kaifeng.[51]

Chief councilor Kou Zhun and Emperor Zhenzong heralded this peace treaty as a great diplomatic success. In modern terms, it was a bilateral agreement to maintain a nonaggressive foreign policy, with minimal concessions: an annual indemnity payment from the Song to the Liao, termed a military compensation, of 200,000 bolts of tabby weave silk fabric and 100,000 ounces of silver (around 3,730 kilograms).[52] The silk cloth, stretched out end to end, would have reached an impressive length of about 2,400 kilometers, but in terms of its financial burden on the Song treasury this tribute payment amounted to around 2.5 percent of the tax income collected in the form of silk fabrics during any given year of the eleventh century.[53] The silver tribute was far more costly for the Song because it depended on the widely varying conditions of silver production. In addition, the rulers agreed not to disturb farms or construct new fortifications and canals along the border they had demarcated, and they promised to detain robbers and fugitives who crossed over from the other side.[54]

Most of his contemporaries and later generations of scholar-officials applauded and admired Kou Zhun, who had adopted a wise and pragmatic policy of pacifying the barbarians by combining defensive military maneuvers with the cultivation of virtue. He succeeded in bringing hostilities to an end at an affordable price without ceding any territory to the northern aliens.[55] Zhenzong introduced coexistence as a reasonable option of Chinese foreign policy. A few officials, however, such as Kou

Zhun's rival Wang Qinruo, criticized his tactics as reckless, dangerous, and humiliating. The problem with the peace treaty, from a Chinese perspective, was that the Song emperor actually recognized the Liao emperor as his counterpart and vice versa, thus creating virtual equality. The ideological fiction that the Chinese "Middle Kingdom" was the center of the civilized world and that the Chinese emperor was the only ruler under Heaven was in danger of becoming mere rhetoric.

The only way the Chinese could maintain their supremacy and authority was by introducing into the agreement the fiction of "brotherhood." According to the old Chinese family model, the Liao ruler had recognized the Song ruler as the "elder brother" and himself as the "younger brother." Nevertheless, the consequences of fraternal treaties such as this which resulted in brotherly states must have been well understood in Song times. The Song dynasty would never be able "to attain the full glory of Tang." This became even more apparent in 1042, when the old treaty of 1005 was renegotiated to strengthen diplomatic parity and the brotherly relationship. The Song's annual payment obligations increased to a total of 300,000 bolts of silk and 200,000 ounces of silver.[56]

In some political quarters the oath agreement was not condemned as humiliating or a sell-out of Chinese supremacy. A fair acknowledgment of the advantageous facts is well reflected in the *Records Following Emperor Yao* (*Zun Yao lu*), a private history written by Luo Congyan and published in 1225, where we learn that Kou Zhun, the architect of the Shanyuan agreement, still ranked among the rather small number of ten famous officials between 960 and 1063.[57] And the fourteenth-century chief editor of the *Dynastic History of the Song* would not have included the statement that "the Song did not at all yield precedence to the Han and Tang" if he had judged the treaty of Shanyuan a national catastrophe.[58]

But even if the treaty of Shanyuan was viewed by many historians as a victory that kept peace with the Liao dynasty for more than a hundred years, Emperor Zhenzong appears to have felt harassed by the perception that he yielded to the barbarian Khitans. Year after year he was reminded of the military weakness of his army by the annual tribute the Song had to pay. Although his peace policy was heavily debated at the time, it was confirmed as a successful model not just in 1042 but again when the Song were negotiating peace treaties with the Tangut Xi Xia in 1044 and with the Jurchen Jin in the twelfth century. The agreement of Shanyuan and the annual payment of tribute set a precedent for coexistence on the basis of peaceful bilateral relations for generations to come.

Kou Zhun fell from power in March 1006, just one year after the treaty of Shanyuan, and his opponents at court had him banished to far away Guangdong province, where he lived until 1023—long enough to witness the decline of Emperor Zhenzong's reign. Zhenzong turned to Kou Zhun's old rival, Wang Qinruo, and asked him "how best to wash away the shame of the Shanyuan agreement."[59] In his attempt to regain imperial prestige and obliterate his feelings of shame, Zhenzong was prepared to accept the idea of supernatural intervention in human affairs and to follow the ancient practice of fabricating Heaven-sent letters, as proposed by Wang. Such letters had been produced in the reign of the Tang Emperor Xuanzong (r. 712–756), and this historical precedent may have given him the courage to participate in the fraud of 1008, the first year of the reign period Dazhong xiangfu (Great Centrality and Auspicious Talisman), which bears testimony to the extraordinary event in its name.

Zhenzong also imitated his Tang predecessor Xuanzong when staging the impressive *fengshan* sacrifices, the Sacrifice to Heaven and Earth, on Mount Taishan, as his predecessor in the year 725 had done for the last time.[60] We are told that 24,375 people—senior and junior officials, Buddhist and Daoist clergy, representatives of the "barbarians," and the elders of counties and prefectures—petitioned the emperor for the *fengshan* sacrifices. The events took place in November 1008 under the supervision of the extravagantly rewarded Wang Dan and the hypocritical Wang Qinruo.[61]

On his way back in January 1009, Zhenzong paid a visit to the Confucius temple and the tomb of Confucius at Qufu and performed rituals in veneration of the sage. He also conferred a posthumous title on Confucius, emulating his Tang predecessor's example. The extremely expensive *fengshan* sacrifices of Zhenzong were the last of this type in Chinese history, but Zhenzong himself continued in the spring of 1011 with other sacrifices directed by his Daoist advisors.

Emperor Zhenzong's personal downfall had started with the banishment of Kou Zhun in 1006. Without the sage advice of his councilor, Zhenzong gave in to his own political weakness and became increasingly dependent on men of minor stature, who gained power over him until his death on March 23, 1022. During the last years of his reign, his authority became more symbolic than real.[62] Nevertheless, Zhenzong's indisput-able achievements in territorial administration, household and tax collec-tion, and the examination system make him a worthy successor to his fa-ther and uncle. And with regard to international diplomacy, Emperor Taizu had already paved the way for a model of coexistence. In the early years of his rule he pondered the idea of buying off from the Khitan the Sixteen Prefectures, "my land and people," which the Later Jin had lost to the Liao empire in 938. Emperor Zhenzong did not succeed in recover-ing these prefectures, but he successfully modified the strategy of his uncle in order to accommodate the changed conditions. He put his faith in long-term bilateral treaties with alien regimes as an alternative to ex-pensive and risky wars. Thus, he innovatively developed what his uncle and father had started and during his first decade of rule completed the consolidation of the dynasty.

3

REFORMING INTO COLLAPSE

REFORM is the keyword for understanding the Song politics of the eleventh century. The government of Emperor Zhenzong, who had set up a successful and long-lasting administrative system, had been able to present well-balanced annual statements. But in the 1030s, after more than a decade of negligence, the state's growing military expenditures created a financial crisis that demanded fresh reform. In the 1040s a proposal was made to remedy the situation but to no avail, and at the end of Renzong's rule in 1063, despite a flourishing economy, tax revenues no longer covered annual expenditures. When Emperor Shenzong ascended the throne in 1067, reforms could be postponed no longer. Yet the initiatives for change promoted by his appointee, Wang Anshi, set off a chain of unprecedented controversies within the ranks of scholar-officials that would outlast the collapse of the Song in north China in 1127.

Fan Zhongyan's Early "Minor" Reforms

Factional strife in imperial China was nothing new. In Tang times the old aristocratic gentry had squared off against the new emerging class of trained officials, and disagreements were sometimes acrimonious. But during the Song dynasty, the lines of struggle were drawn differently. The majority of career-minded bureaucrats belonged to the so-called conservative faction. One of the most famous of them, the chief councilor Sima Guang (1019–1086), expressed the belief that "among the duties of the Son of Heaven, none is more important than ritual."[1] This group of traditional Confucians supported a sometimes impractical pacifism with re-spect to threats from other states.

Opposed to these conservatives were idealistic high-achievers who of-ten hailed from humble family backgrounds and whose professional in-terests tended to focus on benefits for the masses. Their policy proposals were also grounded in a Confucian interpretation of the role of govern-ment. Officials from both factions regarded social and political reforms as essential for the survival of the dynasty, but all proposals met with strong opposition from one direction or the other.

Fan Zhongyan (989–1052), Li Gou (1009–1059), and Han Qi (1008–1075) were on the front line of an early reform movement that culmi-nated in 1045 around the issue of military expenditures.[2] The Song's standing army of professional soldiers had always been criticized for its inefficiency and the heavy burden it placed on the state treasury.[3] In Em-peror Zhenzong's reign, up to 75 percent of the state's annual tax reve-nues went toward military expenditures, and the growth rate was alarm-ing. In 1020, it was reported that 912,000 men held positions in the army. While this number was no doubt vastly inflated, it contributed to the crisis in 1045, when, under Emperor Renzong's rule, 1,259,000 men were reported in the military ranks.[4] About forty years later, at the end of Emperor Shenzong's rule, military expenditures may have consumed 80 percent of the national budget.

The Song conflict over the military gained momentum in 1038 when the Tangut ruler Li Yuanhao (r. 1032–1048), canonized as Emperor Jing-zong, rejected Song tutelage and proclaimed his Xi Xia (or Western Xia) dynasty. The territory of the dynasty covered the Ordos region, parts of present-day central Ningxia, and the Gansu corridor and thus bordered in the south and southeast on the Song and in the northeastern direc-tion on the Liao. Zhongxing (present-day Yinchuan), west of the Yellow River, was the capital. In addition to the Tangut ruling class, the empire's multiethnic population of perhaps three million people included Han Chinese, Tibetans, Uighurs, Khitans, and a number of minor groups.

Emperor Jingzong enjoyed a reputation as a superb warrior and strate-gist. He was fluent in both Chinese and Tibetan languages and read texts on Buddhism, law, and divination. Between 1033 and 1039 he modified a number of rituals that his predecessors had adopted from the Chinese court in order to reinforce native Tangut traditions. Most famous was his order of 1034 commanding all men to shave the top part of their skull and let the hair at the temples grow—a hairstyle that was distinct from the Chinese and similar to the Khitan fashion. Crowds were permitted to kill any man who did not obey the order within three days.[5] In 1036 he also disseminated an ideographic Tangut script comprising over six thousand characters.

The Tanguts did not maintain a standing army but practiced conscription for all able-bodied men between the ages of fifteen and sixty. These soldiers had to supply their own food and equipment adequate for a ten-day mission. When this formidable enemy knocked at the gates of Song China in 1038, Emperor Renzong was not prepared to lose nominal control over the Tangut kingdom and its territory. He immediately gave orders to close all frontier markets that had benefited the Tangut salt traders, and he returned the tribute of horses and camels that the Tangut emperor had paid to the Song. Shortly afterward in 1040 Tangut troops started raiding the northwestern provinces of the Song empire.

In 1039 the reformer Li Gou, realizing the military challenge ahead, finished his *Thirty Plans for Enriching the State, Strengthening the Army, and Satisfying the Needs of the People* (*Fuguo qiangbing anmin sanshi ce*). And as always when reform ideas were proposed in Song times, the author referred to an incontestable textual source; in this case it was Confucius' *Analects* (*Lunyu*). The Master says: "[The requisites of government] are that there be sufficient food, sufficient military forces, and the confidence of the people in their ruler." In Li Gou's interpretation, good government and a sound border defense required a more efficient administration, a stronger peasantry, and more stringent controls on expenditures.

Meanwhile, Fan Zhongyan, a highly talented *enfant terrible* and head of the reform faction, was shocking the political world by advising Emperor Renzong on how to be a good ruler and by criticizing his chief councilor, Lü Yijian, for indulging in favoritism.[6] This breach of the unwritten rule that one does not interfere in matters outside one's own official responsibility led to Fan Zhongyan's demotion to the Shaanxi frontier in 1040.

There he fought the Tanguts for three years, earning a reputation as a scholar-general, a rare species in Chinese history. For most of that time he functioned as a military official rather than a field commander, because more often than not the Tanguts desisted from full-scale invasion against Song forces, preferring instead to raid and negotiate for tribute. Fan Zhongyan was a major participant in this border diplomacy. After Lü Yijian retired in 1043, Fan succeeded him as chief councilor. Given that

Lü had survived twenty years in the government's highest positions and thus must have wielded enormous power at court, it is likely that he did not oppose the appointment of Fan as his replacement. He probably realized that Fan was the right man to come to terms with the Tanguts, who were imitating the Khitan example in demanding diplomatic parity with the Song court.[7]

Fan's appointment to the top position made clear that Emperor Renzong expected all political forces to unite for the common good. But Lü, understanding the emperor's character better than his colleagues, was convinced that this appointment would be only a passing affair. Fan's personal shortcomings were well-known and easily exploited by his opponents. He was stubborn, self-righteous, and insulting to his colleagues, and in certain moods no one—not even the emperor—was exempt from his criticisms.

In a Ten-Point Memorial of 1043 Fan Zhongyan charged forward and outlined a broad program to revamp the civil service system, in particular its protection appointments, in order to make the imperial bureaucracy more efficient. He also proposed down-to-earth reforms designed to strengthen agriculture and silk production, build dikes and reclaim land, and reduce the number of administrative units at the subofficial level, so that the burdens of compulsory service would fall on fewer households. But most important, he wanted to shore up the national defense by organizing local militias, which would lead to a reduction in military expenditures.[8]

Caught up in the implementation of these far-reaching reforms, neither Fan Zhongyan nor his fellow reformers had the talent or diplomatic experience to see through all the maneuvers of their opponents at court. From the outset they lacked broad-based support. But most crucial for the failure of the so-called Qingli reforms (named after the reign period when they were introduced) was the fact that Emperor Renzong was undecided and unwilling to back up Fan. When disputes at court devolved to the level of personal political attacks, the case for reform was lost, at least for the duration of Renzong's reign.

Later historians would credit Fan Zhongyan and his fellow reformers for enforcing integrity and honor and thus raising the political consciousness of Song scholars. But in the turmoil of the time, the reformers' enemies accused Fan of forming a "faction," a term that carried a bad connotation in the Song court. Any notion of a "loyal opposition" to the existing structure of governing, or of disagreement as a form of political engagement, was rejected by members of a conservative bureaucracy trained in subservience based on personal relations and dependence. Ouyang Xiu forcefully justified the forming of factions in his famous memorial *On Factions (Pengdang lun)*, composed in the spring of 1044, by arguing that superior men form factions based on principles, whereas inferior men come together for selfish interests. But the enemies at court were too many, and Ouyang's memorial was too late to save his friend from downfall.

In early 1045 Fan Zhongyan and his fellow reformer Fu Bi (1004–1083) resigned their offices. Fan volunteered for a post at the northern frontier in Shaanxi, and for the remaining eight years of his life he served in a number of administrative positions in the province. He never once returned to court. Much of his energy was spent setting up a charitable estate for the welfare of impoverished members of the Fan clan, which lasted until 1760. The end of Fan's career at court occurred only three months after the welcome peace agreement of 1044 with the Xi Xia, which he had helped to negotiate, went into effect. It committed the Song to annual gifts of 255,000 units of silk, silver, and tea, and to addressing the Xi Xia emperor as "ruler." But it allowed Emperor Renzong to be at ease, at least for the time being.

Immediately, the old career-minded bureaucrats of Lü Yijian's former entourage, whose main concern as officials was to avoid responsibility for reforms, regained control at court. Within a year all of the "minor reform" initiatives of 1043 and 1044 were rescinded. In the 1050s and 1060s Ouyang Xiu and Han Qi pressed successfully for some changes in the examination system, and they introduced a five-grade system of compulsory service at the subofficial level of the imperial bureaucracy. But after witnessing the humiliation of their friend and colleague Fan Zhongyan, they desisted from provoking a political confrontation.

Wang Anshi's "Major" Reforms

During the crucial years of Fan Zhongyan's minor reforms, Cai Xiang (1012–1067)—a brilliant calligrapher and self-appointed policy expert—was sharply critical of the nonprofessionalism of his own class of officials. A *jinshi* scholar himself, he regarded the generalist education coming out of the civil service exam system as insufficient for the variety of professional tasks that officials faced in their careers. Scholar-officials were tested and then assigned to their posts on the basis of their literary skills, but during their service they were expected to deal with fiscal matters, border defense, county and prefecture administration, and a host of other pragmatic concerns. The majority of the Song intelligentsia agreed that the educational system and the larger society would benefit from some re-engineering, but they disagreed on how and what exactly to reform.

In the opinion of the conservatives Sima Guang and Su Shi, simply revitalizing Confucian ideals would bring about the needed social changes. Others favored selective reform as it had been attempted by Fan Zhongyan. But in the 1050s and 1060s, a third group, centered on the official Wang Anshi (1021–1086), asked for fundamental reforms, including an overhaul of the entire civil service examination system. Among other things, Wang asked for useful training in legal and military matters.

The disquieting military maneuvers and changing alliances in the power triangle between the Xi Xia, the Liao, and the Song caused considerable uneasiness among court officials from the late 1030s well into the 1050s. After the fragile peace with the Xi Xia was negotiated in 1044, Song policy-makers tried, for a time, to ignore problems within the military forces that were protecting the empire. But the sheer number of troops made the issue of military expenditures unavoidable: 450,000 troops were garrisoned at the northwestern Xi Xia frontier, 300,000 in Hebei along the Liao border, and another 300,000 formed the central army at the capital.[9] "The constant threat of the barbarians on our borders" figured in Wang Anshi's famous *Ten Thousand Word Memorial (Wanyan shu)* of 1058—a position paper in which he outlined his reform ideas to Emperor Renzong.[10] This memorial turned Wang into an overnight celebrity in reform circles and at court. But the emperor, who by that point was preoccupied with the problem of having no heir apparent, did not show much interest in it.

Emperor Renzong died in 1063. Su Shi, in his preface to the *Complete Works of Ouyang Xiu (Jushi ji)*, compiled in 1091, had this to say about peace and good government during this period in Song history: "For more than seventy years the Song dynasty has flourished without people knowing the perils of war, but enjoying the blessings of affluence and education."[11] In 1092 the Confucian scholar Fan Zuyu also praised Emperor Renzong for his good government, which, he claimed, grew out of the five traditional virtues that distinguished the "benevolent emperor" from all other rulers: "Emperor Renzong feared Heaven, he loved his people, he sacrificed to his ancestors, he was fond of learning, and he obeyed admonitions. Practicing these five virtues is what is called 'being benevolent.'"[12]

After the four-year reign of Renzong's cousin, Emperor Yingzong, the nineteen-year-old Zhao Xu ascended the throne on January 25, 1067. He was Emperor Yingzong's eldest son and was canonized as Emperor Shenzong (r. 1067–1085). His succession rang in the most celebrated reform period of premodern Chinese history. The impatient young emperor aspired to strengthen military defenses at the borders and to reestablish Song authority over the long-lost Sixteen Prefectures and the alien regimes of the north. To achieve these goals, he needed trustworthy advisors and loyal officials.

The emperor's tutor, Han Jiang, recommended Wang Anshi. Wang's reputation at court was bolstered by his prior exemplary career. As a young man of twenty-one from his family's third generation of degree-holders, he had passed the palace examination in fourth place in 1042. He then served for twenty years in many substantive government posts in the lower Yangzi region and honed his skills as an essayist and poet. At the age of thirty, he had already met or worked with some of the major politicians and intellectuals of the eleventh century.

In early 1069 Emperor Shenzong appointed the now 47-year-old Wang to the position of vice chief councilor, the post previously held by the reformer Ouyang Xiu. The appointment of Wang represented a chance for reform "that comes only once in a thousand years," Zhu Xi later remarked.[13] In May 1069 a special commission was formed to inspect the nationwide systems of taxation, agriculture, irrigation, and flood control of rivers. Driven by the emperor's enthusiasm and determination, Wang Anshi lost no time between 1069 and 1073 in setting his "New Policies" in motion.[14]

Wang's reforms fell into three broad categories: economic, military, and educational. His economic program was meant to support farmers, traders, and craftsmen at the wide base of the social pyramid. Wang was convinced that the state as a whole would become strong when the livelihood and well-being of the common people was assured and when local communities prospered. He wanted healthy, affluent citizens who willingly served the interests of the state.

Wang's first economic reform addressed the cash shortage of farmers. The Green Sprouts Act of 1069, named after the spring season when the rice sprouts and financed by the Ever-Normal State Granaries, offered needy farmers two state loans per year, at the low semiannual interest

rate of 20 percent, to be paid back when they made their regular tax payments. The loans were much more reasonable than those offered by private money lenders, whose rates, reaching 70 percent, drove farmers with
small holdings and tenant-farmers who rented land into ruin.

This program caused a great stir in official circles, and many officials
handed in their resignations during the controversy. Opponents argued
that the new policy reinforced centralization and bureaucratization instead of frugality and belt-tightening, as advocated by Sima Guang. And
they complained that it was not the state's business to profit from money
transactions. In a letter to Sima, Wang politely countered that reform of
the money-lending system was in the interest of the state as a whole. Privileged landowners, especially those involved in the highly profitable private credit system, no doubt feared competition from the state-run Green
Sprouts program, and they opposed Wang's reform with all means available to them.[15] At every level of administration, including the local prefectures and counties, the enemies of reform openly or silently interfered,
delayed, and obstructed implementation.

Wang was a southerner, and from the outset his enemies at court—
mostly intellectuals from north of the Yellow River, along with the so-
called Luoyang conservatives of aristocratic heritage—misinterpreted his
intentions, attacked his integrity, and denounced him as a politician ad-
vocating the non-Confucian principle of profit. Wang was undeterred.
Early in 1070, in an effort to train officials in pragmatic professional
skills, he proposed a thorough reform of the examination system. Legal
studies replaced poetry and literary composition, and exposition and policy criticism were added as examination subjects later. But the Green
Sprouts Act and education reform were just warm-up exercises for Wang's
Militia Act and Service Exemption Act, both proposed in early 1071.

The idea behind the Militia Act (*baojia*) was to modernize the local levies, which were a sort of army reserve force, sometimes also called volun-
teers, though in fact the service was not voluntary. In 1076 there were 6.9
million men registered for the levies, which meant that 46 percent of the
empire's households supplied one active militia member.[16] Wang wanted
to make more efficient use of these trained cavalrymen, bowmen, and
crossbowmen in order to cut down the number of regular soldiers and
thus reduce the burden of military expenditures for the standing army.
The costs of the militiamen, who spent most of the year in agricultural
work and provided their own supplies when called into military service,
would be only one-fifth or even less of the cost of year-round professional

soldiers. In addition, when well-organized, well-trained, and armed, they would be more than willing to defend their own locality. The main problems were how to convert farmers into an effective fighting force and how to use that force to defend a distant frontier, far from their homes.

Wang proposed to organize households into military units of ten each, called a platoon. Every household with one or two able-bodied males had to provide one man for the platoon. Five platoons formed a company, and ten companies (or five hundred households) constituted a regimental unit. Bows and crossbows were provided by the government, and in the off-season the farmers were trained in the fundamentals of warfare. In times of peace, the whole system functioned as a police force, and above all it worked as an almost perfect system for mutual surveillance—a role that it played until the twentieth century.

Wang found ideological support for the Militia Act in the Family Unit Act, a precedent taken from the Later Zhou dynasty. Nevertheless, criticism was raised immediately. Feng Jing (1021–1094) asked: "When Emperor Taizu conquered all under Heaven, did he not prohibit the use of farmers as soldiers?"[17] Wang chose to ignore Taizu's precedent, convinced that "regular soldiers are mostly frivolous and reckless people who do not care about death. They are fond of trouble and chaos and are no match [as soldiers] to good farmers." But he conceded that "in an earlier memorandum I have already pointed out that it is not possible to do completely without regular soldiers."[18]

Emperor Shenzong had his own doubts: "Regular soldiers are exclusively for military operations; that's the reason why they are reliable. With regard to the people's soldiers, their profession is half soldier and half farmer. Can they be reliable when fighting and defending?" Wang replied: "Prior to the Tang there were no tattooed [regular] soldiers, and they certainly could fight and defend. I'm of the opinion that there is no difference between the regular soldiers and the people's soldiers. One has to take care to employ good commanders." "The ancient kings made farmers act as soldiers," he pointed out. With training, "the militia units would eventually become better than regular soldiers, and they would be cheaper."[19]

In Wang's view, reform of the militia was the solution to the problem of military weakness at the borders: "Lately the Middle Kingdom has not really stood up to the Four Barbarians, but the Four Barbarians of nowadays would have been no match for the ancient Middle Kingdom. If we had organized the people in [military] units and made provisions that

there are people [strong enough] in all places to take on the enemy, this
would have been the method of the ancient Middle Kingdom."[20] Lü
Gongzhu (1018–1089) defended Wang's militia reform as a return to Tang
efficiency. Although the trained militia in the northern border provinces
constituted a considerable military force that could have been maintained
at reasonable costs, the reform initiated by the Militia Act remained
unfinished. It certainly would have been successful if Emperor Shenzong
had not decided to go to war with the Xi Xia and if the reform had been
continued after his death in 1085. But between 1086 and 1093 the government rescinded the act without replacing it with a functional system.

The Service Exemption Act was Wang's attempt to abolish the ruinous
obligatory local service performed by a comparably small number of
households at the subofficial level in local bureaucracies. Wang introduced a system of graduated taxation on the basis of property and financial assets to be paid twice a year in cash, rather than service, by all but
the two lowest ranks of households, who could continue to repay their
obligation in service. Members of official families paid the tax at half-
rate. The receipts would be used to employ career servicemen, thus opening new prospects for able clerks. As a side effect, Wang hoped to reduce
corruption at the local level.

Critics forcefully attacked this reform initiative because in their opinion it put a heavy financial obligation on some of the poorest groups in
society, who could hardly make a living already. Wang judged the financial situation of the groups differently and put the reform into effect.
New revenues in the government coffers were spent not only to employ
professional servicemen but also to wage war against the Xi Xia ten years
later.

In 1072, to rectify the tax registers, Wang initiated a land survey. This
move to gain central control over provincial bureaucracies for the benefit
of the commonwealth annoyed local administrators. He also initiated a
state trade policy that favored smaller merchants by encouraging trade
and agriculture and stabilizing the market price of goods. This reform interfered with the local business of the hitherto privileged big merchants
and guilds.

In April 1074, after years of struggle with his colleagues, a cabal composed of the empress dowager, eunuchs at court, and antireform officials accused Wang Anshi of having reformed the world into chaos. By
then the vice chief councilor himself was exhausted. He had, in his own
words, "felt like a corpse in office for some time."[21] Although Emperor

Shenzong wanted his service to continue, Wang insisted that he be allowed to resign. When in the second month of 1075 the emperor nevertheless recalled him to court, Wang immediately realized that the political atmosphere had shifted dramatically: his authority was now weak and his reforms were under attack. Even after Wang's final retirement to his favorite city, Jiankang (Nanjing) in the tenth month of 1076, Emperor Shenzong stayed the course for reform and appointed pro-reform officials to leading government positions.

Wang Anshi had gained military experience in the Song's border skirmishes with the Xi Xia between 1070 and 1072, but he had always worked to prevent engagement in a real war. After his retirement, officials at court saw an opportunity to please Emperor Shenzong by making preparations for a great war against the Xi Xia. In 1076 the regular army consisted of at least 568,000 soldiers, in addition to 6.9 million militiamen. In the summer of 1081 the Song army invaded Xi Xia territory from five directions.[22] Almost immediately, the logistics of provisioning and transporting troops turned out to be an insurmountable problem.

In late 1082, after losses of 600,000 Song and allied troops, Emperor Shenzong realized that the war against the Tangut empire could not be won.[23] He abandoned his hopes for reconquering northwest China, and only Lanzhou remained under Song control (Map 4). It may have been a small satisfaction to him that the Xi Xia's loss of manpower, matériel, and goods crippled its economy for years.[24] But to Emperor Shenzong personally, the defeat meant that he, like his Song predecessors, had failed to restore the territorial unity of Tang China.

After Shenzong died on April 1, 1085, the Empress Dowager Gao became regent for the eight-year-old Emperor Zhezong (r. 1085–1100). By this time Sima Guang, the fiercest and most talented antireformer, had exhausted his strength in writing his famous history entitled *Comprehensive Mirror to Aid in Government (Zizhi tongjian)*, and he felt ill. He claimed that he was no longer able to kneel down or ride on horseback, not to mention that he was extremely nearsighted and had lost most of his teeth. Nevertheless, the empress dowager insisted on having him as her advisor and top official. He declined several times and recommended the experienced Wen Yanbo in his place, but Gao wanted an antireformer of public renown who would not just advise her but put her antireform program into practice. He finally gave in to her demands and devoted the remaining few months of his life to the cause of the empress dowager.

Sima Guang was appointed chief councilor, along with Lü Gongzhu

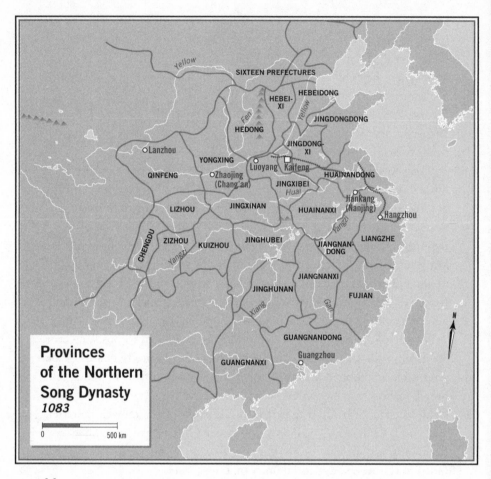

Map 4

and Wen Yanbo, who would assist him. Within seven months, all of
Wang Anshi's New Policies were rescinded. Because of Sima Guang's de-
teriorating physical and mental health and the urgency with which the
project was carried out, the dismantling of the reform bureaucracy did
not take place with the usual degree of care and caution that Sima Guang
brought to his historical writings.[25] Cheng Hao (1032–1085), who belonged to the Old Policies faction, remarked in 1085 after being recalled
to court: "The result [of the reform] is seen in the present sad state of affairs, for which we cannot attach sole blame to Wang Anshi."[26] In his
opinion, prejudiced and unreasonable opposition to the New Policies
was responsible for the chaos as well.

Sima Guang died a few months after Wang Anshi, in 1086. The struggle between reformers and antireformers continued until the end of the Northern Song, but those who claimed to be following in Wang's footsteps did not have his broad view and self-discipline. After the fall of Kaifeng and the collapse of the Northern Song in 1127, Southern Song scholars, searching for a scapegoat, would cast Wang Anshi as the sole architect of the failed reforms, and above all they would mistakenly associate him with the shady behavior of later pseudo-reformers. More than a century after Wang's death, the conservative Neo-Confucian Zhu Xi would sum up the reformer's contribution this way:

> During the final years of the Northern Song period, the government was absolutely powerless in fighting the rebels. This is because the policy-makers were not capable of assessing the true needs of the times. The Xining reign period reform of [Wang Anshi's] government policies was adopted in a time when the government and the society at large were overly relaxed and inactive. The historical force caused them to take the inevitable measures of reforms. Unfortunately, their reforms were not in accord with the Way.[27]

The Fall of the Liao and Rise of the Jin

The many problems reformers and antireformers faced in their debate about the course Song society should take could not deter the Liao court from following the Chinese model of education. Considering the political circumstances, there was no alternative to it. For many years the Liao (Khitan) emperor Xingzong (r. 1031–1055) trained his eldest son Yelü Hongji (1032–1101) to become his successor, and in the process gave him a Chinese education and passed along his taste for the Chinese way of life. The son ascended the throne in 1055 as Emperor Daozong. During a long reign of forty-six years, he promoted the civil service examination system, founded a Directorate of Education, honored Confucius and the sages, and insisted that his officials wear Chinese robes at court. Contrary to tribal preferences, Emperor Daozong also strengthened central authority in his empire.

But in other matters, his judgment was often weak, and he tended to believe the slanderous talk of the court. A few years after ascending the throne, probably in 1061, he ordered the strangling of Xiao Ala, a competent and loyal official. When his own wife, Empress Xuanyi, a poetess and musician, was falsely accused of a sexual liaison, he ordered her to commit suicide. The heir apparent, and the heir apparent's wife, died at the hands of hired killers. Yelü Yixin, who enjoyed the emperor's confidence, played a central role in these intrigues and murders until 1080, when the emperor finally became aware of his devious behavior and sentenced him to death. Though the general atmosphere at court did not change much after Yelü Yixin's execution in 1083, when Emperor Daozong died on February 12, 1101, "his empire still enjoyed power, stability, internal peace, and respect of the surrounding peoples."[28]

Yelü Yanxi (1075–1128), posthumously titled Emperor Tianzuo, began his reign as the last of the Liao emperors in 1101, at the death of his grandfather. One of his first acts was to take revenge on the dead Yelü Yixin, his family, and the members of his faction by destroying their tombs, mutilating their corpses, confiscating the property and possessions of their descendants, and distributing their wealth among the families of former victims. He punished all the evildoers he suspected of having any hand in the death of his grandmother, his father, and his mother. But apart from satisfying his urge for revenge, indulging in countless hunting expeditions, and hosting a number of Song embassies, Tianzuo accomplished little in the early years of his reign.

Until the beginning of Tianzuo's tenure, relations between the Liao dynasty and the Jurchen tribe had been difficult at times but not strained. The Jurchen, whose name first appeared in Chinese history in 903, originally lived south of the Amur River in what is now Russia. After 926, some of them settled on the Manchurian plains and along the Sungari River in present-day Heilongjiang province. In the eleventh century the Jurchen tribes inhabiting the area between the Koryo kingdom (in Korea) to the south, the Amur River to the north, and the Japanese Sea to the east were divided into three broad groups: the "civilized" Jurchens, the "obedient" Jurchens, and the "wild" or "uncivilized" Jurchens.

The Wanyan clan of "wild" Jurchens, living at the Sungari River far away from the civilizing influence of the Liao and Chinese, proved to be the most powerful of the one hundred wild clans. The Jurchens, united under their leadership, started to resist the Liao dynasty. In the first decade of the twelfth century, with Wanyan Wuyashu (r. 1103–1113) as their leader, the Jurchens set up a state with Shangjing, near present-day Harbin, as its Supreme Capital. Khitan overlords conferred on the Jurchen leader the title of military governor but treated the tribe harshly and demanded precious furs, pearls, and hunting falcons as annual tribute. Among the humiliations they suffered at the hands of the visiting

Khitans was the demand, made year after year, that Jurchen virgins serve them as "comfort women" in brothels. Another was the unrestrained sexual abuse of married women from the Jurchen upper class.[29]

In early 1112 the Liao emperor Tianzuo traveled to the Huntong River, a tributary of the Sungari in Jilin province, to take part in the "feast of the emperor's first fish." At this occasion, Jurchen leaders from as far away as 500 kilometers were required to pay homage to the Liao emperor. After they all became drunk, the emperor commanded the leaders to dance, one after the other, in a symbolic gesture of submission. Aguda, a member of the Wanyan tribe from the Korean state of Silla, refused. Later the emperor said in private to Xiao Fengxian, his commissioner of military affairs, that he did not like the behavior of Aguda and suggested that he should be executed. He feared that Aguda, who was extremely tall and imposing in stature, would cause trouble in the future. Xiao Fengxian dissuaded him from this course, explaining the insult as simply a case of bad manners, and asked what harm Aguda could ever do to the powerful Liao?[30]

If Emperor Tianzuo had followed his instinct to extinguish Aguda and his family, he might have postponed the collapse of the Liao dynasty. As the younger brother of Wuyashu, Aguda was elected tribal leader in 1113 to challenge the military dominance of the Liao. In late 1114 Aguda's forces attacked the trading station in Ningjiang prefecture where the Jurchen leaders year after year had paid homage to the Liao emperor. The Liao troops suffered a devastating defeat. In 1115 Aguda founded the Jin or Gold dynasty and became its first emperor.[31] In naming his dynasty after the Anchuhu (Golden) River in the Jurchens' native homeland, he followed the example of the Liao, who had taken the Liao River as their dynastic designation.

The Liao's internal problems, including several court conspiracies to dethrone Emperor Tianzuo, local uprisings, and conflicts with the Jurchens, sapped the emperor's strength and undermined the Khitan clans' confidence that they could put up a strong resistance against the Jin. In early 1122 the Liao army collapsed under a Jurchen attack, and the Jin dynasty proclaimed itself the legitimate successor to the Khitan empire. For the next three years the Liao retreated westward, always one step ahead of Jurchen troops. In early 1122, the Liao Prince Chun deposed Emperor Tianzuo, degraded him to the rank of a prince, and proclaimed himself the new Liao emperor. Tianzuo sought refuge in the tribal regions of the far west. After Prince Chun's sudden death in the summer of 1122, his wife née Xiao took control of what was left of the Liao empire. She joined forces with Tianzuo near the Xi Xia border and reinstated the reign of terror that he had imposed. But she suffered the same fate she had meted out for her former critics and was executed for disloyalty in 1123.

The Jin founder Aguda, canonized as Emperor Taizu, died in 1123 and did not live to see the military successes he had initiated. His younger brother and successor, Wuqimai (Emperor Taizong, r. 1123–1135), continued the dynasty's relentless attacks on its neighbors. In 1124 he successfully concluded a peace treaty with the Xi Xia ruler, who acknowledged the suzerainty of the Jin. In early 1125 the Liao Emperor Tianzuo was captured by Jin troops near present-day Yingxian in Shanxi province. The Jin emperor humiliated him by conferring the title "King of the Seashore," an allusion to the title "King of the Eastern Sea" that the Liao emperor had offered to Aguda in 1119 and which he rejected. The Liao dynasty was finished, though the Khitan people survived for another century in the far west of China as the Western Khitai.

The Collapse of the Northern Song

The Song's irascible, nervous, and indecisive Emperor Zhezong, who was on the throne from the age of eight to twenty-three, died on February 23, 1100. His widow, the Empress Dowager Xiang, helped Zhao Ji (the eleventh son of Shenzong, also known as Prince Duan) to ascend the throne. He became known as Emperor Huizong (r. 1100–1126). In accepting this succession, the court ignored the warning of chief councilor Zhang Dun, who insisted that "Prince Duan is careless and frivolous, and not cut out for ruling all under Heaven."[32]

Emperor Huizong was determined to follow in his father's and brother's footsteps and pursue a course of rigorous reform. But he delegated decision-making to mediocre and corrupt officials like Cai Jing (1046–1126) and eunuchs like Tong Guan (1054–1126), whose pseudo-reform faction wanted little more than to reap the benefits of pleasing their ruler.[33] Claiming to be Wang's successor, Cai Jing participated in the drafting of proscription lists that led to the demotion and banishment of hundreds of reform opponents.[34] This edict dishonoring and degrading reform opponents as "crooked scholars" and expelling them from the political community weakened the Northern Song and contributed to the dynasty's decline.

Emperor Huizong viewed an aggressive foreign policy as integral to his ambitions. Observing the conflict between the Jin and Liao and the weakness of the Khitan empire, he came to believe that the Song had a chance to recover the lost but never-forgotten Sixteen Prefectures in north China that the Khitans had taken from the Later Jin dynasty in the tenth century, prior to Song rule. The Song official Zheng Juzhong strongly advised Emperor Huizong not to ally with the Jurchen "dog barbarians" in order to defeat the Liao. Zheng called to mind the great benefits resulting from the Shanyuan treaty of 1005: "Our soldiers have been spared knowledge of the sword [for over one hundred years], and our farmers spared increases in corvée. Not even the demon-quelling policies of the Han and Tang can match those of Our Song Dynasty."[35]

Between 1117 and 1123 many Jin and Song envoys traveled back and forth in an attempt to negotiate an alliance against the Liao. Emperor Huizong's ambassadors did not realize that while power among the barbarians had shifted dramatically in recent years, it had not receded. In the course of negotiations, the Jin discovered that they could take the Sixteen Prefectures themselves, without help from the Song. In 1122 the Jin army defeated the Liao army single-handedly and took control of north China. Even then, the Song emperor did not recognize the impending danger to his own dynasty.

Though Emperor Huizong failed as a protector of the realm, he gained a reputation as a competent if self-indulgent artist, art collector, connoisseur, calligrapher, poet, and author of treatises on medicine. He was a reformer of court music, court ritual, and education, and he was devoted to Daoism, to the point of imagining himself a Daoist deity. His religious advisors introduced a religious ideology—the Divine Empyrean Daoism —focused on the idolatrous veneration of his image in temples, a Song personality cult of extraordinary dimensions.

Emperor Huizong squandered a fortune on palaces and halls, religious festivities, and landscape design. A famous example was his construction of the Sacred Peaks of Longevity, another name for the Northeast Mountain Peak (Genyue), a gigantic rock garden in the northeast quadrant of the Old City of Kaifeng. This "impregnable mountain" was intended to be many things at once: an exhibition of Song prosperity and virtue, an enigmatic place of rest, an organism where all things start and end and death and birth merge, and a physical expression of the Divine Empyrean Daoism, where at any moment the immortals themselves might descend and acknowledge this earthly paradise. Ironically, Phoenix Hill in Hangzhou, which twenty years later would become the capital of the Southern Song dynasty, served as the natural model for this man-made mountain.[36]

The project was planned in 1117 and construction began on January 10, 1118. When it was completed, it measured 5.59 kilometers in circumference, and its most impressive peak was 138 meters high, a landmark visible from almost any point in the city. The garden consisted of exquisite anthropomorphic rock formations, bridges over crevices, waterfalls and brooks, pavilions and studios high up on cliffs and ridges or hidden deep in bamboo groves, and thousands of exotic trees and shrubs from the far reaches of the empire. The landscape represented an ideal world, a sanctuary, an island worthy of immortals in the center of the busiest metropolis on earth.

The emperor no doubt regarded his landscape garden as a symbol of his virtuous rule, but the common people may have held a different view. To construct this unique habitat (which later served as a model for the Beihai Park in Beijing), thousands of men were forced into service as part of the infamous Flower and Rock Network, which under the direction of Zhu Mian soon became the most powerful and most hated organization in all of China. It was in charge of transporting all the materials and plants, regardless of expense and natural obstacles, on confiscated carts and boats from the remotest places of the empire to the capital. In 1120 when the rebel Fang La started his uprising against the Song in Zhejiang province, one of his goals was to abolish silver and silk subsidies to the Liao and Xi Xia, but the other was to bring the infamous Flower and Rock Network to an end. Fearing that the rebellion might spread to other provinces, officials announced the dismantlement of the network and dismissal of Zhu Mian. Approximately 70,000 regular troops were lost in the effort to squelch Fang La's uprising in May, but once it was over the emperor ordered the reorganization and expansion of the Flower and Rock Network. The Sacred Peaks of Longevity garden was completed in January 1123, four years before the Jurchen troops laid siege to the capital.

In 1123 the Song and Jin mutually agreed on the first formal exchange of oath letters between the two states. Within ten years only Aguda's Jin dynasty had achieved official recognition and political parity with the Song.[37] For a few territorial concessions and an unreliable promise of peace, the Song state committed itself to annual payments of 200,000 ounces of silver, 300,000 bolts of silk, and one million strings of coins— an important subsidy that stabilized the Jurchen war economy. Contrary to the Song's expectations, however, 1123 did not mark the beginning of peace but started a twenty-year period of warfare that threatened the very existence of the dynasty.

After Aguda died in 1123, his brother Wuqimai did not stop at the Chinese border to celebrate the Jin's successful military campaign in the north. On the contrary, he was grimly determined to keep the forward momentum going and to overrun the northern part of the Song empire in one clean sweep. Song officials were shocked when the Jurchens violated the agreement of 1123 by launching a full-scale war against the Song in late autumn of 1125. The well-drilled, ferocious Jurchen horsemen drove a two-pronged advance along the old trade routes deep into Shanxi and Hebei. The Eastern Army under the command of Wanyan Wolibu, a brother of the emperor, made straight for the Song capital, and the Western Army led by Wanyan Nianhan headed for Taiyuan.

The Song government was ill-prepared for a military response. In a last effort to protect his people and perhaps himself, Emperor Huizong abdicated on January 18, 1126, in favor of his son, Zhao Huan (Emperor Qinzong), who reigned until March 23, 1127. In the cold winter of early 1126, the Jin forces crossed the Yellow River and laid siege to the walled capital, Kaifeng. Unable to command an army strong enough to counter the Jin troops, the emperor saw no way out of the desperate situation but to negotiate a withdrawal.

In addition to the loss of the three prefectures of Taiyuan, Zhongshan, and Hejian in Shanxi and Hebei and the continuation of annual tribute obligations, the Song agreed to a war indemnity amounting to several decades' worth of tribute subsidy. The single payment of 300,000 ounces of gold (instead of the 5 million ounces originally demanded), more than 12 million ounces of silver (instead of 50 million ounces), 10,000 cattle and horses, and 1 million bolts of silk fabric would fill the Jurchen war chest for years to come.[38] The Jin troops ended their siege on February 10, 1126.

In March 1126, with alarm bells ringing for the survival of the dynasty, the anti-Jin resistance fanatic Chen Dong—who became famous for his public avowal "I'm a man of the Song"—demanded the capital punishment of officials responsible for the disastrous situation. An estimated 100,000 low officials and candidates, demoralized soldiers, and sympathizers crowded in front of the Imperial City and finally stormed the gate of the Imperial Palace in a desperate public outcry of resistance. This mixed group of loyalists, men in despair, and troublemakers demanded influence over decision-making at court, but any reform capable of changing the fate of the Song would never materialize.[39]

By the summer of 1126 the Jin dominated continental East Asia, and the Xi Xia and the Koryo declared themselves vassals of the dynasty. The Song court, weakened and at the brink of extinction, began to rethink its options. The emperor dismissed the officials and eunuchs who had helped bring about this disaster, among them Cai Jing, Tong Guan, Zhu Mian, and Wang Fu. By the end of 1126 all of the so-called Six Bandits held responsible for the debacle in the reign of Emperor Huizong were dead.

Convinced of their own invincibility and the weakness of the Song army, the Jin commanders looked for more easy booty and a cause to re-kindle the war. In late 1126 the Jin army once more crossed the Yellow River, and two experienced generals besieged the capital on December 10. Most of its inhabitants had already made a hasty escape to the south.[40] With only about 70,000 residents, the city resisted the attackers until January 9, 1127. Emperor Qinzong surrendered and began negotiations with the Jin leaders in their military camp. This time the invaders demanded more than double the amount they had received previously, an exorbitant ransom in gold, silver, and silk. In addition, they wanted 7,000 horses and 1,500 young palace ladies. Otherwise, their troops threatened to pillage private households and public buildings.[41]

The emperor agreed to these demands, but the Chinese officials in charge of collecting the ransom could not meet their quotas. They were able to collect only a small percentage of the total. As punishment for their failure, they were beaten to death in front of the main south gate. Emperor Qinzong abdicated on March 23, 1127, and was degraded to the status of a commoner, along with his father, former Emperor Huizong.[42] When the majority of the Jin troops returned home to the north in May, just before the onset of summer heat, more than one thousand carts loaded with priceless imperial treasures—the imperial art collection, astronomical instruments, the nine cauldrons of state, ritual vessels, the eight imperial seals, jades, pearls, and precious stones, hats and robes of the empresses and concubines—traveled with them. In addition the Jurchen troops took possession of ninety-two warehouses holding more than 3 million gold ingots, 8 million silver ingots, 1.5 million bolts of patterned silk, and 54 million bolts of tabby silk.[43]

After the fall of Kaifeng and the breakdown of imperial power, some scholar-officials refused to render service to a barbarian master, choosing rather to follow the example of the official envoy Dou Jian. When the Song emperor was about to suffer the humiliation of being banished to the north, Dou Jian declared: "I was born to be an official of the Great Song. How could I bear to hand the clan of the Great Song over to enemies?"[44] Thereupon he committed suicide by strangling himself, and thus avoided betraying the dynasty.

On May 13, 1127, a great wind strong enough to move rocks and snap trees blew through the capital. The former emperors Huizong and Qinzong, accompanied by an entourage of three thousand people, left the city through the Nanxun gate on the south side.[45] The empresses, traveling in another convoy, left from the north gate. Several thousand artisans and craftsmen, artists, musicians, and actors—perhaps as many as 15,000—joined the long march to the Jin homeland in Manchuria.

The Jin ruler and his generals did not spare the Song emperors the degradation of being garbed in blue cloth like servants. Nevertheless, Emperor Huizong continued to write poems, and in one of them he confessed:

> With nine generations the great enterprise suddenly stops.
> I was crazy not to listen to my upright officials' advice.
> Willingly I travel ten thousand *li* as a surrendered captive.
> Just think how in my former country I was sad when
> the jade halls grew cool in autumn.[46]

After an odyssey on ox carts through Inner Mongolia and Manchuria, the former emperor arrived in the summer of 1130 at Wuguo City near the northern border of Heilongjiang.[47] The Jin ruler delighted in humiliating his captives, making them bow before Aguda's tablet in his mausoleum and dubbing Huizong "Marquis of Muddled Virtue" and Qinzong "Marquis Doubly Muddled." Qinzong's empress committed suicide by drowning. As many as 11,000 women, including princesses, court ladies, servant girls, and women of upper-class households, arrived in the Supreme Capital (near Harbin) a year later, and most of them became prostitutes in military camps or slaves in households. They lived and died far away from home, never seeing China again.

Zhao Gou, Prince of Kang, had been one of the Song officials sent to the Jin military headquarters in north China in December 1126 to negotiate tribute payments in return for peace. But on his way to the meeting, Song military officials convinced him that, rather than appease the Jin, he should head a fighting force to resist the invaders. Zhao Gou already had some personal experience with the Jurchens. Early in 1126, while they held Kaifeng under siege, he had been a hostage at the Jin court and only narrowly escaped the fate of his father, brothers, and sisters. Well aware of the political danger the prince represented, the Jurchens tried to get their hands on him, but Zhao Gou eluded capture by shifting his base from place to place. On June 12, 1127, following the abdication of Emperor Qinzong in March, Zhao Gou declared himself Emperor (Gaozong) and ascended the throne at Shangqiu, the Southern Capital of the Song.[48]

The collapse of the Song dynasty in 1127 marked the end of what is known in history as the Northern Song period. After north China was lost to the Jin, the Song court and government decamped to the south and embarked on the second phase of the dynasty's history, the Southern Song, which lasted for 152 years until 1279. The terms Northern Song (Bei Song) and Southern Song (Nan Song) are historical constructs not used in Song times. While the idea that the breakdown of the Song dynasty in 1127 had damaged Song continuity and that the dynastic ideology had to be reconsidered was evident in the writings of several contemporaries witnessing the events, none of them would have dared to suggest that the year 1127 marked a turning point in Song history, comparable to the well-known divide of the Han dynasty into Western (Former) and Eastern (Later) periods.[49]

4

THE SONG IN THE SOUTH

It is an irony of history that the Song's loss of the provinces north of the Huai and Han rivers in 1127 corroborated for centuries to come the superiority of the southeastern provinces in production and commerce, and in education, erudition, and the arts. China's population had started shifting southward centuries before the collapse of the Northern Song dynasty, however, as a result of questions about land ownership and alterations in the climate of north China.[1] The migration to the south—clearly reflected in changing population figures from the period—provides a demographic background for political events that continued to challenge both the court and commoners alike.

In A.D. 5 only 10 percent of households lived in the southeast, but by 740, during the Tang dynasty, about 40 percent of the population lived south of the Huai River. Responding to a variety of pushes and pulls, the trend continued into the Song. Among the push factors were the civil wars of the late Tang and the Five Dynasties, which caused many elite households to relocate. Another force was the burden of taxation. By 996 more than 10,000 households had fled from fourteen counties in the metropolitan prefecture around Kaifeng.[2]

But the combination of political turmoil followed by heavy taxation cannot account completely for the migration. China's most fertile land, located on the north China plain and along the river valleys, had been settled and owned by landed gentry for centuries. Peasant families were pulled southward in search of uncultivated land that they could claim for themselves, along with dependable rainfall for their crops. During a change in climate known as the third Little Ice Age, which lasted from the end of the tenth century to the end of the twelfth, the average temperature dropped by as much as 1.5 degrees Celsius.[3] This may seem like a small decline, but farmers who depended on good harvests for their livelihood noticed the changes. They were also aware of increasingly severe and erratic snow, ice, rain, and hail storms.[4]

Extremely harsh winters in Kaifeng are recorded in the late eleventh century and in the early decades of the twelfth century. In some years Lake Taihu, in the lower reaches of the Yangzi, was covered with a sheet of thick ice, unthinkable today. Thirteen disastrous snowstorms are recorded between 1101 and 1127. The colder weather also produced greater flooding. The number of recorded major floods increased from 115 in the Tang to 193 in the Song (including the territory the Song lost to the Jin). From the tenth to the eleventh century alone, the number of floods went up from 49 to 67. The other side of flooding was drought, which often followed. Official Song documents list 183 droughts, a third more than in the Tang dynasty. Between 961 and 1087 we know of 67 natural disasters caused by droughts.[5]

During the Little Ice Age, the Yellow River—sometimes called "China's Sorrow"—was particularly active in changing its course.[6] Climate fluctuation, coupled with negligence in dredging, meant that the river's naturally heavy load of silt and loess—which it picked up in its travels through the Ordos Plateau and the loess landscape of Shaanxi province—not only slowed down the flow of water but also built up the riverbed, causing the river to break through its southern embankment and flood the lowlands. Between 893 and 1019, the main channel of the Yellow River emptied into the Gulf of Bohai to the north of today's delta. In 1019 the river broke through the embankment north of the prefectural city of Huazhou, filling a vast swamp in western Shandong and finally discharging into the Bian Canal, which joined the Huai River. The rivers, lakes, and swamps of the Liangshan area became the home base for a Robin Hood–like band of outlaw heroes described in the Ming novel *Water Margin* (*Shuihu zhuan*), which is set in the last decades of the Northern Song. In 1048 the main current of the Yellow River shifted again, to take its northernmost course and empty into the Gulf of Bohai near present-day Tianjin (Map 5).[7]

The instability of the Yellow River made it a strategic resource. In the winter of 1128 when Du Chong feared a Jurchen attack, he ordered the breaching of the dikes that were holding back the Yellow River some 80 kilometers north of Kaifeng, in order to create a natural moat around the

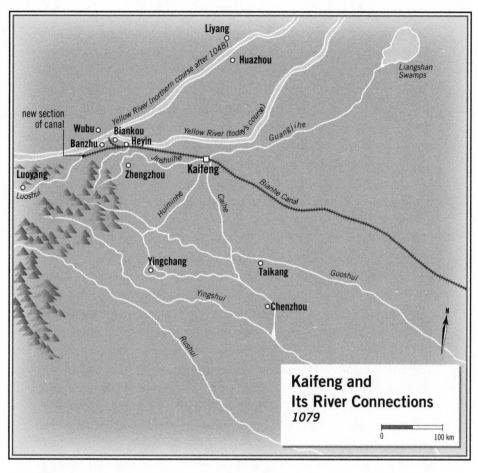

Map 5

capital. The floods devastated the region and returned the river to its southern course. One result of diverting the Yellow River to the south was that it served as the official boundary between the Jin and the Southern Song.[8]

The volume of water diverted from the Yellow River into the Huai River caused it to flood the lowlands along its course, forming Hongze Lake. Surges along the Yellow River in 1187 and 1194 flooded the Liangshan swamps and split the river into northern, central, and southern channels. The mighty central arm changed course in 1194 and 1205 and continued to flow in a southeastern direction, with smaller alterations, until 1853, when it returned to the riverbed it had left almost 850 years earlier.[9]

Faced with such unruly forces of nature, along with settled land ownership in the northern provinces and increasing fear of military incursions
from the alien regimes to the north, Song farmers in the eleventh century
started looking for alternatives, as their families had done for hundreds
of years. They were willing to risk migration into the exotic southern regions, where settlers could open up new and larger plots of land, harvest
several crops a year, and hope that the government's and landlords' control over them and their land would be less onerous than in the north. As
a result of these population shifts, 75 percent of China's 101 million people already lived south of the Huai and Han rivers in the year 1102, a
quarter of a century before the fall of Kaifeng. If we take the Yangzi
rather than the Huai as the division line, 70 percent of all Chinese lived in
the south at that time.[10]

After the Jurchens sacked the capital in 1127, Song household registration collapsed, and population figures are totally lacking until 1159. But
we know that those years witnessed an exodus from north to south on an
unprecedented scale.[11] Assuming a rate of five persons per household, we
can estimate that several million people participated in these migrations.
The population of adult males in the province of Liangzhe, south of the
Yangzi delta, increased by almost 30 percent between 1102 and 1162, to
4.32 million. Fujian registered a similar growth of more than 30 percent,
to 2.8 million adult males. Chengdu registered a 20 percent increase, to
3.15 million. Natural human reproduction could not account for eleva-
tions at this level.

Some of these migrants came from the north, but several of the central
provinces along the Yangzi valley also recorded heavy losses in population. Even these provinces were no longer regarded as safe from the attacks of the Jurchen horsemen. Many counties in the northwest and
north were almost completely depopulated after the collapse of the
Northern Song. It took the Jin several decades and a remigration policy
to entice Chinese farmers to resettle north of the Huai River and raise the
population figures there to the early eleventh-century level of about 25
million people.[12]

In 1110 the Northern Song had registered a total of 20.8 million
households. In 1159 the provinces of the Southern Song registered only
11.1 million households.[13] If these figures were a reliable reflection of the
actual number of inhabitants, the Song population would have dropped
by 45 percent, from 104 million to 55.5 million people, in the decades
immediately following the collapse of Kaifeng. We do not have population figures for the early decades of the Jin dynasty, but provincial and

prefectural population statistics suggest that in 1102 only 25 million Han Chinese lived north of the Huai and Han rivers, which after 1142 formed the borderline between the Jin and the Southern Song. This means that, again, if we are willing to rely on the Southern Song registrars' files, we have to face an unaccountable loss of population in the millions between the end of the Northern Song and the year 1160.

But the Southern Song figures from 1159 have to be discarded as an undercount, due to the concentration of landholding in the hands of the gentry and the inefficiency and corruption of staff employed in land registration. From the population figures for the year 1187 we get the first reliable impression of the demographic situation in the second half of the twelfth century. The Jin census of 1187 showed a registered population of 44.7 million individuals: 40 million Han Chinese, 4 million Jurchens, and several hundred thousand Khitan and Bohai people. Ninety percent of the Jin empire's population was of Han Chinese origin, and in absolute terms far more Han Chinese lived in north China, under Jin rule, than had ever lived there at any point in history. The metropolis of Kaifeng accounted for almost one quarter of all households in the Jin empire.

The Southern Song registers of 1187 provide a figure of 12.3 million households. If we accept that five individuals made up a household, then the registered Southern Song population amounted to 61.8 million people. Thus, in 1187 the aggregate population of China could have reached 106 million people. This figure suggests that due to wars in the 1120s and losses during mass migration, it took almost 80 years for the population of China to recover to the level of the first decade of the twelfth century. If we accept that the real population of the Jin and Southern Song empires far exceeded these conservative estimates, then we can conclude that in the thirteenth century almost half of humankind lived in China.

By 1207 the registered population of the Jin dynasty reached 53.5 million, making this empire more populous than any nation in Europe at that time.[14] This figure may be regarded as an indicator of the economic prosperity that prevailed after the Jurchen conquest of the north. But the prosperity did not last. Population figures took another dramatic turn downward between 1223 and 1264, and by 1292 in the whole of China the population had decreased by roughly 30 million people, or one third of the population, to 75 million people. This was probably due to a combination of factors—warfare in north China, the Mongol invasion, and the bubonic plague or other epidemics. Whatever the causes, this was a decline in human population on a magnitude that the world had seldom seen.[15]

The Road to Coexistence

The rule of Emperor Gaozong lasted thirty-five years—an era during which the Song tried to reassemble what remained of its ideological and material life and consolidate its rule in southern China. Local military leaders in north China still had at least 100,000 troops under their command when Gaozong ascended the throne in June 1127. But under increased pressure from the Jin, the emperor retreated to Yangzhou on the northern bank of the Yangzi River in December of that year. In February 1129 the Song defense collapsed when a commando squad of five hundred Jin horsemen advanced to Yangzhou. Emperor Gaozong ordered the court to decamp to the southern bank. Terrified of the invaders, thousands of Chinese headed for the river and drowned, or died in the struggle for a few small boats.

Emperor Gaozong made a narrow escape by galloping to a crossing point, where a ferry boat awaited him. The Jin horsemen missed capturing him by only a few minutes. Finding himself on the road unattended by the scores of servants and eunuchs that customarily surrounded a Chinese emperor, he had to care for himself in order to survive, and he had to make life-and-death decisions about his own safety. In February he finally reached Hangzhou in the south, where members of the Song government had reassembled under extremely strained conditions.

Two Jin armies crossed the Yangzi, and the one positioned to the east, under the command of Wanyan Zongbi, a nephew of the Jin emperor, headed toward Hangzhou. On January 26, 1130, Jin horsemen captured that city, forcing the Song emperor and his court to escape to the open sea in junks. When the summer heat and rain set in, the Jin troops returned to the north. In June 1130 the Song court settled in Shaoxing, southeast of Hangzhou, at a safe distance from the pillaged city, which was being rebuilt. In 1138 Hangzhou became the capital of the Southern Song.

In a satirical poem, Li Qingzhao made fun of the lords who crossed the Yangzi in flight from the Jin troops, instead of fighting until the end, as Xiang Yu (232–202 B.C.), a hero of the pre-Han civil war, had done. She wrote:

> Alive, one should be an outstanding man,
> Dead, one should be an outstanding ghost.
> Even today, I cannot forget Xiang Yu
> Who refused crossing to the East of the River.[16]

Jin horsemen continued to raid the central plain at will but were unable to control it. Song regional commanders campaigned against them, and the various local militia leaders acted as warlords. The eyewitness Zhou Dunru lamented that the "central plain is a mess." To reorganize the economy of the region and provision its army, in autumn of 1129 the Jin established the buffer state Da Qi under the nominal Chinese rule of Liu Yu (1079–1143?). Operating through the collaboration of Chinese defectors, this state, with its capital at Kaifeng, stood until 1137.

In addition to Jin invaders, central China was also threatened with large-scale banditry and rebellion. A radical religious community under the leadership of Zhong Xiang had existed for decades in northern Hunan and southern Hubei. In 1130 Zhong proclaimed the territory's independence from the Song and declared himself the king of Chu. A celebrated Song general, Yue Fei (1103–1142), put down the rebellion and reestablished social order, and in late 1135 he incorporated the rebels' navy of human-powered paddle-wheel ships of various sizes, called Flying Tiger Warships, into his river fleet. He also folded as many as 50,000 Chu troops into his highly disciplined Yue Family Army.[17] This was not a private army, though its name expressed the strong links between the commander and his individual soldiers. As a rule, when a commander of a military unit was assigned to a new post, he took his officers and his army with him.

In the early 1130s the Jin emperor realized that the remaining Song territory to the south could not be conquered, let alone occupied, and that the Song dynasty could not be eliminated. Unofficial peace talks between the Southern Song and the Jin began in 1132. After Emperor Huizong died on June 4, 1135, in Heilongjiang province, the Jin expressed their willingness to return the coffins of the emperor and his empress.[18] The buffer state of Da Qi was dissolved two years later. But before real negotiations could start, the peace faction at the Song court had to get rid of General Yue Fei, the most successful, popular, independent-minded, influential, and eloquent opponent to a peace agreement in all of China.[19]

On April 27, 1141, Emperor Gaozong wrote a letter to Yue expressing his admiration and encouraging him "to exterminate the caitiffs."[20] But in autumn 1141 the general was jailed for insubordination and malfeasance, and in January 1142 he was poisoned in his prison cell.[21] The intelligent and pragmatic Emperor Gaozong may have viewed Yue Fei's death as a way to curtail the military power of the Song warlords in the north, whose private and largely independent armies posed a threat to the government's peace negotiations. Gaozong may also have hoped to reestablish the priority of civilian control over military force, as Emperor Taizu had done at the beginning of the Song dynasty. A peace treaty with the Jin dynasty replicating the Shanyuan treaty of 1005 with the Khitans would secure a reliable peace for many decades. Taken all together, the power and status of the emperor could only be strengthened by siding with the peace faction.

The most prominent figure among the coexistence advocates was Qin Gui (1090–1155), the official who gave the order to poison Yue Fei. A short time after the general's death, Qin Gui and his counterpart on the Jin side, Wanyan Zongbi, arrived at a peace agreement, drafted on December 25, 1141. The terms were harsh and humiliating for the Song but secured peace between the two states for two decades.

The Song accepted the Huai River as the border between the two empires (Map 6). Thus the dynasty not only wrote off the central plain and two prefectures in modern Hubei but also left millions of tax-paying Han Chinese under the authority of the Jin. The Song promised not to hide fugitives from the Jin state nor to abduct any persons. Furthermore, the Song agreed that in the last month of spring, Jin envoys would arrive at the border town of Sizhou on the Huai River to receive tribute of 250,000 ounces of silver and 250,000 bolts of silk. This annual Song subsidy helped stabilize the finances of the Jin court and kept the Jurchen dynasty intact for almost a century.

For their part, the Jin agreed to return the corpses of Emperor Huizong and his empress to their families and to allow Emperor Gaozong's natural mother, who was still alive, to return to her son. The Jin refused to set Emperor Qinzong free, but this decision was probably good for Gaozong, because Qinzong could have made claims to the throne of the Southern Song.[22] On October 11, 1142, a Jin diplomat presented Emperor Gaozong with an investiture document to sign, which made clear that the Song dynasty was now a vassal of the Jin: "Our insignificant state" pays "tribute" to "your superior state." Emperor Gaozong called himself "your servant [Zhao] Gou."[23] The Jin withdrew its troops from south of the Huai River, and a new period of coexistence began between the Song dynasty as vassal and the Jin dynasty as overlord.

Many people—not just irredentist generals—joined the camp of the treaty's critics, pointing out that the peace settlement threw the Confucian ideology of one world, one ruler overboard. In 1162 the Neo-Confucian philosopher Zhu Xi argued on moral grounds for unwavering military resistance to the barbarians, and in a memorial of 1178 Chen

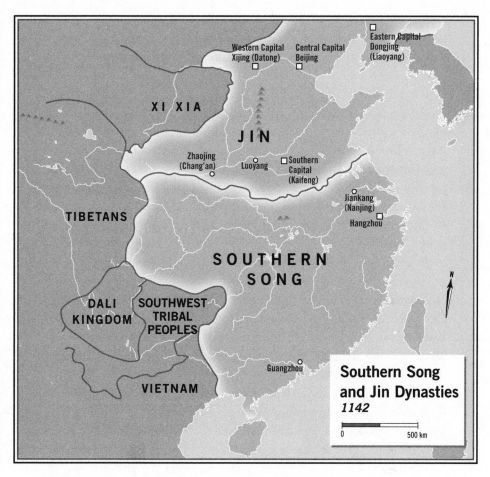

Map 6

Liang called for the reconquest of the central plain. He could no longer bear the thought that China and her civilization were dislodged from the heartland. He wrote: "Your obedient servant ventures to suggest that only China—the standard energy of Heaven and Earth—is that which the heavenly mandate to rule endows, where the hearts of the people gather, where the ritual of civilization cluster, and that which kings and emperors have inherited for a hundred generations. Is it at all conceivable that such a country could be violated by the perverse energy of the barbarians? Unfortunately, it has now been so violated; violated to the degree that we have taken China and civilization and lodged them in this remote, peripheral place."[24] If the Song court did not return to the heartland of China, he feared it would lose its claim to legitimacy.

Given the almost nonexistent alternative of a successful military campaign, however, the treaty establishing the Southern Song was not really a bad deal. Only twice—in 1164, to the advantage of the Song, and in 1208, to the advantage of the Jin—were its terms readjusted.

The Sinicization of the Jin

The Jurchen tribal confederation had made its appearance on the historic stage of East Asia as a distinct group intent on stabilizing its ethnicity and social structure by fighting for independence from its Liao overlord. The Jurchen policy of territorial expansion was critical to this struggle for ethnic survival. But as soon as the Northern Song provinces fell under Jin rule in 1127 and a few million Jurchens became the ethnic minority in power, they had no choice but to make political and cultural concessions to the roughly 20 million Han Chinese subjects all around them.

The question of how to govern this sprawling state—with its 90-percent majority Chinese population living on the former Liao territory and their traditional homeland, the central plain—divided the ruling Wanyan clan. Those who realized the advantages of a functioning administration at all levels preferred the Chinese system of bureaucracy. But the Jurchen warrior-generals, who from the start feared curtailment of their political power and independence, opposed it. Necessity forced the Jurchen rulers to compromise, and this opened the door to sinicization and centralization. The Jin court adopted the Chinese calendar in 1137, reinstituted the civil service examination in 1138, imposed Chinese rules of imperial audience, including Chinese robes for the emperor and officials and Song music at court, in 1139, honored Confucius in 1140, and built imperial ancestral temples.[25] This all happened long before they came to terms of coexistence with the Song dynasty.

In education, the Jurchens promoted the school system they inherited from the Song. While the total number of schools housed in local Confucius temples may have amounted to only 275, sixty of them were built during the Jin dynasty. Schools run by the government were spread all over the country, including the villages. Their financing was secured by a 1196 law that "assigned sixty *mu* of state land to each regional school student, and 108 *mu* to each university student."[26] Tenant-farmers who worked the land were included in the provision.

The main task of the schools was to prepare pupils for civil service examinations. The sound of students reciting the Confucian texts confirmed the view of many contemporaries that the civil principle once again predominated over the military principle. Retaining the education system of old preserved a sense of identity and traditional values among a Chinese upper class who found itself subject to an alien dynasty. Still, education in the classics remained the privilege of a few. The University for the Sons of State had only about 160 pupils, and some schools had only 10. The combined enrollment of all schools at any one time may have added up to only a thousand students. Although the quotas for *jinshi* degree graduates were raised several times, their number was fixed at 600 in 1201. And the Chinese who passed the examination were allowed to enter only the lower ranks of the civil service. The ruling Wanyan clansmen did not share political power easily, especially with outsiders.

In 1149 Wanyan Liang (Prince Liang of Hailing) usurped the Jin throne and initiated a regime of terror aimed at forcing sinicization. Suspicion of his own clansmen, oppression of his critics (including the degrading practice of flogging statesmen in the audience chamber), and bloodshed marked his rule. He constructed Confucian temples in all counties, lifted the ban on Chinese clothing in 1150, and adopted the Song monetary system in 1154. To improve the efficiency of government, he transferred the capital from Shangjing, the old native home of the Jurchen tribes, to Yanjing, a city built in the Chinese architectural style near Beijing. And just to underscore his preference for the urban design of Yanjing, he ordered the destruction of Shangjing's old palaces.[27] Administrative reorganization put into effect by the prince's officials caused many Jurchen nobles to lose their military power and income. These decisions marked the end of the cultural supremacy of the Jurchen traditionalists and left no doubt about the prince's aim to establish a legitimate Chinese dynasty.[28]

In late 1161 Prince Liang of Hailing violated the 1142 peace agreement by moving huge forces across the Huai River to the Yangzi River, the ultimate defense line of the Southern Song. On November 26 and 27, 1161, as his generals attempted to cross at Caishi (modern Ma'anshan), the Jurchens met a well-prepared enemy on the riverbank under the command of Yu Yunwen (1110–1174). Although the Jin losses may not have exceeded 4,000 men, the consequences of the Song victory were far-reaching. On October 27, the prince's nephew, Wanyan Yong (r. 1161–1189), had usurped the Jin throne, and several weeks later, on December 15, 1161, a group of Jurchen officers assassinated Prince Liang of Hailing in his headquarters.

Wanyan Yong had an excellent command of colloquial Chinese and a thorough grounding in the Chinese classics, but he scornfully remarked about his uncle, "Hailing learned Chinese customs; how could he forget his origins?"[29] As Emperor Shizong, the new ruler steered Jin national identity away from sinicization and toward a Jurchen revival. Emperor Shizong was not anti-Chinese, nor did he fail to realize the many advantages of Chinese culture and administration. He retained the Chinese bureaucracy and the practice of recruiting Chinese scholars for public service. But he opposed ethnic integration. In his view, Chinese, Jurchens, and Khitans belonged to different families with different loyalties, and from historical experience he had learned that Jurchens could rely only on other Jurchens.

In Shizong's opinion, imitation of the Chinese had corrupted the Jurchen way of life. He saw before him the rapid disintegration of Jurchen society, the demoralization of its people, and an increasing rate of unlawful behavior. Wide gaps had opened between members of the imperial clan, who mostly resided in the capitals and had adopted the Chinese urban lifestyle, and all the other Jurchens in the countryside, who, unaccustomed to sedentary farmwork, had to struggle for survival. Each of the 170 households of the Jurchen ruling aristocracy owned roughly 1,200 times the agricultural land of the average Jurchen household.[30]

In an effort to remedy this situation to some degree, Shizong confiscated uncultivated land and illegally purchased land from the big Jurchen landowners for redistribution among the poor clans. But this move proved to be counterproductive. In many cases the land quickly changed hands, as impoverished Jurchens sold their holdings right back to Chinese farmers for cash. The emperor resorted to providing sinecures for imperial tribesmen who could not or would not earn a living on their own. But all of this aid could not ward off a loss of economic self-sufficiency.

The emperor's attempts to revitalize Jurchen identity failed for several reasons. First, he had no workable plan of how to strengthen the livelihoods of Jurchen commoners or how to improve the tense relations between the ruling clan and the traditional nobility. Second, the measures he put into effect sent a mixed message and produced mixed results. For example, he decided in 1173 to downgrade the former Supreme Capital at Harbin to the status of a prefectural city, but in the same year he introduced a Jurchen-language *jinshi* degree and promoted the translation of the Chinese classics into Jurchen. The message seemed to be that the Jurchens should use their own language but should study Chinese virtues.

In 1188 he prohibited his people from wearing Chinese clothing, which they had been doing for four decades, but in 1191 he lifted the prohibition on intermarriage between Jurchens and Chinese (which was being practiced at all levels of Jin society regardless of the law against it). In that same year the Chinese were forbidden to refer to the Jurchens as barbarians.[31] Third, Shizong made a fundamental error in assuming that nonsedentary people of warrior origin could, within a few generations, be transformed into law-abiding farmers. All of the economic aid designed to bring about that result was bound to fail. Finally, when it came time to choose Emperor Shizong's successor, his court followed the Chinese principle of primogeniture rather than the Jurchen practice of election by the heads of the clans.

Emperor Shizong claimed that "my country has defeated the Liao and Song and thus holds the legitimate position under Heaven."[32] His successors, Emperor Zhangzong (r. 1189–1208) and Emperor Xuanzong (r. 1213–1224), took this claim one step further by presenting the Jin dynasty as a natural link in the historic chain of Chinese dynasties. But like Shizong, these rulers were also indecisive about adopting Chinese ways, and this alienated both the Jurchens and the Chinese under their rule. Shortly after the fall of the dynasty in 1234 at the hands of the Mongols, Liu Qi would surmise that one of the main reasons for the collapse of the Jin may have been its rulers' inability to make the decision in favor of complete sinicization.[33] A thorough-going adoption of Chinese education and administrative practices would have put able scholar-officials at the top level of political decision-making. The Jin chose instead to permit only Jurchens to hold those positions.

The Jurchens, who kept the Song dynasty under their heel for more than a century, had stretched their potential to the limit. After the Mongol invasion, the tribe finally perished between the Yellow and the Yangzi rivers, far from the forests of their Manchurian homeland.

The Glory and Misery of the Song

In Chinese history the victorious battle of Caishi at the Yangzi River in 1161 was often compared to the famous battle at the Fei River in 383, when Chinese troops defeated the alien Qin dynasty and saved Chinese culture from destruction at the hands of barbarians. The peace treaty signed after the battle no longer used the humiliating term "vassal" for the Song but employed the metaphor of "uncle" and "nephew." The embattled Song dynasty enjoyed a level of confidence and self-esteem it had not known for two or more generations.

After thirty-five years of rule, Emperor Gaozong abdicated on July 24, 1162, in favor of his stepson, Zhao Shen (1127–1194), posthumously titled Emperor Xiaozong, the Filial Ancestor. Zhao Shen was attentive and earnest and tried to live up to Confucian standards of moral behavior. He closely supervised the court and central government in order to ensure that power remained well balanced among his high officials. Reversing the policy of Qin Gui, he rehabilitated the reputation of the military hero Yue Fei and his family, along with many other officials who had suffered humiliation at the hands of the peace faction. Many historians view Emperor Xiaozong as the best of the Southern Song rulers and his reign as the golden age of the Southern Song dynasty.[34]

Suffering from mental illness during the last two years of his reign, Xiaozong followed the example of his stepfather and abdicated on February 18, 1189, after twenty-seven years of rule. Just four weeks earlier, his Jin overlord, Emperor Shizong, whose rule during almost the same period is often called the golden age of the Jin dynasty, had died. Under these two benevolent rulers, the coexistence policy between the Song and Jin had born fruit, for the benefit and welfare of their subjects and their states.

After Emperor Xiaozong's abdication, the gradual but inexorable decline of the Song dynasty set in. His successor, Emperor Guangzong (r. 1189–1194), who also suffered from mental illness, abdicated after five years. His son, Emperor Ningzong (r. 1194–1224), the Tranquil Ancestor, is said to have been the most passive adult emperor of the entire dynasty. He was extremely slow of speech and never seems to have developed a political idea of his own. Decision-making was left to his advisors, who were dominated by his empress.[35] She successfully pushed her uncle, Han Tuozhou (1151–1207), into influential positions at court. Lacking the experience and distinction of having passed the *jinshi* examination, Han instigated one of the most infamous anti-intellectual campaigns of Song history. He also initiated a war against the Jurchens that ended in Song defeat.

In 1195, at the beginning of Ningzong's rule, his chief councilor, Zhao Ruyu (1140–1196), championed a dynastic revival and appointed scholar-officials of reputation, including the Neo-Confucian thinker Zhu Xi, into government positions. After considerable factional strife in 1196, Han Tuozhou took over the position of chief councilor, and Zhao

Ruyu was banished to Hunan province. He died en route.[36] Through Han's manipulations at court, Zhu Xi was impeached after only two months of service and driven from court, and his philosophy was labeled "false learning." Han's example encouraged some of his better-educated but equally treacherous partisans to accuse fifty-nine officials of crimes they themselves had committed.[37] In 1202 the proscription against Confucian learning was retracted, but Han's hostility toward officials who followed the Way prevailed until the end of his term in office.

Han's disastrous domestic policy was matched by an equally ill-informed foreign policy. He hoped to profit from the Jin's troubles, which included border conflicts with the Xi Xia, a new threat from the Mongols, and natural disasters that affected Shandong in 1206. When, on Han's advice, the Song declared war on the Jin on June 14, 1206, a period of peace lasting almost forty-five years came to an abrupt end.

Many of the Song commanders stationed along the border and a number of other patriotic officials welcomed this endeavor to recover territories in the north lost more than sixty years earlier. The Song troops totaled about 160,000 men. In their first offensive, they took the Huai River border town of Sizhou by surprise, but it took the Jurchen only a short time to organize a counteroffensive. They stabilized the central front line at the Han River, and in December 1206 probably 135,000 infantrymen and horsemen made a three-pronged counterattack into the Lower Yangzi region, the Han River region, and Sichuan province. Occupying the north side of the Yangzi River, they conquered Guanghua at the Han River and surrounded the fortressed cities of Xiangyang and Dean. The siege lasted from December 1206 until April 1207.[38] The commander of Xiangyang, Zhao Chun, repulsed several dozen attacks on land and water and saved the city from destruction.

But from the Song perspective, the war was a military disaster. The campaigns failed because of strategic incompetence, logistical failures in provisioning troops, and miserable weather conditions. The Chinese population of the Jin empire did not rise up to join their Song brothers from the south, as Han Tuozhou had expected—on the contrary, the Song dynasty's soldiers deserted by the thousands. Within a few months Han had maneuvered the Southern Song into a most precarious situation. At court the devastating reports pouring in from the front aggravated an already troubled political atmosphere. The peace faction regained the emperor's attention and accused Han of being solely responsible for the military disaster. Emperor Ningzong renounced him.

On March 29, 1207, Song loyalists in Sichuan assassinated the former Song governor Wu Xi, who had defected and declared himself the king of Shu, a vassal of the Jin dynasty. His head was sent in a box to the Song court. This turn of events forced the remaining Jin troops to retreat from Sichuan. By this time it was evident that neither party could win the war. The Jin troops under the command of Wanyan Kuang suffered from disease and exhaustion and were not able to keep up the siege of Xiangyang any longer. Around this time a Song delegation journeyed to the Jin court at Kaifeng to begin peace negotiations.

Complex discussions between the Song and Jin continued throughout the rest of the year. Han Tuozhou was dismissed from court on November 23, and the next day he was assassinated by the commander of the Palace Guard. Four days later the Song throne ordered the execution of Han Tuozhou's confidant, Su Shidan, and banished many others in his faction. The atmosphere of the peace talks shortly improved.[39] On July 29, 1208, the Jin announced that a resolution had been reached with the Song, and October 15 was designated as the day for the official audience proclaiming the conclusion of the peace negotiations. The Song dynasty committed itself to paying a war indemnity of 3 million ounces of silver, making an annual tribute of 300,000 ounces of silver and 300,000 bolts of silk, apologizing for having breached the old treaty, and handing over to the Jin in boxes the heads of the "war criminals" Han Tuozhou and Su Shidan—an unprecedented condition of peace. The heads were lacquered and placed in the ancestral temple of the Jurchen imperial family, but portraits of them were put on display all over the empire.[40] In return, the Jin dynasty agreed to withdraw its troops from Song territory and revert to the old border along the Huai River. The annual subsidy paid by the Song once more helped the Jin ruler to reward his loyal supporters and ensured the survival of the dynasty for a little while longer.

The winner of the factional strife at court was Shi Miyuan (1164–1233), Han Tuozhou's successor, who hailed from a multigenerational official family.[41] Shi Miyuan was involved in the assassination of Han, as we learn from his statement: "I was secretly permitted to assist."[42] This fact clouded his image in Chinese history, but still he ranks among the most influential and independent chief councilors in Song times, along with Zhao Pu (922–992), Cai Jing (1046–1126), Qin Gui (1090–1155), and Han Tuozhou. After Shi Miyuan's tenure, only Jia Sidao (1213–1275), the last Song reformer, was viewed as equally powerful. A man of exceptional talents—well-trained for public office, well-educated, loyal to the emperor and the dynasty, and, when he needed to be, excellent at the art of manipulation—Shi Miyuan worked closely with Empress Yang Yan (1162–1232). An accomplished artist and musician, she was also one of the most politically astute and aggressive empresses in Song history.

Shi Miyuan held his position for twenty-four years, until his death in 1233. His councilorship encompassed the last period of peace and stability in Song history. When Emperor Ningzong died on September 17, 1224, without an heir, Shi and the empress dowager managed to secure the throne for Zhao Yun, son of an obscure clansman of the tenth generation of the second son of Emperor Taizu. He would rule for forty years as Emperor Lizong (Principled Ancestor).[43] His temple name refers to the state's recognition of the primacy of Zhu Xi's School of Principle or Reason within Confucianism. At the same time, his temple name was a political statement reassuring the Song dynasty of its cultural supremacy on the eve of the Mongol invasion.

The Mongol Advance

As if the continuing Jin threat had not been enough for the Southern Song dynasty to bear, at the beginning of the thirteenth century the Mongols turned up on the northern horizon. Under the leadership of Chinggis (Genghis) Khan and his son, in less than ten years the Mongols destroyed the Song's two main enemies, the Tangut Xi Xia dynasty in 1227 and the Jurchen Jin dynasty in 1234. Two years later, the Mongols turned their attention for the first time to the Song empire and invaded the province of Sichuan.

The Mongols were a tribal people living on grasslands near the Kerulen and Onan rivers, several hundred kilometers southeast of Lake Baikhal in the northeast part of present-day Mongolia. They had been self-sufficient for centuries, making a living from their sheep, cattle, and horses. But throughout most of the twelfth century the third Little Ice Age caused a drop in the mean annual temperature, and the worsening climatic conditions may have forced the Mongol tribes to search for better grassland outside their own territory. Conflicts with neighboring tribes were unavoidable. They attracted the attention of Chinese historians for the first time when they defeated the Jin in 1139. In an agreement of 1147 the Jin agreed to pay annual subsidies in cattle and sheep, rice and beans, and fine and coarse silks—much the same kind of arrangement the Jin had made with the Song just five years earlier, except that this time the Jin paid tribute.

Temüjin (1167–1227), better known as Chinggis Khan, meaning the "firm," "strong," or "oceanic" conqueror, did not hail from a powerful and well-settled family. When his father, Yesugei, was poisoned by the Tartars, his father's former followers and all members of the lineage scattered to align with leaders more potent than his son. Temüjin's defenseless widowed mother, Hö'elun, was abandoned with her children. The *Secret History of the Mongols*, written in Chinese characters but giving the sound of the Mongolian language, describes how this courageous woman escaped into the mountains with her children and survived on wild pears, berries, roots, fish, and small game, and how she saved her children from enslavement by her enemies.

Temüjin endured decades of deprivation, endless fights, and years of captivity in the Jin empire, but during this time he built up alliances. In 1206, after the death of the old Mongol leader, a meeting of the tribes was held at the Onan River. At this grand assembly, all the tribal leaders congregated to speak up for the best successor—in most cases a son or brother of the dead leader—who normally had already defeated all his rivals and had thus proven that he could secure the welfare of the tribes. Temüjin's previous efforts aimed at forging a Mongol confederation of ethnic, cultural, and linguistic unity finally bore fruit. He was proclaimed head of all the Mongols.

After Chinggis Khan came to power, the well-being of the Mongols no longer depended on traditional nomadic herding but increasingly on the spoils of war. As the provider of gold, silver, horses, women, captives, and slaves to his people, he demanded obedience and loyalty. Loyalty and revenge formed the basis of his understanding of human relations. Trustworthy tribesmen were generously rewarded, while disloyal ones were cruelly punished. This system of rule worked only as long as the military machine continued to move against the Mongols' neighbors and bring home the booty. Thus, warfare and conquest, along with the intoxication of battle, became ends in themselves.

The Mongol tribal structure was closely connected with its military structure, which was organized in 95 units of 1,000 fighting men each, along with their families and dependents. Appointment to a command depended solely on ability, efficiency, and bravery in battle. This competitive system was highly motivating, because it meant that unrestricted promotion was possible. But it also implied that the khan regarded all soldiers as brothers and as equals-in-arms. His officers and common soldiers shared the same simple food and quarters, and these conditions of equality bolstered the fighting spirit of the men and also their loyalty. In 1227 the number of military units may have increased to 129, encompassing 700,000 people in all—which is to say, the entire Mongol nation.

In 1209 the Mongols intensified their war with the Tanguts, and in 1211 they began to invade Jin territory. In spring 1214 the Mongol forces surrounded the Central Capital Zhongdu (modern Beijing) and forced the Jin to pay a high price for ending hostilities: 500 boy and girl slaves, 3,000 horses, plus gold and silks.[44] In the summer of that year, the Jin Emperor Xuanzong moved the court from Zhongdu to Kaifeng, the Southern Capital, and more than 400,000 households decamped to the south. When Chinggis Khan learned the news, he immediately ordered his troops to attack Zhongdu.

Cut off from supplies and with no chance of getting reinforcements, the capital city surrendered in May 1215 after a ten-month siege. Thousands of inhabitants were massacred. For months afterward, the bones of the slaughtered were piled up in great heaps. The soil was greasy with human fat, and the air smelled of rotting flesh.[45] Chinggis Khan had taken revenge for what he viewed as a cunning maneuver by the Jurchens to strengthen their military forces in the south and then return to attack him. Mukhali, one of the most able of Chinggis Khan's generals, continued his campaigns in the northern Jin provinces of Hebei, Henan, Shanxi, and Shaanxi. Before long, Manchuria, the homeland of the Khitan and Jurchen peoples, came under Mongol rule.

The Scourge of Allah

Displaying the nomad's sense of justice, Chinggis Khan organized his life around the principle of revenge.[46] When the Merkit people abducted his spouse, Börte, he ordered the tribe's extermination. He massacred all males of the Tartar tribe that had murdered his father, and he was responsible for an almost endless list of ferocious punishments meted out regardless of family relationship, former friendship, or tribal affiliation. He destroyed cities and all their inhabitants, often numbering in the tens of thousands. For Chinese living in the northern provinces, the terror spread by Mongol troops was a fact of daily life.

But for the Han Chinese living on the central plain and in the Southern Song state, the former Khitan and Jurchen invaders had been much worse. Chinggis Khan's military campaigns focused on the rich cities along the so-called Silk Road across the Central Asian steppes. Due to previous wars, these states were too exhausted to offer much resistance, and their grasslands were better suited to invasion by his horsemen than the paddy fields of central and south China. The Song dynasty was a demographic giant compared with the easy prey of Central Asia and could not be conquered merely with acts of terror and senseless violence.

The Mongols' reputation as monsters drinking the blood of their victims and devouring the flesh of dogs, rats, and men alike preceded their horsemen and enabled them to conquer vast territories with breathtaking speed. Mongol commanders told their victims that "surrender without fighting" was the key to survival for city dwellers along their bloody route. When a city followed this command, the Mongols plundered public institutions and private households but spared the lives of inhabitants for the most part. After a short respite, just long enough to distribute the booty, the Mongol war machine moved out of the city. Craftsmen who were useful to the Mongols, along with young women, were very often taken into slavery and distributed by the dozens among campaign commanders and their troops.

The military successes of the Mongols raised the ire of the most powerful Islamic ruler in Central Asia, Sultan Muhammad of Khwarazm, who had his own ambitions to conquer the Jin. Khwarazm covered the territory from Transoxania (present-day Turkmenistan), eastern Iran, and Afghanistan and reached into northern India. After fruitless negotiations and the murder of a Mongol envoy, Chinggis Khan prepared for war. But in 1219, before heading out to battle, he summoned a grand assembly to decide the question of his successor in the event of his death. The participants agreed on his third son, Ögödei (1186–1241).

In a campaign lasting from 1219 until 1225, Chinggis Khan's commanders drove their troops into the state territory of Khwarazm and massacred millions of people. The victory cemented the Mongol army's reputation for invincibility and mercilessness and led Arab chroniclers to describe Chinggis Khan as the "scourge of Allah."[47] Bukhara, the Turkic center of learning, religion, commerce, and craftsmanship, was plundered in early 1220, and the city of Samarkand fell in the spring of the same year after a short siege. In both cases the population and Islamic clerics offered surrender and were driven out of the city, but tens of thousands of military defenders were slaughtered. Dozens of other cities suffered a similar fate. By separate routes the Mongol forces advanced as far west as the Kipchak Steppes north of the Caspian Sea and as far south as the Black Sea via the Caucasus before most of the troops returned to Mongolia in 1224 to 1225.

The task of permanent campaigning required more than able horsemen. Each rider was dressed in ox hides enforced with plates of iron, and he was equipped with several mounts, which enabled him to ride for days with only short breaks. Iron stirrups copied from the Jurchen cavalry allowed the mounted archers to stand up and shoot their iron-tipped arrows while moving at a gallop. A great number of carts loaded with supplies and provisions followed the cavalry and the auxiliary forces. Firebombs and rockets armed with Chinese gunpowder were brought along, as well as all sorts of mechanical contrivances indispensable for sieges. Chinggis Khan forced allied tribes and defeated kingdoms to put troops at his disposal, and these forces became cannon-fodder on the front line. The auxiliary troops of Khitans, Jurchens, Koreans, Han Chinese, and other ethnicities often outnumbered the Mongol forces. The civil population in defeated territories also had to provide grain, garments, metals, mounts, and labor services to the invaders.[48]

In his last campaign, Chinggis Khan led his troops in attacking the Tangut capital city, Ningxia, which had earlier refused to provide auxiliary troops. When he died in August 1227, the Mongols exacted a dreadful vengeance, slaughtering the entire population of the capital. The death of the Mongol nation's founder, a ruler of godlike stature, postponed a large-scale invasion of the Jin empire. As soon as Ögödei was accepted as great khan, he resumed the campaigns. In 1230 he launched a great offensive against the Jin—a three-pronged advance through Shandong in the east, through Shanxi in the center under his own command, and through Shaanxi and northern Sichuan in the west, under the command of Tolui. By summer 1232 all three armies had taken positions near Kaifeng. The desperate Jin emperor Aizong (r. 1224–1234) fled to Caizhou, where he appealed to the Song for help. His cries went unanswered. Kaifeng surrendered in May 1233, and Emperor Aizong killed himself on February 9, 1234, bringing an end to the Jin dynasty.

Between 1235 and his death six years later, Ögödei resumed the Mongols' westward advance to secure their claims in eastern-most Europe. His troops took a straight route through southern Siberia, destroyed the Bulgar state on the Volga River in 1237, and sacked Vladimir and Moscow in 1238, before returning to the more familiar Kipchak Steppes. In 1240 the Mongols conquered Kiev, the capital of Rus in the Ukraine, thus severing Russia's religious and cultural links to Byzantium. From Kiev the horsemen invaded Poland, where they defeated the Polish army at Chmielnik and, in April 1241 wiped out the German-Polish knights' army in the battle of Liegnitz in Silesia. Meanwhile, another contingent, after defeating the Hungarian king at Mohi, advanced toward Vienna.

Ögödei died after a severe drinking bout on December 11, 1241, at Karakorum, and his forces returned to Mongolia to elect a new leader. Years of quarrels and competition for leadership between the families of Chinggis Khan's four legitimate sons edged toward civil war and threatened the unity of the tribe. All major military activities were suspended until 1251, when Möngke (1209–1259), the son of Chinggis Khan's youngest son, Tolui, became the great khan through the clever maneuvers of his mother, Sorghaghtani Beki. He proudly asserted that he "obeyed the laws of [his] ancestors and did not imitate the behavior of other countries."[49] In 1253, in a ruthless purge to secure his rule, he almost eliminated Ögödei's family and ordered his brother Hülegü to consolidate Mongol control over Persia. In 1258 Möngke sacked Baghdad, the seat of the Abbasid caliphate, where Christian auxiliary troops joined the Mongols in a great slaughter of the Muslim inhabitants.[50]

The four khanates defined at that time consisted of the khanate of the Golden Horde in south Russia and the Ukraine; the khanate of Chaghadai, formerly the state of Khwarazm; the khanate of west Asia, later called the il-khanate of Persia; and the khanate of Mongolia. In addition to these, he appointed his brother Khubilai (1215–1294) to the khanate of China in 1253 and ordered him to invade the Southern Song territory for grain and to plunder its flourishing cities.

Before starting the Song operation in 1254 by stepping up raids along the northern border, Khubilai took time out to subdue the kingdom of Dali in Yunnan province. On August 11, 1259, Möngke died during the campaign in Sichuan, just as he was about to cross the Yangzi River. A new succession crisis for the khanate granted the Song court a short reprieve. Khubilai emerged as victor from the grand assembly on May 5, 1260, and on December 18, 1271, he proclaimed a new dynasty, to be known later as the Yuan. As Emperor Shizu (r. 1260–1294), he would become the first alien to rule over all of China.

The Lingering Death of the Song Dynasty

After the Mongols turned up on the Song's border in the 1250s, Song officials should have recognized the invaders as a serious threat and not just another horde of marauding barbarians. But the extinction of the glorious Song, which had ruled China for three hundred years, and the conquest of China by barbarians, which had never happened in all of Chinese history, was beyond imagining. Not recognizing the gravity of the problem, Song politicians did not really want to consider a solution that had worked so well for them in the past—establishing diplomatic relations with the invaders in order to buy time until some other military power defeated the aggressor.[51]

A number of domestic problems also got out of control in thirteenth-century Song and set the stage for collapse. In 1234, when the Mongols extinguished the Jin dynasty, the value of paper money, compared with coins, dropped dramatically, causing civilians and soldiers who were paid with money notes to suffer heavy losses. To reduce the amount of paper money in circulation and stabilize its market value, chief councilor Zheng Qing in 1235 suggested an additional land tax of one money note on every *mu* of farmland to be levied. The proposal met with sharp opposition from colleagues representing the interests of the big landowners. They recommended instead a tax on merchants. All of these proposals to save the value of paper money ultimately failed to prevent astronomical inflation by 1246. Although rich harvests kept state revenues high, the disastrous effects on the Song economy could no longer be denied.[52] But nobody dared to take the necessary steps to reform the monetary system, which concentrated wealth in the hands of the landowning class.

To provision the Song's huge armies, the government required that farmers sell their grain to public granaries and accept payment with paper money. In order to stabilize the price of food for everyone else, the new chief councilor, Jia Sidao (1213–1275), tried to reform the method whereby grain was purchased. His Public Field Law of 1263 was a program to reallocate private wealth in order to increase tax revenues. It legalized the state's purchase of agricultural areas from large private landholdings exceeding 500 mu (286,500 square meters) and the conversion of that land into public fields, which were then redistributed to landless farmers. The procedure came close to an expropriation. Officials were also given land in proportion to their rank.[53] Compensation was based on the amount of land sold, and the market value of land depended on the annual tax yield.

Jia Sidao's reform was the most radical and desperate attempt in premodern Chinese history to consolidate state finances, stabilize the value of paper money, limit the acreage held by big landowners, and reduce their economic power and widespread tax evasion. Implemented over a period of twelve years until 1275, his reform enjoyed the support of the emperors Lizong and Duzong (r. 1264–1274) but ran counter to the economic interests of officials whose support the dynasty urgently needed for survival. Their outcry was furious and their resistance fierce. It was Jia's ill luck to be in power right up to the moment of the Mongol onslaught in 1268. Had he died earlier, Chinese historians might have ranked him with the reformer Wang Anshi. Even today, the overall social impact of his reform is difficult to assess, given the rapid deterioration of the dynasty.[54]

When Khubilai became khaghan of the Mongols in 1260, he intended to subjugate the Song, which he regarded as a powerful rival aspiring to reunify China under its rule. But his horsemen were unaccustomed to the terrain south of the Yangzi, with its mighty rivers, vast lakes, mucky rice fields, high humidity, and even higher temperatures. An invasion there would require different provisions and strategies than a cavalry attack on the steppes. For a war against the Song to be successful, the Mongols would have to depend on auxiliary troops and Chinese defectors knowledgeable about the terrain and the Song mentality.

The new Mongol leader also had domestic troubles of his own that demanded attention. His election had not gone unchallenged, and the defection of Li Tan (d. 1262), an influential Chinese warlord in Shandong, had to be handled.[55] He needed to set up an administration in north China to secure the constant flow of tax income to the Mongol court, but he also had to take into account the ethnic and nomadic particularities of the Mongol people. He was caught in the same civilization trap as the Jurchens before him, but it was potentially much more serious. In response, Khubilai established a system of central administration similar to that of the Northern Song. Provincial and local control, however, differed greatly from the Chinese.[56] He divided the population of the khanate of China into three ethnic groups: Mongols, who were dominant; Central and Western Asians, including many Muslims, who were second in command; and Han Chinese, along with Khitans and Jurchens, who were the lowest-ranking group.

The Mongol war offensive started in 1268 with the battles of Fancheng and Xiangyang at the Han River, the heavily fortified strongholds obstructing access to the central basin of the Yangzi. The official Wang Yinglin (1223–1296), who had participated in the funeral of Emperor Lizong in 1264, warned Emperor Duzong again and again that the internal security of the Song empire depended on the fighting strength of these two strongholds. "If they give in," he asked, "how can we find peace again?" He complained that officials at court were negligent, and nobody there was willing or prepared to discuss the precarious situation at the frontier.[57] The Song court was convinced that the fortress could withstand attacks for many years, because in 1206 and 1207 the Jin army had been unable to conquer Xiangyang. Attackers would need naval forces and siege specialists to bridge the wide, deep moat and break the stout wall.

In addition to Mongols, Khubilai recruited Chinese, Persian, and Uighur ground troops, and employed Koreans and Jurchens for his navy. More than 5,000 boats blockaded the river, interrupting the flow of reinforcements and provisions for the beleaguered cities. The breakthrough, however, came in 1272 when Muslim siege technicians arrived at the battlefield. They built a catapult that threw huge rocks over a long distance. These boulders finally cracked the city walls. In January 1273 Fancheng was stormed and all inhabitants, civilian and military—more than 10,000 individuals—were massacred. The Mongols piled up the corpses along the Han River, to provide a shocking view of the fate in store for the defenders of Xiangyang.

After five years of battle, the Song commander at Xiangyang, Lü Wenhuan, defected to the enemy. He later served Khubilai as a military advisor and field commander. In March 1273 the city surrendered in order to save itself from gruesome slaughter. The Song court was shocked, and in the grip of paralyzing uncertainty, officials wavered between heroism, loyalty, and fatalism. They all expected the Mongol forces to advance down the Yangzi River and into the heartland of the Southern Song. But contrary to these expectations, the great invasion was postponed until late 1274. Military expeditions to pacify Korea in 1273 and subjugate Japan in 1274 took priority. As it turned out, the Japan war campaign ended in disaster for the Mongols.

Just three weeks before the unexpected death of Emperor Duzong on August 12, 1274, Khubilai announced a "declaration of war" against the Song, blaming the dynasty for the conflict in the south.[58] Duzong's four-year-old son, Zhao Xian (1270–1323), succeeded him. His grandmother, Empress Dowager Xie Daoqing (1210–1283), the most remarkable woman at the Song court in the thirteenth century, acted as his regent.

The Final Collapse

Khubilai appointed the Mongol Bayan (1237–1295) to lead the great campaign. After elaborate preparations that included the collaboration of many defectors from the Song, his army totaling perhaps 200,000 soldiers, mainly Chinese, crossed the Yangzi River at Hankou in January 1275. The main force followed the Yangzi in the direction of Nanjing and Yangzhou, while a few contingents made for Guangdong and Fujian province. In January 1275 the empress dowager made her appeal: those "having lived on the emoluments of your monarch . . . and those infused with loyal and righteous vigor will offer their services in engaging the enemy."[59] She still held the illusory hope that a concentration of defensive forces might stop the Mongol advance.

In March 1275 Jia Sidao took command of an army of 130,000 soldiers and 2,500 ships blockading the Yangzi River and awaited the Mongol force at Dingjia Islet not far from Yangzhou. The confrontation soon proved that the Song army was no match for the Mongol cavalry and artillery, which blasted the Song fleet to pieces.[60] As the Song defense broke down, officers and soldiers defected or fled. Jia Sidao tried to regroup the remnants of his army, and for his trouble he was held responsible for the entire military disaster. Empress Dowager Xie dismissed him from office on March 26, 1275. His successor, Chen Yizhong (ca. 1228–ca. 1285), demanded his execution, but Xie refused. On his way to banishment in Fujian province, Cheng Huchen, the commander of Jia's guard, had him murdered on October 9, 1275.

Chen Yizhong immediately abolished the Public Field Law and set about reestablishing the prereform system of land ownership. Court officials were in turmoil, divided about the future of the dynasty and as split about Chen Yizhong as they had been about Jia Sidao. The empress dowager rightly complained that the officials were cowards and defectors who did not offer a single proposal for saving the empire. She admonished them that the Mandate of Heaven had not yet changed.[61]

Bayan's troops advanced to the Song capital of Hangzhou. The Song army failed to resist the invasion, and afterward the various negotiation offers sent to Bayan and the Mongol court had no appeal. Most cities had already surrendered without putting up a fight, but a few battles remained to be fought. To intimidate the loyal defenders of the Song, Bayan made of Changzhou, which stubbornly held on, a terrible example. After storming the city in December 1275, he ordered the whole population, civilian and military, to be executed. When the Mongol troops in the early weeks of 1276 closed in on Hangzhou, desertions in all ranks increased. Chen Yizhong advised the evacuation of the capital, a proposal the loyalists Wen Tianxiang and Zhang Shijie had made to no avail ten days earlier in order to save the dynasty.

On February 4, 1276, when Bayan's troops arrived in the neighborhood of Hangzhou, Chen Yizhong deserted the empress dowager and made a secret escape to his home near the coastal city of Wenzhou. Zhang Shijie followed his example one day later and took his troops to Dingzhou. The empress dowager felt betrayed. Now that the Song dynasty was lost, a previously drafted document of unconditional surrender was forwarded to Bayan, along with the imperial seal.

The child emperor appealed to the moral virtue of the emperor of the Great Yuan and reasoned: "Now, the Mandate of Heaven has been restored, Your Servant chooses to depart from it."[62] On February 21, 1276, in the name of the Yuan dynasty, Bayan accepted the document of surrender. When he triumphantly paraded through the gates and on the boulevards of Hangzhou on March 28, 1276, Bayan took possession of the richest, largest, and most cultivated city of the world.[63] The former emperor and his mother, the dowager Quan Jiu (1241–1309), Empress Dowager Xie, and all the imperial consorts and eunuchs were taken prisoner and escorted by Bayan to Khubilai's residence at Shangdu. The former emperor was soon banished to Tibet, accompanied by his mother, where he entered a Buddhist monastery. He committed suicide in 1323.

For Empress Dowager Xie, the humiliating unconditional capitulation to the Yuan dynasty had sealed the fate of the Song. But many of the real and self-styled loyalists, among them Chen Yizhong, Zhang Shijie, and Wen Tianxiang, had fled on differing routes to the south, taking with them the two half-brothers of Emperor Gongdi, Zhao Shi (1268–1278) and Zhao Bing (1271–1279). They tried to organize a military resistance, and on June 14, 1276, they enthroned the elder of the two half-brothers, later known as Emperor Duanzong. A lack of unity, however, weakened this resistance effort from the start. Chased by the Mongol troops, they sailed to the south and fled to the island of Yaishan or Cliff Hill, along with 200,000 other Song escapees. By then, the emperor's younger half-brother Bing, the six-year-old last son of Emperor Duzong, had already been proclaimed emperor on May 10, 1278.

The Mongol fleet crashed the remnants of the Song dynasty in a naval battle on March 19, 1279, claiming countless civilian and military lives, among them the child emperor. Most were killed in action, but many perished by drowning or committed suicide. The real Song loyalists chose martyrdom and death as the moral alternative to service under Mongol rule, and for the women of their households mass suicide became the accepted option, following the precepts of Neo-Confucianism.[64]

One of the witnesses of the battle of Yaishan was the most famous Song loyalist, Wen Tianxiang (1236–1283). In 1256 he had passed the metropolitan *jinshi* examination, presided over by Wang Yinglin, as the first on the list. He was personally honored by Emperor Lizong. Deeply involved in daily politics, he advocated the defense of the dynasty and the capital, but all his efforts and military campaigns failed. He was captured by the Mongols in 1279, and while their prisoner he received several offers to enter public service, but he remained loyal to the Song. This led to a personal dilemma: by ranking his loyalty to the Song higher than his service to family and ancestors, he was in violation of the Confucian ethic of filial piety. Yet in all his years in prison, he refused the Mongol offers, convinced that someone who had been appointed chief councilor by the grace of the Song and had ranked first in the *jinshi* examination list should not serve two masters. He insisted on demonstrating his loyalty through martyrdom. After four years of imprisonment, on January 9, 1283, he was executed at the Mongol capital Dadu (Beijing), in a marketplace crowded with spectators. His last words recorded were: "I have completed my service."[65]

5

THREE DOCTRINES

IN SONG times, under the influence of both Buddhism and Daoism, Confucian thinkers began to reorganize ancient Chinese thought and create the basis of a philosophical system known as the Learning of the Way. Far more than a single philosophical school, this movement—often labeled Neo-Confucianism in the West—aimed primarily to establish a social and political order.[1] It defined and reasserted a system of Chinese values—a fundamentalist ethic as well as a rationalist epistemology—which served as the pivot for Song culture in both the public and private spheres.

The thinkers responsible for this "renaissance" attempted to reestablish the superiority of Confucian philosophy over its Buddhist and Daoist rivals by first clearing out the errors that had infiltrated Confucian learning over the centuries. But during this practical process of rejuvenation, they incorporated aspects of Buddhist and Daoist doctrine and practice that humanized the Confucian program. Throughout the Song dynasty, Confucianism, Daoism, and Buddhism were known as the "three doctrines," and each played a role at every level of society.

Reviving Confucianism

The Song dynasty was the golden age of Chinese philosophy. The Confucian value system of the ancients, revitalized and brought to its highest expression by twelfth-century scholars, became the preeminent ideology dominating the behavior of the Chinese elite and regulating the state's domestic and foreign policy until the end of the imperial period.

Chinese ethical thinking developed into a philosophical system when scholar-officials during the Song dynasty started to examine the fundamental principles in the body of writings attributed to Confucius and his school and to draw their own conclusions, enriching them with their own thoughts. The humanistic and rational Confucianism that grew out of this reconsideration differed greatly from previous understandings of Confucian doctrine. The Learning of the Way (*daoxue*) thus represents a recreation and revival of Confucianism (*ruxue*).[2]

The philosopher Han Yu was the first member of what would become a fraternity of followers of the Way.[3] His brand of Neo-Confucianism was a sort of cultural fundamentalism dedicated to restoring the moral values of the ancients, which had been lost. Han Yu's use of the word *dao* meant something quite simple and straightforward: "What I call the Way (*dao*) and Power (*de*) means combining humaneness (*ren*) and righteousness (*yi*). This is the definition accepted by all under Heaven."[4] Expanding on this basic concept, some branches of the movement focused on applying Confucian principles to the improvement of society and governance, while others sought to define human nature and explain the position of man in the cosmos.

Many Confucians in the late Tang and early Song responded vigorously to the new problems and challenges presented by the widespread acceptance of Buddhism in Chinese culture and the rising influence of Daoism. By the early eleventh century, Buddhist thought had even permeated the examination system. Some modern historians hold the opinion that without Buddhism in China there would have been no Neo-Confucianism.[5] Conceptualizing a new system of individual and universal relations and coherences may have been the Confucian intellectuals' answer to the challenges of Buddhism's growing strength and influence at court and its promises of individual salvation.

In the eleventh century, five pioneers laid the groundwork for a mature Confucian philosophy. They were Shao Yong, Zhou Dunyi, Zhang Zai, and the brothers Cheng Hao and Cheng Yi. These men were thinkers, not politicians or literati, though their achievements cannot be separated from the political struggles taking place all around them. Shao Yong (1012–1077), who called himself Mr. Happiness and lived as a hermit in a hovel, growing his own vegetables and tilling the soil, was the most controversial personality among the Neo-Confucians.[6] Fascinated with the numerological concepts of the book of *Changes,* he considered the *dao* as the basis of Heaven and Earth, and Heaven and Earth as the basis of everything else. The *dao* was not only the creator of the world but was also the good in human nature that became visible in actions. Shao's contemporaries regarded him as a teacher of *lixue*, the learning of Principle (*li*), but his philosophy was closer to that of the Daoist Laozi than to Confucius.

Zhou Dunyi (1017–1073) was a scholar-official who served most of his life in low-level positions in the bureaucracy.[7] Like Shao Yong, he was inspired by Daoism, and his *Explanation of the Diagram of the Great Ultimate (Taijitu shuo)* provided a visualization of the origin of the world. He advanced the holistic view that all material things, including human beings, were one body, but he confirmed that human beings rank highest in the universe.[8] For Zhou Dunyi, sincerity (*cheng*) was the substance of the universe, and the inner Principle was the source of all virtues. His strong commitment to Confucian ethics was what qualified him as one of the five primary Confucian thinkers of the Song.

Like his two contemporaries, Zhang Zai (1020–1077) took his inspiration from the *Changes* as well.[9] In 1056 he became a teacher in the capital, and his lectures were attended by Sima Guang and Zhang's two nephews, Cheng Hao and Cheng Yi. In Zhang's philosophy, the endless interaction of the *qi* of Heaven and the *qi* of Earth creates all things that exist. *Qi* could be visible or invisible, depending on its physical state. Consolidated *qi* is visible in matter, but all matter dissolves and becomes invisible again. Matter is originally made up of *qi* and thus part of a universal Principle.[10] Zhang's clear renunciation of the Buddhist idea of nirvana and the Daoist idea of the prolongation of life, rather than his emphasis on Confucian virtues, consolidated his reputation as a Confucian thinker.

The Cheng brothers—nephews of Zhang Zai, disciples of Zhou Dunyi, and friends of Shao Yong—passed the *jinshi* examination in 1057 and went from there to complete the separation of Confucianism from Daoism and Buddhism.[11] The elder brother, Cheng Hao (1032–1085), was a more successful and honored official than his younger brother, but Cheng Yi (1033–1107) was the more original thinker.[12] Cheng Yi claimed that he and his brother recovered the Learning of the Way, which had been lost since the time of Mencius in the fourth century B.C.[13] With Cheng Hao's encouragement, the *Mencius* quickly became integrated into the intellectual and philosophical mainstream.[14] The Cheng brothers attached so much importance to the writings of the Confucian school that they extracted the *Great Learning (Daxue)* and the *Doctrine*

of the Mean (*Zhongyong*) from the *Record of Rites* (*Liji*) and gave these
two books independent status within the Confucian canon.

The two brothers had quite different personalities, and their ideologies
diverged on many points. Contemporaries characterized Cheng Hao as a
kind-hearted, friendly, conciliatory, and thoughtful man, mild like the
sun in spring. In contrast, his younger brother was cold and harsh like the
hoarfrost in autumn. He stood for respect and sincerity, and appears to
have lived a life of uncompromising correctness, outspokenness, and morality. His arrogance gained him many bitter enemies.

In their interpretations of the classic texts, Cheng Hao was an advocate
of the Learning of Mind (*xinxue*), a forerunner of the idealistic School of
Mind (*xinxue*) established by Lu Jiuyuan in the twelfth century. Cheng Yi
belonged to the rationalist school, and provided the philosophical under-
pinning for a systemization of Confucianism by the preeminent philosopher Zhu Xi. Cheng Yi was the first to build a system on the concept of
Principle (*li*), also called the Heavenly Principle, which had been of little
importance in ancient Confucianism. Mencius had interpreted *li* as a
moral principle but not as a major concept, a law of being. Cheng Yi conceived of *li* as the foundation of all truth and values, "as a single collec-
tive metaphysical Principle, standing in apposition to the physical *qi* or
matter."[15] Principle, which he thought was inherent in all matter and had
existed eternally through time and space, was universal and formed the
pattern for all material things and events. In Cheng Yi's words: "Principle
is one but its manifestations are many," and "Principle of one thing is one
with Principle of all things."[16]

According to Cheng's logic, the exhaustive study of Principle, nature,
and destiny is one single act. In his view, a true knowledge of Principle
leads to an accurate perception of right and wrong. So knowledge forms
the basis for self-cultivation and conduct. And to attain knowledge, one
must apprehend the Principle in things (*gewu*), and to apprehend the
Principle in things one must investigate them. Only when investigation
has been practiced over a long period does it become possible to reach a
free comprehension and knowledge of sincerity (*cheng*); at that point, the
emotional and moral life are in balance.[17]

Cheng Yi's theory of knowledge and comprehension—new to the Confucian tradition—laid the foundation for the many scientific and technological breakthroughs of the Song, and above all influenced the entire
School of Principle (*lixue*) erected by the philosopher Zhu Xi, who lived
approximately one hundred years later. An admirer of the Cheng brothers' work, he would systematize rationalist learning.

During Cheng Yi's own lifetime, many of his colleagues were not supportive of the rationalist school, and in 1097 his teachings were prohibited. Opposition to him was so strong that the five pioneers of Confucianism were labeled "the five devils."[18] Just one year before Cheng Yi died, in 1106, he was finally pardoned.

Zhu Xi, Creator of Systematic Confucianism

In the opinion of many historians, the Song's preeminent philosopher, Zhu Xi (1130–1200), outshined Confucius himself. He was the only person in Chinese history, apart from Confucius and Mencius, whom the official hagiography addressed as Master. Zhu was born in central Fujian province where his father, Zhu Song (1097–1143), served as a county police officer.[19] When he was thirteen, his father died and his mother took over responsibility for her son's education. Before he obtained the *jinshi* degree in 1148, he married the daughter of Liu Zihui, one of his father's friends.

From his excellent education, Zhu Xi learned of three new Confucian doctrines: Principle (*li*), the investigation of things or the apprehension of the Principle of things (*gewu*), and the exercise of sincerity or seriousness (*cheng*). He also knew about a reevaluation of the Confucian texts by the five masters of the eleventh century. Working with Lü Zuqian, Zhu condensed the new Confucian metaphysics into a coherent system and in the process gave Confucian fundamentalism a more theoretical and rational foundation.[20] The result was *Reflections on Things at Hand* (*Jinsi lu*), completed in 1176—the first and best-organized presentation of Chinese philosophical knowledge up to that time. In 1219 Zhu's own philosophical teachings were compiled in the topically arranged *Conversations of Master Zhu* (*Zhuzi yulei*) by Huang Shiyi, published in 1270.

For an explanation of Principle, Zhu Xi referred to Cheng Yi. As in the *Reflections,* he structured a doctrine that put the fundamental Principle of the universe first. Principle, the Supreme Ultimate, governs the five elements (also called phases) and *yin* and *yang* (passive and active forces). Without Principle, no object can exist. All things created in the universe, natural objects and man-made things, have *li*, but *li* has no shape or shadow. It is akin to a natural law. Hence it is unchanging and exists in the metaphysical world.

But there was also a concrete world of shapes which depends on *qi*, the source from which material is produced. *Qi* materializes and individualizes Principle. This means that Principle (*li*) and material force (*qi*) are complementary and interdependent. "Men or things, at the moment of their production, receive *li* in order that they may have a nature of their own, and they receive *qi* that they have a form."[21] In the *Reflections,* Zhu continues with discussions on the nature of man and things, on how to learn Principle, knowledge, and conduct, on the investigation of things and the apprehension of the Principle in things, and concludes with a discourse on how Buddhism and Daoism obscured Principle. "Reality is not something transcending affairs and things. Rather it is like making a ship travel on water or a cart travel on land."[22]

Aside from his philosophical works, Zhu Xi's *Family Rituals* (*Jiali*) cemented his reputation in the Chinese world and in neighboring Korea and Japan. This manual was based on an earlier one by chief councilor Sima Guang, updated with the thinking of Cheng Yi. *Family Rituals* was the often-copied, widely adopted, indispensable, and authoritative reference work for the performance of family liturgies and rites. In popularity it was second only to Confucius' *Analects*. The family rituals designed and codified by Zhu were theoretically available to people from all walks of life, but they were especially influential in structuring family life among the elite—and those who aspired to the elite—from cradle to grave.[23] The validity of these norms as binding for all Chinese was never seriously questioned until the twentieth century.

The *Collected Commentaries on the Four Books* (*Sishu zhangju jizhu*) became Zhu Xi's most important contribution to Confucian philosophy in the Song. Displaying an extraordinary mastery of classical learning from Confucius to the five eleventh-century pioneers, this work became known as the authoritative history of *daotong,* the Transmission of the Way.[24] In 1313, under the Mongol Yuan dynasty, Zhu's *Four Books* became the standard interpretation of Confucian thinking and the basis of education for the civil service examinations until the system was abolished in the twentieth century.[25]

Zhu Xi's career as an official lasted only nine years, but in fulfilling his duties as an administrator he strove to live up to what he conceived as the moral standards of a sage.[26] A member of the Military Academy, he actively engaged in political debate, which brought him into conflict with powerful advocates of peace politics. In the early 1160s, in response to the recent loss of north China to the Jurchens, he attempted to introduce his Confucian learning—and himself—to the highest echelons at court. The classical and political ideals of the eleventh century had faltered by the beginning of the twelfth, and Zhu believed that a return to moral cultivation and education could restore the nation's identity and self-confidence.[27]

But Zhu Xi's elevated interpretation of Confucian ethics rarely matched the personal interests and needs of court officials, and Emperor Xiaozong did not relish being lectured to by a protagonist from one of the several Confucian schools, which at that time still had not yet been consolidated or officially acknowledged. Zhu's program of Confucian education came into harsh criticism from the faction who wanted the examination system to emphasize practical learning. The most vocal of these opponents were Chen Liang and Ye Shi.[28] Ye Shi advocated "utilitarian" knowledge (jingshi), with emphasis on historical analysis of institutions in order to learn from past failures. The welfare of ordinary people were of greater importance to him than debating metaphysical abstractions.

Both thinkers regarded Zhu Xi's teaching—and even more so the lengthy lecturing and general idleness of his disciples—as empty talk. In his memorial of 1178 the strong-willed Chen Liang attacked the followers of the Learning of the Way: "In a situation where the peace of the world depends on taking great revenge for ruler and father, they simply raise their eyebrows and, their hands in their sleeves, talk about human nature and destiny; they do not know what human nature and destiny are really like."[29] In his opinion, all those who are good for nothing belonged to this school. He demanded that politics and philosophical thinking should match the realities of contemporary society. For Zhu, however, the cultivation of personal morality ranked higher than literary endeavors and political achievements.

In 1165 Zhu Xi resigned his office and accepted the sinecure of a temple guardianship. When he returned to public service in 1179, some colleagues accused him of "swindling the world and stealing fame." Zhu became a controversial figure, and his Learning of the Way lost ground.[30] Followers of the School of Mind, led by the idealist Lu Jiuyuan, distinguished themselves from Zhu by underlining the importance of intuitive knowledge rather than learning. Zhu disagreed strongly with Lu's statement that "the universe is my mind. All people own this mind, and each mind owns universal Principle, and thus the mind is universal Principle."[31]

The campaign of defamation and humiliation against Zhu Xi that began in 1195 did not let up until his death on April 23, 1200. His followers, numbering in the thousands, attended the funeral to pay respect and to mourn for the teacher who had been accused of "false learning" by chief councilor Han Tuozhou.[32] At the time of Zhu's death, nobody could have foretold that his philosophical school would survive and his disciples would elevate their master to the rank of a sage second only to Confucius.

Conditions for acceptance of the Learning of the Way improved when Shi Miyuan succeeded Han Tuozhou as chief councilor. In 1227, almost thirty years after Zhu Xi died, the philosopher was posthumously made the duke of Xin, and in 1235 Cheng Yi and others were honored by sacrifices in the Confucian temple. But the decisive and final change in favor of the Learning of the Way occurred in 1241, when Emperor Lizong ennobled Zhou Dunyi, Zhang Zai, and the Cheng brothers posthumously. Now all the Confucian philosophers of the Learning of the Way had secured a place in Confucian temples, where ceremonies attended by teachers and students were held in their honor.

Not coincidentally, the Learning of the Way became state orthodoxy just as the dynasty was once again facing a threat from barbarians. The Mongol empire, which had defeated the Jin in 1234, was starting to take on the trappings of a Confucian state.[33] The Song's claim as the only legitimate government of China required a strong Chinese ideology, and Zhu Xi's updated Confucianism fit the bill perfectly.

Daoism and Buddhism in the Song Dynasty

During the Tang dynasty and well into the Song, Daoism and Buddhism met the religious needs of their followers on many levels of society, from popular practices of devotion among uneducated people to the most sophisticated intellectual discourses between scholars and monks. These religious practices often held even nonbelievers like the Confucian Han Yu spellbound. In his poem of rhapsodic praise for a young Daoist woman, "The Girl of Mount Hua," written in the eighth century, he gave a vivid description of the atmosphere in a Daoist Hall, packed with people, many sitting outside, and an emotional, even erotic, account of a young woman's charismatic appearance and erudite exposition of the Way.

> The girl of Mount Hua, child of a Daoist home,
>   longed to expel the foreign faith, win
>   men back to the Immortals;
>   she washed off her powder, wiped her
>   face, put on cap and shawl.

With white throat, crimson cheeks, long
   eyebrows of gray,
she came at last to ascend the chair,
   unfolding the secrets of Truth.[34]

This Daoist popstar was the attraction of the season, and neither palace ladies nor eunuchs wanted to miss the show. As word of her performance was whispered about, coaches jammed the lanes, and Buddhist temples stood empty. With mind-boggling special effects, she descended, dragon-drawn, through blue-dark skies, a glamorous spectacle. She and the Daoist master Jade Countenance gave a ravishing performance—he obviously had some experience in attracting and entertaining a curious audience and handling the skepticism of staunch Confucians. And even four hundred years later the Confucian Chen Chun critically observed that the Daoists "want to ride on clouds and mount cranes to fly up to the Nine Heavens."[35]

Daoism was China's authentic religion. In the Warring States period from the fifth to the third centuries B.C., it originated as a naturalistic philosophy based on the term Way (*dao*), which, according to the philosophy of Laozi and the *Canon of the Way and Its Power* (*Daode jing*) attributed to him, is a name for ultimate reality. "The *dao* does not age, it floats and drifts, can go left or right, is empty, shapeless, and formless, accomplishes its tasks and completes its affairs, and yet it does not act as their master, thus it is constantly without desires, gives rise to Heaven and Earth and all things—the Chinese call the ten thousand things. If it is spoken of, it is not the constant Way." As energy over time and space, it is the origin of all changes present in each individual thing. The Way asked of its followers that they should live in harmony with nature, free of artificiality, knowledge, and desires, responsible to the natural world.

Daoism started to develop as a religious movement—with clerical hierarchies, noncelibate priests, canonical texts, and a pantheon of deities—in the second century A.D. Breathing, dietary, sexual, and fighting practices, as well as notions about longevity and immortality, became inseparably linked to Tang Daoism. For many, it was an antidote to the public life of Confucian officials. Popular Daoism was also inextricably intertwined with early imperial politics, and this continued in the Song. The Daoist Temple of the Northern Emperor in Kaifeng played a decisive role for the second Song emperor, Taizong. There he received a prophecy from the god General Black Killer that he would become the second ruler of the dynasty. General Black Killer, the Perfected Lord, quelled and destroyed demons and ghosts. He had a human appearance, angry eyes, bare feet, and disheveled hair and was armed with a sword. After the prophecy came true, Emperor Taizong commissioned the construction of the Palace of Highest Purity and Great Peace (*Shangqing taiping gong*).

A few years later in the reign of Emperor Zhenzong, who also favored Daoism, the Perfected Lord was granted the title of Supporter of Sageliness and Protector of Virtue, and the Jade Emperor was made the tutelary god of the Song dynasty.[36] The Palace of Jadelike Purity (*Yuqing gong*), built around 1019, was most probably not only the largest imperial building complex erected in the entire dynasty but also the highest ranked Daoist temple among the hundreds built by Emperor Zhenzong throughout the empire. One hundred years later Emperor Huizong would become the most fervent private and public supporter of the Daoist philosophical tradition and magical practices in Chinese history.

Like Daoism, Buddhism enjoyed the support and protection of many Song emperors. Shortly after the dynasty was founded in 960, Emperor Taizu ordained 8,000 Buddhist monks, and in 971 he encouraged scholastic Buddhism by ordering an edition of the *Buddhist Canon* or *Tripitaka (Dazang jing)*. It was carved on 130,000 woodblocks and completed in 983. With the notable exception of Huizong, all of Taizu's successors refrained from suppressing Buddhist doctrine.[37] Buddhist temples were thought of as places where spiritual power concentrated, and it was believed they could ward off the evil influences of the Song's adversaries.

The Song government made a distinction between public and private Buddhist monasteries. The abbots of public monasteries, which tended to be large and wealthy, were appointed by the local official. The services that public monasteries rendered to the imperial family and the state were, "in order of increasing sanctity . . . memorials for the war dead; religious spaces to mark imperial birthdays and deathdays; repositories of imperial calligraphy; and galleries of imperial portraits."[38] The Song for the first time institutionalized the practice of placing the portraits of emperors in a few large Buddhist and Daoist temples. The cult blossomed in the early decades of the eleventh century, but these imperial shrines met with disapproval from many Confucian scholar-officials. They criticized the practice as a disrespectful violation of the traditional ritual order that designated the imperial ancestral shrine as the place to display and honor the images of the emperors. In 1082 Emperor Shenzong solved the dispute by concentrating the imperial images in a palace with eleven newly built halls.

In 1067 after a long search for new sources of income, the government decided to introduce the sale of Buddhist monk certificates, which exempted purchasers from tax and labor service. Unlike real monks, the owners of certificates did not have to shave their heads or wear clerical habits and could remain at home to continue their business as usual. The first issues of monk certificates could be bought for 130 strings of cash each. As many as 120,000 certificates may have been sold annually between 1161 and 1170.

Buddhist establishments engaged in a wide range of economic activities—operating oil presses, water-powered mills, pawnshops, and hostels. Buddhists owned large estates that were leased in small plots to tenants who worked them.[39] The monasteries flourished, and their numbers increased. In the year 1221 there were 400,000 monks and 61,000 nuns in the dynasty, compared with a total of 260,000 monks and nuns registered in 845. Ordained clerics made up less than 1 percent of the Song population, but their influence on the religious life of all Chinese far outweighed their minority status.

Most of the temples and monasteries belonged to the sects of Meditation (*chan*) and the Pure Land (*jingtu*), both of which had survived the Buddhist persecution of 845. Meditation masters propagated intuition and enlightenment with the help of public discussions in the form of questions and answers, and for a long time they kept a distance from the court and political life. The truth, and their elitist method of teaching it to small circles of believers, was transmitted directly from master to pupil. In Song times, literary (as opposed to spiritual) meditation based on systematized and formal techniques was promoted as a way to achieve spontaneity and realize enlightenment. The followers of Pure Land practiced their religion by repeatedly invoking the name of Amitabha Buddha (*nianfo*), in the belief that the exercise would lead to the individual's salvation. In Song times, Pure Land societies with thousands of members chanting the Buddha's name thousands of times on certain occasions sprang up everywhere. The practitioners of these two popular sects tried to bring them closer together, and Yanshou (904–975) became the first master to teach both Meditation and Pure Land Buddhism.

In the tenth century, two originally Indian Buddhist deities were transformed into Chinese Buddhist deities that were more approachable, down-to-earth, and attractive to uneducated Chinese as idols for worship. Their more humanlike appearance encouraged followers to believe that their personal wishes and hopes would be fulfilled in this earthly life, here and now. The only imported male Buddhist deity transformed into a genuine Chinese goddess was the Indian Bodhisattva called Avalo-kitesvara (in Chinese Guanshiyin), the "one who observes the sounds of the world," the all-compassionate savior. Guanyin, as she is commonly called, accompanies Amitabha Buddha, the central figure in the Buddhist pantheon of the Pure Land. All who call his name and cry out "Blessed be Amitabha Buddha" will be guided by Guanyin to the Western Pure Land, the paradise, a stage on the way to rebirth, which was regarded as the final resting place. Guanyin could assume many faces and appearances, male and female, old and young, sitting and standing. On many frescoes and paintings Guanyin had a mustache, indicating masculinity.[40] Her bare feet provide another hint of her male origin.

A cult of Guanyin took root in Song China as pilgrims to certain holy sites saw visions and reported miracles. These tales went hand in hand with artistic depictions of the deity. The Water and Moon Guanyin gained popularity, as did, from the twelfth century onward, the White-Robed Guanyin.[41] Guanyin appeared with lotus, vase, pearls, and children and was worshipped throughout East Asia as the Goddess of Mercy, the protector of all in distress and misery, the patron goddess of mothers, and the bestower of children. People adored the Guanyin with the Fish Basket as the model of Chinese beauty, and they idealized this seductive virgin as a symbol of woman's liberation from sex and marriage.[42] Guanyin played a key role in the rise of goddess cults in China.

In another instance of Chinese appropriation of an Indian Buddhist element, Maitreya, the Buddha yet-to-come, became the Chinese Milefo, the Laughing Buddha, a jovial pot-bellied reclining figure with heavy jowls and a laugh on his face, present in almost all Buddhist temple halls. His outer appearance and enigmatic expression probably derive from the Meditation sect, though he is often interpreted as the deification of the Hemp-bag Bonze, a person of unknown identity and eccentric conduct. The Laughing Buddha embodies a number of Chinese aspirations: a wealth of material goods, more than enough to eat, and spiritual contentment with himself and the world.[43]

Neo-Confucianism and Buddhism

Many Confucian scholar-officials, among them the eleventh-century historian and intellectual Ouyang Xiu, denounced Buddhist doctrine as foolish, delusional, and harmful to Chinese customs and practices. They regarded Buddhism as a source of trouble for over a thousand years. Shi Jie accused Buddhism of having brought misery to China and concluded generally: "I maintain that three things decidedly do not exist between Heaven and Earth: there are no divine immortals, no method to make gold, and no Buddha."[44] Many Confucians condemned its doctrines as absurd and raised objections to the bald pates of the priests, their dark robes, and their renunciation of domestic ties. Critics claimed that the philosophy offered no basis for a moral society, that it ignored the ways of the ancients, and that the idleness and parasitic existence of monks and nuns contributed nothing to the material benefit of the nation.

Other Confucian thinkers like Cheng Yi and Zhu Xi directed their criticism at Buddhist ontology, which in their opinion denied the substantiality and reality of the world and thus led to nihilism. But still, many Confucians could not resist Buddhist ideas of salvation. Even the influential Zhu Xi, who strongly advocated the abolition of Buddhism and Daoism from China, knew from experience that such a policy would never be realized. So he conceded that teaching the philosophical Daoism of Laozi should be tolerated and placed under the control of the directors of public worship.

Meditation masters promoted the idea that the three doctrines of Confucianism, Daoism, and Buddhism emerged from the same root. And in Jin times, Wang Chongyang, founder of the Daoist sect of Integral Realization or Perfect Truth, pushed the concept that the three religions formed a family. He taught his disciples to study the Daoist *Canon of the Way and Its Power,* the Buddhist *Heart Sutra,* and the Confucian *Canon of Filial Piety.*[45] In this trinity, Buddhism and Daoism represented the inner teaching of the faithful individual, and Confucianism the outer teaching. And fitting to the outer teaching were the rituals distinctive of Confucian practice, particularly ancestor worship, marriage ceremonies, and burials, which managed without a priesthood, church, or liturgy.[46]

Buddhist doctrine as practiced in Song China held that the phenomenal world is not real but only an illusion. Confucians opposed this emphasis on the illusoriness of all phenomena and replaced the Buddhist doctrine of the world's emptiness with the concept of Principle (*li*) and material force (*qi*). In the eleventh century, Zhang Zai explained that *qi* existed at the beginning of the world and consolidated itself into matter, and that all matter arises from *qi* and dissolves into *qi* and then arises yet again. In this view, the material world does not end in nothingness, as the Buddhists claim. Zhang Zai was very skillful in expanding his theory of the ubiquitous *qi* as the vital force of life to humans and human relations and concluded that all people of the world are brothers, including the exhausted, sick, handicapped, maimed, widowed, and orphaned. By extending the Confucian concept of benevolence to include all sentient beings, he implied that every single Confucian had to take social responsibility for the welfare of himself and others. This was a sharp contrast with Buddhists, who advocated escaping everyday tasks by leaving the family. Zhang Zai attacked Buddhism on the one hand, but on the other he drew heavily from its learning as well as its philanthropic concept of the common good.

Notwithstanding their many objections, the Song Confucians day by day were confronted with the embodiments of Buddhist learning, temples and pagodas, monks and nuns, and they inevitably were witnesses of folk Buddhist festivals. They faced a religious reality that could not be ignored but asked for a compatible answer. So they incorporated some Buddhist concepts into their own ethical system, including respect for all life, compassion, philanthropy, meditation, and notions of reality and phenomena, all of which gave Confucianism a new, decidedly humane face.

Ancestor Worship and Filial Piety

Ancestor worship, which began long before Confucius, was the common denominator of all Chinese families, whether Confucian, Daoist, or Buddhist. It defined moral and ethical standards and regulated the spiritual lives of individuals from birth to death. Sacrifices to the ancestors were not dictated from the outside by state, church, or clan but originated in the heart of every person.

For followers of the Confucian creed, an individual was only a link in the chain from ancestors to future descendants.[47] Death finished life, and the individual person was at peace, but death did not sever the relationship between the deceased and the living. The spirit of the corpse in its grave could be beneficial to the living when the rituals were properly performed.[48] In Confucianism, the ego disappeared into the family. For followers of Chinese Buddhism, the ego disappeared into the cosmos, because the ego was an illusion. Reincarnation, which Buddhism held out as a reward or consolation prize for the deceased, did not fit the Confucian view because it upset the order of ancestral lineage.

Imbued with respect for the ancestors, Confucian thinkers also opposed the Buddhist idea that a male member should leave his family to become a devotee or a monk. In their view, the senior male heir of the family or clan was the only person who could legitimately perform the required rituals and offer sacrifices at the ancestral altar. He was also in charge of burials and mourning.

Because humans originate from ancestors and the continuity of the family from the past into the future is a matter of highest priority, filial piety (*xiao*) is the most important characteristic of the relationship between the generations. Long before Confucius, filial descendants expressed their reverence for their ancestors by making sacrifices at the altar in the ancestral shrine. In return, the ancestors were thought (and expected) to reward filial piety by conferring blessings on their descendants. For Confucians, filial piety applied to living parents as well as ancestors long since deceased. Thus, added to filial piety as practiced in the ritual of sacrifice and ancestor worship was filial piety expressed as respect for elders in one's family and clan. The *Canon of Filial Piety* (*Xiaojing*), based on Confucius' answers to questions posed by his disciple Zeng Can, may be viewed as governing the relation of children to their parents and determining the proper way they should behave. As Zeng Can said in the fifth century B.C.: "The fundamental teaching of the people is filial piety."[49] This standard as practiced in the Song was conceived as a lifelong service of obedience from children to their parents.

Buddhists were well aware of the overpowering importance of filial piety for Chinese society. In the Tang dynasty, Buddhist monks composed the *Sutra of Parental Love* (*Fumu enzhong jing*) as the counterpart to, and completion of, Confucian filial piety. In the eleventh century, many Buddhist scholars insisted that Buddhist and Confucian notions of filial piety were consistent, or claimed that Buddhism gave filial piety an even higher moral position than Confucianism did. In this way, filial piety became important in the everyday practice of Buddhism.[50]

Just as the *Canon of Filial Piety* was the undisputed theoretical basis for the conduct of a Confucian gentleman within his family, the *Canon of Women's Filial Piety* (*Nü xiaojing*) was a later supplement written for women.[51] But for a practical guide to model behavior, the Song turned to a collection of twenty-four exemplary stories about the morals of male and female protagonists. These stories gained nationwide popularity, and from the Liao and Song dynasties onward some of them appear as rather crude drawings or quotations carved into the walls of tombs and on artifacts. This practice was obviously in accordance with the general understanding of how to make filial piety visible and lasting in an appropriate and unoffending way to deceased ancestors.[52] The execution of such model scenes of behavior, regardless of their artistic quality, confirmed the patron's self-rewarding understanding of filial piety as expressed by the philosopher Luo Yongyan (1072–1135), who stated in his later years: "The filial piety of the son is the son's happiness."[53]

Most of these twenty-four stories are simple in structure, sentimental, and melodramatic. Some of them merely pander to popular taste, others transgress the limits of good manners, and a few are revolting. Miraculous feats of self-sacrifice, starvation, and dying of grief are common events in the lives of the sons and daughters portrayed in these stories.[54] In one tale, a loyal daughter-in-law allows her old mother-in-law to suck milk from her breast, and in another a son cuts a piece of flesh from his own thigh to use as an ingredient in his mother's medicine or to feed her. In Song times, cutting flesh from one's thigh was not regarded as an act of violence or self-hatred, though eating it oneself was considered taboo. What legitimized this gruesome act in Confucian society was the personal sacrifice for a still-living ancestor.

Such bodily sacrifice conjoined Confucian filial piety with Buddhist self-immolation. *The Lotus Sutra of the Wonderful Law* (*Miaofa lianhua jing*) states that cutting one's own flesh three times a day to feed one's parents can never repay even one day of their goodness. People were encouraged to cut off and sacrifice their own toes and fingers in order to attain enlightenment. Cases are reported of monks and other believers who maimed themselves by hacking off their arms, carving flesh from their bodies for sacrifice to Buddha, scorching their fingers and heads, burning their bodies, or throwing themselves into gorges.

In 955 the Later Zhou Emperor Shizong and in 1020 the Liao dynasty forbade these practices. In *On Medicine* (*Yishuo*), written in 1189, the Confucian Zhang Gao turned the argument from filial piety on its head: "Alas, our body and limbs, hair and skin, we got them altogether from our parents, and so we have no right to maim or wound them. Could any parents, even if dangerously ill, possibly desire their offspring to mutilate their limbs, and make them eat their bones and flesh? These are ideas of stupid people."[55] Although in Yuan times acts of sacrificing one's own body as a fulfillment of filial piety were condemned as "going against the ways of Heaven," the practice continued.[56]

Buddhism in the Liao and Jin Dynasties

The rulers of the Liao dynasty knew their Chinese neighbors to the south and their culture very well, and from early on the Khitans adopted Confucianism, along with all its paraphernalia, as the ideological basis for ruling the Liao state. In private and religious life, however, the shamanistic rituals of the tribe still flourished. The Khitan worshipped the sun, venerated the tribal ancestress and the spirits of the ancestors, made generous sacrifices of horses, oxen, sheep, and geese, and gathered for ceremonial hunts and other occasions. A rebirth ceremony, when the emperor was symbolically reborn, was performed by the emperor himself every twelve years in the rebirth building. It confirmed the emperor's right to rule and renewed the Khitan aristocracy's confidence in him for another twelve years.[57]

Buddhism was the only foreign religion powerful enough to impress the Khitan and other ethnic peoples of the Liao dynasty. The most popular sects were the Pure Land, the Huayan, the Tantric, and the Vinaya School (lüzong). Buddhist scriptures played an important role in the education of the young, Buddha's birthday was celebrated, Buddhist altars were erected throughout the Liao territory, and Buddhist names were chosen by some members of the Khitan aristocracy.[58]

In 942 the Liao emperor provided food for 50,000 monks and in 1078 for 360,000 monks and nuns.[59] By 1078 approximately 5 percent of the total Liao population had become clerics. On some days up to 3,000 people shaved their heads and joined the ranks of the Buddhist clergy.[60] The number of ordained Buddhists increased so dramatically that restrictions had to be introduced. Private ordinations of monks and nuns in Buddhist temples in the mountains were prohibited, but none of the restrictions relieved the situation. The extraordinary increase may be explained by the tax privileges and exemption from labor service that monks enjoyed.

Encouraged and sponsored in particular by female members of the Khitan aristocracy, Buddhist institutions greatly profited from generous donations of land and money. Some of them were so rich that they could afford to cast a Buddha made of silver, as happened in 1054.[61] Emperor Xingzong took the unusual step of vowing to uphold the five Buddhist commandments, and his successor, Emperor Daozong, participated in discussions on Buddhist doctrine and ordered the heir apparent to copy Buddhist texts.[62] Between 1031 and 1064 a Liao edition of the Chinese Tripitaka was published.

At the Yunju Temple in Fangshan, south of Beijing, the Liao emperors continued the gigantic project of engraving many sutras of the Tripitaka on thousands of stone tablets. As if in return for the good will of the leading families, Buddhist temples, with their accumulated wealth, were ex-

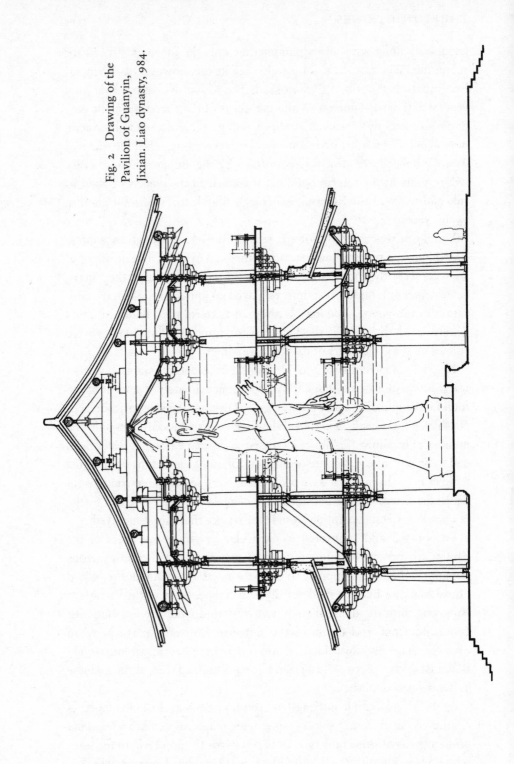

Fig. 2   Drawing of the Pavilion of Guanyin, Jixian. Liao dynasty, 984.

pected to take on the responsibility of caring for the poor. Song officials who traveled on duty missions to the Liao state criticized the Buddhist temples mushrooming everywhere, the licentious monks, and the exorbitant interest rates that were impoverishing the common people.[63]

Approximately one dozen Buddhist wooden buildings still exist in the former Liao territory.[64] Tang and Song architecture provided the models, and Chinese architects and builders no doubt participated in the planning and building of the finest of these structures. Historians of architecture agree that the architects and craftsmen of the early Liao exploited the architectural potential of timber-frame structures and surpassed even late Song architecture.[65] Among the extraordinary designs is a hall housing the ingenious revolving sutra cabinet of the Longxing monastery in Zhengding, Hebei province. The cabinet, a unique specimen of its kind, is based on an octagonal structure and turns on a pivot. The Bojiajiao Sutra Repository—another exquisite library consisting of cabinetwork running along four walls—was built in 1038 in an unimpressive five-by-four-bay hall (ca. 31 by 24 meters) on the compound of the Huayan Temple in Datong. Similar to a balustraded multistory building, the library was divided into two parts linked to each other by a curved bridge designed to house 5,079 sutras in the lower part and ciboria in the recessed upper part.[66]

The Pavilion of Guanyin (Avalokitesvara) of the Dule (Solitary Joy) Monastery in Ji county, east of Beijing and north of Tianjin, was built in 984 (Fig. 2). The five-by-four-bay pavilion (20.23 meters wide and 22.5 meters high) is erected on a polished stone base. A colorful 16-meter-high Guanyin figure made of clay dominates the central space under the earliest known and still preserved example of a sunken ceiling form—a figured ceiling in the shape of a well curb. The pavilion has survived twenty-eight earthquakes, including the Tangshan earthquake of 1976.[67]

Finally, the so-called Shakyamuni Pagoda of the Fogong (Buddha Palace) Monastery in Ying county, south of Datong in northern Shanxi, is the oldest surviving wooden pagoda and the tallest wooden building surviving in China (67.31 meters high). Built in 1056, its nine stories are timber-framed, similar to the Guanyin Pavilion of the Dulesi.[68]

The Jurchens knew about Buddhism from Koryo (Korea) long before they established their Jin dynasty. They inherited flourishing Buddhist communities from the conquered Liao and later from the Northern Song, and continued the Liao practice of patronage for monasteries and monks. The Jin imported Meditation Buddhism from the south and printed the

Buddhist canon between 1148 and 1173.[69] Many women of the imperial household were pious Buddhists, and donations of land, silver, and textiles document the importance and influence of Buddhism at court. The ordination of monks and nuns, sometimes numbering in the thousands, was strictly controlled by the state through a system of imperial privilege. When the state treasury needed money, ordination certificates were put up for sale. Between 1160 and 1190 a virulent sectarianism surfaced in the White Cloud, the White Lotus, the Tantric Sun Buddha, and the Touto ("religious observances") cults. Their messianic rebellions led by monks were often directed against Jin rule but did not succeed in bringing about the dynasty's collapse.

Confucianism and Buddhism in the Face of Change

The political and societal transformations of the tenth and eleventh centuries had immediate repercussions for Confucianism and Buddhism. To be a good Confucian scholar meant transmitting the true learning of the ancients as interpreted by the new philosophical schools, while at the same time curtailing the rising influence of Daoism and the growing acceptance of Buddhism, with its promise of individual salvation. As the doctrine favored by the Song emperors, Confucianism had a clear advantage in this competition, but Confucians as well as Buddhists began to organize and explain their creeds in rational terms in order to respond in a suitable way to the challenges of their time.[70]

The learned Tang Buddhist scholasticism emphasizing sutras and their commentaries, as well as the grand architecture and cave temples, was long gone by Song times. Instead, an easily approachable Buddhism as practiced by the Meditation sect made use of so-called cases that served as aids in realizing enlightenment. They were recorded in collections such as the *Record of the Blue Riff (Biyan lu)*, compiled in 1125. *Recorded Conversations of the Chan Masters (Yulu)*, which included lectures and dialogues written in a semivernacular prose, also became popular. As the Chinese clergy moved to the center of Buddhist religious life in the Song, Buddhism's influence on the Confucian scholar-official class increased. When confronted with Buddhist matters, these elites had to discuss them and define their own ethical system in order to make the differences between Confucianism and Buddhism visible to the outside world. This intellectual discourse covered all fields of scholarly interest and ranged from philosophical explanations to philanthropic pursuits. All of these new forms of pragmatism helped to enrich Buddhism by organizing its thinking and experience and giving it a discursive space. Song Buddhism became a mature intellectual neighbor and competitor of the Neo-Confucian creed.

Song Buddhism with its promise of individual salvation certainly appealed to the majority of the common people and attracted great numbers of followers, but Confucianism provided the ideological basis of a social and political order that supported the dynasty, state, and society as a whole. The individual Neo-Confucian thinker's endeavor was not to create an independent philosophy or a doctrine of salvation fashioned for a single individual, detached from tradition and the individual's responsibility to society, but to provide a pragmatic answer to the pressing needs of a world in transformation. Confucian doctrine was firmly rooted in the Confucian canon, and though the Song philosophers' interpretations sometimes exceeded the scope of the conventional, they never deliberately deviated from the sacred wisdom of the ancients.

Ethical boundaries may have limited the flexibility and imaginativeness of the Song Confucianists, but through the clarity and directness of their interpretations, Confucianism was responsibly brought back into daily affairs and private lives. It served not only as a useful guideline for the educated upper class but also became a state ideology for the first time in Chinese history. Confucian philosophy formed an ethical framework strong enough to support all members of society, but it still left enough space for the transformative processes that distinguished the Song from all other Chinese dynasties.

6

EDUCATION AND EXAMINATION

THE ELEVENTH century of the Song dynasty was one of the most intellectually exciting and stimulating periods in the history of humankind. Its achievements were made possible by an elite—called *shi* or *shidafu*—who defined the dynasty through education and examination, and who solidified their power and preserved its privileges through participation as officials in the government's bureaucracy. When the Song dynasty was founded in 960, the time of the Tang aristocratic elite, the great families, had ended long ago. The officials who replaced them in positions of government and administration no longer originated from a hereditary nobility furnished with birthrights. They were a status—not a hereditary—group. Thus, the Song dynasty became the epoch of civil service families, who on the basis of education and examination formed bureaucratic lineages able to perpetuate themselves.

Defining "elite" in Chinese history, especially after the collapse of the medieval aristocracy in the late ninth and tenth century, is a thorny analytical problem. A common denominator was that the elite enjoyed access to wealth, power, prestige, and privileges.[1] The meaning of the term *shi* underwent several changes over time and is still a matter of debate. But certainly literacy was always a marker of social status in this literocentric culture. In the traditional four-class system of Confucius's time (fifth century B.C.), the *shi* enjoyed the highest social status, followed by farmers, artisans, and merchants. Confucius himself hailed from a family of low *shi* aristocracy who served as advisors, scholars, and officials in various functions. This four-class system expanded in the early ninth century to include two additional classes of Daoist and Buddhist priests. In the eleventh century it grew larger still, to comprise scholar-officials, farmers, artisans, merchants, Daoists, Buddhists, soldiers, and vagrants.

The terms "official" or "civil servant," as they are understood in the Western world, do not capture the status of Song scholar-officials nor their intellectual capacity and political influence. The entwined relationship between Song rulers and their senior officials is evident in Zhang Fangping's bold statement to Emperor Renzong in the 1040s: "The empire cannot be ruled by Your Majesty alone; the empire can only be governed by Your Majesty collaborating with the officials."[2] In 1071 when Emperor Shenzong remarked that Wang Anshi's New Policies were for the benefit of the people, not the *shidafu*, his senior statesman, Wen Yanbo, dryly taught the ruler: "You govern the nation with *us*, the officials, not with the people."[3] This sentence, which could not have been uttered in the presence of the founding Song emperor, reflected a new interpretation of imperial authority and revealed a remarkable independence of mind and self-esteem among Song scholar-officials—not unlike that of Confucius himself.[4]

The Examination System

Advancement into the ranks of officialdom was the only professional career path imaginable for male members of the various scholarly and landowning families in China until the twentieth century. For individuals, the civil service examination system functioned as the door-opener for such a career, and for the Song state the examination system constituted the only methodologically sound way to recruit officials for all levels and fields of the bureaucracy. An edict of 989 confirms the exclusiveness of the examinations for the *shi* class: "The establishing of the examinations serves the class of scholars."[5]

Tang emperors first promoted the examination system in the seventh century in order to curb the political power of the military aristocracy. Holders of the highest degree, the *jinshi*, who made up only 7 percent of chief councilors serving under Emperor Gaozu in the first half of the seventh century, rose to 40 percent during the rule of Empress Wu Zetian half a century later. Yet over 90 percent of Tang officials did not enter the civil service via examinations but got their positions through the traditional and well-developed recommendation system.[6]

In Song times, candidates sitting for the civil service exams numbered not in the hundreds as in the Tang but in the hundreds of thousands. The first of these tests was the prefectural examination, which was conducted by local officials in early autumn. Graduates who passed this test were qualified for employment as teachers in local or family schools, as administrators of granaries or temples, and as subofficial local administrators. By the middle of the twelfth century, roughly 100,000 candidates registered for the prefectural examination each year, and in the middle of the thirteenth century it reached 400,000 or more. Those sitting for the prefectural degree for the first time had not only to present a declaration of surety issued by the county administration but were also required to study for at least 300 days in a school. If a candidate had previously failed the exam, he was allowed to try again after 100 days of additional preparation.[7]

What made the Song examination system particularly stressful, in addition to the long preparation and the rigor of the prefectural test itself, was the restriction imposed on the number of candidates who were allowed to pass. In 1009 Emperor Zhenzong introduced quotas on degrees awarded. He favored elite selection and wanted to make sure that only the most qualified candidates received degrees. By 1106 only about 3 percent of people taking the prefectural exam (2,334 out of approximately 80,000) became graduates.[8] The austerity of the regulation can be seen in Fuzhou prefecture in 1090, where only 40 degrees were awarded to 3,000 candidates. This meant that only one degree would be offered for every 75 test-takers. In the thirteenth century, quotas became even more stringent, and only 1 percent of candidates, or less, was allowed to pass the prefectural examination.[9] By the end of the Northern Song the total number of graduates may have numbered 15,000, which represented only 0.015 percent of the population of 100 million. Holders of the prefectural degree constituted a real elite.

While most graduates used their degrees and connections to obtain employment as teachers or bureaucrats, men of extraordinary talent and ambition proceeded to the metropolitan examination for the *jinshi* ("presented scholar") degree, which as a rule took place in the capital once every three years in late spring. Artisans, merchants, clerks, Buddhist and Daoist priests, and persons with a criminal record were barred from participating in the *jinshi* examination, although exceptions to honor the talent and conduct of a few artisans and merchants were granted.[10] Candidates ranged in age from eighteen to sixty-five years old, with the average candidate around thirty. Those who had previously failed the test were permitted to try again, as long as their conduct was not publicly criticized and their finances allowed them to repeat their effort.

Taking part in this last series of tests was indeed expensive, and candidates had once more to invest a lot of time, energy, and money to prepare for the examination. In most cases they relied on their families or other sponsors to cover the cost of several months' traveling on roads and barges and of staying at inns or guesthouses in the capital. But this price was paid willingly because having a high-ranking official in the family promised to be most rewarding. In addition to financial backing, each *jinshi* candidate needed someone in the official hierarchy to act as his patron—a person who would vouch personally for the integrity of the candidate. This relationship was a mutual act of confidence binding the political fate of the two people together. The emperor himself presided over the last test in the series, called the palace examination.[11] This ritual allowed the emperor to get a personal impression of his future high officials, and it strengthened mutual ties between the ruler and his closest advisors from the very beginning of each official's career.

By the middle of the eleventh century, between 5,000 and 10,000 prefectural degree-holders, who had graduated in different years, took part in the metropolitan examinations in a given year. Only a small percentage of them passed. In 1002 a mere 1.5 percent of candidates (219 out of 14,562) was awarded the *jinshi* degree. In 1109 the rate rose above 10 percent (731 out of 7,000), and in Southern Song times the average revolved around 6.5 percent.[12]

Local histories record a total of 28,933 *jinshi* scholars during the entire Song dynasty—roughly one third in the Northern Song and two thirds in the Southern Song. But other authoritative sources list about 40,000 degree-holders between 960 and 1223, and some estimates go even higher. Including the facilitated *jinshi* degree-holders—a benevolent concession to candidates who had previously failed several times—and degree-holders in various specific fields, the total number may have amounted to 70,000 persons between 960 and 1229. In any one year, the number of active officials who held the *jinshi* degree ranged from 5,000 at the beginning of the eleventh century to 10,000 in the early thirteenth century. In 1046 this highly qualified work force filled just over a third of the bureaucratic positions that existed (7,085 of 18,700 positions). The disproportion grew dramatically worse in the Southern Song—only 8,260 *jinshi* degree-holders for 38,870 positions in 1213.[13] Under the

Northern Song Emperor Huizong, the bureaucracy ballooned to over 50,000 jobs, and the Southern Song never corrected this deplorable state of affairs—even though the territory to be governed had been reduced in size by roughly one third.

This inflationary growth in government can be understood, for the most part, as the response of influential families to the encroachment of degree-holding "nobodies" upon their privileges, status, and power. The quota system kept a tight lid on the number of people who passed the examinations, but many Southern Song officials entered the bureaucracy via a back-door system called appointment by protection. This privilege, introduced as early as 963, allowed officials high up in the official hierarchy to nominate their sons, nephews, and grandsons for the civil service. After 1009, personal recommendation was not enough, however; candidates also had to study at the Directorate of Education. After completing the prescribed course, nominated candidates sat for the examination, which more than 50 percent of them were allowed to pass. Jobs far exceeding the needs of the state, particularly at lower levels in the capital, were then awarded to these members of the Southern Song elite. Protection privileges helped the old families regain ground near the end of the dynasty, and over time the career value of the *jinshi* degree eroded somewhat.[14] Nevertheless, the elite position of *jinshi* degree-holders within Chinese society did not change fundamentally until the end of imperial China in 1912.

The Song civil service examination system offered excellent opportunities for intelligent and ambitious candidates without direct forebears in the civil service to advance into the ranks of officials. In the Northern Song, degree-holders made up almost 40 percent of officials, whereas they had made up only 15 percent of Tang officials.[15] In late Tang times, 69 percent of prominent officials originated from big clans or high officials' families, while in the Northern Song only 19 percent did so. When E. A. Kracke investigated the biographies of degree-holders for the years 1148 and 1256, he found that approximately 57 percent of the successful candidates originated from families without a father, grandfather, or great grandfather in the official ranks.[16]

But the examination system was not devised as an instrument to foster upward social mobility among the talented poor. Rather than being a meritocratic tool of social engineering, the civil service examinations were designed to ensure exclusivity at the top. Assuming that the Song dynasty, over its entire course, employed 220,000 officials and that in any given year roughly 20,000 officials were active as civil servants, this would mean that around the year 1100 only 0.02 percent of the population of 101 million people held office in the bureaucracy. The roughly 5,000 officials with the highest degree represented only 0.005 percent of the population, a figure that remained steady in the thirteenth century. Around 1200, when the population sank to 63 million, the figure of the metropolitan and prefectural degree-holders may have risen to 0.102 percent.[17] Compared with the population as a whole, what the number of officials demonstrates is the absolute dominance of a few hundred, perhaps a few thousand, families at any given time. Social inequality was prevalent and widely accepted in the Song dynasty, as it was throughout Chinese history until Western ideologies started to have some influence in the twentieth century.

When Robert M. Hartwell and others revisited Kracke's data and took into account the influence and protection rights of the wider family, including uncles and great-uncles, they concluded that almost all Song graduates had a relative in the civil service system.[18] Well-to-do families with no scholar-officials—for example, merchants—climbed up the social ladder by marrying their daughters into families with an elite lineage. For talented young scholars of humble origin, the promise of success in the examinations made them attractive husbands for the daughters of the moneyed classes. In this interpretation, marriage across social classes was the key to upward mobility in the Song dynasty.[19]

A scholar may have lived in poor and distressed conditions in his village or town, but as soon as he passed his examinations he became a man of utmost distinction, influence, and power. Ouyang Xiu described the scene in the eleventh century when a successful candidate returned home: "Once a scholar rides in a high carriage drawn by four horses, flag-bearers in front, and a mounted escort forming the rear, people would gather on both sides of the road to watch and sigh. Ordinary men and stupid women rush forward in excitement and humble themselves by prostrating themselves in the dust stirred up by the carriage and the horses. This is the elation for a scholar when his ambition is fulfilled."[20]

Educational Institutions

Chinese women were often well educated in the classics, but they were not allowed to sit for examinations or to hold office in imperial China. In households where husbands served far away on official assignments, women were the driving force promoting education, and their role was to act as the early teachers of their young sons. As their children grew, large families who could afford to do so employed house teachers or sent their sons to family or clan schools. Some of these family schools developed into academies offering such attractive courses as mathematics and law.[21] Other students continued their education in local government schools, usually located in Confucian temples. The goal of all this effort was to raise sons who could pass the prefectural and perhaps even the metropolitan examinations and obtain an official position, which would bring honor and wealth to the whole family.

The founding of local schools built on plots of land allotted by the government gained momentum after 1009. During the reform periods of the 1040s and 1070s, great numbers of prefectural and county schools were set up. The reformer Fan Zhongyan and his followers established sixteen schools between 1035 and 1046. Ouyang Xiu donated 1.5 million cash for building a school in his home prefecture, and Han Qi contributed to education in a similar way. In 1071 the next wave of reformers succeeded in raising the prefectural school-land allocations, which put educational institutions on a sound financial foundation. Children from wealthy families made as much use of local government schools as did children from poor backgrounds.

The official and Confucian philosopher Cheng Yi (1033–1107) provided a description of how this system worked: "Boys entered [private primary] school at eight and [government prefectural] college at fifteen. Those whose talents could be developed were selected and gathered in the college, whereas the inferior ones were returned to the farm, for scholars and farmers did not exchange occupations. Having entered college, one would not work on the farm. Thus scholars and farmers were completely differentiated. As to support in college, there was no worry about sons of officials. But even sons of commoners, as soon as they entered college, were sure to be supported [by the state]." The philosopher Zhu Xi, who incorporated many of Cheng Yi's thoughts in his own philosophical system, did not agree that schooling and farming were divided in this way, remarking that students "farmed in the spring and summer and studied during the rest of the time. I have never heard that the government had to support them."[22]

In 1044 the government ordered that schools were established in all counties and prefectures. The order was repeated in 1102 by Emperor Huizong.[23] In addition, the government-run Military School, first established in 1043, and Law School, founded in 1073, prepared students for special careers. Most families of standing disliked seeing their sons take up a military career, because "good men should never become soldiers, as good iron should not be used to make nails."[24] Physical exertion ranked low among members of the upper class, and the use of muscles was viewed as unseemly. Young men were taught to be polite and gentle.

The Supreme School, commonly known as Imperial University, can be traced back to 124 B.C. It reopened as the Hall of Learning in 960 under Emperor Taizu. Later the Imperial University admitted seventy students, mostly from families of lower-rank officials and refined commoners. As the number of applicants increased, the lesser renowned School of the Four Gates opened in 1043.[25] Students received stipends, meals, and a place in a dormitory. They had to study for a total of 500 days, but they enjoyed the privilege of being exempted from the prefectural examination; they were allowed to proceed directly to the metropolitan exam. After the reform movement failed in the 1040s, the Directorate of Education confiscated the property of the School of the Four Gates and reduced its annual budget. But despite all these adversities, the school survived the antireformers, and by 1068 there were 900 young men enrolled.[26]

The Imperial University struggled with a shortage of classrooms and dormitory spaces. In the 1070s—this time under the reforming influence of Wang Anshi, who had been a student at the school—the university was divided according to the ability of the students into three houses.[27] The freshmen lived in the Outer House. From there, they could advance to the Inner House and finally to the Superior House. In 1080 Li Ding and Cai Jing suggested extending the Imperial University to comprise 80 buildings housing 2,400 students, of whom 2,000 belonged to the Outer House and only 100 to the Superior House.[28]

In 1102 Cai Jing made the revolutionary suggestion that the best graduates of the Imperial University should be selected for appointment in the civil service without having to take the civil service exam at all. He even toyed with the idea that a reformed school system might completely replace civil examinations. These initiatives immediately met strong resistance from officials at court and ultimately failed. His opponents viewed them as a direct attack on their role in fashioning the education of upcoming generations of officials. Despite this setback, the famous architect Li Jie, vice-director of the Board of Works and author of the *Treatise on Architectural Methods* (*Yingzao fashi*), was commissioned to plan and build new lecture halls and dormitories for the Imperial University. In

1104 the school enrolled 3,800 students, many from poor families. The admission fee was 2,000 cash, roughly the income of a low-category farmer in four months or 15 percent of the monthly salary of a low official. After the Song dynasty lost its northern territory, the Imperial University was reopened in Hangzhou in 1142 and continued to flourish in the capital of the Southern Song.[29]

Examination for the *Jinshi* Degree

The high stakes of the metropolitan examination were vividly mirrored in the way it was carried out. In 1007 impartiality became the keyword.[30] A number of practices were put in place to create ideal conditions for fair grading, such as covering the names of the candidates on exam papers, sealing the cover sheet, and having clerks copy the papers before they were handed over to examiners, to disguise the candidates' handwriting. In many years, candidates' bodies were searched for illicit aids before they were allowed to enter the examination hall. Inside, the chief examiner took his place behind a curtain where he could be seen but remained beyond reach. As the candidates' names were called out, they took their assigned places on mats laid out on the ground. Guards supervised the exams, and the candidates were not allowed to talk to one another nor to have food or beverages brought in from the outside. If they were thirsty, they could drink from the water available for their ink-stones. The use of candles was prohibited, even when it grew dark in the hall.

Li Gou gives a lively description of his feelings as he sat in the examination hall:

> The chief-examiner sits behind his curtain;
>   not to be reached, although he is seen.
> The eunuchs stand right in the front entrance;
>   they search every candidate from top to toe.
> Then the names are called;
>   everyone sits on a broken mat, placed on the cold ground . . .
> A man may be known since his youth to be good in learning;
>   and that he has learned how to behave himself.
> When he is in the prison of the examination hall,
>   he is wide-eyed and speechless.[31]

Examination requirements for the *jinshi* differed greatly over the course of the dynasty, depending on the political predilections of the influential senior examiners. In 1044 the testing consisted of three parts: discourses on policy, a discussion essay, and composition of a poem and rhyme prose.[32] The four books (*Analects, Mencius, Great Learning*, and *Doctrine of the Mean*) and the five classics (*Odes, Documents, Rites, Spring and Autumn Annals* with the *Zuo Commentary*, and *Changes*) of the Confucian tradition served as the basis for all political and historical discussions, and exposition of this canon allowed candidates to display their powers of persuasion and intellectual brilliance. The ordeal tested the capacity of candidates to memorize long passages from the *Analects* and the *Mencius*, and also stressed written responses to ten questions taken from the *Annals* or the *Rites*.[33]

In a memorandum of 1043 the reformers Fan Zhongyan and Han Qi criticized the poetic composition test, which was traditional in the Tang but on the decline in the Song. They also decried the system's emphasis on learning by rote: "Only ten to twenty percent of the scholars at the court are knowledgeable men with imagination. This is especially dangerous in times when the nation lingers in a deep crisis and is in need of talent. Thus students ought to be taught the profession of managing the nation and the people, and select only those who are talented in these arts."[34] By 1071 candidates were asked to answer five questions from one of the five classics and to compose an essay and three discourses on policy, drawing on the classics as their source for logical argumentation.[35] Very often in such essays the answer to a problem of the past had to be elaborated and explained in terms of its applicability to the present.

The emperor conducted the final "palace examination" himself. Only a small percentage of candidates passed it. They all aimed to place among the top two of five groups, which meant passing with distinction. The best result, however, was to rank first on the list of all passers, to be honored as the principal graduate, the "first in appearance," the "dragon head," or, at the time when the names were published, "the first name on the list." The principal graduate and the two men in second and third place had the best chances for a top-flight job offer.

The early reformers of the 1040s had a clear idea of the qualifications required of a future official: he ought to be morally responsible, culturally conscious, a well-educated all-rounder. They did not want to appoint degree-holders whose essays flaunted novelty and obscurity. When Ouyang Xiu headed the examination board in 1057, he rejected such writings and asked for substance over style. Thus the metrical parallel-style prose that had dominated Chinese prose writing for hundreds of years was pushed into the background by the nonpoetic ancient-style prose, which was regarded as better suited to espouse moral and philo-sophical messages. The essay "Punishment and Rewards as the Ultimate Expression of Loyalty and Generosity" by the candidate Su Shi signaled the new style. He was ranked second by his examiners.

In addition to the prefectural degree and the *jinshi* degree, the "various fields degree" was a comparatively comfortable way to advance into the civil service system. Wang Anshi abolished it in 1073, probably to cut down on the number of degree-holding officials who specialized in learn-ing by rote only one category of literature. In the reformer's opinion, the nation urgently needed highly qualified generalists who could be effi-ciently employed in all administrative areas and on different levels of the complex bureaucracy. With this reform, the *jinshi* degree gained in im-portance.

The Ancient Prose Movement

For budgetary household reasons, Song officials of the eleventh century pushed for political, economic, and military reforms. And for ideological as well as philological reasons tightly interwoven with the rejuvenation of Confucianism and the classics, these reformers also paved the way for the acceptance of prose written in the ancient (*guwen*) style in the *jinshi* examination. This generation of scholar-officials, more than any other before it, was deeply concerned about the art of writing, but they were also concerned about how the highly idealized ancient standards of Chi-nese society and government could become a living model of the Chinese cultural heritage in the present. Their concern with language was much more than a matter of philological heritage; it was about creating a means of linguistic expression that corresponded to the challenges of the societal transformations they were witnessing.

For Su Shi and others, the literature of the past eight dynasties repre-sented a period of decline, and many scholar-officials began to doubt whether the parallel-style prose that had dominated Chinese writings be-tween the Han and Tang dynasties would be adequate for addressing pressing questions raised by Confucian philosophy and morality. How-ever, it was not the practicality of the nonpoetic, nonparallel ancient writ-ing style that led to its acceptance in the eleventh century but its underly-ing ideological message: the revival of the spirit of Confucianism. The ancient prose style had originated in Zhou and Han times long before alien Buddhist thoughts infiltrated Chinese learning. By intentionally

modeling their own texts on these illustrious ancient examples and by returning to an authentic Chinese literary style that combined theory and
practice, form and content, they hoped to bring the underlying values of
Confucianism to their deliberations as scholar-officials. The syntax had
to be studied and cultivated for years before an author was able to produce an excellent essay that met the expectations of the *jinshi* examiners.

Although the ancient prose style is tightly linked to Confucian learning
of the eleventh century, the movement actually started more than two
hundred years earlier, in the late eighth century, when essayists began to
promote the virtues of ancient prose as being particularly well suited for
putting into words a Confucian understanding of the world and its relationships. Han Yu (768–824) was the ancient prose movement's major
spokesman, and it is with him that the story of *guwen* and the revival of
Confucianism as an ideology began.

At one time the junior tutor of the crown prince, Han Yu believed fer-
vently in the power of teaching and education. In the year 802 he put his
ideas to paper in his *Discourse on Teachers* (*Shi shuo*):

> Students of antiquity must have teachers to pass on the Way, give in-
> struction, and solve doubts; since men are not born with knowledge,
> all have doubts . . . A man who loves his child selects a teacher to in-
> struct him, but is ashamed to take a teacher for himself. This is puz-
> zling, indeed. The teacher of a child is one who instructs him on
> books and practices syntax and reading. This is not what I would
> call passing on the Way and resolving doubts. Taking a teacher for
> syntax and reading but not for resolving doubts means learning the
> minor things and neglecting the major ones. I do not see the wisdom
> of this.[36]

In Han Yu's view, literary form was inseparable from content when
transmitting the Confucian Way. Both needed to be direct and clear.
"When I write ancient prose do I merely keep to its syntax because it is
not similar to the present one? No, I think of the ancient whom I cannot
meet. When I learn the Way of the ancients, I also wish to understand
their phrases which are based on the Way of the ancients," he wrote in a
postscript to the dirge for Ouyang Zhan, his classmate in the *jinshi* examination of 792.[37]

Taking up this cause in memorials to the throne over the next two centuries, many scholars argued that the nonpoetic ancient prose promoted

by Han Yu was well suited to the task of guiding the people and governing the empire in the Confucian Way. Writing about official matters, they argued, should be free from the strictures of balance, syntactical parallelism, refined diction, endless literary allusions, and figurative language of metrical identity that characterized the parallel-prose style favored by the Han and Tang literati.

Han Yu, Ouyang Xiu, and Su Shi are considered the most influential of the eight masters of Tang and Song prose. Ouyang Xiu signaled his position on ancient prose when he announced a preference for substance over style in the 1057 *jinshi* examination papers. This bold declaration encouraged others to become acquainted with the new writing style, which could take years to master. Ouyang Xiu succeeded in elevating the ancient prose of Han Yu as a model that history-conscious scholars aspired to, and after the 1050s a rugged and eccentric *guwen* style, resembling a beautiful piece of uncut jade (as Shi Jie described his own style previously), no longer met the expectations of the examiners—they required polished prose. But at the same time Ouyang Xiu did not condemn the parallel style as long as it accomplished its task.[38]

Identifying himself with the learning of Han Yu, Ouyang Xiu promoted the idealistic notion of "reviving the way of antiquity." As a skillful politician, he did not hesitate to make use of his influence at court, and he gained a reputation among his contemporaries for his outspoken and frank memorials and remonstrances, which were mostly well received by the emperor. In the preface to the *Literary Writings of Ouyang Xiu (Jushi ji)*, compiled in 1091, Su Shi praised his master as a modern Han Yu: "Since Master Ouyang appeared, all scholars under Heaven competed with one another in purifying and cultivating themselves, and took the thorough study of the Classics and the study of the Ancients as their priority, and benefiting their own time they acted in accordance with the Way."[39]

Su Shi was convinced that Han Yu's writings pointed out the Way and saved all under Heaven from drowning.[40] But it was Hu Yuan (993–1059)—often regarded as the personification of the spirit of the Confucian revival in the eleventh century—who successfully synthesized Han Yu's understanding of the unity of literary form and content in transmitting the Way. For him, the Way consisted of substance, literary style, and function. Substance was found in the relations between prince and minister, father and son, and in the values of humaneness, righteousness, propriety, and music, which are unchanging through the ages. Literary style was embodied in the *Odes,* the *Documents,* the official dynastic histories, and the Zhou philosophers. Function consisted of activating substance, enriching the life of the people, and ordering all things to imperial perfection.[41]

After acceptance of the Learning of the Way in the thirteenth century, the literary anthologies—the backbone of the civil service examination culture—included the prose of the *guwen* masters along with the writings of the *daoxue* philosophers.[42] In practice, many scholar-officials failed to conform to this stern and unbending standard, but the ancient style lived on through the dynasties. As late as 1695 the most famous anthology published for Chinese students, *The Finest of Ancient Prose (Guwen guanzhi)*, included 220 texts written in the ancient style.

Career Patterns, Salaries, and Privileges

The Song bureaucratic hierarchy was made up of graded officials, ranging from the lowest administrators to the top level of senior chief councilors. In theory, Song officials were ranked according to their examination results, character, and moral behavior, but in reality an official's career was still influenced by family background and the favor of the emperor, whose incontestable decisions in personal matters overruled anything else. There were exceptions, of course, as old traditions intersected and overlapped with innovations.[43]

The grading of positions could be traced back to the Three Kingdoms of 265 A.D., which recognized nine ranks. The Song adopted the Tang subdivision of the nine ranks into eighteen classes.[44] Before the reforms of the 1080s, as many as thirty classes were in use. The Song's founding emperor Taizu devised a new classification system, known as the protocol list, that ranked all offices in order of their prestige.[45] Basically it included two kinds of offices. The first were titular offices such as grand master and court gentleman, whose holders were entitled to a certain position in ceremonies but that often involved very little actual work. Titular offices originated in previous dynasties, where hereditary positions in the financial and military administrations were common. In the second category on the protocol list were functional offices such as assistant magistrate and prefect, which came with tasks (called duty assignments) that an official was expected to perform and responsibilities he was expected to assume.

During the reforms of the 1080s, a new protocol list comprising sev-

eral hundred offices was devised and introduced. This new system survived with only minor changes until the end of the dynasty. While it preserved the old titular distinctions, they were now tied to a functional
office as well. Thus the functional offices gained ground. Several smaller
reforms followed under the rule of Emperor Huizong, and a bigger reform after 1131 emphasized functional positions rather than titles.[46]

This two-pronged classification system was not only confusing but also
wasteful. On the one hand there were office-holders who did not perform
any real duties, while on the other hand less honored officials shouldered
the burdens of government on all levels and in all fields. To remedy this
situation somewhat, it became common after the 1080s to award a civil
or military titular office to officials who were appointed to a functional
position. Ideally, the rank of the titular office matched the rank of the
functional office. In practice, however, an official who entered the civil
service through a protection appointment would be given a functional
rank (and duties) somewhere near the bottom of the hierarchy but a titular office one or two notches higher than his functional position. In this
way, the newcomer would gain a career advantage of several years over
the typical degree-holder, along with improved salary, benefits, and privileges. During the Southern Song, this strategy helped old families regain
their social prestige and influence.

Officials were generously rewarded for their service—not just with a
monthly salary in cash but also with various benefits in kind, such as
grain, silks, fuel, wine, salt, writing materials, and other goods. A system
of cash payment and grain allotment had already existed in Tang times,
and before the reform of the 1080s one third of compensation was paid
in coins and two thirds in kind. Later, officials received their salaries in
cash, and in Southern Song times they were paid with paper money. Although the salaries of officials in the lower ranks may not have been
enough to support a fashionable high-society lifestyle, these men were far
from being underpaid. And if they ran into a financial bottleneck, taking
a bribe was, for many, an easy way out. Although the Song paid its officials the highest salaries of all the imperial dynasties, corruption was
ongoing at all levels of the bureaucracy, and calls for reform were regularly issued.

The salary structure was extremely complex, requiring many accoun-
tants at various levels of the bureaucracy to document receipts and expenses and to control income. In the Northern Song, compensation was
closely keyed to titular office, but in the Southern Song these honorary

salaries lost importance compared with compensation from functional assignments.[47] This slow change in the source of income came about as a way to give ambitious officials of the younger generation a monetary incentive to take on duty assignments as part of their functional office. Duty assignments became more attractive as the salary schedule attached to them improved, and this shift automatically reduced the weight of the titular office.

In accordance with an edict of 976 issued by Emperor Taizu, the salaries of officials serving in counties and prefectures, along with all their administrative expenses, were covered from the returns of land allocated to them by the state and leased to tenants.[48] In Song times the acreages given to officials ranged from 200 *mu* (114,600 square meters) for a low-positioned official to 2,000 *mu* (1.14 million square meters) for a high-ranking official. In the second half of the eleventh century the annual harvest of 31 tons of rice from 200 *mu* of official land may have had a market value of almost 620,000 cash, more than seven times the annual cash salary of a low official. The harvest yields depended on the climate, local weather conditions, quality of the soil, tillage patterns, and the skill of tenants. In Tang times this state-allocated "land for official post" had been considerably less.[49]

Low-ranking officials made up between 60 and 80 percent of the civil service force. They all started their careers in a county, and as a rule not in their home prefecture. Each of these duty assignments lasted three to four years. Thereafter they were transferred to another locality and position. This rotation system kept most officials on the move and far away from their native county. The majority of them toiled for years, hoping for a positive evaluation of their performance in order to make the great step toward the administrative ranks.

The salary differential among these officials was surprisingly small.[50] The comprehensible salary scale and its transparency may explain why the system worked for such a long time. Leaving aside the small number of top officials at the court (rank 1), the monthly salary of rank 2 officials amounted to only about 8.5 times more than that of the lowest official in the executory rank, who earned a salary of 7,000 cash. An official bearing the title gentleman for meritorious achievements, who ranked low in the new titular office list and could have served as assistant magistrate on the county level, got a monthly salary of 12,000 cash. His equally ranked colleague in Tang times would have earned only about half of his annual income (including his allotment of grain).

High performers and officials enjoying the most elite family ties often received appointments to economically and politically important counties, especially metropolitan counties where they could double their income. When Zhao Rugua was honored with the title of grand master for closing court a few years before he died in 1231, his remuneration amounted to 35,000 cash a month, thirteen bolts of silk tabby in spring and winter, one bolt of gauze in spring, and thirty ounces of silk floss in winter. But the top earners of the Song system were the three seniors who acted as chief councilors and took part in policy deliberations in the Council of State.[51] Their compensation consisted of a monthly salary of 400,000 cash (prior to the 1080s reform, 120,000 cash) plus, in spring, 3 bolts of gauze for garments (previously 1 bolt), 30 bolts of small damask (previously 14 bolts), 40 bolts of silk tabby (previously 30 bolts), and, in winter, 30 bolts of small damask for garments (previously 10 bolts), and 200 ounces of silk floss (previously 50 ounces).

Most sources give the impression that salaries fixed in the 1080s were never raised afterward and, as a consequence, lost a good deal of their purchasing power near the end of the dynasty. Even if that is true, officials and their households were still far better off than everyone else in China and enjoyed a higher standard of living than all their forerunners in office. In addition to salaries and payment in kind, officials were partially exempt from tax on their own land (depending on the rank they held) and from the humiliating and physically demanding corvée service. In the event of a legal proceeding, officials from the seventh rank and above could not be tortured to force a confession, and the grandparents, parents, brothers, sisters, wives, children, and grandchildren of officials from the fifth rank and above could not be tortured under similar circumstances.[52]

Another privilege reserved exclusively for officials was fifty-four holidays, divided into short periods of three, five, or seven days. Usually these were taken during annual festivals, such as the winter solstice, the New Year, and the anniversaries of the death and birth of emperors. Every three years an official was allowed to journey to his home to spend two to four weeks with his family. Other important events that allowed him to leave office and travel home were the capping ceremony commemorating a son's coming of age (revitalized in Song times) and the marriage of one of his children. The only break of significance in an official's career came about when his father or mother died. On that occasion he was allowed to stay at home for three years (though in most cases not the entire time), and during that leave he could devote himself to the favorite pastimes of his social class: books, music, poetry, painting, and calligraphy.

The ultimate test of any educational system is how well it prepares students for the demands of a changing society, how efficiently it achieves this mission under both normal and stressful conditions, and how it innovates in the face of new challenges. Considering the long and peaceful rule of the Song in the eleventh century and over many decades in the twelfth and thirteenth centuries, we can reasonably conclude that the Song system of education, examination, and recruitment of civil service officials, developed at the beginning of the dynasty, passed this test with flying colors. Song scholar-officials laid the foundations of a bureaucratic system that would last for more than a thousand years.

7

LIFE CYCLE RITUALS

Two rituals were of outstanding social and financial importance to a Song family: marriage and burial. In addition, the pinning ceremony of girls about to become engaged, the sacrificial rites of the four seasons, the service to ancestors, and the capping ceremony of young men at the age of fifteen (when they put on the long robe and received an adult name) played important roles as life cycle rituals. Unlike capping, which was a reinvented ceremony patterned after the rites of antiquity, weddings and funerals were not just hollow acts but were part of a living tradition in Song times.[1] Beyond their significance for individual families, they were central to definitions of Chinese cultural identity and as a means of accommodating the past to the present.[2]

The Song Marriage System

The Chinese family was patriarchal, meaning that the father or grandfather was the ruling authority recognized by law. When three generations lived together, the grandfather had legal responsibility for the whole family and all its members, including his wife and concubines, his sons and their wives, grandsons and unmarried daughters, junior relatives and servants. He was the authority for all matters of importance to the family, especially ancestor worship, which was regarded as central to the perpetuation, solidarity, and prosperity of the lineage.

The head of scholar-official families worshipped the ancestors of three previous generations in the ancestral hall, which was the spiritual center of a household.[3] Marriage was designed to produce legal male descendants whose foremost obligation was to continue the rituals of ancestor worship—an institution that upheld the spiritual connection between the living and the dead for the benefit of both parties. The authoritative source *The Meaning of Marriage* (*Hunyi*) in the *Record of Rites* (*Liji*) explains that "marriages are for the good of two surnames joined together. Looking back they serve the ancestral temple, looking ahead they continue the family line."[4]

But a good marriage fulfilled other social and economic functions in addition to producing heirs. It built up family networks and secured political influence, privileges, and economic prosperity. In Chinese society a person's standing within the family was defined by position (as head of household, older brother, younger brother, wife, concubine, daughter, daughter-in-law, and so on). Hierarchy within a family mattered even more than gender, and the husband and wife of the oldest generation still living held the key position and could demand subservience from everyone else.

Although the state did not maintain an office in charge of registering marriages, families of equal social standing viewed marriage as a serious business and generally accepted certain legal constraints on its practice. For example, monogamy in China meant that a man could live with several women (his wife, concubines, and maid servants) in his household at the same time, but he had only one legal wife. She ranked at the top of the female hierarchy, especially after her sons brought home wives and she attained the status of mother-in-law. By law and under penalty of penal servitude, a man was forbidden to take another wife while he was still married to the first one. Only the death of his wife or a divorce ended the marriage and allowed him to remarry.[5]

Most families turned to female matchmakers to arrange good marriages for their sons and daughters. Matchmakers knew the local market and initiated the communications that allowed families to eventually agree on betrothal gifts from the groom and the dowry to be paid by the bride. In these negotiations, the wealth of the bride's family weighed heavier than her beauty or other personal attributes. The eligible young men and women seeking to wed were only pawns in the marriage game, and prearranged marriages between children were quite common. They generally married within their own generation, unlike their barbarian neighbors. In the eleventh century the preferable age of marriage for girls was between fourteen and twenty; young men married between sixteen and thirty.[6] Marrying at an even younger age was permissible, but being older and unwed was regarded as a misfortune.

During the Tang dynasty upper-class families preferred to choose their daughters-in-law from families with an eminent reputation in the past. In Song times, a daughter from an affluent household would place first on a family's list of ideal partners. Cai Xiang complained about this trend: "Nowadays [the eleventh century] it is common that a man considering a marriage does not take into account the status of the family but solely the family's wealth."[7] In the opinion of Neo-Confucian philosophers, the corruption of this new system was evident. The man's property, his betrothal gifts, and the wife's dowry became the deciding factors.

Well-to-do Song families belonging to the landed gentry and merchant classes, who as a rule furnished their daughters with rich dowries consisting of personal trousseaus and landholdings, collected information on young, well-placed examination graduates in the capital, whom they viewed as the best choice for a future son-in-law. The whole family expected to profit from having a *jinshi* graduate as a relative. And for an educated, wealthy, lovely daughter in her midteens, whose parents had allowed her to read history books and literature, compose her own writings, excel in conversation, and master household affairs such as weaving and embroidery, a scholar-official seemed to offer the best chance for happiness and prosperity. Sometimes a family even invested in the education of the future son-in-law, "tying [him] up when he grasps the money."[8]

Finding a suitable mate for an educated young woman could be challenging. A famous case was the daughter of the philosopher Cheng Hao (1032–1085). Her uncle, the staunch moralist Cheng Yi, did not want her to marry a man who was not up to her intellectual level and thus not worthy of her. After she died of exhaustion at the age of twenty-four, old Cheng Yi stated, "I deplore her death, but not her failure to marry."[9] To avoid any chance of a failure to marry, upper-class families in the Northern Song cultivated marriages among the families of friends, colleagues, and relatives. Local connections became especially important in the Southern Song.

According to a description of 1147, complex negotiations and technicalities were practiced by matchmakers to safeguard both of the families from errors and deceptions. A matchmaker engaged by the young man's family started the process by presenting a "draft card" containing a list of all sorts of information about the family's pedigree, the young man's standing within the family, his date of birth, and his mother's surname.[10] If the girl's family was interested in him, her matchmaker would return a draft card containing the same kinds of information.

The next step for the young man's family was the presentation of "detailed cards" with much more personal information, including the time of his birth and conditions in the household where the daughter would be living. The girl's family would reply by providing additional information on the quality and quantity of her dowry. At this stage, if one or both families judged the conditions for a marriage to be unsatisfactory, they still could withdraw without losing face. The next step was inspection of the bride by female members of the groom's family. In Southern Song times the groom himself was allowed to view her at this point. If he approved of his prospective wife, he inserted a gold hair pin in her headgear.

The groom's family signaled its approval of the match by sending four or eight decorated jars of wine to the bride's family. To complete the engagement, the groom's family had betrothal gifts sent to the bride's family. Depending on the wealth of the groom's family, these gifts comprised not only foodstuffs, women's clothes, and bolts of silk but also three items made of gold—a bracelet, a chain, and a pendant. The bride's family commonly sent gifts in return, creating a relationship of mutual obligation. By the time the families and an astrologer had decided on an auspicious day for the wedding, everything including the dowry had already been settled.

The social importance of the Song wedding was evident in the garments that grooms were allowed to wear. In Tang times the eldest son of an official born by his legal wife was entitled on his wedding day to wear an official's robe one rank lower than his father's. In Song times, if the son of an official had not yet passed his examinations, he was allowed to dress in the robe of an official of the ninth rank. A groom who had already passed the civil service examinations wore his own official robe on his wedding day. Commoners in the Tang and Song were allowed by law to wear a festive garment to their weddings but no official robe.

The weddings of commoners entailed only four comparatively simple steps, whereas the children of officials had to follow six or more elaborate rituals.[11] Theoretically, these rites were the same as those performed in antiquity, but in reality they had undergone considerable alterations within a mere one hundred years, as the texts of Sima Guang and Zhu Xi make clear.[12] The thoroughly choreographed series of ceremonies in-

cluded the bride's farewell and her procession, her ride with a completely
veiled face in a curtained sedan chair, chants, the arrival and greeting of
the wedding company, the entry of the young woman into her husband's
home, the preparations for the wedding festivities, the bowing and kneel-
ing, the many formulas to be repeated, her promise never to deviate from
the commands of her parents-in-law, the bowing of the newly wedded
couple to the ancestral altar of the husband's family, the closing of the
curtains to the bedchamber, the wedding banquet, the ritual undressing,
and later the visit of the couple to the bride's family. Each step in this
elaborate rite had to be performed in accordance with traditional rules
and local customs.[13]

Women's Education and Property Rights

"If you love your daughter do not give her to a mediocre man."[14] This
line reveals a lot about the worries of parents when giving their daughter
away to another family. The status and intellectual capacity of the husband within his own family was important to the bride's future for several reasons. A man who married did not have to change his way of life—
his relations with his parents and the outside world remained more or
less the same. A daughter or a widow who married not only changed
her family identity but started a new life. Her new position within her
husband's family was, more than everything else, that of a daughter-in-
law, a role well described in the *Canon of Women's Filial Piety* (*Nü
xiaojing*).[15] The daughter-in-law's priority and purpose in life were to
concentrate on the fulfillment of all the rules of filial piety, putting others
first, herself last.

These rules, which were far too theoretical and strict to be practiced
perfectly in daily life, dictated that the daughter-in-law must wear the
clothing prescribed by rites and doctrines, that her speech must follow
the classics, and that she must act sincerely and virtuously in all things.
She was expected to serve her parents-in-law as respectfully and lovingly
as though they were her own father and mother. At the cock's crow, she
washed her hands, rinsed her mouth, and dressed. She spun thread, tailored garments, and supplied the sacrificial food for the ancestral altar. In
winter she warmed her parents-in-law, in summer she cooled them. She
was their servant day and night.

Women in upper-class households no doubt found ways to modify or
elude some of these strict rules. But if in-laws found enough fault with

their daughter-in-law, they might insist on a divorce, and if the young husband was not strong-willed he would give in. This is what Lu You did shortly after his marriage. He was only twenty years old when he divorced his young wife, Tang Wan, and he later lamented his decision. In 1155 when by chance he met her again in the garden of the Shen family in Shaoxing, she offered him a cup of "golden-branded wine," which led to an exciting and unconventional exchange of poems. In a verse of 1183, he revealed his deep fondness for his former bride after almost thirty years, and described in her voice the desperate situation that led to the divorce:

> I was stupid to be sure, yet I knew
> that Madam, my mother-in-law, must be obeyed.
> Out of bed with the first cock's crowing,
> I combed and bound my hair, put on blouse and skirt.
> I did my work, tidied the hall, sprinkling and sweeping,
> in the kitchen prepared their plates of food.
> Green green the mallows and goosefoot I gathered—
> too bad I could not make them taste like bear's paws.
> When the least displeasure showed in Madam's face,
> the sleeves of my robe were soon damp with tear stains.
> My wish was that I might bear a son,
> to see Madam dandle a grandson in her arms.
> But those hopes in the end failed and came to nothing;
> Ill-fated, they made me the butt of slander.
> Driven from the house, I did not dare grumble,
> only grieved that I'd betrayed Madam's kindness.[16]

This remarkable relationship gives evidence that the lives of adult women and men were not always modeled after the reinvented rules of Neo-Confucian moralists.

Many daughters from affluent families received a literary education, especially in works on the proper conduct of women. Sima Guang instructed that girls should start learning women's tasks at the age of six, and at seven years old they should read the *Canon of Filial Piety* and the *Analects*. At nine they should get an explanation of the *Biographies of Women* (*Lienü zhuan*) and the *Admonitions of Women* (*Nüjie*). However, they should not be allowed to sing, compose poetry, or play music.[17] If her parents had obeyed the rigid restrictions of Confucian doctrine, Li

Qingzhao, the most famous female poet of Song times but also a book collector and connoisseur of antiquities, could never have composed her pure and elegant poems so full of emotional intensity.

In the reality of daily life, after the marriage ceremony was over most families did not care so much about a young lady's classical education or her idealized natural disposition, as summarized by Sima Guang in his "six female virtues," as they did about her subservience and practical talents. Knowing how to keep a household in good order and cope with all the tasks related to it—preparing food and beverages, serving, cleaning and washing, birthing and caring for children, rearing silkworms and reeling silk, spinning, weaving, embroidering, and sewing—ranked higher in the minds of in-laws than literacy. Expertise in such practical matters helped upper-class girls find good husbands and keep their in-laws happy, and it allowed commoners to land jobs in wealthy families as maid servants, cooks, embroiderers, weavers, laundresses, or whoever was needed.

Also in reality, feelings often triumphed over convention. Many men felt sympathy and affection for their women and daughters and did not judge them by the rigid concepts of the Neo-Confucian philosophers.[18] For example, a number of scholars wrote of their concern for the fate of their wet nurses, and men often displayed intense grief when a daughter or niece died. The full-dress burials they sometimes prepared for these girls and young women were not at all in keeping with the generational ranking of the dead. Confronted with the dilemma of whether to re-bury his five-year-old niece Jiji, the ninth-century poet Li Shangyin remarked that he was doing more than what propriety would allow for a child and assured her soul: "Wandering about, you will not be frightened of anything. Come and enjoy the pretty dresses, sweets, and fragrant drink that I have brought for you."[19] The thirteenth-century Song loyalist Wen Tingxiang expressed his love for his two young daughters in a vivid and worried description of them that he composed in a Mongol prison:

> Daughters I have two, both bright and sweet.
> The older one loved to practice calligraphy
> While the younger recited lessons sonorously.
> When a sudden blast of the north wind darkened the noonday sun
> The pair of jade whites was abandoned by the roadside.[20]

Here he alludes to the miserable circumstances he has left his daughters in and the somber fate that awaits him. In contrast with boys, who had to behave in an exemplary manner from an extremely young age, girls—this poem suggests—were allowed to be children, and that difference was no doubt part of what endeared girls to both fathers and mothers.

When a husband died, his family expected his wife to remain a widow until the end of her days. Confucian moralists considered such conduct the correct way of the universe, but the many cases of remarriage indicate that this restriction was too stern. Against the advantages of remarriage for young widows—ensuring the further prosperity of her children and enjoying life in a new partnership—morality ranked high in theory, but it often could not compete with the demands and opportunities of real life.

A critical factor in the economic independence of wives and widows was the legal status of their dowries. Song laws entitling women to own property clearly contradicted the Confucian scholar-officials who demanded that all belongings of a daughter-in-law should be turned over to her parents-in-law. Sima Guang and others claimed that the dispossession of women would strengthen family ties.[21] But the state had an interest in providing a certain financial protection for young widows, orphaned girls, and divorced wives, and even before Song times women's property rights had been moving away from the Confucian ideal of patrilineality.[22]

A woman received her inheritance in the form of a dowry when she married, and in the case of rich families the dowry consisted of considerable landholdings, silver ingots, silver and gold jewelry, hundreds of silk bolts and garments, furniture, and many other furnishings. The "wife's assets" were always kept separate from other property in her husband's household, rather than being merged into the common fund.[23] Landed property owned by a woman was regarded as her personal private property, in contrast with the ancestral land held by the males of a household for the benefit of the family. A wife's property stayed with her permanently; if she became divorced or widowed, she could take it with her into a new marriage.

The ownership and management of property by women corrects the overall impression that traditional China always adhered to the patrilineal ideal. Although Song society as a whole functioned along these lines, women enjoyed considerable independent control of their assets. In addition, women managed large households, and when their husbands were away on official duty assignments, often for the better part of a year, wives took over the financial affairs of the family estate. They occasionally went into business themselves, to enhance the wealth of the lineage. Men, in the opinion of Zhu Xi, were more profitably employed in the pursuit of self-cultivation and scholarship.

The Mongol invasion that ended the Southern Song empire brought about a fundamental change in gender relations by imposing Mongol marriage rules on Chinese women. Wishing to preserve their nomadic customs, the Mongols placed women at the disposal of the family and curtailed their legal, financial, and personal autonomy, beginning in 1260. This played right into the family-strengthening ideology of orthodox Neo-Confucians. The wishful thinking of Song family autocrats that "all authority and economic power resided with the family head" became a reality after the fall of the dynasty.[24] The ancient admonition to widows to stay chaste, serve in the husband's household, and relinquish control of their personal property gained legal support for the first time under the Mongols.[25] The cult of chastity began to prosper, the condemnation of re-marriage grew stronger, and the property rights and financial independence of women evaporated.

The Khitan and Jurchen Marriage Systems

During the Liao dynasty, the Yelü family was the imperial clan, while the Xiao clan supplied the emperors' consorts. All other Khitans belonged to tribes with place names but no surnames.[26] Intermarriage between the Yelü and the Xiao, which may well have occurred in predynastic times, allowed these two lineages to dominate the other Khitan tribes. In a similar exclusivity, the ruling Wanyan clan of the Jin dynasty chose their partners from only eight of ninety-nine Jurchen clans, and as a rule the rest of the Jurchens married within their own clan. Concubinage was legal, and adultery was tolerated. Intermarriages between the ruling clans of the Khitans and Jurchens, as well as among other tribal clans and neighbors, were common, but not intermarriage with the Song.

The Liao dynasty integrated many features of Chinese culture into its own society. The Yelü clan adopted the customs of ancestor worship and sacrifice to the spirits of deceased emperors but continued a marriage system practiced by nomadic and pastoral peoples of Inner and Northern Asia for hundreds of years.[27] Khitans married outside their own generation, and they allowed a man to marry his brother's widow. For the Chinese, marrying the widow of one's brother constituted incest, and marrying outside one's own generation was a shocking taboo. The imperial lineage of the Liao dynasty, however, benefited from this way of marriage, which secured its political position.

In 941, Khitans of the southern region who held Chinese offices received permission to marry Chinese women, but the dominant clans did not encourage such departures from nomadic rules.[28] Men of the ruling Yelü clan often married Chinese women, as happened when Emperor Shizong famously promoted a Chinese lady to the rank of a Liao empress. When Han Chinese women married Khitan men, the daughters of that union often married Han Chinese dignitaries. More research is needed to answer the question definitely whether a Han Chinese official was allowed to marry a Khitan clan woman of his own free will. As late as 1095 the Khitans living in the border regions were forbidden to intermarry with other barbarian tribes.[29]

The Jurchens were opposed to intermarriage as well. We do not know when intermarriage between Jurchens and Chinese was prohibited, but intermarriage seems to have become common among the people anyway. With so many Chinese imperial consorts at court, the Jurchen Jin Emperor Zhangzong finally gave his permission for intermarriages in 1191.[30] Under the alien dynasties of both the Liao and the Jin, Chinese subjects kept up their own traditions of marriage and continued to live in family households accommodating several generations.

While court marriages are reported in Chinese sources on the Khitans, there is no information on commoners' marriages. The widespread customs of marriage by elopement and wife-stealing with the girl's consent as practiced by the Khitans and Jurchens may have been the traditional way of marrying. The Chinese viewed both methods as barbaric. Khitan commoners and the lower nobility probably married in their own generation, as did the Yelü clan at the beginning of the dynasty. But starting with the third ruler, Emperor Shizong, the Yelü emperors adopted the practice of marrying into ascending generations of Xiao, which means they married contemporaries of their mothers and grandmothers, and their Xiao wives married contemporaries of their own sons and grandsons.[31] So, for example Emperor Daozong married Empress Xunyi, who was his father's mother's brother's daughter (that is, a contemporary of his mother).[32] This marriage system served the purpose of gaining political support and strengthening the supremacy of the imperial clan. Polygamy was common among upper-class Khitan, but at times they adopted the Chinese system of one legal wife plus concubines.

From the marriage of a Liao princess we may get an impression of how the marriage ceremony of the Khitan aristocracy was influenced by Chinese ritual. One of the princess's uncles served as master of the wedding. A revered "red woman" impersonated the Khitan ancestress. The ceremony started with choosing an auspicious day for the wedding. In the early morning the go-between went to the groom's family. At the court the groom waited until the emperor and empress arrived at the private hall and led his clan in for an audience. Wine was served. The members of both clans drank it in pairs. The next day a further audience took place, with the princess and groom participating. The emperor and empress gave a feast for them, and afterward the farewell gifts were presented. The princess received two blue-curtained carriages with dragon-head ornaments and coverings decorated with silver drawn by camels. She also got a funeral carriage drawn by oxen. The presents for the groom consisted of court clothes, garments for the four seasons, saddles, and horses. An imperial clansman escorted the prince to his home.[33]

Khitan society was patriarchal in structure and patrilineal in succession, but the realities of nomadic life, especially the preoccupation of men with hunting and war, ceded to women a great deal of economic and political influence. The wife of the Liao founder Abaoji gained a reputation for her sharp mind and strategic planning. She entertained a military force of her own, campaigned against tribal rebels, and seized power as a temporary regent. Other ladies followed her illustrious example. Emperor Jingzong's wife, who possessed an army of her own and was influential during her husband's lifetime, gained complete political and physical control over her son after the emperor died. She was the driving force behind the wars against the Song and the Shanyuan agreement with the Song in 1005. Unlike their Chinese sisters, Khitan wives of the nobility could divorce their husbands comparatively easily and marry again. One Khitan princess married four times. Throughout the dynasty, Khitan women succeeded in creating a sphere of personal autonomy that they safeguarded against male incursions.

Burial Customs of the Han Chinese

When the head of a Chinese household died, an almost endless number of regulations had to be observed and a tomb had to be built by his family. An inscription composed by an unknown son who buried his parents in 1191 provides a good idea of his motives and the preparations he undertook: "A tomb built of brick provides lasting protection for its occupants, and therefore is a work of merit and filial piety. My father and mother were hardworking, compassionate, and filial. After amassing the funds, I requested the services of artisans. Now I rebury here the bodies of my parents, so that their memory may be passed on among their descendents."[34]

The necessary behaviors such as washing, dressing, and laying out the corpse, wearing mourning garments, preparing for the burial, composing the epitaph, selecting the tomb site and burial date, arranging the procession of mourners, and performing various sacrifices followed a long established ritual that can be traced back to late Zhou times in the second half of the first millennium B.C. It is described in the *Record of Rites* (*Liji*) and the *Etiquette and Rites* (*Yili*). Sima Guang wrote his *Notes on the Yili by Master Sima* (*Sima shi shuyi*) to provide practical guidance to scholar-officials on how to perform burial rites with the appropriate deference to the dead and respect for the social hierarchy.[35] Ouyang Xiu wrote that instructing people in these rituals "not only would prevent disorder but also would teach them to distinguish superior and inferior, old and young, and the ethics of social relations."[36]

One century later when Zhu Xi lectured on *Family Rites,* he was no longer interested in establishing complicated rituals but described ideal and at the same time simplified and comfortable-to-use ceremonies. His work explained the formal proceedings, but it did not say a word about why the rituals had to be performed exactly the way he described them. Perhaps it was the handbook-like structure of his *Family Rites* that led to its unparalleled acceptance as the standard publication on rituals for centuries to come.

The family manuals—which were products of Song Confucian fundamentalism—and the official literature give the impression that the proper rules for burial as laid out in the classics were the standards followed by everyone. This was certainly not the case. On the contrary, Buddhist rituals had already infiltrated the mortuary territory that the Confucians vainly claimed to be their own, and Daoist priests made inroads into this lucrative market as well. The Buddhist "purificatory fast [for the spirits] of water and land" and the Daoist "retreat of the yellow register [for the salvation of ancestors]," both of which originated in the tenth century, gained immense popularity and proliferated widely. The Buddhist food-offering ritual for the gods, conducted on running water, and for ghosts, conducted on land, was a Song phenomenon and only one of many ecumenical, egalitarian, and universal Buddhist rites that promised redemption.[37]

Burial in tombs had always been a luxury and privilege of the educated political elite in China. During Song times the majority of commoners could not afford to buy a coffin or a plot of land for a grave, nor could they spend enormous sums on a proper burial. They, along with all who died anonymously as paupers, travelers, or victims of battles, massacres, epidemics, and natural disasters, were buried in various kinds of public cemeteries. These so-called charity gardens, charity grave paths, charity graveyards, or mercy gardens were fenced in and situated outside the city gates on wasteland, preferably close to Buddhist monasteries. The Southern Song capital Hangzhou alone administered twelve of them.

Charity—an underlying principle of Confucianism as well as Buddhism—embodied social obligations toward others, and it had a long-established claim on government resources. Although the maintenance of the charity graveyards was covered by the Stabilization Fund Bureau, the public budget never covered the costs for the Buddhist and Daoist monks who were responsible for all the funerals to be carried out. Members of socially responsible and powerful local families stepped into the breach, and many local officials gained a reputation for their benevolent administration when they purchased land and turned it into charity graveyards for several tens of thousands of corpses and skeletons. But despite its good intentions, Song society was just as inefficient as contemporaneous European societies in solving the urgent problem of managing deaths on a large scale.[38] After battles, epidemics, or other natural disasters, the corpses of unknown persons were often buried in mass graves and drained canals. In 1131, after the massacre of Nanjing, Ye Mengde, the commander of the city, ordered the burial of 4,687 complete and more than 70,000 mutilated corpses in the eight graveyards of the city.[39] Males and females were buried separately in registered mass graves.

An excellent example of a well-organized and perfectly kept mercy garden, in use from 1104 to 1116, was excavated south of present-day Sanmenxia city in Henan province.[40] The excavation team brought to light 849 vertical shaft tombs uniformly arranged in rows and columns oriented north-south. Most of the dead were buried in different postures in pottery vats made especially for this purpose. Information about the deceased and the graveyard comes from 372 epitaphs in the shape of square and rectangular bricks bearing engraved inscriptions. These inscriptions give not only the name, age, place of death, and date of burial of the deceased but also a tomb code indicating the organization of the graveyard. Sometimes the name of individuals or groups who arranged for the burial is given.

The majority of the dead were soldiers from the local garrison and men fulfilling menial labor service. Many of the people buried in this grave-yard—their age of death ranged from nine to eighty-two years—had been in the local Public Hospital for the Poor and in old people's homes that cared for men and women over seventy years old. All burials took place under the auspices of the local administration, which wrote on all epi-taphs (sometimes in abridged form): "Record of the burial in accordance with the rules completed."

To leave corpses and bones unburied contradicted Confucian ethics, but even mass burials were comparatively expensive because of the scar-city of suitable uncultivated land for graveyards. Corpses could not be lawfully thrown onto an open field or into ditches outside walled towns and villages, though this happened often. The financial burden of burial, as well as the demands of public health and hygiene, may explain why these alternatives to timely burial of the dead were tolerated. The bodies of poor people sometimes awaited burial in coffins stored in a sort of de-pot containing several thousand corpses.

The Neo-Confucians stated again and again their contempt and indig-nation over the barbarian practice of destroying bodies through crema-tion. They objected because cremation did not differentiate between the corpses of the poor and the rich, or the laborer and the scholar, and thus disrupted the social hierarchy. Nevertheless, starting in the tenth century, cremation became a widely accepted type of funeral rite until its prohibi-tion by law in 962. Buddhist institutions were in charge of cremations and storage of ashes. As a rule the corpse was put in a sitting "Buddha" position before the flesh was consumed by fire. Sometimes instead of cre-mation, the dead were exposed to the sun—a practice with roots in Ira-nian Central Asia. The bones left over after the fire or the sun had done its work were believed to nourish the *yang* energy that descendants re-ceived from the ancestor.[41] The bones were buried or piled up on Bud-dhist ground or halls.

Following but not copying the rules for burials stated in the *Record of Rites*, Sima Guang declared that "in ancient times, the Son of Heaven [the emperor] was buried after seven months, feudal lords after five months, great officers after three months, and gentlemen after one month. They were buried on the north side with their heads to the north." Zhu Xi stated that "after three months, bury the body. Prior to that, select a suit-able place for the burial." There was a general understanding that burial should take place as fast as possible, but certainly by three months after death in most cases. In reality, however, three obstacles prevented a timely burial.[42]

First, most officials died far away from home, and time was required to transport the corpse back to its burial place, usually the hometown of the deceased. Second, it took some time to select and purchase an auspicious burial ground and fix the date of burial in accordance with geomantic practices. Furthermore, the family had to arrange for building the tomb, fashioning the wooden inner and outer coffins, preparing the burial objects, finding someone to compose and inscribe the epitaph in stone (a privilege reserved for dead officials), inviting and entertaining hundreds of guests, honoring their attendance with reciprocal gifts, and finally performing the actual ceremonies and organizing the funeral procession.

According to Sima Guang "the Son of Heaven was allowed to make an underground passage [to the coffin chamber]. All the others lower the coffin [into the grave] and bury [it]."[43] The commentary says: "Nowadays in regions with coarse soil, coffin pits are made straight down. Either stone or brick is used to make the grave, just big enough to hold the coffin. [The people] cover it with stone. Every time after having spread one *chi* of soil on it, they make it solid by stamping. After having reached a layer of five *chi* or more [c. 150 cm], they ram it with a pestle."[44] A later commentary confirms his statement: "This is the method that should be used today."[45]

These vertical-shaft graves cannot be compared with the miniature residences the Tang aristocracy had built as underground tombs. The burial "chamber" had just enough space to take the coffin together with an epitaph and its covering slab, both cut in stone. They were usually placed near or just in front of the coffin. The function of the epitaph was to represent the deceased as faithfully as possible, introducing him in the other world as the kind of person he had been during his lifetime so that he would be granted the same place in its hierarchy. A large number of land deeds excavated from Song tombs was intended, like epitaphs, to introduce the deceased and establish his status in the other world.[46] Land deeds were used as substitutes for inscription stones by all classes who were not entitled to epitaphs.

The typical tombs of scholar-officials and their wives—who as a rule were individually buried in Song times—were very simple. They were built of stone, brick, and wood and have been found in most provinces of

China. The coffins placed in single tombs were also of modest design. The *Dynastic History of the Song* states: "In all their burials [the ranked officials] should not use stone for the inner and outer coffin and the tomb chamber. The coffins should not be carved [with ornaments] or colorfully painted or display windows and doors at the sides, the inner coffin should not contain gold, treasures, jewels and jade."[47]

The majority of Song tomb occupants did not belong to the aristocracy, as had been the case in Tang dynasty tombs, but were members of other elite groups within Chinese society, especially scholar-officials.[48] This elite class abandoned the Han and Tang architectural tradition used for aristocratic tombs, in keeping with Confucian principles and rules of a society that was no longer dominated by a genealogy-conscious aristocracy but was based on a new more meritocratic political and social order. Song scholar-officials imitated and revived the simple tombs of Zhou antiquity as an antidote to the extravagance and wastefulness of tomb architecture in Tang times. That these simple tombs were affordable to most scholar-official families helped to popularize this Confucian type of burial. They refused to build underground residences for the dead, in particular corbelled dome-type structures with several chambers that corresponded to the idea "in death as in life."

But even the simplest tomb required a number of preparatory steps before and after the coffin was placed in it. The coffin consisted of an outer casing around an inner coffin that held the corpse. The Chinese term for the inner coffin, *guan,* reflected the understanding that the coffin was designed for officials, also called *guan,* and should be made of wood. The outer encasing could be of various shapes and styles, though as a rule it was larger at the head and smaller at the feet and made of straight wooden boards.[49] The archaeological evidence demonstrates that stone tombs and stone coffins continued to be built, however, especially in Jiangxi and Sichuan.

In many ways the Song followed the well-established traditions of the burial trade. The outer coffin was positioned in a narrow pit on a layer of charcoal, lime, or limestone to protect the wood from water and insects and to delay decay. The narrow pit was filled with a special cement made of fine sand, lime, and yellow earth which became as strong and solid as metal or stone (Fig. 3). The idea behind the use of durable material for coffins was that filial sons had to fulfill the obligation to preserve the dead bodies of their parents fully intact. No harm should be done to their

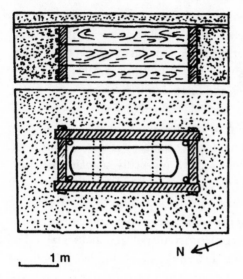

Fig. 3   Outline and longitudinal section of the wooden outer coffin tomb of Madame Sun Siniangzi (996–1055). The outer coffin is surrounded by mortar and covered with a layer of white clay. Northern Song. Jiangying-xian, Jiangsu province.

parents' flesh, because "the *yang* energy of the dead parents was expected to transmigrate to their sons," thus helping them to become prosperous.[50]

The simple construction and the lack of decoration of scholar-officials' tombs stand in sharp contrast with their social status and influence. Yet this type of tomb was consistent with the notions of economy, modesty, and simplicity in burials that Neo-Confucianists propagated in their ritual books. The strengthening and perpetuation of this ancient tomb tradition, which had been almost lost in Tang times, helped this elite class create their own nationwide identity and define their social responsibilities and privileges through their cultural consciousness. Such a remarkable social and cultural effort, which was also visible in the composition of epitaphs, brought aristocratic tomb building almost entirely to an end. It was taken up and continued for a while by nonofficial landowners in north China, but scholar-officials finally succeeded in imprinting their cultural values and ethnic norms on Chinese society as a whole, including aristocrats, landowners, and merchants.

The rapid acceptance and diffusion throughout the empire of the simple tomb—which after Song times became the standard tomb for all Chinese aside from the high aristocracy and members of the imperial family—may be interpreted as a victory of the cultural and consequently political ideals of the scholar-official class over the hereditary nobility.

Khitan and Jurchen Burial Customs

How different and incomprehensible the burial customs of the Khitans must have appeared to the Han Chinese. In the early years of the Liao dynasty, the Khitans followed the ancient custom of placing their dead in trees on mountainsides. Family members gathered and cremated the bones after three years.[51] A Khitan who wailed over the death of his parents was regarded as a weakling, whereas the Chinese would have condemned such stoic behavior as a failure to display filial piety. Persons who did not belong to the Khitan aristocracy were cremated or buried without much ado, just as Chinese commoners and paupers were.

After the establishment of the Khitan khanate in 907, various methods, in addition to cremation, were practiced to prepare corpses of the Khitan aristocracy for burial. One method, recorded after 1055, was to hang the corpse from the feet and pierce the skin all over with straws. This allowed the bodily fluids to drain off, and the result was desiccation. The corpse was then treated with alum, which caused the body to shrink so that only the bones remained. The dressed-up skeleton was interred in a tomb. Another method consisted of opening up the abdomen with a knife, removing the intestines, cleansing and washing the body cavity, and filling it with aromatic herbs, salt, and alum. Thereafter it was sewn up with a thread of five colors in order to preserve it. This burial rite was still practiced after the Liao dynasty ended.[52]

After the corpse was properly prepared, it was dressed in the traditional manner according to rank. The face of the deceased was covered with an individually fashioned mask of gold, silver, or copper, and the corpse was dressed in a special death garment made of gold, silver, or other metal wire.[53] The custom of dressing the deceased in a metal wire suit may have derived from the jade burial suits of the Chinese or, as some scholars believe, may have been introduced from Central Asia.[54]

To their Chinese contemporaries, the burial customs of the Khitans must have been revolting. According to the Han understanding of the proper way to treat an ancestor, the corpse had to be unscathed when buried. And yet Khitan practices, which resulted from the need to reduce the size of the remains, were not so far removed from fourteenth-century practices in Central Europe. One method consisted of disjointing the corpse like a piece of game and boiling the pieces to remove flesh from the bones. Another method, also practiced among Central Europeans, was to remove the entrails and organs before burial. It was only in the second half of the eighteenth century that a preference for keeping the corpse intact gained ground in Central Europe.

Seven emperors of the Northern Song, twenty-two empresses, and more than a thousand members of the imperial household were laid to rest on the imperial burial ground in hilly Gongxian county between Kaifeng and Luoyang. By contrast, the mausoleums of eight Liao emperors are distributed over the mountain slopes of four regions. When the dynasty's founder, Yelü Abaoji, died in 926 and was buried one year later, several hundred of his courtiers were killed so that they could follow him to the other world.[55] The Song, by contrast, did not practice human sacrifice for the purpose of populating imperial tombs. The custom of human sacrifice gradually declined among the Khitans, but it did not completely disappear. In the fourteenth century, in accordance with Mongolian custom, it was revived for the burial of the Ming emperor Taizu.

Unlike their Song counterparts, Liao tomb builders took up the Han and Tang style in the tenth century and developed it in new directions. The Yelü and Xiao clans, along with the upper echelons of Han Chinese in their service, created impressive subterranean dome-shaped tombs whose purpose was to preserve the social hierarchy among the dead. These many-chambered structures, with their corbelled roofs, were axially symmetrical. An approach ramp led to an antechamber, and from there into the burial chamber. On each side of the antechamber were side chambers built on the same level and generally in the same form—either round, square, hexagonal, or octagonal, with domed ceilings in corresponding forms or in different forms.

The interior of one of these chambers was usually furnished with an architectural structure of wood and stone that served as a room or coffin for the corpse. Several of these structures were unique to the Liao dynasty. One of them, a wooden interior tent, was a doorless, windowless structure very often built in log-cabin fashion, topped with a domed roof. In plan and elevation it closely followed the interior walls of the burial chamber, measuring several meters in height and diameter. In this closed-off room, the dead individual or couple was buried after having been previously prepared. The deceased lay in full attire inside the wooden tent, generally not in a coffin but on a coffin platform or a sort of pedestal bed surrounded by curtains.

The earliest wooden interior tent, datable to the tenth century, was discovered in the tomb of Xiao Qulie, a son-in-law of the emperor. All later constructions that have been excavated were octagonal in shape, apart from the most famous round interior tent, fashioned in the early eleventh century for the Princess of Chenguo (1001–1018) and her husband, Xiao Shaoju (Fig. 4). They were dressed in death garments made of silver wire, and their faces were covered with individually modeled masks made of pure gold. Khitan tombs, with their remarkable interior furnishings, form the final, most impressive, yet still mysterious high point of aristocratic tomb architecture in China.

The Jurchens of the Jin dynasty kept to their own burial customs, as we are informed in the *History of the Great Jin Kingdom* (*Da Jinguo zhi*). When a Jurchen fell ill and all herbal remedies failed, the shaman sacrificed a pig and a dog for the sick person, and someone packed him or her onto a cart headed for the big valley in the deep mountains. Relatives and friends avoided the sick person until death came, and afterward relatives cut their own forehead with a knife so that blood and tears could flow together. This ritual was called escorting blood and tears. Thereafter, the dead person was buried without inner and outer coffins. Although changes occurred in the burial customs of the Jurchen, in general they cremated their dead or interred them in simple graves and tombs built of stone.[56]

The Han Chinese of the Jin dynasty continued to build corbelled dome-type tombs in keeping with the model of Song antecedents. While most of these tombs did not attain the grandeur, structural density, and impressive complexity of Liao structures, their interiors, with many representations of floral ornaments and Confucian filial piety, incontestably reached a high point in interior decoration.

Weddings, Funerals, and Chinese Identity

In marriage and burial customs, the Han Chinese of Song times differed greatly from the Khitan and Jurchen peoples to the north. Although they were neighbors, in everyday life they lived in different worlds. Intermarriage between the two Khitan clans and the rather limited options of the ruling Jurchen clan served the preservation of political power. In Song society, on the other hand, marriage was clearly designed to produce legal descendants whose foremost obligation was to continue ancestor worship. In the Song marriage ritual, the Zhou Confucianism of the first

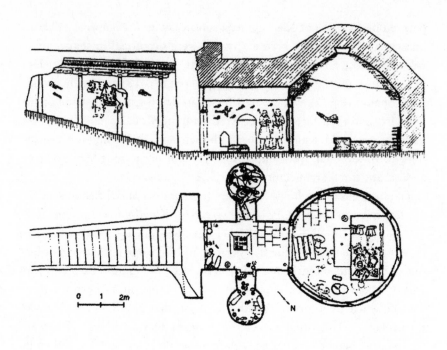

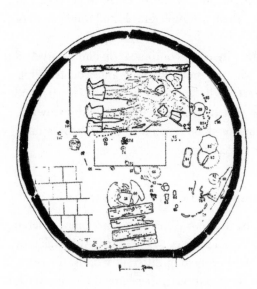

Fig. 4 The tomb of the Princess of Chen (1001–1018) and her husband, Xiao Shaoju. Liao dynasty, 1018. Naiman Banner, Inner Mongolia.
Top: Longitudinal section and plan of the complex tomb, furnished with side chambers and a wooden interior tent.
Bottom: Detail of the burial chamber and the fully dressed couple.

millennium B.C. fused with the scholar-officials' interest in building up family networks and securing privileges, influence, and economic prosperity.

With respect to burial practices, the Khitan kept their own distinct traditions alive, but at the same time their subterranean burial architecture brought aristocratic tomb building in the Tang style to its highest expression. In the Song revival of the more modest burial practices described in the classics of Zhou antiquity, scholar-officials expressed their continuing and conscientious search for models of correct behavior. As Song perceptions of antiquity came full circle in their Neo-Confucian concepts of appropriateness, the cultural identity of the Han Chinese was strengthened.

8

EXPLORING THE WORLD
WITHIN AND WITHOUT

THE Chinese held literature, the preserve of a tiny minority, in high esteem as an art. As with all cultures based on writing, the Chinese way of thinking, reasoning, and describing facts, theories, events, and emotions in prose and lyrics is reflected in the style of writing and the vocabulary used. From early in Chinese history, poetry was part of education and communication at every level of society. In Tang and Song times, it also figured prominently in the "memorization corpus" of examinations. To paraphrase Shao Yong, poems, as history, were good at recording intentions, not events; poems, as painting, were good at depicting emotions, not things. So poetry captured the essence of both history (which was motivation) and painting (which was emotion).[1] During the Song, poems were written to reveal the inner pattern of a process, and covered all aspects of cognition and being, including the dangerous sphere of politics. Being talented enough to compose excellent poems of the various types was regarded as the hallmark of an outstanding mind. So for Song writers, the essence of the inner world was concentrated in poetry but at the same time was intricately related to the perception and understanding of affairs in the outside world and in nature.

Poems formed a natural bridge to painting, especially when written as colophons for these works. In Song times scholar-officials created a secularized world in art composed of atmospheric landscapes, genre scenes, figure painting, animated sketches of birds and insects, and still lifes of flowers and fruits. Many of these works provided virtual places for meditation and for metaphysical exploration of invisible mental imaginings in the search for eternal truths outlasting the trivialities and anxieties of everyday existence. Others focused on the realities of daily life and re-corded the artist's observations of natural phenomena. It was in this readiness to observe and investigate the natural and material world that the intellectual curiosity of painters and scientists found common ground. Though they approached their shared interest with specific and individual techniques, in Song times the exploration of the inner and outer world went hand in hand.

Chinese science, in the words of Nathan Sivin, embraced "everything that was thought systematically, abstractly, and objectively about nature."[2] Joseph Needham concluded from his extensive investigations in the history of Chinese science and technology that "whenever one follows up any specific piece of scientific or technological history in Chinese literature, it is always at the Song dynasty that one finds the major focal point."[3] In Needham's opinion, the Song was the time of the greatest flowering of indigenous Chinese science. The three great technologies that Westerners associate with China—movable-type printing, the manufacture of firearms, and the invention of the compass—are tightly linked to the Song.

For Song society itself, printing allowed the growth of a publishing business that served all sorts of public and private interests, especially the education system. The invention of gunpowder in the ninth century and the development of firearms thereafter led to an armaments industry that employed several tens of thousands of technicians and workers. Although the invention of the compass did not transform Chinese society, its introduction into Europe as a navigation instrument turned European kingdoms into maritime powers operating worldwide. In 1620, at the dawn of the scientific age in the West, Francis Bacon stated that these three advances had "changed the whole face and condition of things throughout the world."[4]

Poetry—the Art of Revealing Inner Patterns

Poetry in Song China came in various forms, including the regulated verse poem (*shi*), with its narrowly set five-character or seven-character lines, and the song lyric or song words (*ci*), which made use of all the rhetorical resources of the Chinese language. The Tang geniuses of the eighth century, Li Bai and Du Fu, and several other influential poets set up the "classical" standard for regulated verse, and this tradition carried on through the centuries in various forms. "At the beginning of the Song dynasty," the critical observer Yan Yu noticed around the year 1200, "the poets still slavishly copied the Tang masters."[5]

The best known form was the Xikun-style poem, composed in parallel lines using an ornate and allusive language that displayed the erudition of its author. These poets were criticized for their failure to convey Confucian morality through their verse. Far more influential than this separatist poetic school, which continued to excel in a slightly outmoded style of poetry, were the regulated verse poems composed by the titan of Song literature, Su Shi, and others.[6] Charles Hartman observed: "The great Song poets of the eleventh century—Mei Yaochen (1002–1060), Ouyang Xiu (1007–1072), Su Shi (1037–1101), and Wang Anshi (1021–1086)—were the last poets ever to command a mastery of the entirety of the Chinese poetic tradition."[7]

The oldest of the four, Mei Yaochen finally passed the *jinshi* examination just nine years before he died. Unlike his poetry-writing contemporaries, he was a keen observer of simple, unimportant, casual, even ugly everyday objects and events. He wrote poems about earthworms swarming in a muddy hole and about maggots, lice, and other unattractive creatures that had only rarely appeared in verse. The even, bland style of his early work fit well with the new realism in painting. As he grew older, his poetry became more and more forceful, and many of his verses criticized society and its elite members.[8]

In *Ploughing Ox (Gengniu)*, he pointed out the differences between landlords and the poor, between idleness and tedious work. In this poem, the ox symbolized the farmer, while in *Swarming Mosquitoes (Juwen)* the mosquitoes represented corrupt officials who exploited the poor and protected the rich. As soon as the sun set, they would fly from their hiding places in the cracks of walls, swarm in the void, and dance like a veil of mist. The rich could protect themselves by encircling their beds with fine silk nets, but the poor and starving were victims of these blood-sucking insects seeking self-increase.[9] Mei Yaochen's contemporary, Wang Ling, a bright young man aided by Wang Anshi, also composed ballads about social evils. In one of them, called *Dreaming of Locusts (Meng huang)*, nightmarish insects lecture him that human beings should be regarded as the real pests to humanity.[10]

Su Shi belonged to the political faction opposing the reforms of Wang Anshi, but the two men shared a sense of humor and a feeling of sympathy and mutual respect, which can be appreciated in Su Shi's *Reply to Wang Anshi, Former Chief Councilor* of 1084:

Riding an ass, I come from afar to visit you,
Still imagine you as healthy as I knew.
You advise me to buy a house at your next gate,
I'd like to follow you, but it is ten years late.[11]

Su Shi founded the influential literary group known as the Four Schol-ars at Su Shi's Gate (*Su men si xueshi*), which consisted of Zhang Lei, Chao Buzhi, Qin Guan, and Huang Tingjian. Their political fate and ca-reers as poets depended to a large extent on Su Shi's political fortune and his up and downs as an antireformer.

Song lyrics (*ci*) written for musical performance already existed in Tang times and became very popular in the ninth and tenth centuries. They were composed by literati and performed by singing girls. By Song times, lyrics were the most fashionable and expressive poetic genre. In the words of Stuart H. Sargent, "The song lyric embodies in its very form the experiencing of emotion . . . [Its] characteristic prosody reminds us of the genre's musical origins and of the fact that it was once preeminently per-formance literature."[12]

A text of the song lyric was composed to fit existing tunes. To make the interaction of text and tune work and to accomplish perfection in perfor-mance, the genre of song lyric is governed by rigid tonal requirements and also by verse pattern and rhyme scheme. The total number of tune patterns amounted to over 2,300 variations. None of these melodies has been preserved, but their titles suggest that they covered a range of inter-ests, from the observation of nature, as in "The Moon over the West River" and "Wind through Pines," to dancing songs such as "Dance of the Cavalry" and "Bodhisattva Barbarian," to love songs such as "Telling the Innermost Feelings," "Song of Picking Mulberry," and "Joy of Eternal Union." Lyrics drew on colloquial language and gave it expres-sion in musical performance. From very early on, the words were written down and later printed, increasing the lyrics' circulation.

Two forms of song lyrics can be distinguished: the shorter form *xiao-ling*, originally meaning "commands," as used in drinking games, and the longer form *manci*, which means literally "lengthened" or "slow-paced tunes." The shorter form is usually composed of three to six lines in each of its two stanzas. The longer form is roughly twice as long, and its prosody displays extreme variation of line length (between two and ten syllables), allowing more irregular and extended rhythmic texture.[13] A translation of a song lyric from Chinese into a Western language (which should not be squeezed into a rhyme scheme) can never convey the sound and rhythm of the original but may succeed at conveying the poem's sensitivity of feeling, creating its atmosphere, and perhaps giving an impression of the composition's beauty.

In contrast to regulated verse, the song lyric consists of lines of unequal length. It was the verse form of choice to describe a state of mind, the pace or struggle of contemporary urban life, heartbroken loneliness, longing for love, erotic touch, romantic desire, a scene or image of natural beauty, and departure and farewell. Lyrics also conveyed private, hidden, ambiguous, and suggestive messages that could be delivered in a public context. The metaphorical complexity and symbolism varied widely, depending on the talent of the poet who selected and composed the characters.

The official and poet Ouyang Jiong, who compiled and prefaced the collection *Among the Flowers* (*Huajian ji*) in 940 in Sichuan, wrote that lyrics express aesthetic contemplations of beauty and refinement, emotional pleasures, and deprivations. They do not stress Confucian moral ideals and cannot be read as political allegories.[14] The "flying minister" Wen Tingyun, a nonconformist who failed the *jinshi* examinations but excelled as an innovative poet, figured prominently in this anthology. For a period of time he formed a liaison with the famous poet, courtesan, and Daoist nun Yu Xuanji (844–868), though he seems to have been no longer infatuated with her by the time she was accused of murdering her maid servant and publicly decapitated in the capital, Chang'an.

Although critics disagreed about the poetic merits and imaginative creativity of Wen Tingyun, and objected especially to his erotic bedchamber descriptions, there can be little doubt of his long-lasting influence on his colleagues and on later poets such as Liu Yong.[15] The poet Li Qingzhao did not try to camouflage both her admiration and her reservation: "Liu Yong transformed old music into new . . . Although the musical tones of his song lyrics are harmonious, the language is vulgar."[16]

The Southern Tang excelled in poetry as well as painting. The most famous of these poets was Li Yu, the last ruler of the dynasty, who surrendered to the Song and died in captivity in 978. He expanded the range of song lyrics from love affairs to political and philosophical reflections and made fine use of a colloquial language. In his short verse lyric to the tune "Dance of the Cavalry" he contrasted the once glorious past in the first stanza to the depressing present in the second, which is translated here.

Over night I surrendered to being a prisoner,
Thinner I grow, my hair turns grey
The day when we parted in greatest hurry from the ancestors'
   shrine,
Farewell songs were played,
And I shed tears standing before my palace maids.[17]

The story is told that in another of his lyrics the line "the spring waters flowing eastward"—expressing his nostalgic feelings for his lost kingdom—aroused the Song emperor's suspicion and finally sealed his fate as a captive until death.[18]

Political enemies capitalized upon a widespread inability to distinguish the persona (or voice) of a song lyric from the opinions of the poet himself, especially in the eleventh century, when song lyrics were the domain of romance and love. Taking advantage of Ouyang Xiu's reputation as a man of principle as well as an eminent lyric writer, his opponents may have forged some songs under his name in which the male protagonist is infatuated with a young girl.[19] At one time in his career Ouyang Xiu was charged with illicit relations with his niece Zhang, who lived with his family, and a lyric written about Ouyang by Liu Yong is an example of this type of personal slander. The victim would have stood no chance of vindicating himself.

To the tune "West of the little market"

I'm thinking of someone
Sweet face, just sixteen
Born beautiful—
She has got to be a minx.
Where she is most remarkable
Is when she laughs and her dimples show.
She has a hundred ways and a thousand charms,
And the more you embrace her
The more sweet and slippery she gets.
I've neglected her a long time.
Last night in a dream
We made love
Like old times.
Then just when I was happy

The cock next door woke me up.
Everything was quiet
But I could not get back to sleep;
The setting moon outside my window was wasted.[20]

Ouyang Xiu complained that anonymous poems were being circulated in the capital as a means of harming or even ruining the careers of loyal and competent officials. Although songs of romantic love, erotic potential, and desire for a young girl (usually a professional entertainer or courtesan) were heavily criticized, even tabooed, literati still went into raptures over the beauty and attractiveness of adolescent girls and were unable to desist from composing provocative lyrics full of intimate descriptions or promises of sexual pleasure.[21] Erotic topics and metaphors certainly enjoyed popularity within the circles of professional singing girls.

Most song lyrics deal with less offensive subjects, and in the long form, with its slow-moving melody, try to capture delicate landscapes and atmospheres. Li Qingzhao, the greatest woman poet of Song times and perhaps in all of Chinese history, grew up in an open-minded and unconventional scholar-official family, and as a teenager she was already aware of her talent.[22] Several decades later in 1133 we learn from two poems that the status of her formerly prominent clan had declined and that family members were scattered and living among the humble classes. When the Jurchens invaded Shandong, the collection of books and antiques she and her husband had collected in ten storage rooms went up in flames. She was separated from her husband, and she suffered from his early death in 1129.

Despite her despair, Li Qingzhao was convinced that her poetry would be remembered.[23] To pour out her misery in her lyrics, she made use of allusions and repetitions, and injected colloquial and onomatopoetic expressions into classical Chinese poetic language, which gave her lyrics an unequaled intensity and directness. Still, she knew the rules she had to observe, and her verses "reproduced a horizon of expectation defined not only by the genre, but also by her gender."[24]

To the tune "Every sound slowly"
Search. Search. Seek. Seek.
Cold. Cold. Clear. Clear.
Sorrow. Sorrow. Pain. Pain. Pity. Pity.
Times of hot flashes and sudden chills.

It's hard to come to rest.
Three cups, two bowls of tasteless wine,
How should he late burst in like a gust of wind?
Wild geese fly, wrenching my heart.
Really, from old days we know each other.
Golden flowers pile up on the ground,
Faded, dead.
Who would pick them now?
All alone, waiting at my window,
How does it become dark?
The wutong trees blend drizzling rain.
Until dusk falls. Drip. Drip. Drop. Drop.
This condition, can the mere word melancholy suffice?[25]

The best poets of the Southern Song are known for their patriotic and heroic loyalty to the Song empire and Chinese culture.[26] Xin Qiqi, in 1161 barely twenty years old, operated as a guerrilla leader of two thousand uprooted farmers on Jin territory, and later was appointed a commissioner of the Flying Tiger Cavalry before being forced into retirement in 1181. He was the most prolific writer of song lyric in the entire Song dynasty. His contemporaries praised his poems for their unbridled vigor and sensibility. As a military man, he relived in his nightmares the loss of the north to the Jurchen. In his songs, he asked the rhetorical question: "Where is the central plain when gazing beyond the Northern Tower?" "I gaze afar on land long lost in the northwest," and how "to recover the lost land for the emperor."

His friend, the philosopher Chen Liang, complained that "still are the northern steeds around" and asked, "Is there none who thinks it is wrong to submit to the foe, whose stink of mutton spreads for miles and miles." Liu Guo, another follower of Xin Qiqi, cried out: "When can we recover the lost central plain? Our men, united, should start now and here." With the carefree life of the Northern Song over, the burden of reconquering the northern territories weighed heavy on the patriotic officials and officers.

But love for and loyalty to the fatherland was not limited to Song poets and officials. Yuan Haowen, who like all Jin dynasty intellectuals was well aware of the problem of the Jin's political legitimacy in an age when China was divided, left a collection of poetry that breathes depth and gravity.[27] His poems embodied Confucius' *Doctrine of the Mean*

(*Zhongyong*): "Unless there is sincerity, there is no substance." Five years after the Jin dynasty collapsed and the last Jin ruler committed suicide, Yuan Haowen composed a five-character regulated verse poem entitled "New Year's Day, 1239":

> At fifty, one is not really old,
> Yet my appearance keeps worsening.
> As the hair on my head grows thinner,
> So too the image in the mirror changes.
> My unofficial history just outlined,
> Yet undetermined is the site of my retreat.
> It would not do, riding my gaunt horse,
> To re-enter the world's red dust.[28]

In those years, as he restlessly traveled from one patron household to the next, he began to draft the *Dynastic History of the Jin* (*Jinshu*), which was officially completed about one hundred years later.[29]

Reflecting Nature and Daily Life in Painting

A refined gentleman of the Song period was expected to master four arts: calligraphy, painting, Chinese chess, and the lute. Calligraphy and painting were techniques of communication, vehicles used by knowledgeable people to make the invisible visible. They depicted the condition and state of mind of an individual's inner self by making them appear in the form of Chinese characters and in the shape of physical objects. The quality of a work of art was judged by the presence or absence of vigor in the style of communication. Throughout Chinese history, the literati were regarded as the true artists. They normally painted with special brushes and paints on paper or silk in the form of horizontal and hanging scrolls in a variety of formats. These scrolls could be rolled up and easily carried. In addition some artists painted on fans and album leaves.

Aside from works of art created by and for the educated elite, a deep-rooted popular tradition of colorful murals could be found in temples, palaces, and tombs. These wall paintings were traditionally created by skilled but mostly unknown professional artists who earned their living from commissions.[30] The preserved paintings convey a lively impression of the everyday life of the wealthy landowning Song households and the Liao aristocracy.

While there are generally no doubts about the authenticity of the murals in tombs, the situation is less certain for paintings of the literati. The early founders of Chinese landscape painting in the tenth century created the models for a unique understanding of nature and landscape, but we know their art solely from paintings ascribed to them and from copies of their work. In Chinese custom, the imitation of the style or spirit of an earlier master was considered a sort of hallmark of artistic quality and a legitimate continuation of an established tradition.[31] To date, the authenticity of only one landscape hanging scroll, a painting from the hand of an unknown provincial master, which may well have been executed between 959 and 986, has been ascertained. However, its execution does not represent the artistic style of the period in its most mature form.[32]

In the pre-Tang era, depictions of nature and landscape were subordinated to human figures, which formed the focus of interest. Tang landscapes took on a didactic function, allowing the informed observer to read depictions of a landscape and figures in it as a "historical" document. The emancipation of landscape from this primarily narrative function was inseparably bound up with the removal of the Chinese cultural centers from the north to the southern and western regions of China in the late ninth and tenth centuries.[33] Human figures, historical events, and religious ceremonies were subjected to reinterpretation, in the course of which their importance, compared with that of landscape, diminished. Landscape painting depicted nature itself as an all-embracing organic unity.

The essential innovations in landscape painting—"the painting of mountains and rivers"—are linked to the names of a small number of artists. In the north, Jing Hao (ca. 870–930), the creator of the concept "landscape of truth," may have served as a model.[34] In the south, the painter Dong Yuan (active ca. 937–962) produced remarkable landscapes that were praised by connoisseurs in the eleventh century, as did his pupil, the Buddhist monk Juran (active ca. 960–980). None of Juran's paintings survives, but fortunately he and a colleague were commissioned to decorate the Jade Hall of the Northern Song Hanlin Academy. These murals featured a morning scene with lofty peaks and small rounded rocks surrounded by mountain mist, which created an illusionistic effect.[35]

The most important transformation in Song landscape painting can be seen in a hanging scroll that was traditionally ascribed to the tenth-century master Li Cheng but which was probably painted one century later (Fig. 5).[36] A solitary Buddhist monastery amid towering mountains

Fig. 5 *A Solitary Temple amidst Clearing Peaks*. Attributed to Li Cheng (919–967), Northern Song dynasty. Hanging scroll, ink and slight color on silk. Nelson-Atkins Museum of Art, Kansas City, Missouri.

and parting clouds was a central motif in his compositions. The mountains, misty valleys, waterfall, and individually placed trees and architectonic elements were perhaps intended to reflect the painter's belief in an ordering principle inherent in nature, in accordance with Confucian cosmology and the doctrine of the unity of Man with Heaven: "By expanding one's mind, one is able to embody the things of the whole world."[37] Completely absent here are the exaggerated, melodramatic effects evident in the heroic and exuberant landscapes of later masters of the Northern Song era, such as Guo Xi.

In the Southern Song era, landscape artists preferred smaller formats, often album leaves and fans, and painted more intimate, selective scenes. Especially famous were the "one-corner" compositions of Ma Yuan and Xia Gui, who were both active around the turn of the thirteenth century. Their works reflect the idea of a reduction to essentials, a purity of view. In an easily visible corner of the lower foreground, a few simple strokes depicting a group of trees, a scholar's hut, or some other feature offer an initial focal point for the eye, thus creating a suggestive atmosphere of emptiness, a deep perspective articulated through mists and vapors, a striking openness within a very small format.

Just at the time when many Song painters were trying to capture the essence of landscape in a drastically reduced pictorial format, depictions of real life started to appear in pictures. This new receptivity to representation, as reflected in both the subjects and the execution of paintings, coincides with Zhu Xi's *Reflections on Things at Hand (Jinsi lu)*, which brought Confucianism back to a vital concern with daily life. Comparable to one-corner composition in painting, his *Reflections* illustrate that the structure and analysis of the details of everyday experience can provide essential insights.

This attention to the common detail resulted in a body of work that can be described as genre painting. Groups of artists with a special focus on painting flowers and birds, for example, were centered in Chengdu and Nanjing. The most renowned and influential painter living at the court in Chengdu was Huang Quan. He served the Shu rulers for nearly fifty years, and in 965 was appointed a member of the Academy of Painting in Kaifeng. Huang Quan's life and work bridge the period between the end of the Tang period and the beginning of the Song, when phantasmagorical subjects gave way to real animals and flowers that could be observed in nature. His contemporaries judged his depictions of nature to be unsurpassable, and later connoisseurs like Shen Gua referred to them

Fig. 6 *Sketches of Precious Creatures*. Attributed to Huang Quan (903–968), copy from the early decades of the twelfth century. Handscroll, ink and color on silk. Palace Museum, Beijing.

as "sketches of life" or, literally translated, "writing life."[38] His mastery is evident in the double album leaf ascribed to him and his son with the title *Sketches of Precious Creatures (Xie sheng zhenqin)*, although the sketches still extant are probably from the early decades of the twelfth century (Fig. 6). His taxonomic approach to detail, which seemed in some ways more realistic than life itself, remained authoritative in the Academy of Painting until the mid-eleventh century.[39]

In Nanjing, the capital of the Southern Tang, a number of painters specializing in flowers, birds, cats, and bamboo motifs were active until around 975. Whereas Huang Quan in Chengdu strove for fidelity to real life through the accurate use of outlines, shadows, and color, Xu Xi in Nanjing employed a thick paintbrush that he wielded with strong, free strokes to paper or silk. His wild, free style seemed to capture not so much the formal details as the forces of nature. Fidelity, realism, "writing life" were not enough for him, which is why later commentators maintained that he expressed in his work the "vital principle" and embraced the "idea of vitality."[40] His pictures were enthusiastically appreciated by the Emperor Taizong, but it was not until the eleventh century that painters like Cui Bo adopted his style and restored animals and plants to a more natural composition within an open, free landscape.

Emperor Huizong, who was known for his idiosyncratic slender gold style of calligraphy, greatly appreciated the flower and bird paintings of his court artists. His own meticulously accurate portrayal of these subjects depicted nature in a way that had already been outdated for several decades, but they were distinctive and admired in their own time. Practical functions, more than courtly taste and personal ability, defined the message of these paintings, which may be divided into "auspicious omen" and "auspicious presentation" paintings. The auspicious omen so important to Emperor Huizong's rule appeared to him on the evening of February 12, 1112, during the Lantern Festival, when suddenly rainbow-hued clouds brushed the roof ridge of the Imperial Palace's Duanmen Gate. Cranes—immortal birds proclaiming good auspices—descended from the sky, two of them resting on the roof and the other eighteen wheeling in the sky for some time.[41] In Mary Bickford's interpretation, the cranes were "the designated agents of congratulations between the parallel courts of Huizong at the Song capital city and the eternal Daoist realm of the immortals."[42]

Emperor Huizong described this event in his inscription and in the poem added to the short handscroll *Cranes of Good Omen* (Fig. 7), which he signed as usual with "First man under heaven" (*Tianxia yi ren*). Hence his artistic endeavors should be viewed as more than just a hobby. He may have aimed at the integration of governmental and cultural functions and thus linked himself and his undertakings to many of the Daoist activities of Emperor Zhenzong one hundred years earlier.[43]

The artistic renaissance at the court of the Southern Tang in Nanjing sprang from a long and creative tradition in the south. New subjects became increasingly popular—both intimate domestic interiors and scenes of work and travel in the outside world. The narrative handscroll *Han Xizai's Night Revelry* (*Han Xizai yeyan tu*) from the mid-tenth century has traditionally been ascribed to the Southern Tang court painter Gu Hongzhong (Fig. 8). More probably, in view of the dating of the landscape portrayal in the background, it is a copy from the late Song era.[44] Han Xizai spent his entire fortune on festive entertainments and courtesans and ended up a beggar. His profligate pleasures, as depicted on this handscroll, ranged from the performance of an instrumental piece on the Chinese lute by the sister of the acting director of the Imperial Theatre,

Fig. 7 *Cranes of Good Omen*. Emperor Huizong (r. 1100–1126). Handscroll, ink and color on silk. Museum of Liaoning Province, Shenyang.

Fig. 8 Detail from *Han Xizai's Night Revelry*. Attributed to Gu Hongzhong, southern Tang dynasty, mid-tenth century, copy from the Song dynasty. Palace Museum, Beijing.

whose playing Han Xizai listened to while relaxing on a sofa, to a bed scene where only a courtesan's stockinged golden lotus foot is visible but is nonetheless quite unambiguous.[45] The representation of individual scenes and the portraitlike features of the figures underscore the painting's narrative content. Two guests are sitting on chairs with backs, indicating that a shift in custom away from floor mats had already taken place, at least for the newly rich and fashion-conscious.[46]

A horizontal scroll ascribed to the Southern Tang court painter Zhao Gan bears the title *Travelers along the River in Early Snow, in the Manner of the Academy Painter Zhao Gan (Jiangxing chuxue huayuan xuesheng Zhao Gan zhuang)*, which the Jin Emperor Zhangzong, an important collector of Chinese art, inscribed on the scroll (Fig. 9).[47] Its motifs, execution, and realistic detail ensured its place in the palace collections from the Song to the Qing dynasty. This unique work depicts the difficulty of water travel and in particular the struggle of fishermen to earn a living under inhospitable conditions. In a wintry, partly snow-covered riverscape, these men steer their flat boats through the wind-blown water, inspect the contents of their open nets, which are raised and lowered by

Fig. 9   Detail from *Travelers along the River in Early Snow.* Attributed to Zhao Gan (fl. 961–975), southern Tang dynasty. Handscroll, ink and color on silk. National Palace Museum, Taiwan, Republic of China.

means of an intricate mechanism, and seek refuge from the bitter wind in barrel-shaped shelters made from woven rushes on wooden posts.

Zhao's depiction of men engaged with the forces of nature provided material for philosophical speculation and suggested Confucian and Daoist influence. Fishing with a rod was seen as a selective activity, which in a metaphorical sense could be applied to political decisions too. By contrast, fishing with a net corresponded to the Daoist notion of the net of heaven, the unity and totality of the world.

Entertainment and travel were often the subjects of tomb paintings that immortalized the deceased. Liao tombs especially had developed the traditional Chinese underground tomb architecture and wall decoration style of northern China and Inner Mongolia from the Han to the Tang era, and this architecture offered optimal opportunities for murals. The pictorial programs were executed on the walls of the approach to the tomb, the burial chamber, and the dome of the tomb. Among the themes treated were landscapes depicting the four seasons, animal and flower painting, the twenty-eight lunar mansions (on the tomb domes), the twelve Chinese symbolic animals, the twelve Western zodiacal symbols, a wide variety of religious and profane figures, and scenes from daily life (found mainly in burial chambers).

An excellent map depicting the Chinese lunar mansions and the Chinese and Western symbols was discovered on the ceiling of the dome-shaped tomb of Zhang Gongyou from 1117 in the Liao dynasty (Fig. 10). The Western zodiac was probably introduced into China around the end of the sixth century.[48] The theme of departure was captured in a large group of travelers with a horse, wagon, and entourage, and several smaller groups setting off, journeying through a landscape, or returning home. This theme enjoyed special popularity on the walls of the long approach to the tomb, whereas a banquet theme often appeared in the burial chamber.

In terms of artistic execution, the best depictions of preparations for a banquet as well as lesser household events have been found in a range of northern Chinese tombs, above all those of the Zhang family in Xuanhua in the province of Hebei.[49] They show official helpers, a woman and a man warming and serving wine, and also cheerful scenes such as children playing in a scholar's study while tea was being prepared. Another room features writing utensils (doubtless intended to indicate the scholarly class that the family belonged to). A female servant holds a dish and clearly warns a dog not to jump up at her. An intimate scene in the richly

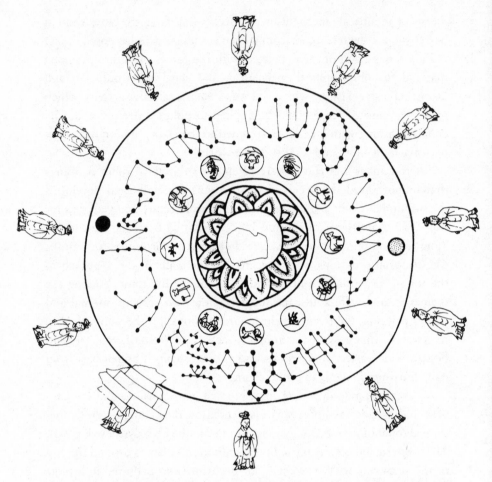

Fig. 10 Drawing of a ceiling painting depicting the Mesopotamian twelve zodiacal symbols, the twenty-eight lunar mansions, and the Chinese twelve symbolic
animals representing the twelve earthly branches, arranged around a lotus design
with a mirror in the center. Liao dynasty, 1117. Tomb owner Zhang Gongyou
(1069–1113), tomb no. 2 of Xuanhua, Hebei province. Tao Zongye et al.

painted tomb of Zhang Gongyou depicts the tomb's owner, his son, and
his wife viewing his art collection in a well-furnished and nicely decorated room.[50]

    As the composition of these interior scenes and above all the outstand-
ing rendering of the figures' faces indicate, the professional tomb painters
at the end of the Liao era reached a level of artistry that their Song colleagues would never attain. We can only speculate on the reason. The
Liao probably wanted to maintain the high Tang standards in aristocratic

tomb painting, and investing in a professional tomb painter was worth the expense. In the Song, however, high officials and important scholars did not build architecturally significant tombs. Elaborate tomb building became almost exclusively the passion of landowners, who used tombs to emphasize the local prestige of their families.

Most of the pictorial records in these landowners' tombs are reliefs carved in brick or stone, sometimes intensified by the application of colors in order to achieve better contours with sharper contrasts. Aside from religious motifs such as guardians or fierce warriors or the twenty-four scenes of filial piety, most of these depictions reflect a peaceful, secluded, and cultivated atmosphere, the lifestyle of the landed gentry. As a rule, they show the married couple sitting opposite each other on chairs at a table, their hands buried in their long, wide tunic sleeves, being served by the daughter-in-law or by servants (Fig. 11).

The physiognomies of the deceased are clear and distinct. Portrayal of the deceased man was quite common, although it was not considered appropriate by stern Confucians to uncover the face of the woman and "copy her likeness."[51] This orthodox view of scholar-officials, who preferred idealized nonindividualized portraits of their wives, must have differed from the view of the local elite, who insisted on portraits of the deceased that captured the individual's features—otherwise, not so many mural paintings of couples showing individuality would be extant. Many tombs were furnished with mock doors, mock windows, and household furnishings, including table and chairs, clothes racks, mirrors, and high stands with arms to hold oil lamps. This tradition can be traced back to Han times.

An outstanding and rare pictorial document allows us a glimpse of women at work in a household.[52] On the far right of the mural painting, a boy is carrying up pails of water hung from a pole (Fig. 12). In the center two women are stretching silk fabric, while a third woman is smoothing its surface. The silk working process required pounding in order to soften the fabric. The earliest handscroll depicting this step may have originally been painted in the eighth century by Zhang Xuan, and later copied by the Song Emperor Huizong. Further to the left, another woman is standing on a low bench and taking bolts of textile materials or articles of clothing from a large chest. In the background, clothes and pieces of textile are drying or being aired while hanging over a pole. This picture clearly takes up a theme already popular during the Tang dynasty.

Fig. 11   Mr. Zhao and his wife served by his daughter and servants. Northern Song dynasty, 1099. Mural painting in tomb no. 1. Yuxian, Henan province. Su Bai.

Most Song architectural tombs did not contain the epitaphs that are typical of officials' tombs. This absence confirms that the tombs belonged to long-established wealthy landowning families who lived and were buried in great style.

Apprehending Principle in Things

In the three centuries of the Song dynasty, investigating things—or, as the Confucians put it, apprehending Principle in things (*gewu*)—went far beyond the domain of ethics and personal moral cultivation. It included

Fig. 12 Women pounding and softening silk fabrics (*daolian*). Early twelfth century. Mural painting in tomb no. 6. Shizhuang, Jingxingxian, Hebei.

also a perception of reality that can be attained only through a thorough study of objects, events, and behaviors in the natural world.[53]

For hundreds of years Chinese scholars had observed the sky and recorded their observations. Though in most cases they did not draw conclusions in a modern scientific sense, their accurate descriptions made an enormous contribution to the history of astronomy. In 896 astronomers reported the break-up of a comet (called a traveling star). During one evening in 1064, Shen Gua heard what sounded like thunder and saw an object on the southeastern sky that appeared to be the size of the moon. A meteorite as big as a fist fell into a garden. It felt warm and had the color and weight of iron.[54] In 1112 an observer recorded the appearance of sunspots the size of chestnuts, which he observed by looking at a reflection of the sun in a basin of oil.

Roughly ninety novae (called guest stars by the Chinese) were reported in China prior to the modern period, but the supernova of 1054, near p Tauri 6,500 light years from the solar system, was the most impressive. It was visible to the naked eye for twenty-three days in daylight, and after two years it disappeared. In 1839, using a telescope, astronomers rediscovered the remnant of a supernova in the same part of the sky, and in 1921 the remains of the giant stellar outburst of 1054 was named the Crab Nebula.

Various sources in the eleventh century reported the use of the "south-pointing fish," a magnetized thin leaf of iron. When floating on water in a bowl, its head pointed south. The clumsy fish was eventually replaced by a south-pointing needle, which was magnetized by rubbing it with a lodestone. Shen Gua's report of this invention is the earliest description of a compass needle known in world literature. Through experimentation, he concluded that his needle always pointed slightly to the left of south; what he had discovered was the difference between the geographic and magnetic poles of the earth.[55] The magnetic needle set on a disk—used by magicians, necromancers, and geomancers in Song times—was an early prototype of the modern magnetic mariner's compass. Chinese sailors employed the navigational compass as early as 1090. Within the next century it traveled to Europe, and in 1190 Alexander Neckam, an English monk who had studied in Paris, described the advantages of a magnetic needle for sailors.[56]

In 1247 Song Ci, who for many years during his official career served as a judge, published his *Collected Writings of the Washing Away of Wrongs* (*Xiyuan jilu*), the first systematic work on forensic medicine. The manual was quickly taken up for use by officials holding inquests on ho-micides and other suspicious deaths.[57] Many of his ideas and explana-tions, especially concerning the investigation of corpses, were grounded in superstition, but others were thoroughly rational. Song Ci instructed his colleagues in the art of autopsy, and he described tests for sulphide poisoning, warned against arsenic poisoning, understood the symptoms of carbon monoxide poisoning, and recommended ligature of limbs to prevent snake venom from spreading through the bloodstream.

The most important single work describing scientific phenomena in Song times is the *Notes Taken in Mengqi (Mengqi bitan)*, composed be-tween 1086 and 1093 by Shen Gua. His quest for knowledge led to a Confucian-based Song Enlightenment, which permitted an understand-ing of the Principle in all individual things and the universe as a whole. This high-achieving, career-minded executive, court politician, and tech-nocrat belonged to a like-minded group of professional officials with sci-entific and technological inclinations, although an institutionalized scien-tific community did not exist at the time. Most famous are his entries on the invention of movable-type printing by Bi Sheng in the 1040s, which preceded Gutenberg's invention by four hundred years, his description of cartographic techniques, and his explanation of fossil remains. In an-other entry he wrote that from the way the moon waxed and waned, he could tell that the shapes of the sun and moon were spherical. The moon does not radiate light, he wrote; it only shines when shone upon like a sil-ver ball. When light strikes it from the side, it appears to the human eye as a crescent.

Shen Gua delighted in strange occurrences, and not all entries were of the highest quality or written with the same purpose. Included were "trivial didacticisms, court anecdotes, and ephemeral curiosities," as Na-than Sivin observed.[58] Explanations of natural phenomena were based on the existing cosmological theory of the cyclical order of the five phases or elements: metal, wood, water, fire, and earth. When the wind blew over a salt pond and the salt crystallized, Shen did not explain the process as an increased rate of evaporation but as the principle of the mutual produc-tion circle, which means that fire (here wind) produced earth (salt).

The use of water clocks and the positions of 1,350 stars in relation to the sun for each of the twelve months of the year had been known for some time. In 976 a student in the Bureau of Astronomy, Zhang Sixun, built a water-driven astronomical clock placed in an elaborate three-story tower 10 meters high in the capital Kaifeng. But it was the scientific scholar Su Song in the Ministry of Personnel who brought the previous time-measuring devices to perfection. The idea behind the design of his armillary clock was three-fold: astronomical demonstrations, astronomical observations, and time-keeping.[59] The mechanism of the clockwork linked time-measuring to the rotation of an armillary sphere used for the observation of star positions, and to a celestial globe used to tell the exact time and correlate it with the motion of the heavenly bodies, including the sun, moon, and the five planets, for calendrical verifications. This brought time and space into harmony; hence, the device was called the "cosmic engine."

The motive behind this unprecedented and costly project goes back to the year 1077, when Su Song was sent as ambassador to the Liao court to offer birthday congratulations to the Liao emperor. It turned out that the Song calendar was ahead of the Liao calendar by one day. Su informed the Song Emperor Shenzong of what had happened. He had all the officials of the Bureau of Astronomy and Calendar punished. In 1086, for obvious political reasons, Emperor Zhezong ordered Su Song to build an armillary clock that should exceed all previous instruments in precision. In 1088 a small wooden model of the clock for testing was finished. In 1090 the full-scale structure with all its complex functions, including a sphere and globe cast in bronze, was set up in the Imperial Palace at Kaifeng (Fig. 13).[60] In *New Design for an Armillary Clock* (*Xin yixiang fayao*), completed in 1094, Su Song explained the workings of his invention.

The wooden tower was 12 meters high with an armillary sphere on the platform at the top level. This allowed the astronomer to observe the sky and the positions of the stars when weather allowed. The armillary sphere as well as the revolving celestial globe in the upper story were ingeniously geared to the driving mechanism of the clockwork, thus giving the astronomer an opportunity to calculate the position of the heavenly bodies regardless of the weather. Below this chamber was a five-story pagodalike structure for announcing the time. Numerous wooden jacks appearing at windows and holding a tablet with an inscription displayed the time by day and night on the hour, the quarter hour, and other intervals. These were signaled not only visually but also by ringing bells, striking gongs, and beating drums. The whole mechanism was geared to a water wheel fitted with scoops that were filled by a steady flow from a water tank. The wheel measured more than 3 meters in diameter. In the opinion of Joseph Needham, a special device comparable to a clock's escapement

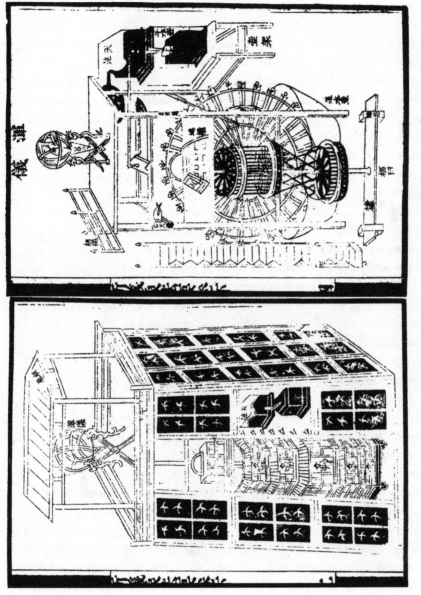

Fig. 13　Water-power-driven astronomical clockwork set up in the Imperial Palace at Kaifeng. Northern Song, 1094. Su Song.

was used to regulate the motion of the wheel. This mechanism broke time into a series of precise "ticks."

Shortly after the huge water clock's completion, political controversy at court between conservatives and reformers intruded into the realm of technology and science, and in 1094 some politicians demanded the destruction of the astronomical water clock for ideological reasons. Chief councilor Zhang Dun, who later warned against Zhao Ji ascending the dragon throne in 1100, averted the catastrophe, but roughly three decades later the victorious Jurchens carted all the astronomical instruments to their capital. Only the fifteen-ton armillary sphere remained intact. In 1195, in a heavy storm, it was struck by lightning. The armillary sphere was repaired and placed in an observatory tower, and that is where the Mongols found it after they expelled the Jin from Beijing.[61]

Su Song also invented a slowly rotating artificial sky to train observers in the positions and motions of celestial bodies. This "planisphere" was set up in 1092, and a great number of astronomers and calendrical pundits flocked to watch its operation. Because of its spherical structure built around an axis, it is often called the first planetarium. The axis pivoted 23.5 degrees to the vertical, thus corresponding to the inclination of the earth's axis.[62] Approximately six hundred years later, the first planetarium in Europe was built by Germans for Peter the Great of Russia.

Advances in the observation and description of natural phenomena, particularly in astronomy, time-measuring, cartography, earth sciences, medicine, and the study of plants and animals, went hand in hand with new conceptions of how to reproduce visual realities in illustrations— how to picture landscapes, people, and all other creatures and materials. The investigation of the natural world, the relations between the inside and the outside world, and the depiction of their visual reality led to previously unknown insights into the interdependence of the "ten thousand things" and a new understanding of the role of humans between heaven and earth. The activities of scholar-officials in the fields of arts and aesthetics as well as science laid the foundation for all the later developments, and support the claim that the Song elite functioned as catalysts in a process of secularization that was consistent with the growing influence of the Learning of the Way.

9

TRANSFORMING THE CAPITALS

WELL before the end of the first millennium B.C., Chinese cities already fulfilled the criteria that distinguish a city from a settlement. People occupied a limited space, they organized themselves into nonfamily groups, they used script, created works of art, bought and sold commercial goods, specialized in particular crafts, applied rational or proto-scientific thought to solve problems, invented a social structure for governance, and established a public architecture.

In ancient times and well into the twentieth century, walls formed the skeleton of every Chinese city. "There is no such a thing as a city without walls."[1] Walls not only provided a defensive perimeter but also divided cities into lots and compounds. The Chinese used the same word, *cheng*, for a city and a city wall. Walled cities originally grew up on locations where ancestor worship and religious sacrifices to the Earth god were made. Some of them gradually developed into political centers and eventually became capitals. Since the Chinese thought Heaven was round and the Earth was square, only a square layout for a capital could create an urban living space that harmonized with Heaven and nature.[2]

Chang'an, the Capital of the Son of Heaven

Throughout imperial history, the glorious Tang capital of Chang'an (Xi'an) was always regarded as the Chinese capital par excellence. When the Tang emperors adopted this city in the Wei River valley as their main capital, they changed its Sui name, Daxing (Great Prosperity), back to its ancient name, Chang'an (Long-Lasting Peace), by which it had been

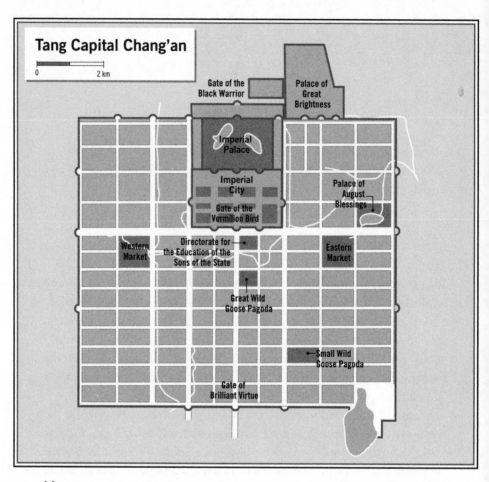

Map 7

known for almost a thousand years. The city's almost square layout was gigantic, measuring 8.6 kilometers north to south and 9.7 kilometers east to west (Map 7). The planning of the capital followed the cosmological ideal of antiquity: as the locus of imperial authority, the capital must reflect the harmony between Heaven and Earth and the absolute control of the Son of Heaven. The formal severity and rigidity of the city's architecture was a materialization of an all-pervading imperial law and public order.

The capital walls were aligned on a compass grid. Three city gates on each side allowed entry. There were nine main longitudinal avenues and twelve main latitudinal avenues. In Chinese numerical categories, the number three referred to the three powers of nature: Heaven, Earth, and

Man; the number nine represented the nine provinces of the legendary Emperor Da Yu; and the number twelve corresponded to the twelve months of the year. Additional avenues and streets in both directions ran parallel to the main avenues, creating a strict grid system of 110 square or rectangular walled wards. This regular cityscape was punctuated with gates to the wards (many with towers) and pagodas of the major temples. Two markets served the needs of the local population, in the eastern and western parts of the city.

Chang'an was thought to be the center of all under Heaven, and the emperor was the mediator between Heaven and Earth. The aristocratic families who lived in the many two- or three-story palaces near the Imperial City ranked just below the emperor, followed by families of officials with respected genealogies. Rich merchants and well-educated people, including important members of Buddhist monasteries and temples and other religious institutions, came next in the social hierarchy. The houses of commoners may have numbered in the tens of thousands but they were not thought of as part of the architectural landscape of the city. Strict distinctions by class—which kept aristocrats from living near officials, and officials from living near commoners—were reflected in the size and location of the walled wards.

According to the Arab traveler Ebn Wahab, who visited the city in the third quarter of the ninth century, "The emperor, his chief ministers, the soldiers, the supreme judge, the eunuchs, and all belonging to the imperial household lived in that part of the city which is on the right hand eastward; the people had no manner of communication with them."[3] The grounds of the eastern wards were spacious enough to play polo and practice archery, and they were close to the heart of the empire, which consisted of the walled Palace of Great Brightness and the Imperial City, to which only the privileged had access.

The yellowish earth-colored walls of the wards were built at a distance of several meters behind wide drainage ditches on either side of the avenues. These walls of rammed earth measured 3 meters high, and the width at their base was between 2 and 3 meters. Each ward and crossroads was guarded. Wards were not only physically separated from other wards and thus functioned as discrete living units, but social contacts between wards were limited to official hours.

A ward headman, also called a village headman, controlled one hundred households. He was responsible for keeping order and for seeing that taxes were paid and labor duties were fulfilled by members of his "village." Urban living in most wards of the capital—particularly in areas situated far from the markets—resembled life in the countryside. On the headman's command, the wardens opened and closed the gates to the wards at dawn and sunset. "At sunset, the drums were beaten 800 times and the gates were closed . . . Mounted soldiers employed by the officers in charge of policing the streets made the rounds in silence. [Before dawn] the drums were beaten 3,000 times and stopped only when night had changed to day."[4]

Commoners lived in the interior of the wards. Their houses were low and simple, generally without any decorative elements. Sumptuary laws dictated the size and style of officials' residences. As we learn from a police report of 831, high officials were allowed to build a private gate in the wall of their ward to provide them with direct access to the main avenue.[5] The same privilege was granted to aristocrats, whose large residences covered as much as an eighth of a ward, and to temples, which could take over a whole ward by themselves. In most quarters there was enough ground space to grow crops for a family's daily needs.

The ward system in the Tang capital was designed for the strict control of the movements and activities of its inhabitants, and apart from crowded markets and spacious temples, people lived rather segregated lives in their own circles. Families who had lived in cities for several hundred years became accustomed to this degree of surveillance, restriction, and curfew, and they enjoyed the high degree of personal security and protection from the spread of fire that the ward system offered.

Shopping and trading activities concentrated on Chang'an's busy Western Market, where the so-called Silk Road began and ended, and the more fashionable Eastern Market, which catered to the tastes of the wealthy. In the ninth century the Western Market was the commercial hub of traders. Thousands of stalls and shops lined narrow alleys, so that all merchants offering one type of merchandise—silks, lacquer products, basketware, ceramics, perfume, wine, or slaves—were congregated in a small area. The markets also included an endless array of restaurants, snack booths, wine shops, guesthouses, brothels, cattle markets, horse barns, butcher shops, fishmongers, and the stalls of artists and craftsmen.

The Eastern and Western markets were the downtowns of their day, and people from all quarters—men and women, Chinese and foreigners—crowded into these tight spaces to exchange news. Officials above the fifth rank were not allowed to mingle with commoners in the markets.[6] The opening of both markets at noon was announced by 200 beats of the drum, and their closing at sunset was signaled by 300 beats. Most people who worked in the market lived behind, in, or near their stalls in unimaginably cramped conditions.

A special spot near the Western Market and close to the southwestern corner of the Imperial City was called Lone Willow. It functioned as an execution ground where criminals and other offenders, including officials, were publicly decapitated or cut in half and their heads displayed. Another execution ground named Dog-Spine Hill was located in the northwestern corner of the Eastern Market. Public executions were thought to be of educational value. Officials of the capital were required to attend, and commoners were drawn by the gruesome spectacle.

In the ninth century the situation in the wards of the capital changed, some would say deteriorated. The strict sumptuary laws were neglected, or the police were unable to enforce them. Curfew hours were disregarded, and trade spilled over into residential areas, where commercial activities went on day and night. Unauthorized markets were established in great numbers, and in 817 the New Market was opened near the Imperial City.[7] Some people illegally broke holes in the walls of residential wards or built unauthorized gates, while others erected solid structures, such as shops and stalls, on the major avenues. Night markets were prohibited in 840, but to no avail. All-night musical performances at religious shrines were not uncommon.

As the Tang emperors lost political control of their empire, they witnessed the slow but inexorable decline of their formerly well-controlled capital. Chang'an had been the model for urban development for the whole of East Asia, especially the new cities of Nara and Kyôto in Japan, and it was the largest city of the medieval world, with a population of more than one million people. Yet by 904, when the warlord Zhu Wen ordered all the buildings pulled down and construction materials transported to Luoyang, the city had reached its existential limit, after almost a thousand years in existence. Chang'an would never recover from the annihilation of its aristocratic elite, and it never again became the capital of a Chinese dynasty.

Kaifeng, a Change of Urban Paradigms

When the emperors of the Five Dynasties took control of the miserable remains of the glorious Tang cities of north China, they used them as strongholds for consolidating their military and political power. Kaifeng,

on the Yellow River, served as the capital of four dynasties during this period; only the Later Tang (923–937) preferred Luoyang. In order to in-
fuse new life into urban areas, these rulers encouraged private initiative
and investments that would entice people to settle on unoccupied urban
territory and rebuild the cities. The ward system still existed in theory,
and the borough, a term borrowed from military organization, was introduced as the administrative unit ranking above the ward.[8] But in practice
the general situation of land ownership and property demarcation in the
interior of the cities was probably chaotic.

This new right to buy and sell property as a commodity within urban
boundaries changed the traditional perception of real estate in China.
Property prices now depended on the commercial attractiveness and use-
fulness of a plot of land. Business considerations dictated the appearance
of the cities' downtown areas, and the old principle—valid for more than
a thousand years—that trading and commercial activities had to take
place at a specific place called a market was disregarded.

Major repair of Kaifeng's city wall did not take place until 951. In the
meantime, the Old City had become crowded, the streets were narrow
and damp, and people suffered from the heat and humidity. The Later
Zhou Emperor Shizong, noting that "of the tens of thousands, all want
an easy and comfortable life," ordered in 955 that "the city must be expanded . . . for the convenience of the state and the people."[9] According
to legend, Emperor Shizong ordered Zhao Kuangyin (who would later
found the Song dynasty) to gallop from the Gate of the Vermilion Bird
straight in a southern direction until his horse showed signs of exhaustion. That spot, at a distance of 2 kilometers from the old wall, was
marked as the location of the city's new perimeter.[10] The emperor ordered
more than 100,000 conscripts to build the new wall 27 kilometers long
and to provide twenty-one gates, including nine gates for rivers and canals (Map 8, schematic drawing). The whitewashed outer wall, reinforced with defensive towers, was built up to an awe-inspiring height of
more than 12 meters. The moat dug around the city, called Guarding the
Dragon River, measured more than 30 meters wide. In the early 1080s
another moat more than double this width was laid out around the city.
This willow-lined moat measured an impressive 76.8 meters wide and
4.6 meters deep.[11]

This truly imperial planning not only quadrupled the size of the city
and transformed it into a giant urban defensive bastion but also encompassed the immense suburban population that had been living and work-

Map 8

ing just outside the Old City walls. In designating how land would be used, the dynastic government and all its official institutions still got first choice, but after that, in contrast to earlier dynasties, all city dwellers, including officials, merchants, traders, artisans, and craftsmen, were free to settle and build wherever their purse allowed them to buy.[12]

So, ironically, the civil disruption from the late Tang to the early Five Dynasties favored the formation of a more open city plan than China had ever known before. Streets and alleys with residences and shops opening onto streets replaced the walled wards. And even beyond the New City gates, commercial suburbs began to flourish.[13] Thus Kaifeng, in the words of Robert Hartwell, "became a multi-functional urban centre, quite possibly unsurpassed by any metropolis in the world before the nineteenth century." It was the place where the powerful, the rich, the educated, the followers of fashion, as well as uprooted drifters, mingled and became urbanites, where money, property, and economic success made their mark on the Chinese lifestyle, where in a short period of time a fortune could be made, spent, or lost. As Mark Elvin concluded, "China at this time was the most urbanized society in the world."[14]

Kaifeng was a new sort of capital on a geographical site never previously used, displaying a hitherto unheard of urban layout and lifestyle. Its location in the heart of China, well-connected by roads, rivers, and canals, meant that all kinds of foods and other commodities from the fertile southern and southeastern provinces could easily reach the city's residents. But as a capital, Kaifeng had several disadvantages, as Emperor Taizu and his officials were well aware. First, never before in Chinese history was a site chosen for a capital on the open north China plain, which was threatened by flooding of the Yellow River, vulnerable to military attacks by northern tribes, and difficult to defend.

Second, the layout of the capital lacked symmetry, proper north-south alignment, and a strict boundary defined by a city wall. Kaifeng was continuously growing outward, from the walled Old City to the walled New City and eventually into the rural suburbs beyond the new wall. Viewed from nearby Wangniu Mound, Kaifeng had the shape of a "crouching-cow" rather than a perfect square.[15] This shape could hardly have pleased the traditionalists, and it obviously lacked auspicious cosmological symbolism. But for defensive reasons, the first Song emperor, Taizu, who extended the outer wall in 968, insisted on irregularity. As a consequence, the streets also lost their gridlike organization. This too represented a sharp contrast with the Tang capital Chang'an.

An irregular layout of streets and lanes lined with houses of different types whose doors opened onto the streets was not well suited for establishing wards. As the interior walls came down or were opened up and as the market system expanded in the early decades of the Song, Kaifeng became a beehive of commercial activity. In 965 Emperor Taizu encouraged this entrepreneurial development by extending the curfew to one o'clock in the morning.[16] Curfew was finally abolished altogether a hundred years later. This meant that many shops carried out their business almost twenty-four hours a day. And by this time, urbanites were taking these bustling day and night activities for granted. The flourishing of small businesses led to a new evaluation of urban property, and probably for the first time in Chinese history commercial buildings became more expensive than private residences.[17]

About 890,000 people may have lived in the entire Kaifeng prefecture between 976 and 984, and about 1.3 million in 1103.[18] If these figures are accurate, Kaifeng under the Northern Song was the most populous city the world had ever seen until the nineteenth century. As the population proliferated, buildings grew in height. Towers of restaurants and the pagodas of temples became landmarks. The walled capital covered about 49 square kilometers—almost thirteen times the size of medieval Paris in 1292 but of modest size in comparison with the 84 square kilometers of Chang'an under the Tang.

The Imperial City of the Song accommodated not only the most important government offices and institutions but also the Imperial Palace itself, called the Grand Inner. Though the size of the Imperial City increased to about 0.7 square kilometers after its wall was extended to a length of 3.3 kilometers in 962, it was still no match for the grandeur of the Imperial City in Chang'an, which was seven times the size of the Song compound.[19] The Tang emperors' palaces had been separate from the Imperial City, whereas the Song emperor's living quarters were squeezed into its northwestern quadrant. The cramped conditions under which the court and government operated were alleviated when Emperor Huizong doubled the size of the Imperial City.

The eastern parts of the Old City and the New City were densely crowded in the late tenth century. The northeastern boroughs of the Old City housed 79,500 inhabitants, while the eastern borough of the New City was home to 134,000 residents.[20] Fifty or more individuals per 1,000 square meters lived door by door, not including an unknown number of unregistered households. Compared to Paris, with its 59,200 inhabitants in 1292 living on 3.78 square kilometers (sixteen persons per 1,000 square meters), the population in the Song capital was two to three times as dense.[21]

The centers of the various boroughs of the capital were full of people from all walks of life, and their activities on the streets and in shops filled the air with noises, smells, and stenches. Contrary to the impression we get from the famous handscroll *Traveling up the River at Qingming Festival* (*Qingming shanghe tu*), where men dominate the street scenes, and despite the statements of Confucian moralists who tried to restrict the world of women to child-bearing, serving parents-in-law, and household activities, the life of many women in the big cities was more colorful and self-determined than the male upper class was willing to concede in their family instructions and domestic regulations. Married women were not the property of their husbands.[22] In theory women did not take part in affairs outside their homes, but in practice they ran snack booths, restaurants, guesthouses, and beauty parlors, along with shops selling textiles, garments, and shoes for ladies.

Women also managed the finances of their urban households, while their scholar husbands concentrated on self-cultivation, scholarly matters, government affairs, and their own careers. Women negotiated the buying and selling of land, supervised the building of houses, kept accounts of rents and taxes, and dealt with most other financial and commercial activities outside the family. Knowing how to handle money was essential, because their dowries often included large amounts of land, and widows were entitled to inherit their husbands' property outright. Women were accepted as household bursars in charge of preserving and enhancing the family estate. Efficient management of household affairs was classified as a female virtue.

Prior to the thirteenth century, when women began to bind their feet, they moved freely about the city without requiring transport, as they performed their many tasks. Even the stern Confucian Sima Guang demanded only that women who left the inner quarter should cover their faces with a veil.[23] Privacy and quiet were the privilege and luxury of very few, and commoners spent most of their time in the streets and alleyways. Nevertheless, the city was attractive overall, and it offered unrivaled prospects for making a living. Catering and entertainment businesses, service facilities, and commercial activities boomed, and energetic women as well as men could earn a lot of money. These prospects for financial gain made up for all the other adversities of crowded urban life.

The capital as well as the flourishing cities of the southeast attracted people from the countryside, and in Kaifeng a shortage of affordable living and working space soon extended to the New City between the Old and New City walls. Accommodations catering to officials as well as sheltering the flood of illiterate commoners from rural areas sprang up just outside the New City wall—workshops, guesthouses, and all sorts of food stalls and markets. These newcomers, who were accustomed to living in the country, could do without the sense of security that came from living inside city fortifications if more affordable space could be had just outside the walls.

From *Traveling up the River at Qingming Festival* (*Qingming shanghe tu*), painted near the end of the eleventh century by Zhang Zeduan, a member of the Imperial Painting Academy, the viewer becomes aware that the countryside, with its thatched huts and hamlets, well-tended fields, and irrigation channels, has gradually merged with the suburban sectors of Kaifeng outside the city walls.[24] Zhang's quiet landscape in the distance, where the seasons still dictate the rhythm of life, stands in sharp contrast with the bustling suburbs, where huge warehouses, wine restaurants, commercial establishments, and entertainments crowd around a city gate (Fig. 14).

From an economic viewpoint, the advantages of suburban life outweighed the dangers, but from an administrative point of view everything in the heavily populated boroughs, whether inside or outside the New City wall, was far from ideal. From the start the government feared that it might lose control of the capital to profiteers. In addition to merchants and property owners, members of the ambitious and privileged class of scholar-officials, who were no longer confined to the studio, engaged in all sorts of business transactions. They began to explore new opportunities for financial gain, venturing beyond real estate to more atypical investments. With the help of front men acting as their agents, they made fortunes by renting out property, running guesthouses, and founding companies.

These changes in the personal conduct, ethical understanding, and commercial activities of members of the educated class clearly indicated that the traditional hierarchical distinctions had softened and a new social order was in the making. In 977 Emperor Taizong had attempted to restore the old order by issuing an edict prohibiting officials from engaging in commercial activities through agents.[25] This had little effect, simply because the court itself was the biggest landlord in the capital and thus deeply involved in the real estate and rental business, as we know from the existence of the Office for Houses and Shops, which was in charge of managing this part of the government's portfolio. Rent was paid on a daily basis in order to avoid accumulating debts, and the government often spent this income frivolously. For example, in 989 the daily bill for cosmetics used by ladies of the imperial household amounted to 100,000 cash.[26]

Emperor Taizong made a serious effort to reestablish old administrative values in 995 by ordering his chief councilor, Zhang Ji, to relabel the eighty odd wards of the Old and New cities in a more rational and

Fig. 14   City gate, street life, and a first-class wine restaurant with welcome gate. Late eleventh century. Detail from *Traveling up the River at Qingming Festival* by Zhang Zeduan. Palace Museum, Beijing.

harmonious way.[27] Kaifeng had been divided into two metropolitan districts along the north-south Imperial Avenue of the Old City: an eastern one, called Kaifeng, and a western one, named Junyi (after 1008, Xiangfu). Apparently, this metropolitan organization no longer met the imperial demand for control, and in particular for securing tax revenue from households, maintaining public order, and ensuring fire protection. Zhang decided to divide the whole capital into eight boroughs consisting of 121 wards.[28] The Old City comprised four boroughs of varying sizes, with a total of 46 wards. The New City was also divided into four boroughs but with a total of 75 wards. This more rigorous and formal division of the capital was, at least theoretically, an administrative improvement over the earlier chaos.

Population growth was immense, however, and the task of efficient tax collection became ever more complicated, especially in the proliferating suburbs outside the New City walls. In January 1009 Emperor Zhenzong expanded the administrative structure to encompass eight boroughs in the suburbs. In 1021 another one was added, making nine boroughs containing a total of fourteen wards.[29] Theoretically, the new administrative wards should have simplified policing and increased civil order and security, but in practice the administrative system was no longer compatible with a city that had no interior walls. The long walls of the Tang wards, which had separated aristocrats from commoners, had given way to narrow lanes, canals, waterways, bridges, small houses, mansions, and towering gates. Streets were now shared by city residents from every class, and the unwalled wards, consisting of areas near a street, canal, bridge, or gate, a Buddhist temple or shrine, or neighborhoods centered around or along streets, were hard to regulate. An administrative reform in 1021 informs us that a combined force of 172 officers, or only one to two officers per ward (not including the suburbs), were responsible for maintaining law and order.[30]

Among the new wards east of the capital, the famous Qingming Ward along the Bian River ranked as number one. The canalled Bian River linked the capital to the Huai River and the Grand Canal in the south, and to the Yellow River in the north. It was the most important waterway in Kaifeng. It entered the New City by two water gates in the southeastern city wall, followed a course through the Old City, probably as a single wide canal, and split into two canals before leaving the city through two water gates in the outer west wall. A traveler who arrived on this waterway in the capital had to disembark in the suburbs and hire a small boat

to carry him into the heart of the city. During the daytime he entered the
city through one of the water gates, and in the evening when a gate of
iron bars closed this entrance, he could walk through one of the neighboring gates situated on both sides of the river.

The Bian River served as the capital's lifeline, a sort of circulatory system allowing bulk transport of commodities on tens of thousands of
large barges and smaller boats, along with the removal of tons of waste
and refuse out of the city (Fig. 15). Since the water level varied according
to the season, most goods had to be stored in warehouses near Ware-
house Bridge or reloaded onto smaller flat boats to enter the city. To keep
the river navigable, it had to be dredged regularly to a depth of about 2
meters. The navigability of the Bian River improved considerably after
1079, when the river was linked by the Bian Canal to the Luo River instead
of merging with the dangerous waters of the Yellow River (see Map 5).[31]

The Imperial Avenue, also called the Heavenly Avenue, formed the central north-south axis of the Old and New cities. It connected the Gate of
Imperial Fragrance on the outer wall with the Gate of the Vermilion Bird
on the inner wall. The avenue was about 4 kilometers long. A specially
marked central lane for the emperor was often used to parade horses and
men in front of the Street-Overlooking Pavilion, from which the emperor watched the colorful spectacle. The Imperial Avenue was lined with
shopping galleries, officials' mansions, and densely crowded commoners'
quarters on both sides. Soldiers stationed at intervals of about 450 meters
patrolled it day and night.[32]

East of the Imperial Avenue were the Southern Bureau of Medical Relief, the Directorate for the Education of the Sons of State, and the Imperial University. Nearby, the Relief for the People Canal was dug as a wide
bend through the central southern boroughs of the New City. Dragon
Ford Bridge, located just south of the Gate of the Vermilion Bird, was one
of the thirteen bridges over the canal. After crossing Longjin Bridge and
entering the Old City through the Gate of the Vermilion Bird—a spectac-
ular, colorful, gigantic gate measuring more than 150 meters wide, with a
towering hall built on top of the Old City wall—a pedestrian would have
found himself on one of the busiest sections of the Imperial Avenue.
Many sorts of food stalls and restaurants stretched all the way to Zhou
Bridge, a landmark of stone bridge architecture, also called Heavenly
River Bridge. At 17 meters long and up to 30 meters wide, this bridge
spanned the roughly 15-meter-wide Bian River traversing the city from
east to west. Zhou Bridge and Xiangguo Bridge, built in a similar way

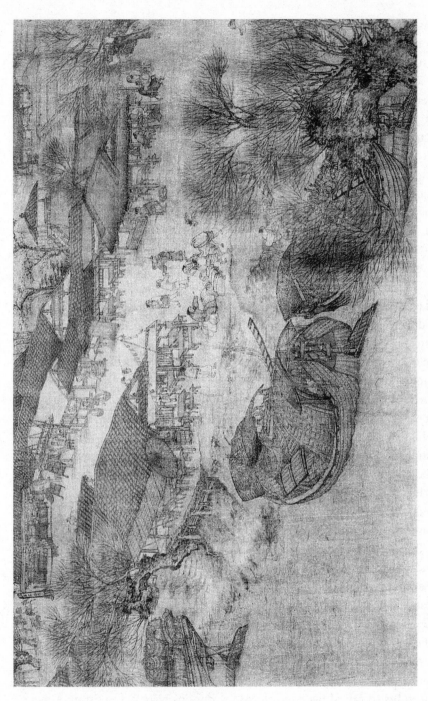

Fig. 15 Bulky transport barge on the Bian River in the suburbs of Kaifeng. Song, late eleventh century. Detail from *Traveling up the River at Qingming Festival* by Zhang Zeduan. Palace Museum, Beijing.

east of Zhou Bridge, were rather low structures that allowed only flat boats to pass. The most famous Buddhist temple of the capital, the Assisting the State Temple, was nearby.

Walking several hundred meters north on the Imperial Avenue, a traveler would pass by several government buildings, including the Court of Imperial Sacrifices and the Bureau of Imperial Music to the east and the Capital Hostel for accommodating foreign guests and envoys to the west. Crossing the lateral street leading to the Department of State Affairs, which was some distance to the west and close to the Altar for Offering Sacrifices to Heaven and Earth, a pedestrian would have soon reached the great square in front of the Gate of Displayed Virtue, which was the main southern entrance to the Imperial City. The gate tower sat above five gateways with doors lacquered in vermilion red and embellished with gold nails.[33]

During the rule of the Song's third emperor, Zhenzong, the Gate of Displayed Virtue stretched more than 300 meters in length and was splendidly decorated with glazed bricks. From an awe-inspiring, lavishly decorated hall on top of the gate, the emperor could look out over the city, as he did at the end of every New Year's Festival. On that occasion, a yellow canopy of silk with the imperial seal billowed above the gate, and in the early hours of the morning the emperor himself made a ceremonial public appearance wearing his red silk robe. He ascended the stairs to the gate while music played, and he sat down behind a table flanked with his attendants. Top-ranking aristocrats and officials sat in curtained boxes, and commoners stood in front of the gate to witness this grand spectacle. When the red silk lamps on top of the gate were pulled up into the air, the people knew that the emperor had returned to his palace. Soon snapping whips were heard. The lights were extinguished all at the same time.[34]

Restaurants of various kinds in the area catered to all sorts of guests and tastes. Southwest of Zhou Bridge was the famous pancake kitchen of the Zhang family. A little farther to the west was the Fresh Breeze wine restaurant, where guests congregated to relax and cool off in the hot summer. There were 72 first-class wine restaurants, which could be identified by their lavishly decorated welcome gates several stories high.[35] Some of these restaurants had up to 110 separate rooms in which guests could spend a few hours or several days, hold banquets, or engage prostitutes. Just north of the educational institutions near Wheat Straw Alley, the restaurant Highest Graduate Tower, along with several brothels, met the needs of academic and well-to-do guests. Small and less fashionable wine taverns waved a colored flag with the character for wine written on it, or displayed a broom to attract guests. Some places offered a bowl of water and a towel so that guests could wipe the dust from their faces before attendants served drinks and food.

Abattoirs for the daily slaughtering of thousands of pigs were situated south of New Bridge on Slaughtering Pig Street, located—delicately enough—near yet another neighborhood of brothels. There were a number of shopping areas furnished with workshops and stores specializing in garments, accessories, pearls, lacquer articles, gold and silver wares, incense and drugs.[36] On other streets, the products of weaving workshops and the services of medical practitioners could be bought. There were 68 markets to hire maid-servants and buy slave girls, and many places where all sorts of workmen and attendants could be enlisted for a job. Business continued in night markets such as the one south of Zhou Bridge, which was famous for its pig meat, game, fowl, and other delicacies.[37] The famous eleventh-century poet Su Shi was impressed by the resplendent light of the lanterns in the night market at Dragon Ford Bridge.

The capital never rested. Entertainment and pleasure establishments called "tiles," composed of theaters, wine taverns, restaurants, and houses of prostitution, spanned a wide range of prices and services. At a crossing in one of the busiest areas of the city, the Market for Local Products was famous for selling bamboo poles in unimaginable variations. At the next crossing to the east, teahouses entertained their guests. And at the Ghost Market, lit with lanterns and closed only at dawn, people sold and bought clothes, pictures, flower rings, collars, and many other goods. A famous wine restaurant, the Central Mountain, was nearby.

Yuan Menglao writes about entertainment in the Song capital:

Going eastward [on the Street of Family Ban's Tower] there is the Calabash Mutton Stew Shop of the Xu family, and just south of the street is the neighboring Pleasure Quarter of the Sang family. And close to the north is the Central Pleasure Quarter and next to it the Inner Pleasure Quarter. In these quarters are more than fifty theatres, big and small. In the Central Quarter the Lotus Theater and the Peony Theater, and in the Inner Quarter the Yaksha Theater and the Elephant Theater are the largest, providing a capacity for an audience of several thousand people.[38]

In these quarters, frequented only by male clients, the pleasures of penciled eyebrows and white powder, refined entertainment, romance, and sexual intercourse were for sale. Vendors of herbs, hexagram fortune tellers, hawkers of old clothes, sellers of drinks and snacks, paper cutters, and singers of all sorts took advantage of the area's easy-going customers to make a living. "Here one can stay all day and never become aware when evening falls."[39]

The inexhaustible vitality and prosperity, welfare and commerce, luxury and fashion, entertainment and decadence of Kaifeng lasted 166 peaceful years. But after the Jurchen troops invaded the city on January 9, 1127, Kaifeng immediately lost its charm, and in almost no time an urban center that had once set the pace of cultural and commercial development for the whole empire was remembered only in diaries and other literary sources. After its occupation by the Jurchens, who were accustomed to living in tents and did not need cities or understand their function, the former Eastern Capital became a political and cultural backwater. Despite a resurgence of the Han Chinese population living under the Jin during the late twelfth century, the city never recovered its former glory.

Unlike the capitals of the Han Chinese, the capitals of the Khitan empire (which the Jurchens also overran) served the purpose of seasonal sojourns. The difference between the nomadic Khitans and the sedentary Han Chinese is captured in the following statement: "South of the Great Wall [where the Chinese live] there is often rain and heat in the summer. The people there plow and sow for food, grow mulberry trees and hemp for clothing, have palaces and houses to live in, and capitals to rule from. Between the great deserts [where the Khitan live], it's often cold and windy, the people rear animals and go fishing for food, use leather and wool for clothing, they lead a migratory life at all seasons, carts and horses are their home."[40]

The Khitans founded five capitals between 918 and 1044. The politically most important was the Supreme Capital built in 918 by the Chinese architects Kang Moji and Han Yanhui on orders from the founding emperor of the Liao dynasty. The layout of the capital followed the ideal of a Chinese walled capital, but the east-west wall divided the city into a part north of the Bayan-gol River, which accommodated the Khitans, and a smaller part south of the river, which housed the Chinese and other non-Khitan residents. The function of this divided city, which all barbarian dynasties imitated until the Manchu Qing dynasty abdicated in 1912, was to segregate ethnic rulers from their Chinese subjects. Although these capitals had an Imperial City in the northern part and a number of administrative and religious buildings, the Khitans themselves lived in tents.

The Liao capitals, like their counterparts in the Jin dynasty, were no match for the Song cities in China, but were only copies adapted to the administrative needs of a still nomadic society.[41]

Hangzhou, a "Temporary Residence"

From the perspective of Han Chinese living on the north China plain, Lin'an (later, Hangzhou) in southeastern Zhejiang province was located in "a lost corner of the empire," in a peripheral area of the world where the dynasty was no longer able to participate in the flow of psycho-physical environmental energy (qi) on the central plain.[42] In 893 more than 200,000 conscripts had extended the city and fortified the city wall to a length of about 35 kilometers, and in the tenth century, when it was briefly part of the kingdom of Wu Yue, Hangzhou was made a capital for the first time (Map 9).

After Kaifeng fell to the Jurchens in 1127, Emperor Gaozong decided in 1129 to make Lin'an his "traveling palace." The more orthodox Song scholars among those who migrated south with the Song court considered Hangzhou unacceptable as a capital city. The streets were narrow, overcrowded, and noisy, filled with merchants, traders, and craftsmen. More important, the city plan did not match the traditional rectangular or square layout of a Chinese capital, though it met astrophysical requirements. But in troubled times Hangzhou had the strategic advantage of being securely situated behind a natural barrier of waterways, lakes, rice fields, and hills and thus was difficult for Jurchen raiders to attack. Despite objections from scholar-officials, Emperor Gaozong in 1138 proclaimed Lin'an his "temporary residence." The term reflected the Song hope that one day the dynasty might be able to regain north China and return to the capital city of Kaifeng. Formally, Hangzhou remained the seat of the Southern Song empire until December 11, 1277, fifteen months before the dynasty perished on March 19, 1279.

By 1085 more than 200,000 households, or at least a million people, were registered in the city. An eyewitness observed: "Lin'an city has vastly expanded and suffers from overpopulation. The houses are high and tightly built. The roofs border on each other, the eaves combine. There is not an inch of space left between them."[43] Under these cramped conditions, the construction of two-story buildings became the architectural norm, and this distinguished the appearance of Hangzhou from other Chinese cities, whose skyline was generally lower.

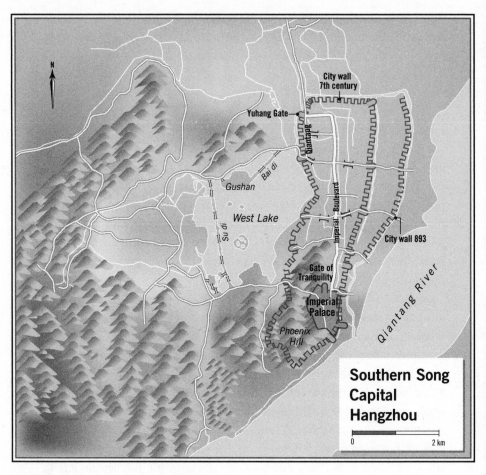

Map 9

The main avenues and other central locations were so packed with commercial activities that hardly any place was left to accommodate an imperial court, administrative buildings, or the residences of several thousand officials. The emperor moved into the modest buildings of the prefectural administration at the northern foot of Phoenix Hill. Later, the Imperial City, with a limited number of government buildings, moved in here as well. The halls and residences of the Imperial Palace were built on the wooded hillside higher up.

The fact that the emperor resided on the southern side of the city was awkward. When the emperor held audience or performed his official duties, the ritual rules prescribed that he had to face south, which in Hangzhou meant that he practically turned his back to the city. In an attempt to obscure this inconvenient urban plan, rigidly drawn maps of Hangzhou arranged the whole city, with all its avenues, canals, and wards, in a rectangular format and squeezed the imperial palace into a ridiculously oblong shape positioned parallel to a straight southern city wall, which in reality was full of bends.[44] The idea was to suggest that the layout of the capital was geometrically perfect, though in fact it was far from it.

The Imperial Boulevard, the axis of the capital, linked the Yuhang Gate in the north wall of the city with the Gate of Tranquility, the main gate of the Imperial City. But unlike the Imperial Avenue of Kaifeng, it did not run in a straight north-south line, dividing the city into an equal eastern and western part, but twice shifted to the west. The Imperial Boulevard had to give way to commercialism in the port area of the Grand Canal and thus met the city wall at its northwestern corner. The city map was a fiction designed to give later generations the impression that an ideal capital had existed in Southern Song times.[45]

"Quinsai [Hangzhou] . . . is the greatest city which may be found in the world," maintained Marco Polo in 1298, "where so many pleasures may be found that one fancies oneself in paradise."[46] His enthusiasm corroborated the Chinese saying that "above is heaven, on earth is Suzhou and Hangzhou." The vitality of urban life in Hangzhou, "the naval of the world," between 1241 and 1275 was captured by Wu Zimu in this enthusiastic description: "The population is abundant, merchants and traders are ten times more than in previous times, and the traffic flocks together here. There is no prefecture like this one." "Hangzhou is the place of the temporary residence, where everything is available. And if one views all the guilds and the hundred markets which line up from outside the roadblock at the Gate of Tranquility to the Bridge of Inspection there is not a single family which is not in the trading business."[47]

Throughout Chinese history, merchants have been regarded as both indispensable and disreputable, and their families have had to suffer from many restrictions as a consequence. Confucius once said: "The mind of the superior man is conversant with righteousness; the mind of the mean man is conversant with profit." In 1044 Ouyang Xiu confirmed that statement when defining the quality of friendship on the basis of a distinction of classes. He rigorously declared in On Factions (Pengdang lun): "In general, gentleman and gentleman share the Way [as a basis] for their friendship, small people share the profit [as a basis] for their friendship."[48] The unworthy man, in this view, follows the practice of the market, desires profit, and seeks wealth, which was a false, dishonest, and disloyal basis for any social relationship.

If in theory the status of merchants in Song society was hardly better than that of previous dynasties, in practice merchants actively took part in shaping urban and cultural life in Kaifeng and especially in Hangzhou. Their families improved their social status through marriage with scholar-official families, and affluent merchants were in some ways the envy of scholar-officials. In 1187 Lu You composed a poem about the upward mobility of Hangzhou's merchants and the deprivations suffered by the city's scholar-officials. Here are a few of his lines:

> In singing-girl towers to play at dice, a million on one throw;
> By flag-flown pavilions calling for wine, ten thousand a cask;
> The Mayor? The Governor? We don't even know their names,
> What's it to us who wields power in the palace? . . .
> See what Heaven gives me [an official]—luck thin as paper.
> Now I know that merchants are the happiest of men.[49]

Every morning in the southern capital, as soon as the Buddhists had beat their iron gongs or wooden fish to proclaim the new day and announce the weather conditions, all officials and commoners prepared for work and left home. To help early risers get going, curbside traders offered a liquid potion or pills which, they claimed, either stimulated or lowered life energy (qi), depending on what the individual needed for good physical and psychic balance. While officials' lives centered on pushing and promoting their professional careers, commoners set out to earn as much money as possible.

Both groups had to answer the basic question, what do we eat today, and where? Certain places in Hangzhou were famous for the exquisite dishes they served: the sweet-bean soup at the Market of Miscellanies, the pickled dates of the Ge Family, the thick soups of the Guang Family, the fish soups of the Five Song Sisters outside the Qiantang Gate, the mutton hotpots of the Zhi Family, the dumplings of the Zhang Family, the meat dishes of Wei Dali at the Cat Bridge, the honey preserves of Zhou Wuliang in front of the Five Bay Tower.[50] And when the day markets closed at suppertime, the tireless and insatiable flocked to the crowded, noisy night markets with their special food stalls.

Markets were spread over the entire capital but especially along the Imperial Boulevard. Trade flourished almost without restriction. Until the end of the Northern Song, Hangzhou had been the terminus of the Grand Canal, but in Southern Song times it became the canal's southern starting point. Agricultural products and commercial goods were imported from the hinterland on this extensive waterway, which relied on an efficient system of boats and barges provided by the region's shipyards. The gigantic warehouses lining the canal in the north of the city were stocked with building materials, timber, firewood, charcoal, coal, textiles, iron, along with an abundance of food, including rice, pork, fresh seafood, poultry, salted fish, tea, vegetables, fruits, sugar, and alcoholic beverages.[51] The Song treasury had a keen interest in these commercial activities because of its income from taxes, especially the high taxes imposed on monopolies such as salt, alcohol, and tea.

The proliferation of workshops, markets, and family businesses was without parallel elsewhere. "In every ward and lane, at bridges, gates and remote places, everywhere are shops and stalls selling the essentials of life. The reason is that people cannot be without firewood, rice, oil, salt, soy sauce, vinegar and tea and even need luxury items. Rice and soup, however, are essential, and even the poorest cannot do without them."[52] But in addition to these essentials, specialized ceramic kilns, lacquer workshops, tanneries, mat weavers, and wax and candle producers served a pampered clientele accustomed to luxury products in every domain of private life. The insatiable demand for books and the growing publishing business required the production of high-quality paper and ink.

Trade guilds flourished in Hangzhou. The Song system of guilds originated in Tang times, when merchants or craftsmen who sold, bought, or manufactured the same products crowded together at a specially designed place of business. The guild headman secured the professional and financial interests of the group through price fixing and acted as the middleman between the state and the guild.[53] The names of guilds corresponded to the taxation categories for specific products. In the southern capital, an olive merchants' guild could be found on Muddy Road, an orange dealers' guild on the Back Market Road, and a dried salt fish traders' guild at the Turbid Water Gate. Even fortunetellers, common laborers, and scavengers belonged to guilds. There were guilds for dried fishmongers, fresh fishmongers, crab mongers, hog traders, chicken and geese traders, vegetable retailers, waternut dealers, and wine merchants. A number of guilds existed for those manufacturing and selling fashionable and luxurious articles such as combs, jewelry, fine cloth, and hats.

Traders of the seven treasures—gold, silver, emeralds, crystal, rubies, amber (or coral or diamond), and agate—joined together in the so-called antiquity guild. The jewelers who threaded pearls named themselves the separators' guild, while bootmakers called themselves the guild of the double thread.

In contrast to Europe, where in the early twelfth century craftsmen began to band together for the purpose of forming guilds, artisans in China were often conscripted for labor service into highly specialized workshops. These workshop conscripts, as they were called, included fine-toothed comb makers, tailors, belt and girdle makers, goldsmiths and silversmiths doing inlay work, jade grinders, makers of stickers for mounting scrolls or pasting layers of textiles together, makers of oiled paper and paper articles burnt at funerals, rope makers, carpenters, brickmakers and bricklayers, stone-cutters, bamboo masters, oil millers, nail and hinge smiths, coopers, mat and basket weavers, soap producers, and many more.[54]

But it was the family-owned trading houses, shops, and restaurants—selling or serving products from all over the empire—that formed the backbone of commercial life in Hangzhou.[55] In the close neighborhood west of the Market Ward were the Chen and Zhang family banks, which handled orders for gold and silver credits; the shops of the families Liu, Lü, and Chen, which sold a wide range of colored silk fabrics; and shops for hemp, ramie, and cotton cloth near the Bridge of the Plain Ford. North of the Ward of the Western Market the Niu family sold colored silk fabrics, as did the Gu family in the Ward of Clear Harmony. For fashionable garments, ladies called on the Xuan family, while the best haberdasheries belonged to the Xu and Zhai families.

In the Ward of the Southern Market, the Shen family made the white garments of hemp, ramie, or cotton that were worn by commoners without rank. Nearby, the Niu family sold broad woven girdles. In front of the red-washed house at Baoyou Ward, the Kong family's shop displayed various sorts of headgear, and Kong Balang owned a hatter's shop in Sand Skin Lane. The Cloud-Ladder silk shoe shop of the Li family specialized in luxurious shoes, while the Peng family dealt with oiled waterproof boots. The fan shop of Xu Mouzi's family was just in front of the Central Entertainment Quarter. For folded fans, the fashion-conscious consumer would visit the shop of the Zhou family, but for round painted fans the shop of the Chen family was a better choice.

Many family businesses sold pearls, necklaces, and jewelry in the shape of flowers, along with beautiful feathers of the kingfisher. In front of the

Great Temple, Mother Chen applied facial masks to protect the complexion from wind, and Zhang Gulao specialized in cosmetics and rouge. Ivory combs were a specialty of the Wei Family on Official's Lane. Everybody probably knew Ran Hongwang's beauty parlor. Gu Si sold his flutes at the Gate Awaiting the Flood, while the Qiu family offered bamboo whistles at the Great Entertainment Quarter. The shops of the Shu and Xu families specialized in paper articles for burning at funerals, the Tong family shop manufactured candles from the fat of the tallow tree, and the families Wu, Xia, and Ma offered all sorts of incense, candles, and headgear.

The Zhang family was well-known as hardware dealers, and the You family's lacquer shop was exceedingly popular. The Qi family at Clear Lake Bridge sold lacquer products made to look like rhinoceros skin, while the Peng family traded only in local lacquer wares manufactured in Wenzhou. Near the Bridge of the Scholar Li the Teng family opened a gold and silver shop, and the Wang family offered gold-spotted paper for sale in their shop. Other shops sold Qingbai porcelain, baskets, paper, and many other articles used by commoners in their daily life or in an attempt to imitate the luxurious lifestyle of Hangzhou's upper classes. Expensive imported goods from outside China (ivory, herbs, spices, and timber) were also available to those who could afford to buy, in addition to local products from throughout the empire. A great number of drugstores specialized in the preparation of medicines of all sorts.

The list of family shops and enterprises and the high degree of specialization in manufacturing and trade support Wu Zimu's assertion in 1275 that in the capital there was a demand for everything, and every demand was met. Changing urban fashions and the desire for products that exceeded the bare necessities of survival expanded the capital's consumer markets far beyond anything that state authorities could effectively control. This opening up of urban space and its transformation into an unprecedented center for trade transformed the lives of the southern capital's residents. Hangzhou was unequaled in Chinese history as a commercial center. In Wu Zimu's assessment, the capital was "the hub of the universe and there is no prefecture outside equaling [it]."[56]

The Fate of Chang'an, Kaifeng, and Hangzhou

Chang'an during the Tang dynasty—the city that provided the model for an urban aristocratic culture and embodied a set of cosmological ideals for capital-city planning that would influence the whole of East Asia—

sank into insignificance for hundreds of years after its destruction in 904. Tang notions of city planning survived in China in the Southern Capital of the Liao dynasty (present-day Beijing) until 1122, when the Jurchen troops captured it. At that time the Southern Capital was still divided into wards with walls and gates, while Kaifeng had become an open city with extensive suburbs, twenty-four-hour activities, pluralistic neighbor-hoods, and urban-conscious inhabitants.

After the Jurchen troops took Kaifeng from the Northern Song on January 9, 1127, they began dismantling it almost immediately. The Jin ordered the Bian Canal to be filled in and transformed into a housing area. By 1214 when the Jin government, in its turn, was forced to decamp from Beijing to Kaifeng under pressure from the Mongols, the outer city fortifications had been demolished long since and the city itself had shrunk to its Old City dimensions. In spring 1233 Mongol troops looted the city, and Kaifeng fell into insignificance until 1370, when the Ming Emperor Zhu Yuanzhang designated it his Northern Capital, a designation he withdrew just seven years later. In late 1642 the troops of the rebel Li Zicheng opened the dikes of the Yellow River and flooded Kaifeng, causing as many as one million people to perish. The city was buried under mud and silt until 1662, when it was again made habitable.

With the Mongols' march into Hangzhou in 1276, this dynamic southern city ceased to be "the hub of the universe." But Hangzhou fell without bloodshed, and the city continued as a vibrant commercial center. Eventually the Mongols would base their provincial government there.

10

A CHANGING WORLD
OF PRODUCTION

THE Song dynasty, like the dynasties that preceded it, depended on a system of efficient household registration in order to be able to control agricultural production and tax income. The imperial economy prospered only when self-managing farming households were able to harvest high yields per acre and move food and other raw materials to market efficiently. The mechanization of agricultural work, along with the development of sophisticated textile machinery, increased production and raised the standard of living, while a well-developed transportation system provisioned the capitals and the court with food and other items that were part of the new urban lifestyle.

Farm Production

The Northern Song state covered 2.6 million square kilometers, and this entire territory—"all under Heaven"—was the property of the emperor. In this ideological construct, the emperor owned the ground and acted on behalf of the Chinese people, who regarded him as the guardian of their interests and welfare. In theory, the emperor could give away, sell, expropriate, and confiscate land at will. In actuality, apart from distributing large estates among members of the imperial family, he rarely made use of this unique privilege.

Landowners in China were people whose tracts of land were registered in the Residence Registration Files. They tilled the ground and paid taxes on its production. They were allowed to bequeath, sell, and lease the property they held to family members and others. Prior to the twentieth

century, the percentage of Chinese who did not make a living from agriculture, the marketing of agricultural products, or the making of farm
tools was negligible. During the Song dynasty, as military expenses rose
continuously, state revenues depended more than ever before on a reliable system of tax income from rural households. Good harvests allowed
the dynasty to purchase peace by exporting grain to its northern nomadic
neighbors, whose average yield from agriculture, even in good years,
barely fed their population.

In 959, one year before the Song dynasty was established, about 108
million *mu* (one mu was equivalent to 573 square meters), or roughly
62,000 square kilometers in total, were registered as agricultural acreage.
From a tax collector's point of view, this figure was far below the actual acreage under cultivation. After a great administrative effort at the
county level, by 1021 there were 524 million *mu*—five times the acreage
of 959—on the registration rolls, the highest taxable acreage of farm land
recorded during the Song dynasty.[1] Several types of agricultural land
were tax-exempt. About 6.3 million *mu* may have been under the direct
administration and official use of the state. The emperor and his family
probably owned about 3.7 million *mu,* and the landholdings of monasteries came to roughly 35 million *mu.* Altogether, this made up 570 million *mu* or roughly 330,000 square kilometers of agricultural acreage.
Thus, more than 13 percent of state territory in the Northern Song was
farmed as agricultural land, compared with 10 percent in the People's Republic of China in 2004.

A Song reform of 1022 reduced the nine categories of farming households that had existed in Tang times to five categories. All five of these
groups consisted of self-managing farm households that owned and
worked state farmland and were listed in the tax and labor service registers. As before, the agricultural land of these "tax households" could be
bought, sold, leased, and bequeathed by the registered owners.[2] The first
category of households owned between 300 and 10,000 *mu.* According
to official figures, grain production of these farms ranged from less than
20 kilograms to more than 200 kilograms per *mu,* depending on the quality of the soil and rice seedlings. The households of the second and third
categories owned between 100 and 300 *mu.* An annual average harvest
of 100 kilograms per *mu* extracted from 200 *mu* of acreage would have
been enough to feed more than 110 people for one year (assuming a daily
consumption of 0.5 kilograms per day per person). These three categories included many old, established, and privileged landed families. To-

ward the end of the eleventh century, according to one estimate, roughly 14 percent of the population, including officials and farm households ranked one to three, owned roughly 78 percent of the land under cultivation.[3] But if the question of land ownership is answered on the basis of household register calculations—that is, by taking into account the total acreage worked by households of the fourth and fifth categories—these two categories could theoretically have owned as much as half of the tax-registered acreage.

Households of the fourth category—which were by far the majority of self-managing households—held between 20 *mu* and 100 *mu* of land. An agricultural acreage of 50 *mu* (about 29,150 square meters) of highest-quality soil allowed a maximum crop of 10,000 kilograms, which was enough to feed almost 60 people for one year. The ancients regarded this as the ideal acreage for making a living as a farmer.[4] Though this fourth category of nonprivileged or tax-exempted small-holding families may have owned only 30 percent of the land under cultivation at the end of the eleventh century, the taxes collected from them, paid in cash and kind, along with the required labor service they rendered, the investments they made, and their administrative contributions at the local level, formed the economic backbone of Song agriculture and the primary support for the entire state financial system.

The fifth category of Song farmers worked 3 to 20 *mu* (roughly 11,500 square meters) of land. Under very good conditions, a farmer and his family working 20 *mu* of land would have harvested more than five times his family's annual rice consumption, assuming that a family of five needed no more than 2.5 kilograms of rice a day.[5] While this level of income may not seem large today, it represented a doubling of the per head grain consumption of the ninth century (0.25 kilograms per day). Under average conditions of soil quality and annual yields, a household of five persons that farmed less than 10 *mu* would eat up most of its harvest and would not be able to store adequate food for winter or times of famine. In this case an individual's annual income would be less than the yearly salary of a servant or employee in the capital Kaifeng. To secure an income above subsistence level and stay out of debt, these families had to double their acreage by renting additional land to farm, or else they had to hire themselves out as farmhands.

This fifth category, which should be labeled half self-managing households, actually straddled the largest division that existed in Song agricultural households—the division between self-managing farmers and guest farmers (or tenant farmers), who leased all of the land they worked. Guest-farming households, which made up about one third of all farming households, ranked far below self-managing households in their standard of living and social status. Owning neither land nor the means of production, they leased land from the state land administration or from private landlords for a defined period of time. This land-leasing relationship in many cases resulted in the complete dependence of tenants on their landlord, though it had one big advantage: at least in theory, tenant farmers of landlords were exempt from taxes and labor services. The landlord took care of these obligations.

In underpopulated areas of southern central China, landlords were heavily dependent on reliable tenant farmers: without their labor, no harvest could be reaped and no profit made. Uncultivated agricultural land represented a grave financial loss, and so experienced landlords offered good or at least acceptable conditions to their tenants and provided them with tools and animals at reasonable fees. Nevertheless, most guest farmers in China lived from hand to mouth under degrading circumstances, and their standard of living deteriorated even further after crop failures, when they were often forced to give up their land lease and survive on daily wages.

In the 980s, self-managing farming households numbered about 3.5 million, or 58 percent of all farming households, compared with 2.5 million guest-farming households. Due to more efficient tax registration or better economic conditions or both, the proportions after 989 slowly shifted toward self-managing farming households. By 1067 this class of farmers had increased to about 9.8 million households, or 69 percent, the highest percentage recorded during the Song dynasty. The average percentage of self-managing farming households throughout Song rule was around 65 percent.[6]

By 1078, all farming households nationwide, including guest farmers, totaled approximately 16.6 million. Of this number, around 45 percent lived in just fourteen provinces. These provinces, which included the capital prefecture, were home to 70 percent of all self-managing farming households, which contributed a decisive share of the empire's agricultural output. The never-ending flow of revenue directed toward the capital, especially from these fourteen provinces, supported the high expenditures and extravagant lifestyles at the city's upper echelons. Households tilling their own ground were the wellspring of Song prosperity. Any rise in the percentage of self-managing farming households went hand in hand with above-average rates of productivity. If the tax rate was about 10 percent of the agricultural output, the aggregate amount of the annual grain harvest in 1085 was around 245 million *shi* (or 18.7 million tons). If each individual consumed 0.5 kilograms per day, this production—at least in theory—would have sufficed to nourish the entire Song population of more than 70 million individuals.[7]

In the chilly north, millet, barley, and wheat were the staple crops. Small-seed millet was grown for food in north China, and sorghum or "tall millet," better known as Sichuan millet, was used to make a tasty, clear, high-proof alcoholic drink. Wheat, a hard grain, was ground into flour for noodles and bread, while barley was consumed mostly as porridge. But above all, the Song Chinese ate rice, "the most diverse and adaptable crop known to man."[8] Most of it, in a range of varieties, was cultivated in the warmer, wetter climate of central and south China. By the sixth century, twelve nonglutinous varieties of rice and eleven glutinous varieties were under cultivation. Exotic strains included fragrant rice used to perfume dishes, red rice grown to reclaim saline land, and other varieties well-suited for making spirits or cake.

But the most important distinction made by farmers was between *geng* (japonica) and *xian* (indica) rice, which differed in shape and cultivation requirements. Japonica rice was short-grained and round, while indica rice was long-grained and thin. A third type, early-ripening Champa rice, gained special economic importance because it was drought-resistant and could be grown on any land, fertile or not. Often it was harvested twice a year: 60 and 120 days after seedlings were transplanted. In 1012 Emperor Zhenzong gave the order to introduce this variety into China from Vietnam. The propagation of Champa rice immediately increased the food supply, filled state granaries, and put extra cash into the purse of farmers. In 1021 grain collected as land tax reached the astronomical figure of more than 32.7 million *shi* (or roughly 2.6 million tons). Only a few decades after the grain's introduction, 70 percent of the rice grown in Jiangxi province was Champa rice, and shortly before the close of the century 80 to 90 percent of the wet rice grown in the Lower Yangzi were improved varieties of Champa rice.[9]

Nearly all rice cultivated in China is wet rice, grown in irrigated, diked fields. Growing wet rice requires experience and knowledge and is labor-intensive. The farmer has to take care of the shoots and prepare seedbeds; the fields have to be freed from weeds, tilled, and harrowed before the seedlings are transplanted. Constant attention must be paid to the plants and the irrigated fields before harvest time. Rice agriculture led to the invention of a number of tools such as the turn-plough and special harrows and sickles, and it required special working techniques.

The main centers of rice cultivation harvested enough to cover not only their own needs but to export large quantities to other regions. It was said, "When Suzhou and Changzhou have harvested, the empire will have enough food." The rice trade was brisk in the cities of Hangzhou, Jiankang (Nanjing), and Ezhou (Wuchang) in Hubei. As the national rice market grew, the share of tax to be paid in cereal and delivered to the court increased to 6.2 million *shi* (471,000 tons) by 987, and by 1077, a year of modest tax income, it reached 17.8 million *shi* (more than 1.35 million tons). But these large tax payments in kind were not enough to cover the government's needs, and every year additional rice had to be purchased on the open market. In 981 barges on the Bian River shipped approximately 2.4 million *shi* (or 182,400 tons) of *geng* rice and millet into Kaifeng. The government alone required an annual average supply of 1.5 million *shi* (or 114,000 tons), of which almost half had to be purchased on the rice market. Every year the residents of the capital Hangzhou consumed between 1.1 million and 1.4 million *shi* (or 106,000 tons) bought on the rice market.[10]

Rice farmers with small tracts and very little extra grain to sell were the weakest link in the rice trade. The price they could realize depended not only on the quality of their product but also on the fluctuation of supply and demand. Sometimes they carried their extra rice on their back or on a pole to market and sold it to a rice merchant. Many of these middlemen traveled from village to village purchasing comparatively small quantities, either because they did not have the cash to buy more or they did not have access to transportation.

More commonly, rice farmers pooled their rice in the granaries of rich households or sold their harvest directly to them. Rich landlords in the Suzhou region owned granaries with a storage capacity of several thousand tons. The transport of this rice to the larger rice markets took place on so-called rice boats. For their service in making these arrangements, agents charged a brokerage fee of 10 to 20 cash per 6.6 kilograms, which was equivalent to 5 to 10 percent of the value of the goods. Rice brokers sold the rice to shops or directly to consumers. Of the many people in the rice business who reaped profits as grain made its journey from farmer to consumer, the rural laborer who tilled the soil far away from the centers of trade usually pocketed the smallest amount.

The rice market was a seasonal business, and merchants could make real profits only during the few weeks after the farmers had cropped the rice paddies. Between August and September, as the supply of rice suddenly increased, for a short period the price would be low. This was the most opportune time for rice merchants to buy up rice and fill their granaries, because farmers who did not own storage facilities or whose financial reserves were depleted had to sell their harvest right away. Merchants put pressure on small farmers to sell below the market price, and farmers who were in desperate need of cash to pay off loans for seeds, tools, draft animals, salt, and tea usually agreed to these unfavorable terms. One month later the year's harvest was stored in the granaries of merchants or rich landlords, who held back supplies until the price returned to normal.

Legumes played a large role in the sustenance of the Song people because they could be sown and harvested through four seasons. In 981 barges on the Bian River transported approximately 800,000 *shi* of pulse into the capital. The most important legume grown for food was soybeans, which provided high levels of much-needed protein and vitamins A and B. A soybean crop was easy to grow even on poor soil, and through its release of nitrogen it improved the soil's fertility for other crops, which could be grown in rotation.[11] Thus soybeans qualified as a valuable plant food in good times as well as in famine. Various kinds of soybeans could be cooked in porridges and gruels, fermented and shaped into bean curd, and made into tasty sauces. Soybeans could also be used as fodder for cattle and horses. "Lesser beans," such as green beans, broad beans, and silkworm beans, as well as peas, were cooked as a fresh vegetable or made into noodles or dumplings.

A great variety of other vegetables were grown in patches and gardens, including various cabbages, melons, gourds, garlic, leaks, and onions, along with aquatic vegetables—water chestnuts, lotus, and water caltrop. The Chinese larder also contained bamboo shoots, mushrooms, radishes, and ginger. In addition to native fruits of north China such as peaches, plums, apricots, pears, and persimmons, many fruits cultivated in the south were available in the cities of the north: oranges and tangerines of all kinds, bananas, lichees, olives, loquats, and longan. In the peaceful years between 1161 and 1189 many of these foods and fruits were sold on the market of the border town Sizhou on the Huai River, and from there they were traded into the Jin empire.[12]

By Song times, tea was no longer viewed as a luxury but as an everyday beverage available even in the households of commoners. Around the middle of the eleventh century the official Cai Xiang published his *Monograph on Tea* (*Chalu*) in which he not only described the plant itself but also the taste, color, and scent, the aesthetic enjoyment to be gained from the beverage, and methods of preparation. The main regions of tea cultivation produced annually more than 600 tons each, and in some years 2,000 tons. Tea merchants did a big business, and the state treasury profited from the tea monopoly and its tax revenues.[13]

Textile Machinery and Water Mills

Silk-reeling was a technique for producing a continuous thread of silk several hundred meters long. With the use of chopsticks or a brush, filaments of raw silk were removed from cocoons that had been soaked in a hot or cold water basin. Six kilograms of cocoons yielded about 480 grams of raw silk. The filaments were wound together around a reel, forming a single thread. To achieve a fine, round, even thread of proper tension, the silk reel had to be operated by hand in a rotary motion.

Silk-reeling had been practiced for more than two millennia by the time the Song dynasty was founded. But the earliest extant textual source in any language that describes the technique in detail is the *Book on Sericulture* (*Canshu*) written by the scholar-official Qin Guan around 1090. Here we read about the guiding-eyes, the roller, the ramping-board, and the silk reel itself.[14] The reeling frame operated by Qin's wife was a highly sophisticated machine, an extraordinary achievement of engineering (Fig. 16). As we know from a depiction on a handscroll, many silk reels were operated by two workers and were furnished with a treadle. If two frames were used for reeling, a daily output of up to 2,869 grams of raw silk thread was possible—a figure that compares favorably with the daily output of factory workers using steam-powered silk reels in the nineteenth century. The use of silk-reeling frames of this make can be documented from the eleventh until the twentieth century.

Silk fabric was reserved for Song officials. Ramie and hemp—perennial plants harvested several times a year on a comparatively large scale— were the textile materials used for commoners' clothing before the triumphal march of cotton during the Yuan dynasty. All textile threads from whatever source that are to be woven into fabric on a loom have to be twisted for better elasticity and strength. The *Book of Agriculture* (*Nongshu*) of 1313 contains two types of big spinning frames, one type

Fig. 16   The northern silk-reeling frame. Detail from *Sericulture*, attributed to Liang Kai, Song dynasty, thirteenth century. Handscroll, ink and color on silk. Cleveland Museum of Art, Cleveland, Ohio.

driven by hand or animal, the other by water power, both ideally suited for twisting fibers of ramie and hemp (Fig. 17).[15] Both types of frames had already been set up for operation in the thirteenth century in many villages of the central plain in north China. When there was a lot of thread material to twist, many households came together, weighed the spinning material they brought to be processed, and shared the output of yarn according to individual input.

The length of the machine measured more than 620 centimeters, its width about 155 centimeters. All functional parts were worked by three driving belts, their speeds dependent on the velocity of rotation of the big driving wheel. The general structure and functional parts of the frame were borrowed from silk machinery. The material to be twisted and wound was placed in circular layers in thirty-two cylindrical wooden boxes, which could produce almost 60 kilograms of low-twisted yarn in twenty hours. With ramie, the water-driven frame could be worked all year round except during the few weeks in winter when the river froze. The twisted yarns were used for summer cloth, underwear, mosquito nets, and so on.

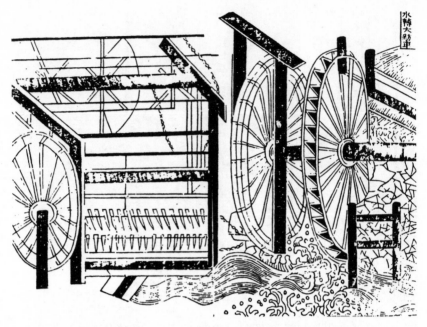

Fig. 17   Water-powered bast-fiber thread-twisting frame, thirteenth century.
Nongshu, j. 20:17ab.

   These spinning frames were early predecessors of the box-spinning machine, but they did not lead to a revolution in textile production in China.
Several centuries later in mercantile Europe, however, all the features of
the Chinese silk-reeling frame and the twisting frame would be adapted
for Italian silk manufacture and British cotton technology. They formed
the mechanical basis for the industrial revolution in Europe.
   Water mills have a long history in China, going back to the Han dynasty. The earliest paintings depicting water mills belong to the tradition
of Guo Zhongshu and Wei Xian, tenth-century architectural painters
whose original works have long been lost. Water mills can also be found
in mural paintings and book illustrations.[16] But the most famous depiction of a water mill is a horizontal handscroll dating from the early decades of the thirteenth century (Fig. 18). A viewer unfolding the handscroll can follow the production sequence at a mill. On the right side, a
man carrying his grain crosses the river on a ferry, rests at the winnowing
scene with the two suspended sieves, grinds his grain on the millstones,
and sifts it in a rather large-framed open mill. The millstones and sieves
are driven by horizontal water wheels placed far below the workroom
just above water level. The flour is sun-dried on the terrace, put in sacks,

Fig. 18 *Water Mill*. Attributed to Wei Xian (fl. 960–975), copy from the early decades of the thirteenth century. Handscroll, ink and color on silk. National Palace Museum, Taiwan, Republic of China.

and again ferried across the river, before it is loaded onto freight carts that disappear to the left.

Apart from the forty laborers at work in this depiction, there are two officials—recognizable from their full court attire—and three attendants. The presence of officials checking the accounts, managing the work force, and monitoring the products clearly indicates that the government owned and operated this mill. Milling was a profitable business, and the government's participation in it was a novelty of Song times. In 970 Emperor Taizu established two water mill agencies, one in the west of Kaifeng and one in the east, each of them operating a mill that provided the Imperial Palace and residents of the capital with flour.[17] Each of the mills was headed by two officials and staffed by a total of 205 workers.

Later, more water mills were set up. The emperors Taizu and Taizong, in the company of hundreds of courtiers, officials, and servants, visited water mills eleven times, in a grand public display of imperial glory. The government-run mills were strictly controlled, and private flour transactions and embezzlement were heavily punished. During the many heated conversations about reform in the Song dynasty, the question of public versus private ownership of water mills came up frequently. But as long as 400,000 strings of cash from government-run water mills filled the coffers of the treasury every year, proposals to close them down were of a rhetorical nature only.

Transportation of Goods and People

The Song empire was held together geographically and economically by a road and canal network that provided a lifeline for official and private communication and for the transportation of goods and people (Map 10). Cartography was highly developed in Song times, and references to two maps of grain routes along the Grand Canal in 996 and 1006 suggest that route maps existed for other corridors of travel and transport as well.[18]

The Qin dynasty (221–207 B.C.) was the golden age of roadwork in China, when "speedways" 11.5 meters wide were built around the capital Xianyang (near modern Xi'an), and even small roads were calibrated to the width of the axle of a cart. The old Qin network of roads with flagstone paving and hard shoulders radiated from the capital to many places in north China. Built exclusively for the emperor's regular inspec-

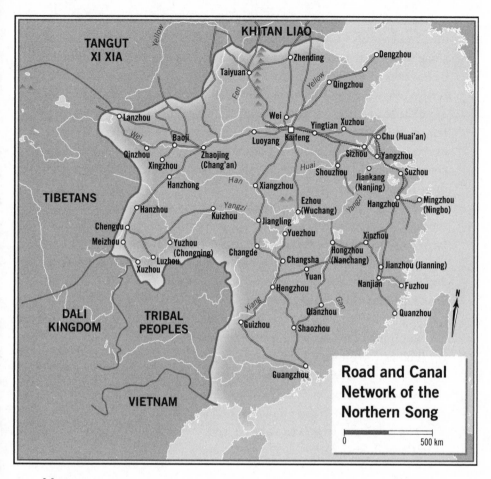

Map 10

tion tours, this network served as the basis for the Tang government's courier relay routes and relay stations, which were placed every 20 kilometers or less along the way.[19] Here, couriers, who rode at a rate of 15 kilometers an hour, could change horses and recover from their exhausting ride. The Tang road network also included stone bridges and ferry services over rivers that could not be easily forded. During the Song dynasty, private guest houses and restaurants offering food, washing facilities, and accommodation to all sorts of travelers grew up around the official relay stations.

Even though the road network in north China was not as dense as it had been in Tang times, the early Song emperors supported a number of initiatives to improve the flow of traffic.[20] To make travel safe, especially for merchants, who paid a toll of 2 percent on the value of their commodities, road towers or mounds with a watchtower built of earth, wood, or stone were erected every 2.5 kilometers along the roads. For the comfort of travelers in the border regions of Hebei, in 1012 Emperor Zhenzong ordered that elms and willows be planted along the right and left sides of public roads. Elsewhere it was quite common to plant trees along courier routes and public roads, as may be seen from an old paved Sichuanese courier route flanked by gigantic cedar trees in the north of Zitong county. Around 1116 there were 338,600 fir and pine trees along prefectural and county roads in Fujian.[21]

The roads in north China allowed big ox carts with wheels of 180 centimeters in diameter to transport bulk goods to Kaifeng. Some were so large that they needed twenty mules to move them over longer distances. But on the north side of the Yellow River, road conditions in early spring and winter were often treacherous. Wang Yucheng (954–1001) informs us in his poem "Facing the Snow":

> But think of the people north of the River
> Pulling carts to supply the border towns.
> Each cart heavy with its load of grain,
> Roads stretching for hundreds of miles.
> The skinny horses can't move in the cold,
> The ice-locked wheels can't be budged.
> Where do they camp when nightfall comes?[22]

Some of the earliest known travel diaries record conversations between Song envoys and Liao officials in the early eleventh century.[23] In one of these secret-service reports, Su Che described his journey to the Liao in 1086. He complained about road conditions so poor that travel for more than 30 kilometers a day was impossible: "When I and the others were sent to the Northern Dynasty [Liao], each of the barbarians was responsible for six carts carrying secret and official items. The carts were low and small and lasted only one or two journeys before breaking down. The construction of the coast road was not yet finished . . . One should not make use of big carts to travel in this country. Due to the continuing bad weather conditions [all roads] became marshy. For a short time we got carried, but we also had to walk a lot, exhausting ourselves."[24]

Only a few roads linked the major cities in the Liao empire, and information about road construction there is scarce.[25] We know that 200,000 laborers were mobilized to build a road through the mountains in one day in 984. Five years later, roads were built to connect the Southern Capital with other places in the newly captured areas in northern Hebei. In 1027 an order was issued that all official highways should be cleared on either side to a width of thirty paces. These wide roads allowed the Khitan to travel with their huge "carpet carts." Khitan roads were probably made of earth, sand, and gravel and were not covered with flagstones. Since they were not constructed in a way that caused water to run off the surface, most of these roads washed away and had to be rebuilt almost every year. Dusty in summer and muddy during the rainy season, they were unpleasant to travel on.

In comparison with north China, where well-kept main roads linked the Song capital with faraway provincial capitals or other important places, the road network of central and south China appears to have been underdeveloped.[26] There, people preferred to journey by water. Roads connecting minor towns may have resembled the country roads described by foreign observers in the early decades of the twentieth century, who complained that, outside cities, they found only narrow paths, inadequate for wheeled carts and scarcely wide enough for foot passengers. Scholar-officials usually rode on horseback with servants, but many preferred donkeys and mules to indicate their humbleness. In flat regions, farmers used wheelbarrows to transport goods. In the mountainous provinces, however, travelers needed a hardy physical constitution to climb steep paths on mountain ridges and walk on the slippery ground between the terraced rice fields. The general situation improved only during the Southern Song, when road construction intensified in the southeast. Traveling on roads was exhausting: "Take a long trip—then you learn how hard the road can be."[27]

A special type of road composed of wooden planks anchored to cliff faces connected a few places in the Wei River valley of western Shaanxi with towns south of the Qinling Mountains in the Han River valley and Sichuan province. These regions could not otherwise be reached by foot but only by sailing or towing a boat upstream on the Yangzi through the Three Gorges. The longest was more than 100 kilometers long. Solid enough to walk on, ride a horse over, and transport goods, these wooden roads also served the Tang emperors well when they were forced to decamp from the capital Chang'an to the safe haven of Chengdu in Sichuan, and they were probably life-saving for Chinese refugees of Gansu and Shaanxi as they fled from the invading Jurchen and Mongol troops.[28]

Traveling on board a boat or barge was preferable to traveling on any sort of road, whether on the Grand Canal, the Bian River linking Kaifeng to the Huai River, the Yangzi and Yellow rivers, or the many other rivers of central and south China. Boats ran the risk of capsizing, especially during hellish rides through gorges and currents, but generally they were faster, more comfortable, and a lot safer for the transport of heavy, voluminous, or bulky goods than ox carts or mules.

Between 605 and 610 the Sui emperor Yangdi had ordered the construction of an enormous canal network. It posed a heavy burden on the treasury, but it joined China's grain supply and its centers of silk and tea production in the southeast to the densely populated north. It also provided an efficient way to transport troops and military equipment. Hundreds of thousands of commoners and convicts were forced to build several tens of thousands of kilometers of artificial waterways, which were often furnished with pound-locks. The Universal Benefit Canal connected the Yangzi River with the Yellow River, and the Eternal Benefit Canal linked the Yellow River to the Bohai Sea. The canal system was eventually extended southward from Yangzhou to Hangzhou.[29]

The assistant commissioner of transport for Huainan Qiao Weiyu first described the pound-lock in 983. Instead of hauling barges over slipways made of inclined stone aprons from a waterway at one level to a waterway at another level, he had pound-locks built with two hanging gates arranged at a great enough distance from each other to accommodate a long barge. Water flowing into the lock raised or lowered the barge to the level needed to continue on the river. This was the fastest and safest method to overcome differences in altitude along a river's course.

By the Song period, boats and barges of various types and tonnage had almost completely replaced overland transport in southern and central China, and traffic carrying rice and beans dominated the inland waterways. One of the biggest storehouses for grain was situated where the Bian River connected with the Yellow River at Bianliang River Mouth. Li Ao wrote in his travel diary on February 11, 809: "[I] left the Luo River, traveled down the Yellow River, and stopped at Bianliang River Mouth. Thereupon we traveled the current of the Bian River, which provides passage between the Yellow River and the Huai River."[30] The successful re-routing of the Bian River in 1079 in order to link its canal extension directly to the clear waters of the Luo River—and away from the silted Yellow River—allowed safe transport on the Bian River all year round.

Some barges on the canals measured less than 30 meters in length, whereas passenger ships, some at 90 meters, transported 700 to 800 passengers on two decks. Ferries crossing the turbulent Yellow River could be more than 20 meters long and almost 6 meters wide.[31] River and canal boats were built according to local traditions based on the experience and peculiarities of their owners and crew and according to the goods and passengers they were intended to carry. They relied on a wide variety of modes of propulsion. On the Yangzi River, boatmen made use of paddle-wheel boats. On the smaller rivers of Jiangnan they used small craft called flying shuttles or flat-bottom boats. Some were rowed and some punted, some had flat bottoms and others were reinforced with nails to allow them to scrape over shallows.

In the tricky waters of the Yangzi gorges and at the rapids on the Han River, boatmen used oars and hawsers to tow boats upstream. The poet Lu You described an ascent up the Yangzi through the Three Gorges in 1170, a practice that would continue until the twentieth century:

A hundred men shouting at once, rattling the oars;
in the boat, face to face, we can't even hear ourselves talk.
All at once the men have scattered—silence, no more scuffle;
the only sound, two winches reeling out hundred-yard tow-lines;
whoo-whoo, whaa-whaa—how fast the winches unwind,
the boatmen already standing there on the sandy shore.[32]

Towing boats from paths cut into cliffs high above rivers—sometimes several hundred meters away, where draft animals could not be used—posed a dangerous challenge to boatmen. In other sections of the big rivers, sails made of mats from reeds or bamboo were hoisted to catch the wind, but traveling by boat was still a wearisome and noisy business. In the early evening when darkness filled the deep-cut gorges of the Yangzi River and the boatman docked at the shore, the traveler could expect only modest comfort—a spicy noodle soup and a hard bed in rough surroundings where people from all walks of life met to find shelter for the night.

An idea of the transport capacity and facilities needed to secure the food supply and other goods to the capitals and big cities may be gained from freight transport figures. In 981, 3 million *shi* (ca. 228,000 tons) of rice and millet and 1 million *shi* of pulse were shipped on the Bian River, while the total shipped on the Bian, Yellow, Huimin, and Guangji rivers amounted to 5.5 million *shi* (ca. 418,000 tons). By 1065 the freight transported on the Bian River had increased to 5.7 million *shi* (ca. 433,000 tons), and on the combined rivers to 6.7 million *shi* (ca. 509,000 tons). Almost one third of the total rice tax revenue traveled on barges from the coastal regions to the capital. The roughly 12,000 grain-carrier barges displaced 18 tons in Jiangxi, 60 tons in Anhui, 100 tons on the Grand Canal, and 600 tons on the Yangzi. The largest English ship in 1588, half a millennium later, displaced a mere 400 tons.[33]

The fleet of privately owned barges and ships may have amounted to several times the number of grain-carrier barges. By the end of the thirteenth century as many as 15,000 ships may have operated in the Lower Yangzi alone. In coastal waters, vessels displacing 180 tons and more were common. A vessel 24.2 meters long and 9.15 meters wide with a capacity of 300 tons was excavated in Fujian province. Its body consisted of thirteen waterproof compartments—wooden boards sealed with a plaster of hemp and tung oil. In comparison, the maximum displacement load of Columbus's 1492 flagship, the *Nina,* was about 110 tons. The city of Quanzhou, in Fujian province, had eleven wharfs building sea-going vessels. The construction of the barges had many ingenious features, such as square hulls, sternpost rudders, fore and aft sails, and watertight compartments. Unlike European ships, which were streamlined like fish plowing the sea, Chinese ships were shaped like ducks swimming on the surface of the water. These big-bellied barges embodied what the poet Li Qingzhao observed: "Great ships sail only for profit."[34]

Around the year 1021, the government ordered the fifty-one shipbuilding centers to construct 2,915 barges specialized for the transport of rice, millet, and other grains. This number probably represented the number of ships that had to be replaced annually. Forty-two of these shipyards were located in the provinces of central and southern China, five in Sichuan, and only four in north China.[35] From the number of ships ordered and the location of the shipyards, we may deduce that shipbuilding took place mostly near the sources of the raw materials required—timber, nails, tong oil, lime, and hemp. In the central and southeastern provinces, people could not do without ships. They were a necessity of daily life.

The Exploitation of Natural Resources

A society's mastery of mining and metallurgical technologies speaks volumes about its economic development. During the Song dynasty, coins cast from copper and iron, and ingots from silver and gold, allowed the growth of a money-based economy and the proliferation of nation-wide trade, both of which contributed to political unity. But metal coins were just the tip of the iceberg. The annual output of iron in the eleventh century supported the manufacture of weapons, armor, horseshoes, axles, knives, chisels, nails, locks, cooking pots and pans, hatchets, hoes, spades, ploughshares, axes, hammer heads, and other tools of critical importance to workers and consumers.

The most profitable mines were placed under government control. From all the others the state collected taxes of 10 percent for iron and copper and 20 percent for silver and gold, and mine owners were required to sell their production to the government. Around 1065, of the 271 metal-working places in China, 123 locations or 44 percent worked as iron and copper smelting foundries, and 84 places smelted silver. The average taxed annual iron production may have ranged between 5,000 and 10,000 tons, and in peak times around the year 1078 it may have ranged between 17,000 and 20,000 tons.[36]

Because of high production, the market price of iron was kept low, and this led to more affordable finished goods. In 1080 the ratio of the value of iron to rice was 177 to 100 in Sichuan and 135 to 100 in Shaanxi. Iron production had its downside, of course. Because the blast furnaces for smelting required immense quantities of fuel, nearby forests were chopped down and erosion was the result. As the forests receded in the eleventh century, foundries began to substitute coke for charcoal.

Gold and copper were mined in China from earliest times, but during the Song dynasty comparatively efficient mining methods gave impressive results. Demand for copper from the private sector as well as from the Northern Song government led to a dramatic rise in production. The annual tax quota increased more than fivefold, from 2,460 tons in 997 to 12,982 tons in 1070. This was far more than the total global production of copper in 1800, and exceeded the total Chinese production in 1952. After 1078 and the end of the reform period, copper production sharply declined, and exploitation of deposits resulted in a shortage. After the southern migration, production appears to have suffered an almost complete breakdown. For the year 1162, a meager and highly unreliable copper production of 157 tons was given.[37]

Silver became an important metal only after craftsmen succeeded in separating it from argentiferous sulphide ores found deep underground. The technological difficulties of its production made silver a relatively scarce commodity compared with gold. In the middle of the ninth century when the annual silver production reached around 14 tons, silver for the first time in Chinese history became economically more important than gold. The annual silver production during Song times was somewhere between 15 tons and 60 tons.[38] Some silver was probably imported during this period, and importation of silver would become a big business a few centuries later.

Gold was imported through barter trade from Siberia and other locations along the Central Asian Silk Road. According to Bo Juyi, writing in the early ninth century, many peasants left their land and joined the gold washers and silver miners. Silver, so he wrote, came from faraway places in the hills of Chu, and gold from the shores of the Po River in Jiangxi. The miners cleared away the gravel and chiseled into the rock all year round, he said, not caring for themselves, only for the profit to be made. But gold and silver are not things one can eat or wear, he moralized, and so they do not help men who are hungry and cold.[39] Apart from a few mining experts, most workers in mining-related activities and in foundries were farmers, poor or landless folks who in the slack season tried to supplement their income. It was a low-status, impoverished occupation that offered no real prospects.

Taken together, several factors account for the outstanding economic performance of the Song. First was an enormous increase in agricultural acreage on the tax registration rolls—from 2.5 percent of state territory in 959 to 13 percent in 1021—which underwrote Song prosperity. Land registration went hand in hand with a reform of tax households that helped to make self-managing farmers (constituting 66 percent of all farming households in 1078) the backbone of Song agriculture. The flourishing agricultural economy required all sorts of technical improvements and especially new tools, which created a demand for more efficient mining methods and a higher production of iron and copper. As these metals became more readily available, they were cast into coins on a great scale—an essential medium of exchange for an almost insatiable national market.

11

MONEY AND TAXES

CASH currency played a key role in commerce, money lending, taxation, and foreign policy during the Northern and Southern Song. In 801 the Tang scholar-official Du You proclaimed the metalist doctrine that cash in the form of metal coins was the only medium of exchange that could meet the needs of commerce. Monetary instruments such as grain and silk were too bulky and fragile for this purpose, while gold and silver were too rare and valuable.[1] According to this theory, the face value of a single coin should correspond to its value as a metal.

In the Qin and Han dynasties, one thousand round copper coins with a square hole in the center were threaded on a string, and thus strings with one thousand cash were regarded as the full unit (*guan*) of cash currency. As soon as the Song unified the country, the emperor abolished the various currencies of the former regimes still in circulation and replaced them with the dynasty's own currency bearing the inscription *Song yuan tongbao* (primary circulating treasure of the Song). After 983 the name of the reign period when the coin was cast was indicated on its surface.

In 820 copper coins were cast for 150,000 strings of cash, each holding one thousand coins. This number rose to approximately 1.83 million strings of cash in 1007. In 1080, after decades of "currency famine," it reached an unprecedented 5 million strings. In that same year, 800,000 strings of iron coins were brought into circulation. Seventeen mints produced copper coins (consisting of 65 percent copper, 25 percent lead, and 10 percent tin), while nine mints produced iron coins. When copper supplies were low, more lead was substituted for copper, thus diminishing the value of cash. In the Southern Song, up to 60 percent lead was used in coins.[2]

Between 1077 and 1088 in the central regions of the Song empire, a standard string held 770 copper coins weighing 4.5 *jin* (2.85 kilograms). The exchange rate for one string of iron cash, which threaded between 1,020 and 1,100 coins, was equivalent to one string of copper cash.[3] The considerable increase in the supply of cash from the end of the tenth century until the last decade of the eleventh century is a strong indicator of the growing significance of the Song's money-based economy. In 752 only about six coins were available per head. This increased to 17 coins around 995, and to 212 coins per head in 1080. The number of coins in circulation in the whole of the Northern Song has been estimated at 200 million strings, which would have totaled around 145 billion coins.[4] Never again in the history of imperial China would the supply of coins reach such a scale.

Paper Currency

In modern monetary theory, everything that performs the functions of money is money. According to this definition, not only cash currency—"the circulating treasure"—but also the various sorts of paper money in widespread use were money, even though many Song scholars refused to accept this reality. Song paper money was the first viable paper currency system used in a national economy in world history, although not a single authentic specimen is known to exist today.[5] The Mongols adopted paper money almost two decades before they defeated the Song. The "silk notes" they issued in 1260, which were backed by silk yarn, reached Persia in 1294 and Korea in 1296. The Japanese created their own paper currency in 1334, and the Vietnamese adopted paper in 1396. In Western countries, paper money was a rather late arrival. It started in Sweden in 1661 and was adopted in America in 1690, France in 1720, Russia in 1768, England in 1797, and Germany in 1806.

Paper currency came into use in Song times because several preconditions were met. First, the Song's flourishing national economy created a high demand for iron and copper in the production of all sorts of articles, and the introduction of paper money helped to free up these metals for use in manufacturing. Second, the technology for printing paper notes became so advanced that currency could be printed in good quality (making counterfeiting difficult) and in high numbers (Fig. 19). Third, Song

Fig. 19   Relief plate for printing paper money (*huizi*), Song dynasty, twelfth century. The text below the ten coins says: "With the exception of Sichuan, [this] may be circulated in the various provinces, prefectures, and counties to make public and private payments alike representing 770 cash per string on presentation." Peng Xinwei.

scholars who paid attention to the monetary system had a very good understanding of money as a means of payment and exchange, not as a value in its own right, in the way that silver or gold was valuable. As Ye Shi (1150–1223) explained, "Money, one of those magic things created by man, is useful to its creator only when it is in constant circulation; it loses the meaning of its existence when it is taken away from the market and locked up in an iron-chest."[6] In his view, ease of circulation was the very function of currency, and paper money fulfilled this function better than coins.

But perhaps the most critical factor in the growth of paper currency had to do with the Song's foreign policy. The government constantly feared that bronze coins, with their high percentage of copper and a face value worth less than the actual metal they were made of, would be taken out of circulation, particularly by the Song's northern and western neighbors. The resulting shortage of cash would damage the national economy while strengthening alien regimes. The stability of the Liao dynasty's economy in particular depended heavily on cash imports from the Song. To keep control of metals and safeguard the stability of its currency, the Song government established segregated currency zones in the border regions.[7] In the 1040s iron cash was extended to all the frontier provinces bordering the Liao and Xi Xia dynasties and copper cash was prohibited. In the middle of the twelfth century the Jin also tried to safeguard their own currency system by prohibiting the use of copper cash in border provinces, especially in the affluent Huainan region. Low-value currency zones on both sides of the border not only made the lives of commoners in these regions more difficult but also complicated all nationwide commercial activities and tax administration.[8]

The year 994 is the earliest documented date for a privately issued "order to pay," also called a promissory note or exchange bill. This note or bill was a privately agreed-upon deed, and the earliest mention of it that has come down to us was in the context of the uprising of Li Shun, the leader of a short-lived insurrection of craftsmen, artisans, and farmers in Sichuan province. These insurgents objected to the heavy iron coins that had replaced the small copper coins in use for thirty years. In response to this unrest, and after some further administrative irregularities, the government established a Bureau for Exchange Bills in 1023 in modern Chengdu and introduced the official exchange bill—a clever, highly efficient, profitable, and comfortable invention for buying and selling goods and services.

This piece of printed paper entitled its holder to receive the amount of cash strings printed on the surface of the exchange bill when he presented it at one of the bureaus. Originally, one exchange bill was one string's worth of cash and was valid for a circulation period of three years. Later, the printed exchange value could vary between one and ten strings, and exchange rates of 770 coins and less per string became common.[9] For merchants who needed a large amount of cash to purchase commodities, paper bills immensely facilitated the transfer of funds from one place to another. Nobody had to carry bulky, heavy iron coins over dangerous mountain paths. Very soon the new exchange medium found its way into regions of the north, as merchants and officials saw its value in solving a number of problems related to commodity transfer and payment.

Paper money was made from the bark of the paper mulberry tree, which is why it was also called mulberry paper money. The government manufactured, issued, and controlled paper notes, starting with the raw material and continuing through distribution. Usually silk or other fibers were mixed in to make counterfeiting as difficult as possible. Both the Northern and Southern notes had elaborate and difficult-to-copy patterns and usually bore technical data (date and series of issue, serial number, exchange value in strings, time limit of circulation, seal stamps, and so on) verifying the genuineness of the printed paper. The punishment for counterfeiting bills was usually printed on the note: "By imperial decree: Criminals who counterfeit paper money are to be punished by beheading. The reward [for informers] shall be 1,000 *guan*."[10] The government-run Chengdu printing house was established in 1068, and in the late twelfth century the treasury near Hangzhou employed 204 craftsmen. The size of a single note may have measured 11 by 19 centimeters. Exchange bills—and, later, money vouchers—were multicolor prints using multiple impressions.[11]

For better control of use and distribution, the government set up certain restrictions and conditions for the issuance and circulation of exchange bills. From 1023 until 1107 the Song government circulated forty-three issues, each limited to a total worth of 1,256,340 strings per circulation period (which was three years until 1069). A liquidity backing of 360,000 strings (or 28 percent) per circulation period helped to avoid insolvency. After three years the old exchange bills had to be replaced by new ones or exchanged for cash. A handling fee of 30 coins was charged for each string paid out and each order renewal.

Liquidity backing was decisive in the early success and the later failure of paper currency. Toward the end of the eleventh century some scholars insisted on 100 percent liquidity backing, while others erroneously thought that the convertibility problem could be solved by introducing a fixed rate of exchange from paper to cash and vice versa. Some scholars insisted that the government should maintain a cash reserve as liquidity backing. Emperor Shenzong thought liquidity backing for exchange bills was unnecessary, because income and expenditures would cause the people to trust the value of money.[12] He held the strikingly modern opinion that the economic power of a national economy was sufficient backing for paper currency. His advisers did not agree.

In 1071, after some of Wang Anshi's fiscal reforms were put into practice, the demand for exchange bills doubled. Six-year circulation was introduced shortly thereafter, and in 1093 the whole system started to run out of control when exchange bills equal to 13.3 million strings of cash were issued. In 1105 a reform, effective with the forty-fourth circulation issue printed in 1107, replaced the exchange bill with the money voucher. The bureaus were renamed accordingly.[13]

At the end of the Northern Song in 1127, the total number of old exchange bills in circulation may have amounted to about 70 million strings.[14] When the Song Chinese began their southward migration, the old credit line no longer satisfied demand. The total worth of money vouchers had to be increased by 30 percent to 1,886,340 strings of cash, and in 1141 the sixtieth issue climbed to an inflationary 5,886,340 strings. In 1145, after the Song had come to an agreement with the Jin and political security at the northern border eased the strain on state finances, the government reduced the issue of money vouchers to the old figure of 1127.

It would not last long. In 1161, the year when the Jin attacked the Southern Song, the issuance of money vouchers rocketed to 23 million strings of cash and remained there, more or less, until the end of the century. In the thirteenth century, the circulation period would be extended to four, six, nine, and finally ten years, and the number of issues increased as well. Issue ninety-nine, the last, came out in 1234, the year when the Mongol invaders crushed the Jin dynasty.

Besides exchange bills and money vouchers, Song merchants purchased credit instruments, or receipts, from the government and exchanged them for monopolized commodities such as salt, tea, alum, and perfume. A receipt entitled its holder to obtain the monopolized good in a specified quantity and quality at a certain place. Receipts of this nature implied long-distance travel and transport of bulky goods and the willingness of merchants to take risks. But the profits to be had in specialized stores in the capital and other trading localities, where holders of the receipts and the monopolized goods could meet to negotiate business matters and explore price differences, made the risks worthwhile.[15] Here, merchants had a place to buy and sell receipts and goods with the intention of making even more profit at lower risk. In order to secure its control over the receipt trade and participate in commerce, the government established its own Buying Receipt Office. The receipt system was immensely important for securing military supplies and provisioning troops at the northern border.

Paper Money

To relieve the shortage of cash caused by the war with the Jin, in 1160 Song officials created yet another kind of paper money, called *huizi* here to distinguish it from exchange bills, money vouchers, and other paper instruments. The introduction of *huizi* was not an entirely new idea but was a sort of convenient-to-use exchange bill designed to succeed the "flying money" of Tang times.[16] "Flying money" was a certificate for cash used by merchants. In 812 the government in Chang'an took over the issuance of certificates as a means of forwarding local taxes and revenues to the capital.

Huizi were already circulating among merchants and private people in Sichuan in the 1020s. The theoretical advantage of these money notes over exchange bills or money vouchers was their full convertibility into hard currency, as indicated in the twenty-nine-character inscription printed on the face of the note: "With the exception of Sichuan, [this] may be circulated in the various provinces, prefectures, and counties to make public and private payments alike representing 770 cash per string on presentation."[17] In practice, however, the holder of a *huizi* could not assert a claim for cashing in the note, and big discrepancies with the exchange rates showed up soon.

At first the face value of a *huizi* equaled one string of cash, but soon *huizi* with smaller denominations of 200, 300, and 500 coins were printed. In 1169 a circulation period of three years and an issue limited to the worth of 10 million strings was determined for each series. During these early years the cash value of a *huizi* was very good, and it was a vast improvement over all the methods of cashless money transfer ever imagined in the Northern Song. Although the commercially engaged public received the *huizi* with some reservations, the government succeeded in creating confidence in its paper money for several decades. *Huizi* were printed in three colors (red, black, blue) as well as monochrome from wood blocks or copper plates.

The Song interpretation of the advantages as well as the problems of paper money, especially after 1160, can be viewed against the background of old theories of the "real" (*shi*) and the "empty" (*xu*). During the Han dynasty, goods were regarded as "real," whereas cash was "empty." There was a widespread fear that in a growing economy "empty" cash currency would do away with "real" payments in kind. In Song times, when cash currency was well established as the basis of the national economy, the concepts of "empty" and "real" shifted to paper money (which was "empty") versus cash currency (which was "real"). Yang Guanqing (b. 1139), who understood the monetary difficulties of his time and supported the issuance of paper money, explained the point of view of its opponents by using this old terminology: For them, "paper money is empty, and the damage it causes cannot be expressed in words. Coins are real. They can be stored without damage. Now paper money is issued from above without limitations. People [buy it] to pay [their taxes] to the government and this is the reason why copper cash is regarded as expensive. Why should I take the 'real' to get the 'empty'? Day by day the old cash [currency] is getting scarcer and paper money cheaper."[18]

Yang explained the scarcity of cash this way: "Because today the rich families and merchants store copper cash so profitably and do not want to spend them cheaply, there is a daily shortage of copper cash."[19] He was right. Paper money was being used for everyday business and payment of debts because people were hoarding coins. Especially during wartime, thousands of coins disappeared from circulation as affluent merchant families and local administrations buried them in the ground. In the past thirty years, thirteen batches of iron cash were discovered in the area of Baoji in Shaanxi province, adding up to about 28 tons.[20] The result of hoarding was that "bad" money gradually edged out "good" money. This observation in eleventh-century China would become known as Gresham's Law when it was pronounced in the sixteenth century by Sir Thomas Gresham (1519–1579), an economic advisor to Elizabeth I, Queen of England.

Emperor Xiaozong, who is said to have spent ten sleepless years after issuing *huizi*, was the driving power behind attempts to stabilize the monetary system. In 1166 he even bought back two million silver ounces' worth of circulating *huizi* and burned them. In addition, he decreed that paper notes should be accepted for payment of taxes and fees. Thus, he tried to regulate the market value of paper money by limiting the quantity in circulation. His attempt to curb inflation was so effective that by 1175 the value of the *huizi* stabilized. On the one hand there was an increasing demand for *huizi* because not enough cash was available to satisfy the market, and on the other hand the government tried to control the exchange value of *huizi* through curbs on distribution and variations in the circulation period, which after 1171 ranged from six to thirty years.

The interrelation between the value of a note and the number of notes in circulation had been known for a long time. In 1178 Huang Chouruo stated in a report to the throne: "If [*huizi*] are few, they are expensive, if there are many, they are cheap." In 1186 the issue increased to more than 20 million strings of cash, before rising in 1209 to more than 110 million strings, following another war with the Jin. Liu Kezhuang (1187–

1209) remarked: "*Huizi* became cheap as dirt, and the issue was halted."
Traveling merchants could not exchange *huizi* for coin, and paper money
was not accepted for the purchase of commodities. In 1168 a *huizi* for
one string of cash was worth 770 copper cash, but by 1208 the value had
dropped to 600 coins.[21]

After 1209, Li Fan aptly described the monetary problem and offered a
solution that reflected his advanced and well-balanced understanding:
"There is a shortage of cash, and the paper money gushes forth. Children
[paper money] and mother [cash] do not suffice to balance each other. Paper money should not circulate because coin currency cannot balance it.
Paper money does not circulate and people should be prevented from
hoarding it. This is a waste. It should be used carefully. As a means [to
balance it] in the first place there are still cereals. Only if one does not
have to accept paper money, then paper money is of real practical use."[22]

By 1224 *huizi* worth about 240 million strings of cash were in circulation. The internal exchange value dropped further, and after 1236 exchange rates of 240 cash per string and less are given. In 1246 an astronomical 650 million strings' worth of *huizi* were on the market. The
ruinous effects on the Song national economy could no longer be ignored. But it was easier to print more notes than to reform the monetary
system. By this time the government was also failing at keeping counterfeit money out of circulation. Of the printing plates that have survived,
almost all were clearly the work of counterfeiters, and this prevalence
lends support to contemporary concerns about rampant counterfeiting in
the thirteenth century.[23]

In 1264 the *huizi*—and all the regional substitutes that had been created to rescue it as a means of payment—had lost value so dramatically
that the whole paper currency project collapsed. Even before the first currency reform of 1287, the Mongol Yuan dynasty would try to solve the
problem by breaking away entirely from traditional cash currency and
relying on paper money as the medium of exchange.

Inflation and Money Lending

In the early ninth century, the annual income of a Chinese farm family
living at subsistence level may have amounted to no more than 5,000
cash, or approximately 416 cash per month. The living conditions of
farmers in Song times probably did not change from this standard by
much. Farm labor in China was always regarded as inferior work and

was underpaid. Estimates of the daily income of lower-class people range between 10 and 100 coins. A Song farm hand on one of the profitable tea plantations of Sichuan earned a monthly wage of about 1,800 cash, while an employee or servant in Kaifeng could earn as much as 3,000 cash. In the second half of the eleventh century this monthly income would have bought about 200 liters of rice—roughly double the amount of rice needed for a family of five persons. By contrast, an official of the lowest (ninth) rank could earn a salary of 12,000 cash per month, not including additional payments in kind. High officials with monthly salaries in the hundreds of thousands could afford to entertain dozens of relatives and retain scores of servants and other employees.

During the Northern Song period, when the state was comparatively stable and economically prosperous, one string of cash held between 700 and 800 coins, depending on the region. The number of coins, which indicates the exchange rate, influenced the value of a string: more coins, less strings; less coins, more strings. But in times of threatened security, the number of coins on a string dropped dramatically and the price of commodities increased proportionately. During the Southern Song, the value of a string fell from 770 coins in 1168 to fewer than 240 coins around the time of the first Mongol invasion in the 1230s.

In 1007 one *dou* (about 6.6 liters) of tax rice (that is, rice collected from farmers as tax and sold to nonfarmers) cost 20 cash, about the same number of coins a guest in a restaurant had to pay for a typical meal in Kaifeng. After the war with the Xi Xia in 1043, the price for one *dou* went up to 100 cash. Following the collapse of the Northern Song in 1131, more than 600 cash was charged for the same amount of rice. Gradually, the price settled down within the range of 300 to 500 cash per *dou*. Then, just after the Mongols started to invade Song territory, the rice market finally collapsed, and the government charged 3,400 cash for one *dou*. The rice market price debacle was accompanied by a dramatic increase in the prices for monopoly commodities such as salt, wine, and tea but not on the same scale as rice.

Inflation in the price of tabby silk per bolt followed a similar pattern. In 980 one bolt was assessed, for tax purposes, at 1,000 cash. This price held more or less steady until 1107, when it suddenly doubled to 2,000 cash nationwide. Rising almost in parallel with the market value of rice after the breakdown of the Northern Song, the price of one bolt rocketed to 10,000 cash by 1134. The market calmed down again and settled in the range of 4,000 to 5,000 cash per bolt until 1156. Over the course of the dynasty, from approximately 1000 to 1220, the prices for rice and silk increased by 2,500 percent and 400 percent, respectively.

As for precious metals, from 976 until 1125 the exchange rate of one Chinese ounce (39.6 grams) of gold remained at 10,000 copper coins, while the rate of one ounce of silver fluctuated between 1,000 and 1,500 coins.[24] The standard weight of a silver ingot or "shoe" was 50 ounces (1980 g), but other weights of ingots were also on the market. There are no indications in the Northern Song of a flight of capital from copper cash into precious metals. The situation was much different in the Southern Song. Around 1126 as the Northern Song empire was collapsing, the exchange rate for one ounce of gold rose to 20,000 cash, and in 1209, after the disastrous war against the Jin, to 40,000 cash. A comparable price hike occurred for silver: from 1160 to 1252 between 3,000 and 4,000 cash had to be paid for one ounce. Marco Polo reported that gold was worth five times as much as silver in thirteenth-century China, but other evidence suggests a ratio of one ounce of gold to ten ounces of silver.[25] It is highly improbable that gold lost value with respect to silver shortly before the end of the Song dynasty, though the price of silver in relation to gold in China may have been the highest in the world.

Inflation in the price of gold and silver was moderate compared with the escalation of real estate prices. Rich families invested in farm land, not in precious metals, and this drove property values skyward. These investments reflected a Chinese understanding of sound business practices. They were in harmony with the Confucian ethical system and at the same time created economic security and profits that benefited the family.

Money lending was much more widespread in the Chinese economy than in the European economy of the medieval period, where it was forbidden among Christians. By contrast, exorbitant interest rates were common in China. In Song times, private money lenders were allowed to charge an interest rate of 4 percent per month, and the government lent money at 5 percent per month. In the Tang dynasty, pawnbrokers charged much higher interest rates for short-term loans. For just a one-day loan, 50 coins had to be paid in interest to retrieve an unlined silk garment with small patterns. To retrieve one bolt of tabby silk after six days in pawn, 120 cash had to be paid in interest. This amounted to an annual interest rate of several hundred percent—many times the object's market value. Such crushing interest rates, which violated the emperor's prohibition of 982, led to concern among scholar-officials about the public welfare and to a number of attempts at fiscal reform.[26]

The Two-Tax System

In 780, Yang Yan, a high Tang official, established the two-tax system with the intention of unifying the multifarious existing taxes and alleviating some of the burden on poor farmers. Under this plan, taxes were collected according to local conditions in either one or two payments per year, in summer or in autumn. In 1077, 31 percent of the annual taxes were paid in summer and 69 percent in autumn. This innovation was a first step toward setting a state budget that would project the government's annual expenditure and attempt to reconcile it with projected annual income. "An estimate of the national expenditures should first be made every year," Yang Yan wrote, and on the basis of that projection, the required amount of tax would be apportioned among the various tax counties.[27]

The two-tax system replaced an old system consisting of a land tax paid annually in the form of cereal grains, duty paid in form of textile fabrics, and compulsory service provided in the form of time and labor. The new tax was a combination of a land tax and a house tax, which included wealth other than land, and it was to be paid in both cash and kind.[28] This reform was intended to rationalize the tax system and in the process get the inflation rate caused by thirty years of civil war under control. Tax on land remained the most important source of government revenue, and for this reason many officials (who at that time belonged to the landed aristocracy) opposed it.

In the first decade of the ninth century, when Liu Zongyuan was demoted to Hunan province, he wrote a story about a snake-catcher and his right to pay his tax in kind. Part of Liu's job had been to collect taxes, and when he suggested to the snake-catcher that he should pay his taxes in cash instead of snakes, the snake-catcher burst into tears and cried:

> Can you take pity on me and let me go on living? Unfortunate as my service may be, it is not as unfortunate as returning to pay taxes in cash. If I had not done my service this way, I would have come into trouble long ago. It is sixty years since the three generations of my family settled in this village. As time passed by my neighbors incurred more difficulties to earn their living from day to day. They

have used up the produce of their land and the income of their houses, appealed for help and finally had to move. They suffered from hunger and thirst, wind and rain, heat and cold, and breathed poisonous air. So they have died in confusion . . . I alone have survived on account of my snake-catching.[29]

Liu Zongyuan concluded that the poison of onerous taxation was worse than that of snakes, and he expressed his hope that those whose duty it is to observe the people's way of life before making government policy should take note of this case and allow that taxes are paid in kind.

Theoretically, the two-tax system abolished compulsory labor service. However, it soon became apparent that no Chinese government could do without it. During the Five Dynasty period the rate of conscripted laborers increased dramatically, and the service continued to exist in the Song. All men between the ages of twenty and sixty years of age except officials, the household members of officials, monks, and the military were subject to labor service.

Ouyang Xiu, in his position as censor to the emperor, complained about imperial extravagance and the hardship it imposed on forced laborers: "I am informed that in consequence of the recent birth of a princess, a demand has been made on the treasury for no less than 8,000 pieces of silk. Now the rigor of winter is just at its height, and the wretched workmen of the Dyeing Department, forced to break ice before they can get water, will suffer unspeakable hardships in supplying the amount required. And judging by Your Majesty's known sentiments of humanity and thrift, I cannot believe that this wasteful labor service is to be imposed, though rumor indeed has it that the dyers are already at work."[30] We do not know the outcome of his complaint. Furthermore, local people had to fulfill various lower administrative services at the local level without pay.

During the Tang dynasty, local tax revenues were divided three ways. One third went to the Central Imperial Treasury at the capital, one third was transferred to the provincial administration, and the remaining third was used to cover the local expenditures of the prefecture. This tax distribution system granted local authorities a certain degree of freedom in managing fiscal matters, but it also represented the central government's willingness to abandon efficient control over local authorities in return for the benefit of fixed and regular tax returns.[31] In a financial system where the government could not run the state into debt—because the

financial instruments for this kind of borrowing had not been invented—
the annual tax income had to be sufficient to cover expenditures. Collecting tax in advance was the only method available to pay for impending expenses.

But in practice, the annual revenue of the two-tax system did not cover
annual expenses, and thus the state reinstated its monopoly on alcohol,
tea, and salt. The sale of these commodities produced added revenue.
During the rule of Emperor Xuanzong in the early ninth century, the salt
monopoly alone contributed half of the state's annual income. These monopolies extended into the Song dynasty, when perfume was added to the
list.[32] By the 1170s the salt monopoly still accounted for half of state revenues, to which were added taxes from distilleries and breweries (of
which 1,861 were reported in 1077).

The Song dynasty also adopted the system of dividing local revenues
into three streams, but the Central Imperial Treasury now got most of it:
about 61.5 percent of income from silver, 49 percent of income from silk
fabrics, 67 percent of silk wadding, 53 percent of cloth, and 35 percent of
cereals.

The Song Tax Burden

The household registration of the five classes of self-managing landowners provided the demographic data that allowed local officials to set
taxes. The taxes levied on Song commoners differed from region to region and seemed to comply with previously fixed quotas based on soil
quality and other criteria rather than the actual annual yield. The tax
burden normally amounted to 10 percent of the annual harvest, paid in
one or two installments (spring and autumn), plus a substantial contribution in silk and other fabrics. Farmers were allowed to substitute other
products, such as silk or oil, for cereals at a previously fixed exchange
rate, and they were allowed to pay in cash.

From a comparison of fabric requirements, we know that tax payments went up considerably from the Tang to the Song. During the Tang
dynasty, standard bolts of silk tax fabrics measured between 12.04 and
12.64 meters long and 54.18 centimeters wide; bolts of other textile materials were 15.8 meters long. The most important Song tax fabric, silk
tabbies, were not only longer but also wider: 13.29 meters long and 64.78
centimeters wide.[33] Farmers' households had to invest more material,
time, and effort in producing them than in Tang times. Working condi-

tions were hard for the weaver, throwing her shuttle to and fro and filling the cloth beam inch by inch to come up to the county tax quota. In 750, the annual figure of silk tabby weaves amounted to 7.4 million bolts, but in Song times it was only 2.9 million bolts. The figures clearly indicate that the Song dynasty shifted away from taxes in kind to taxes in cash.[34]

In addition to paying annual taxes in kind, the economic situation of silk-weaving rural households was further aggravated by the introduction in 999 of the "harmonious beforehand selling" principle, whereby the government gave tax credits to farmers, which were paid back in silk fabrics. This system amounted to a compulsory sale to the state of enormous quantities of silk (30 million bolts in 1047) at vastly reduced prices. The average overall annual tax income (including all sorts of taxes) amounted to more than 11 million bolts of silk fabrics and almost 560 tons of silk wadding.[35] The revenues collected in cash, cereals, and silks not only financed the peace policy and all the subsidies in kind paid to alien regimes but also supported the military forces along the northern border.

Apart from the two-tax system, an additional five kinds of taxes were levied on Song citizens. First, self-managing farmers had to pay taxes on any farm land they rented from the government. Second, urban residents owning property had to pay a combined house tax and land tax comparable to that of farmers. This tax on city dwellers became important as a source of revenue by the end of the Northern Song, when around 7 percent of the Song population may have lived in cities. Third, all male adults between twenty and sixty years of age were required to pay a poll or capitation tax in cash. Fourth, many products such as hides, sinews, horns of beef, agricultural implements, mulberry trees, silkworms, salt, tea, and vinegar, as well as the seven sorts of cereals, the ten types of silk fabrics, threads and cloth of the vine creeper, the so-called four products of gold and iron, and local products were charged with taxes when they were bought and sold. Local products included domestic animals, bamboo wood, hemp straw, fruits, herbs, oil, paper, firewood, coal, lacquer, and wax. Finally, traveling traders were subject to a 2 percent tax on their commodities, which could be levied several times, and merchants who sold their goods at market had to pay a 3 percent tax on the products' value.[36]

In some periods and places a number of products produced by farmers were tax-exempt. This seems to have applied to agricultural tools, cereals, firewood, and a few other items of daily use. Nonetheless, the tax burden weighed heavily on farmers, commoners, and merchants. Farmers may well have agreed with Lu You, who wrote in 1202: "Pleasantest of all, to think taxes have been paid on time—for this year at least, no officials banging at my wicker gate."[37] Only privileged people with good connections to clerks and officials in the local tax registration office could avoid rapacious state administrators seeking to collect ever higher revenues. With income from all these sources, the Song treasury's annual tax income rose enormously compared with Tang times—perhaps as much as seven-fold—and the economy grew prodigiously.[38]

The commercial tax income in the 1070s—a result of multiple taxation of goods—amounted to 5 to 10 percent of the total goods that changed hands, which had a cash value of 100 million strings. Commercial taxes in 1077 came to about 8.7 million strings of copper and iron cash. This represents more than a doubling since the late tenth century. One reason for increased tax revenues may have been the rapid increase in the number of market towns functioning as trade centers, though no doubt much trade in kind occurred in these towns that alluded the tax collectors.[39]

From 995 to 997, when the state's total income in cash amounted to 22.2 million strings, the monopolies contributed approximately 5.25 million strings, or more than 25 percent. By 1064 revenues reached 116 million strings, including about 21 million strings from the alcohol and salt monopolies. At that point, however, expenditures were outpacing revenues, which means that the government had to balance its accounts from other sources. Revenues stored in the state storehouses and the profit extracted from the issuance of millions of exchange bills, sold in exchange for cash, may have helped to cover the excessive expenditures. Between the years 997 and 1085, the percentage of taxes paid in cash increased from 40 to 70 percent. Clearly, the entire economy of the Northern Song was based not only on monopolies and commercial taxes shifting toward a dependence on cash payments but also on the income from monopolies and commercial taxes surpassing the income from farmers levied in the two-tax system.[40]

Comprehensive figures for total state income and expenditures during the Southern Song are not available, but from what we know we may conclude that the share from the two-tax system declined as the landed gentry perfected their techniques for tax dodging. Nevertheless, the annual state income in strings of cash from various sources remained at a high level in the second half of the twelfth century. Silver may also have played a major role during the second half of the twelfth century and onward, when a considerable portion of taxes, especially consumption and capitation taxes, was paid in silver.[41]

Fiscal Policy of the Alien Regimes

For its settled population—not including the Khitan clans—the Liao practiced modified versions of the Tang two-tax system in combination with a rather irregular demand for labor service. After the settlement in 1005 between the Song and the Liao, the annual subsidy paid by the Song in silk and silver made up a good part of the total annual revenue taken in by that government. The economic situation of the northwestern Xi Xia regime of the Tanguts did not differ fundamentally from that of the Liao. The Xi Xia regime was also supported by Song peace payments. The Song's national economy had no problem with the annual silk tribute but could hardly have afforded annual payments in silver to the Liao and Xi Xia amounting to 20 to 30 percent of its annual national production if the Song had not recaptured a large percentage of this outlay through increased border trade.[42]

When the Jurchens annexed the territory of the Liao dynasty and the northern provinces of the Song dynasty, with all their towns and cities, it took control of all government reserves in the treasuries of the capitals. In early 1126, in a desperate effort to meet the peace terms of the Jurchen invaders, the Northern Song Emperor Qinzong agreed to a war indemnity of unprecedented value, including silks, livestock, and metals. He ordered—by threatening with decapitation all who disobeyed—the collection of all the reserves of gold, silver, and coins held in treasuries, garrisons, and households of officials and commoners and thus stripped the capital of its precious metals. According to the *History of the Great Jin Kingdom (Da Jinguo zhi)*, in the capital of Kaifeng alone the Jin made a haul of 3 million ingots of gold, 8 million ingots of silver, 54 million bolts of silk fabric, and 15 million bolts of satin.[43] This booty was of higher value than the total of the average annual subsidies the Song contributed to the Jin economy for the remaining 110 years of the dynasty.

When the puppet state of Qi was dissolved in 1137, the Jin cashed in once more. This wealth may have been spent by the government in the form of gifts and rewards handed out to imperial relatives, other dignitaries, and loyal subjects. In 1142 a victorious general, for example, received 1,000 slaves, 1,000 horses, 1 million sheep, 2,000 ounces of silver, and 2,000 bolts of fabric. In 1142, in the oath letter terminating hostilities between the Jin and Song, the Song once again committed themselves to enormous annual tributes of silk and silver.[44] Financial subsidies from the Song dynasty, which had secured the survival of the Liao empire in the eleventh century, would support the enormous military budget of the Jin empire for almost another 100 years.

The Jin tax system followed the Song model, to which it added a commercial tax in 1180. The dynasty was less successful in copying the Song monetary system. Lacking not only the raw material but also the technical skill to produce a significant quantity of cash, the Jin relied heavily on legal and illegal imports of Northern Song coins.[45] When the Song monetary system suffered an almost complete breakdown during the southern migration, the Jin dynasty also suffered from a coin shortage. But after the treaty of 1142, which committed the Song an annual indemnity, the Jin's currency shortage diminished. The Jin government introduced its own exchange notes in 1154 and began to cast copper coins and issue paper money in 1157 but was never able to stabilize the exchange rate.

Compared with the Song, the economic history of the Liao, Jin, and Xi Xia dynasties is confusing to the point of mystification.[46] All three of these regimes profited immensely from subsidies supplied by their southern neighbor. The fact that the Song involuntarily financed the courts of these alien powers for more than two hundred years distorts any assessment of the real performance of their national economies.

I2

PRIVATE LIVES IN THE
PUBLIC SPHERE

IN ALL medieval societies of East Asia, a hierarchical social order prevailed, and people for the most part complied with its strict rules in all spheres of daily life, both public and private. In China, however, the Confucian revival during the Song dynasty gave this tradition added impetus. The lifeways of Song Chinese were circumscribed and often highly regulated by their social position, and this reality affected the choices they made—and were allowed to make—in housing, transportation, personal appearance, entertainment, and health.

Song society enjoyed a degree of early *laissez-faire* liberalism that distinguished it from contemporary societies outside China. This economic liberalism granted a good deal of freedom in the marketplace, with the result that innovation in the production and distribution of goods thrived. Yet in keeping with the prevalent Confucian ideology, Song merchants and traders ranked far below the humblest scholar-officials in terms of family status, personal prestige, and privileges even if they became quite wealthy.

Homes and Furnishings

The majority of the Song population lived in the countryside in small windowless sheds built with local materials according to the custom of the region. These one- or two-room dwellings were dark and poorly ventilated, their earthen floors were frequently damp, front doors were often broken, and roofs usually leaked. People of the lowest classes in Tang and Song times—slaves and servants in affluent households—shared their

sleeping spaces with others or with the livestock. The houses of commoners, both rural and urban, were limited to a front gate of a specified
width, and commoners were forbidden to improve the appearance of
their homes with paint or decorative motifs.

The residences of wealthy landowners and officials were considerably
more spacious, comfortable, even luxuriant. Yet here, too, strict building
codes dictated the size and style of buildings, depending on rank.[1] The
number of rafters, beams, and corbelled brackets, and the colors, symbols, and decoration on all structural elements, were subject to regulation
according to the social status of the owner.

The first priority of household architecture among the affluent was an
ancestral hall, as Zhu Xi spelled out in his *Family Rituals* (*Jiali*), first published in 1305: "When a gentleman plans to build a house, he first erects
an ancestral hall to the east of the main room of his house." The ancestral
hall, where male descendants sacrificed in front of an altar to the spirit
tablets of the ancestors, was the spiritual center of the upper-class family.[2]
In addition, most upper-class residences included a reception hall, master's rooms, private spaces for family members, and servants' quarters.
A garden with a pond and a pavilion created the contemplative atmosphere that was considered indispensable for a scholarly lifestyle. In
the Northern Song capital, Kaifeng, the tile-roofed compounds of high
officials may have covered a walled-in area of three *mu* (1,700 square
meters), as we learn from Su Shi's poem of 1084 to Wang Anshi. Most
private homes consisted of one story only, though in the crowded southern capital of Hangzhou, two-story buildings, offering more space and
better ventilation in the stifling summer heat, emerged along the main
street.

Even emperors had to contend with building restrictions set by the
founding Song emperor, Taizu, who forbade any colors other than purple
and white in the Imperial Palace. Successive sacred rulers respected his
will.[3] Regardless of the many regulations, the rich and powerful managed
to build luxurious residences, spending 200,000 cash and more on just
one hall. At the beginning of the dynasty, Zhao Pu (921–991), Taizu's influential advisor, used only the best building materials on his own home.
"When Zhao Pu had his residence built he spent more than 1,200 strings
of cash for [special] hemp-pounded plasterwork . . . All [his] houses were
covered with wooden boards instead of coarse bamboo mats."[4]

In 1202 the politician and eccentric dandy Zhang Zi gave a short description of his residence on the northern outskirts of Hangzhou, boast-

ing more than eighty halls, houses, pavilions, bridges, ponds, and gardens, thus dwarfing the famous estates of Luoyang in Northern Song times.

> In the fall of 1187 I turned my old residence into a Buddhist temple
> . . . Thirteen years later in 1200, my mind gave birth to new plans
> that varied with the landscape . . . The East Ancestral Hall is the
> place to requite the emperor's favour and to worship the ancestors;
> the West Residence is the location for resting and for bringing up
> children; the South Lake takes care of the wind and moon; the North
> Garden is for entertaining guests and relatives; Mâdyamika Hut is
> for morning retreat to offer blessings in order to accumulate good
> karma; the Frugality Studio is for reading books during the day to
> cultivate learning in my old age . . . Indeed the "Maker of Things"
> [Nature] has not turned its back upon my small desire for peace and
> tranquility.[5]

"Limitless sums are squandered on the construction of lofty and elegant mansions, something which used to be forbidden," we learn from his contemporary Wang Mai (1184–1248), who disapproved of this practice.[6]

In the ninth century, the size of rooms was given in numbers of mats. Members of the upper class preferred to sit and sleep on woven bamboo mats spread on the swept floor. Sitting on the ground was regarded as the most appropriate posture for people of distinction. More than two centuries later in conservative families such as that of chief councilor Sima Guang, household life was still organized around mats spread over tiled floors. He vigorously opposed the fashionable habit of sitting on chairs, particularly in the case of women. In the late twelfth century Lu You noted that in the past a woman of a well-bred family was ridiculed for her lack of manners when she sat on a chair. But now tables of various heights, along with stools and screens, had become indispensable, and most upper-class households had moved from the floor to wooden chairs with a back rest.[7]

The rich embellished their residences with patterned silk curtains, blinds of various styles, and embroidered wall hangings, while the water clock's "drip drip . . . slowly pushes the day to dawn."[8] The members of affluent families expressed their status even in the selection of everyday household articles. They distinguished roughly woven mats and rattan mats from elegant bamboo mats with dragon and phoenix patterns. They preferred chests made of five colors of canes or of white rattan. They knew that Taizhou manufactured the finest gold lacquered articles, Guangzhou was the source for tortoise leather, and shark skin leather had to come from Wenzhou and other coastal places.[9] In the ladies' quarter, translucent and embroidered curtains of gauze and other materials, gold incense burners in the shape of lions, rhinoceros horn cups, embroidered silk quilts, scarlet net tassels, carved jade dragons, and jade mirrors were regarded as essential.

Compared with the Tang dynasty, only a few Song gold and silver objects have come down to us, although the names of a good number of goldsmiths are known. In the Tang dynasty, dishes, plates, cups, bowls, cases, jugs, incense burners, phoenix hairpins, perfume bags, and jewelry made of gold, silver, and gold-plated silver reached near-perfection. One reason for the scarcity in the Song may be that objects made of solid gold were reserved for the emperor and his family. Officials could use gold goblets and bowls only if these items were gifts from the emperor.[10] But another reason may have been a fundamental change of aesthetic values among the educated Confucian elite. The excellent, diversified, affordable, and technically new and thus fashionable Song ceramic wares from the five famous kilns of Ding, Ru, Jun, Guan, and Ge embodied a new taste with respect to purity, shape, and materials. Monochrome glazes mirrored the refined taste of imperial households and those of scholar-officials. The masterly execution of flower, fish, bird, dragon, and cloud motifs hand-painted, carved, or impressed on these items from the kilns of Dingzhou and Cizhou, along with ink-painted scenes from daily life or nature, displayed a fresh appreciation of reality and a new understanding of beauty.

In the kilns of Ru, Jun, Longquan, and Jingdezhen, the repertoire was expanded by a wide range of superb glazes using special effects, in particular *craquelée,* which was renowned for the fineness, smoothness, and coolness or warmth of the glaze to the touch.[11] In Song ceramics, unchallenged standards of artistic achievement and a demand for high-quality wares were brilliantly matched with mass-production techniques dictated by a growing consumer economy. The production of ceramic wares in Jingdezhen, the Town of Manifest Virtue in Jiangxi province, started during the reign period called Manifest Virtue (1004–1007) of Emperor Zhenzong. A few centuries later Jingdezhen would become the most famous porcelain production center in the world.

The government had an interest in the change of taste from precious metals to ceramics, and indeed may have had a hand in promoting it. If the use of gold and silver for household articles had continued on the same scale as it was practiced in the Tang dynasty, this would have presented a number of difficulties for a striving economy dependent on the circulation of metal coins and a government buying peace by subsidizing alien regimes with silver. The upper classes did not stop hoarding metal dishes or collecting dragon and phoenix hairpins and small cups and plates made of precious metals. But as the range of ceramics available on the market increased—from the attractive yellowish-brown coarseness of a bowl to delicate and refined wares suitable for a scholar's studio or tea ceremony and precious enough to be collected—gold and silver wares no longer held the same sort of attraction and social prestige for their owners as they had in Tang times.

Personal Transportation

Sedan chairs, closed to all sides and carried by porters, were not common in early Song times. During the eleventh century, many scholar-officials considered sedan chairs, carried by four or eight porters, to be an inappropriate substitution of human labor for work that should be done by animals.[12] Only when officials became old or suffered from bad health were they privileged to use sedan chairs. When the emperor resided in the capital, officials were obliged to ride on horseback, though top-ranking officials might ride in a leather-decorated horse-drawn carriage with red curtains drawn. Upper-class ladies preferred perfumed carriages.

Restrictions on the use of sedan chairs were removed toward the end of the eleventh century, and by Southern Song times sedan chairs had become a common means of transport. The reason for the change of attitude may have had to do with the new capital of Hangzhou, where streets were paved and thus a sedan chair was safer than riding on horseback. Sedan chairs also allowed officials to flaunt their exclusive status in full view of the public. Commoners always had to immediately dismount and stand away from officials when they passed by. Apart from old and sick women, who might enjoy the comfort of a curtained sedan chair, commoners were not allowed to hire sedan chairs under any circumstances.[13] They had to walk, or—if they could afford it—they made themselves comfortable in roughly fashioned bamboo chairs carried by two laborers.

Sometimes they endured a bumpy ride in a small cart pulled by an ox or mule.

Khitan warriors and their wives journeyed on saddled horses, while their family members rode in carts furnished with tents and pavilions. Nobles moving their households across the wide plains and hill country of the north preferred huge and rather comfortable carpet carts drawn by a two-hump camel. Fitted with wheels whose diameter was taller than a man, these carts were lightweight but sturdily constructed. The long-bodied cart, which was narrow in the front and wide in the rear, consisted of three compartments. The front compartment was covered by a large carpet and reserved for the master. During daytime travel, curtains made of blue felt were rolled up to the top. When resting at evening the curtains were let down. The central compartment, closed to all sides, was situated just above the axle of the cart. This was the place where the mistress sojourned. The third compartment for the servant was structurally similar to the front one but considerably smaller. To the Song, these huge camel-drawn carts appeared rather exotic and un-Chinese.

Hygiene and Cosmetics

Sima Guang informs us that servants and concubines of the inner (women's) and outer quarters had to rise at the first crow of the cock. After combing their hair, washing, and getting dressed, they started their daily work. Unlike officials, who every tenth day were entitled to take one day off from work, commoners, merchants, and farmers worked every day except during annual festivals. From ancient times it had been the custom that officials used their day off to take a bath and wash their long hair, which was normally tied up under their official hat or other headgear. Commoners and peasants covered their heads with pieces of cloth or large broad-rimmed bamboo or straw hats fastened under the chin. Khitan men followed the northern nomadic practice of shaving their heads bald, or leaving only a fringe of hair at the back of the head. But at the temples they grew their hair so long that it would sometimes hang down to the shoulders.[14]

Normally, upper-class men and women washed their face and hands in the morning with liquid herbal soap in a bowl of water, and the men shaved their faces clean. If a man grew a beard, it was a moustache and goatee. Many people regularly bathed in their own homes, but for those without this private luxury, commercial bathing establishments number-

ing in the hundreds in all major cities and towns provided comfortable facilities. The keepers of bathing establishments in Hangzhou were
organized into a "fragrant water guild." As a rule, baths were taken in
cold water, but hot-water bathing was not uncommon. The Arabs, with
whom the Song traded, considered the Chinese to be dirty because "they
did not wash themselves with water after having defecated, but wiped
themselves with Chinese paper."[15]

Hygiene in the coastal provinces was better developed than it was
among the northern Chinese. Bo Juyi (772–846), who was a northerner,
describes in a poem how one morning he took a bath for the first time in
a year. The Sichuanese had a reputation for washing their bodies only
twice in their lifetime—after being born and after dying. But even some
famous contemporaries who hailed from the cleanliness-obsessed southeast accepted the practice of bathing only reluctantly and preferred to appear untidy in public. The chief councilor Wang Anshi was known for
the dirtiness of his person and his repulsively unkempt head of hair. Not
surprisingly, most people were tormented by parasites of all sorts, especially lice "swarming together behind the belt and robe, then climbing in
droves to the edge of the fur collar." Insects and other pests were unin-
vited but frequent visitors in bed.[16]

The general condition of teeth seems to have been lamentable and a
matter of great individual concern. Instead of using a toothbrush, the
Chinese wiped their teeth and gums with a piece of cloth after eating. In
the early ninth century the famous Han Yu describes how "last year I lost
an incisor, this year a molar."[17] By the time he was forty-two, two thirds
of his teeth were gone, probably a result of vitamin B1 deficiency (a disease known as beriberi). He knew that, for a person of his age and position in society, his appearance shocked people, and he admitted to having
problems eating and pronouncing words clearly.

We do not know the bathing habits of women, but we may deduce
from the many poets who expressed admiration for the court ladies' delicate and smooth complexions that women cared a lot more about maintaining a clean and attractive appearance than did their male partners.
From finds among the extravagant wardrobes of Huang Sheng and
Madame Zhou, who lived in the thirteenth century, we have material evidence that towels, kerchiefs, perfume, and sanitary napkins made of silk
were among the standard toilet articles of a lady (Fig. 20).

In late Tang times women wore their hair in extravagant styles bound
together in various forms of artful buns or horns, sometimes adorned

Fig. 20 *Madame Zhou Doing Her Morning Toilet.* Northern Song, 1099. Mural painting in tomb no. 1, Yuxian, Henan province. Su Bai.

with the ice-blue feathers of the kingfisher. Many depictions of Song ladies sitting in front of a mirror at a toilet table and being attended by servants give evidence that elaborate hairstyles were still in fashion.[18] Girls arranged their hair in coils, and when a woman "tied up her hair," it was a symbolic act meaning that she had married. Hairstyles very often indicated which stratum of society women belonged to. Women from the lower classes wore a modest bun held together with a hair-band. Towering tied-up hair—often treated with paste to make it appear sleek and shiny, sometimes boosted by additional hairpieces, and often decorated and kept in place by headdresses, jewels, various single- or double-forked hairpins, and voluminous hats—clearly help to identify a woman as a member of the official or gentry class. A portrait of Empress Liu, wife of Emperor Zhenzong, painted in 1033 or shortly thereafter, shows her wearing a crown decorated with pearls and beads, adorned with twenty-two female Daoist immortals and dragons surrounded by floating clouds and blossoms (Fig. 21).[19]

Fig. 21 Portrait of Empress Liu (969–1033), ca. 1033 or after. Her crown is
adorned with twenty-two female Daoist immortals, nine dragons, another
dragon-riding female immortal, clouds and blossoms, pearls and beads.
National Palace Museum, Taiwan, Republic of China.

Men who spent time in the outside world showed considerable tanning of the skin. With women it was different. By the age of eleven or twelve, many girls used a mirror and learned how to take care of their complexion. Cosmetic parlors specialized in facial masks to protect against the biting winter winds. Such treatments, it was said, ensured that faces uncovered in spring would have the beauty of jade.[20] The portrait of Empress Liu suggests that a great variety of facial cosmetics were in use. The early Yuan scholar-official Wang Yun commented on the portrait in 1277: "Purple pigment in the shape of two rectangular leaves covers her face from the eyebrows downward including her cheeks. The [b]ridge of her nose is emphasized by leaving the natural skin unpainted. One gets the impression that the face was partially covered by a thin purple gauze veil." This make-up was known as the "pretty smile."[21] Fashionable ladies in the capital wore white make-up and powder of a deep rose shade on their cheeks. A pallid complexion seems to corroborate the seclusion of women and was thought to reflect the purity of a woman's conduct and character. Pallor, along with make-up, was also consistent with Song Chinese notions of eroticism, though to suggest such a thing would have scandalized the most liberal Confucian critic. Yet we read in an anonymous song lyric,

> In my transparent purple silk nightgown
> my white skin glows
> fragrant and smooth as snow.[22]

Another cosmetic treatment that seemed to introduce an element of eroticism was plucking eyebrows and penciling them back with a black line—a fashion carried over from Tang times. Men also plucked hair for reasons of vanity, especially white hairs on the day they appeared among the black ones, as Mei Yaochen explained. In Tang times women painted flower motifs on their faces and applied red lip color in such a way as to give the impression of a small mouth in the shape of a butterfly. In Song times, lips almost regained the natural shape of the mouth, though they continued to be painted red. Fingernails were also artificially tinted.[23]

Tattooing has a long history in China. Criminals were tattooed or branded on the face with small or large characters, depending on the seriousness of the crime. Tattoos on the forehead, the cheeks, or behind the ears often resulted in mutilation. When tattooing became a fashion rather than a punishment, the dandies of Kaifeng sometimes tattooed their whole body with blue pigments in designs of dragons, birds, human figures, landscapes, and poems.[24] They may have envisioned their bodies as a powerful and symbolic work of art. Such extensive tattooing caused considerable pain during execution, however, and was also risky and expensive. At the beginning of Southern Song times, whole-body tattoos disappeared, though the tattooing of a single motif continued. Many jealous wives of scholar-officials had the faces of maid-servants marked with a tattoo in the shape of the moon or a coin. These marks were intended to punish and humiliate their bearers, in the same way that branding soldiers on the lower limb—a practice known as "patterning the leg"—discouraged them from desertion.[25]

Foot Binding

Tang poets do not mention foot binding. This crippling practice seems to have begun among the upper classes of the Song Chinese and then spread into all good families. Bandages were used to wrap up the feet of young girls so tightly that the four small toes were forced under the foot and the arch was distorted and exaggerated. The objective was to fit the deformed foot—about half the length of a normal foot—into tiny shoes fashioned of silk in various styles.[26] This excruciatingly painful process started when girls were very young and their bones still malleable and continued over many years until the feet assumed their final tiny "golden lotus" shape. At this point the bandages became indispensable for stabilizing the feet when walking.

The name "golden lotus" may have been adopted from a concubine's dance performed on lotus blossoms made of gold-leaf strewn on the ground. The foot binding practice made its appearance in the tenth century among professional dancers, who may have wanted to beautify and strengthen their feet and make them "elegant-looking."[27] *Talks While the Plough Is Resting (Chuogeng lu)* of 1344 confirms that "the custom of binding the feet first appeared under the Five Dynasties and was not widely adopted before the reign periods Xining and Yuanfu [1068–1085]. But recently this fashion has become so common that it is considered shameful not to adopt it."[28]

Foot binding continued to be rare in the eleventh century, but archaeological evidence from the thirteenth century, including silk shoes, socks, and pointed-toe shoes made of silver sheet, whose shape resembles a "small foot boat," as well as a 210-centimeter-long and 9-centimeter-

wide bandage made of yellowish silk gauze, give evidence that by this
time foot binding had become widespread among women in scholar-official and landed gentry households. Many names appeared for the bow-
shaped shoes intended to beautify the "golden lotus." These included
"ornamented to the base," "quickly mounting the horse," or "palace
style firm."[29]

The foot binding craze did not go uncontested in word and deed. The
women among the sixth-generation descendants of the Confucian philosopher Cheng Yi (1033–1107) refused to have their ear lobes pierced or
their feet bound. And around 1274 Che Ruorui voiced his disagreement:
"When foot binding appeared I do not know. I wonder what good it is to
have atrophied small feet by making an innocent child of five or six years
old to undergo such endless torture."[30] Critics of foot binding could certainly be found, but they constituted a small minority. The silk shoes of
Madame Zhou, who lived in the middle of the thirteenth century, measured 22 centimeters long, 6 centimeters wide, and 4 centimeters high,
which means that her feet were not bound. But most upper-class women
mastered foot binding techniques and inflicted them upon their young
daughters, transforming the fashion of a professional group from the entertainment quarters into an unmistakable symbol of Chinese femininity
that lasted until the end of the imperial period.

Foot binding can most accurately be thought of as a sort of surgery
without a scalpel. It permanently altered a woman's body, mobility, and
agility and thus changed her perception of agency as a physical being in
the outside world.[31] Women with "golden lotus" were forced to walk
with small steps, and for the most part they preferred sitting. Stepping
outside the inner quarters in thin silk shoes with soles made of hemp and
then walking over long distances with crippled feet was painful. In the
thirteenth century, if an upper-class woman wanted to go out, she had to
rely on some means of transport other than her own two legs.

During the Southern Song and continuing for the rest of the imperial
period, this limited mobility meant that women were more or less confined to the domestic sphere. The polo-playing, horse-riding ladies of the
Tang dynasty, not to mention the voluptuous and well-fed concubines of
that time, were a far cry from the feminine ideal praised by Song literati
and painted by artists. The perfect woman was smaller than a man, slender, soft, and fragile. She stayed at home, serving her parents, husband,
and family and educating her small children. Song women who bound
the feet of their daughters were behaving in accordance with the Neo-

Confucian orthodoxy that a woman's place was in the home. Over the centuries, as foot binding became common among the wives and daughters of most households, including commoners who could afford the loss of labor that it entailed, the personal freedom of women as it had existed in the Tang and Northern Song was abolished. Foot binding made women dependent on the master of a household, and the subjugation of women to men continued from the second half of the thirteenth century until the end of the empire.

The ideal upper-class man also changed over the course of the Song. He was thought to be a refined person of slim stature and effeminate behavior. For many of these men, the small steps and movements of women with bound feet may have had an irresistible erotic appeal. The unbound foot may have been seen as a private part of a woman's body—not unlike genitalia—and the ritualized, eroticized unbinding of the foot may have aroused the male libido. But the women who practiced and popularized foot binding could have been responding to another change in Song times: the presence of concubines in the household and the growing entertainment market that was transforming girls and women into commodities.[32]

In Tang times a husband took a concubine only when his wife did not bear him a son. He chose her through the connections of his family network. By Song times, when the money economy permeated all quarters of society, well-to-do men purchased women to serve as concubines at home. As concubinage flourished in a highly competitive market, female attractiveness gained ever more importance in the minds of all Song people, including wives and other family members. "Golden lotus" feet may have tipped the scale in favor of one concubine over another, and wives may have adopted the practice so that their daughters could compete for the affections of future husbands. To maximize the chances for a good marriage, mothers in good families not only groomed their daughters to become virtuous and modest wives but also enhanced their attractiveness by binding their feet, in keeping with a new standard of female beauty that would go unchallenged for hundreds of years.

Clothing

The famous official Shen Gua (1031–1095) maintained that there were no fixed rules in the old sources for formal clothes and hats.[33] In Song times, however, dress regulations stipulating the materials and colors of the wardrobe followed the Tang model for the most part. Outer garments of officials were divided into official robes and private clothes for daily use. In addition, there were many types of half-length loosely fitting leisurewear with long sleeves—mostly pictured on paintings—made of silk or other materials. The style of clothing worn for leisure was simple and followed practicality and fashion but was not formally regulated.

Song garments and robes worn by scholar-officials in both private and official settings had several features in common. They were usually made of silk and tailored with a round collar and closed along the right side, following the ancient tradition praised by Confucius. Official robes were roomier than private ones, and the sleeves were extremely long and wide. Under their robes, men wore several layers of different jackets and shirts, special types of short skirts and half-length trousers, and silk underwear. Some of these garments were lined or silk-wadded for added warmth in the winter. The colors of official robes changed several times in the dynasty, but usually officials of ranks one to three were allowed to wear purple, ranks four and five wore crimson, and ranks six to nine wore green or blue. Wives and mothers of officials were allowed to dress in colors indicating the rank of their husbands or sons, as they had done in Tang times.[34]

The Chinese wardrobe incorporated some elements of "barbarian" origin, such as a short tight-sleeved jacket useful when riding and shooting, with a girdle whose ends hung down. The outfit was completed with protective high boots. Only officials were entitled to use jade, gold, silver, or rhinoceros horn to decorate their belts. In winter, people who could afford them wore fur coats. When inspector Mei Yaochen made his rounds in the Yongji granaries on a chilly winter night in 1052, he remarked that "the warmth is gone from my tattered fox-fur robe, mended with patches of yellow dog skin." Commoners were allowed to wear white (and sometimes black) clothing made of hemp and ramie. The poorest of the poor—exploited miners and boat-towers on the Yangzi—worked naked. Old men in remote villages were seen "with no robes to wear holding grandchildren in their arms."[35]

In the eleventh century, the clothing of barefoot country women was simple—a farm dress with a blue skirt. The wardrobe of affluent women, on the other hand, included hundreds of robes, open coats, long and short jackets, trousers, skirts, vests, and underwear of various cuts, made of silk, cotton, and ramie woven in different weaves and richly patterned.

Long ritual robes, opened on the front, were fitted with extremely long sleeves that reached down over more than half the length of the robe. A long skirt was fitted under the bust. Very often a collar measuring more than 2 meters long but only 10 centimeters wide was worn like a scarf and held in shape by weights made of jade appended to both ends. As life-size clay sculptures of ladies in waiting made in 1087 and preserved in a prominent shrine in Shanxi make clear, it was also common to dress in several layers of garments under a long open coat with tight sleeves in bluish or greenish colors.[36]

Emperor Huizong captured the appearance of a cultured and culti-vated palace lady in this short verse:

> Fine eyebrows, cinnabar cheeks, and a tiny waist,
> She's perfect for the long tight-fitting dress now in vogue.
> Her hair adorned with palace blossoms, in the kingfisher style,
> The jeweled cicada and pearled butterfly are about to fly away.[37]

In Southern Song times, elegant translucent sleeveless vests came into fashion for womenswear.

The weavers of Hangzhou produced silks for ladies' wardrobes bear-ing appropriate names for the months in which the articles were to be worn, such as spring streamers, lantern globes, and boat racing. Floral motifs also symbolized the seasons. Ladies of aristocratic families were allowed to use gold along the borders of clothing worn in the private sphere. Garments and adornments that appeared on women in the inner quarters of the palace in the morning became the latest fashion among commoners in the evening.

Archaeological finds suggest that the heavy, colorful *jin* brocades pop-ular during Tang times—and often decorated with foreign motifs and symbols—gave way in the Song to gauze (leno) weaves.[38] The Tang bro-cades gave the impression of being woven with gold (*jin*) threads, while the Song silks were mostly patterned with rather unobtrusive floral ten-drils and other delicate designs such as peonies, hibiscus, plum blossoms, bamboo leaves, lotus, chrysanthemum, and camellia (Fig. 22). The Song elite's preference for light-weight, elegant silks may be viewed as a textile equivalent to their predilection for glazed ceramics over heavy metal housewares. The preference for leno weaves over *jin* brocades is best doc-umented in the figures of annual tax production. Here leno production

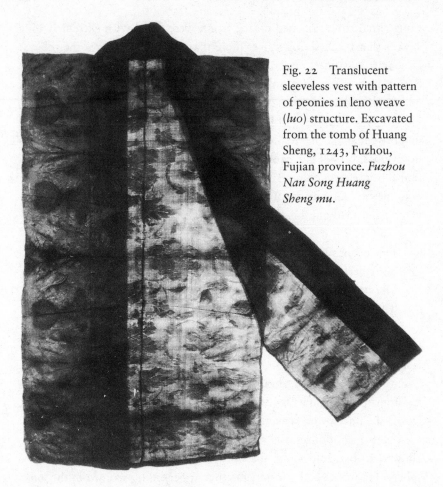

Fig. 22   Translucent
sleeveless vest with pattern
of peonies in leno weave
(*luo*) structure. Excavated
from the tomb of Huang
Sheng, 1243, Fuzhou,
Fujian province. *Fuzhou
Nan Song Huang
Sheng mu.*

outnumbers *jin* brocades by thirteen times. The pictorial evidence from
the Song and Yuan periods shows drawlooms dressed for the production
of leno weaves, not *jin* (Fig. 23).

The Khitans were culturally closer to the Tang than to the Song, as may
be seen from the gold and silver items they continued to produce.[39] Under
Tang influence, their "barbarian" clothing had gradually shifted to conform with the customs of their sedentary neighbors to the south, as they
expanded their wardrobe of wool, felt, fur, and leather to include silk
jackets and robes fashioned in the Chinese style, though not identical.
Khitan men wore a tight-sleeved long gown with a round collar and a
leather girdle to which was attached "the bow and sword, a towel, a
leather bag with counting sticks, and a grindstone." Their embellished
felt hats, called "swinging headgear while walking," were also distinc-

Fig. 23   Loom (*zhiji*) for weaving leno (*luo*) fabrics. Southern Song dynasty, thirteenth century. *Nongshu*, j. 24:7ab.

tive. Khitan women dressed in tight-sleeved coats, with a jade ring attached to the waistband of their skirts. In most cases even the tight sleeves were fashioned wide enough to bury their hands. Both men and women wore various sorts of trousers under their coats. Leather boots and sometimes leather shoes completed the wardrobe. The preferred colors of the Khitans' comfortable unlined garments were red and green. Khitan nobles wore sable furs of a purplish black color and pure white ermine. Even the lower classes dressed in warm furs of sable, sheep, mole, and desert fox.[40]

In the tenth century, Khitan rulers favored garments in the Chinese style, and in 937 Emperor Taizong of the Liao dynasty donned the attire of a real Son of Heaven. In 947, Han Chinese officials in service to the Liao wore Chinese garments, while ethnic Khitan officials (as well as the empress) continued to wear their national garments, including the indispensable felt hat. In the opinion of Song Chinese, these garments were buttoned the wrong ("barbarian") way, meaning on the left side, but at least they were distinguished in cut and style from the Han garments that the Khitan had inherited from the Tang. After 970, all Khitan top officials were ordered to dress in Chinese style, whereas lower officials of Khitan origin dressed in the native garments worn for the Great Willowtree Shooting ceremony, which included prayers for rain. In 1055 the emperor ruled that all Khitan officials, not just the top tier, must wear Chinese-style clothes.[41]

In addition to the characteristic Khitan and imperial Han symbols of sun, moon, and mountain, the Chinese dragon made an appearance on the Khitan wardrobe around this time, as did the twelve insignia known from the Tang and earlier Chinese dynasties. The residents of the cities were "all accustomed to wearing Chinese clothing, [but] there are among them those who wear 'barbarian' clothing," and the Liao emperor wore "Chinese clothing with a yellow gauze robe" when he received Chinese envoys.[42] Thus, the Khitan in the southern region underwent a thorough sinicization in clothing during the tenth century.

The Liao dynasty continued to manufacture well-established *jin* brocade patterns, but they added new, large designs that employed gold-thread weaving techniques not previously known in China. After the Jin dynasty conquered the Liao in 1125, it acquired this expertise. A Liao order of 1027 prohibiting garments fashioned from variegated silk and fabrics woven with bright gold thread indicates that a wide range of luxurious silk fabrics were available to the Khitan nobility for tailoring into glamorous garments, though even imperial relatives had to ask permission before wearing them.[43]

Entertainment and the Floating World

The Chinese calendar included a number of annual festivals in which most people of the Song empire participated. During these periods of days off from work, people made family visits, gathered with their social peers, took sight-seeing excursions, and engaged in other sorts of entertainment.[44] The most celebrated festival was the lunar New Year between the fifteenth of January and the fifteenth of February, but there were many others. At the Lantern Festival around the middle of the first month, the residents of big cities displayed their illuminated, colorful lanterns in the shapes of flying dragons and playful lions, and the guilds held big processions in the streets of the capital. After eating the feast of cold food (*hanjie*) and sweeping the graves of the ancestors (*qingming*) in early April, people participated in the famous Dragon Boat Race on the Lake of Golden Brightness just outside Kaifeng and, later, on the West Lake of Hangzhou.

In October in Hangzhou the viewing of the tidal wave rolling up the

Qiantang River drew a crowd in the tens of thousands. Who would have missed an event described as a silver thread appearing at the horizon, approaching as a wall of jade, a snow-laden ridge, convulsing and shaking, roaring like thunder, swallowing up the sky and inundating the sun? Several hundred youths with tattooed bodies loosened their hair and went swimming in the roaring waves, holding up colored banners.[45] On other festival days Hangzhou residents visited the superb garden landscape of the West Lake, rented a boat for a rowing party, enjoyed the changing atmosphere and colors during the four seasons, and went on picnics, which were popular even in the winter snow.

Zhou Mi described the fairy-tale quality of late twelfth-century life among Southern Song elites, reserved almost exclusively for men: "I dragged my robe to the residence of prominent people . . . We sang songs in the morning and made merry in the evening, passing the years and the months in drinking and play. We thought that man's life should be like this, not realizing that happiness in times of peace was difficult to come by."[46] In the late twelfth century, the rich and powerful were often invited to the enormous Riding-the-Mist Pavilion of Zhang Zi, where highly ritualized and elegant peony parties were enjoyed. More than a hundred singing girls and musicians performed the famous songs about peony blossoms of previous masters, while courtesans served wine and food.

> After all the guests had arrived and were seated in an empty hall, there was nothing but silence . . . From behind the screen an unusual fragrance came forth, pervading the entire hall . . . There were ten famous singing girls all dressed in white, with their head ornaments and collars shaped like peony blossoms. They each had a "hall-illuminating" red peony blossom on their heads . . . After the singing was over and music played, they retired from the hall. The screen was then rolled down and the guests chatted with each other at ease. A long while later the fragrance was again issued and the screen rolled up as before. The famous singing girls came out in different garments and flower decorations. If they pinned white blossoms in their hair, they wore purple garments, purple blossoms, pale yellow garments, and yellow blossoms, red garments. In this fashion they served ten rounds of wine and changed garments and blossoms ten times . . . In the candle light and fragrant mists, with singing and music resounding all at once, the guests felt they were on a fairy trip.[47]

Men of the upper class had many ways to spend their spare time and money in the congenial company of colleagues and friends. They could join the Poetry Society of the West Lake, the Society for Vigorous Debates, the Dark Red-Green Society, which concentrated on literature to be performed on stage, the Society of Painted Leather for the friends of shadow plays, and various music societies. Officers of the army became members of the Club of Archers or the Club of Crossbowmen. There were clubs for physical exercise, for playing ball games, for boxing, wrestling, and fishing. Even the rough game of polo was organized into clubs.

Wine shops attracted male customers by hanging out a red-painted twig, crimson curtains, and gardenia lanterns. Taverns serving only wine, where guests could stay as long as they needed "to hit the cup," were called strict wine taverns. At the multilevel wine restaurants, called "mountains," a selection of food on a tray was presented to patrons, who made their choices and placed their orders.[48] If someone did not know the custom and started eating the samples with his chopsticks, he would be laughed at. A small order of food would have cost 100 to 5,000 cash. A lower-rank official earning a monthly salary of 12,000 to 15,000 cash would have to settle for the medium-priced dishes. "Nunnery wine shops" were furnished with separate bed chambers, and prostitution was part of their regular business. The government monopolized alcohol production and thus sales, and establishments that combined alcohol with prostitution served as a source of state revenue. Some of the largest of these houses were reserved for officials and run by the treasury.

Eating was a great source of pleasure in Song times. Apart from fervent Buddhists who lived as vegetarians and Daoists who abstained from cereals, the Chinese did not observe religious taboos around food. A great banquet could consist of more than forty different dishes of fresh meat (not including beef), fish, and poultry, more than forty dishes of fruit, sugar, and honey, almost thirty dishes of dried fish, and more than fifty desserts, sweets, and biscuits. The region of Hangzhou alone brewed and manufactured more than fifty-four varieties of rice wine, spirits, and liquors.[49]

Formerly in [Kaifeng] there were restaurants serving noodles in the southern style and tea shops with Sichuan style cooking for clients from south of the Yangzi River who did not like the northern kitchen. Since the southward migration started more than two hun-

dred years ago, people got acquainted with the water and soil and
the origin of dishes and beverages was mixed up. Now people no
longer distinguish between the southern and northern kitchen.[50]

Tea prepared with boiling water was consumed at home, at street vendors' stalls, and in special teashops. The eleventh-century official and calligrapher Cai Xiang described the quality, color, fragrance, and taste of
tea and the tools used for its preparation in his *Monograph on Tea*
(*Chalu*).[51] Highest quality teas such as Best Tea under Heaven or Dragon
and Phoenix Tea cost up to 75 grams of gold for 600 grams of tea leaves.
People of all trades came together in teashops to enjoy this stimulating
drink. In some of them people met to play music and sing songs. In others, known as "market heads," the guests consisted of merchants and
craftsmen negotiating commissions or looking for good workmen. Some
teashops were famous for their exhibition of hanging scrolls.[52] Musicians
played plum blossom songs, which earlier had always been performed in
summer, when guests enjoyed plum blossom wine. In winter, salted soybean soup was served instead of tea. Other teashops operated brothels
camouflaged as "water teashops" and "flower teashops."

Hangzhou hosted no fewer than twenty-three entertainment districts
and fifty-five classes of entertainers: imperial poetry laureates, members
of the Imperial Painting Academy, masters of the narrative arts including
storytellers of historical subjects and Buddhist sutras, female singers and
other musicians, joke tellers and dialect imitators, comedians and puppet
players, clowns, acrobats, jugglers, rope dancers, wrestlers and boxers,
weight lifters and archers, and animal trainers. New forms of literature originated in these districts, and texts were set to popular melodies
for performance there. For Song men though not for respectable women,
the entertainment quarters were the amusement parks of the thirteenth
century.

Health Care and Welfare

In premodern times, most sick, old, and handicapped people in need of
health care and welfare depended on private households, not on public
attention and allocation. In the Confucian system where the younger generation was expected to care for and support their elders in a loving and
respectful way, families were understood to be social as well as economic
units. If families did not fulfill the tasks expected of them, however, the

situation of a destitute and sick individual became desperate. Government institutions were hardly ever able to cope with this social problem, though sometimes Buddhist monasteries supplied minimal relief. Despite these challenges, the medical system as it existed in Song times worked better than in any previous dynasty.

Before Song times, most upper-class households had a family retainer skilled in medicine. But Song scholar-officials, who regarded themselves as the only true experts in almost all fields of life, took on the task of looking after the sick. When an upper-class man felt ill, he would consult a colleague for diagnosis and treatment. There were academically trained physicians employed in government institutions, but their medical and anatomical knowledge may have differed little from that of run-of-the-mill practitioners whose knowledge and reputation came from their fathers or other family members. These male practitioners made their living by peddling drugs or offering massage, and their social status was rather low. They were not even organized into a guild.

All serious healers, whether trained academically or not, learned how to make a diagnosis by feeling someone's pulse and relating the sounds to a complicated pulse system handed down through the ages. Most practitioners used the traditional techniques of acupuncture and moxibustion (burning substances on the skin to heal or relieve pain) and knew recipes for preparing herbal drugs of various sorts. In the eleventh-century understanding of scholar-officials, a human disease resulted from unbalanced living and working conditions. Sima Guang explained in a letter to his friend Fan Zhen that "human diseases arise if something is either present in excess or is lacking. They are based on a surfeit of *yin* or *yang*, wind or rain, darkness or light. They result from imbalances of hunger and satiation, cold and heat, work and leisure, joy and anger. If both sides are balanced, there is no disease. *Yin* and *yang*, wind and rain, darkness and light all derive from Heaven. Hunger and satiation, cold and heat, work and leisure, joy and anger—these are affected by humans . . . If humans do not maintain equilibrium in their actions, they are invaded by diseases."[53]

Women folk attended the sick and nursed the invalid and aged in their own households. Consultation with a doctor was far more delicate when the patient was a woman, since a physical examination of a sick woman by a male physician would have violated the Confucian code of ethics. Diagnosis had to be made solely on the basis of the patient's description of her symptoms and the taking of her pulse. Poor families could not afford to consult a medical practitioner or purchase medicine under any circumstances, although a number of drug stores offered their services. Midwives of all social classes, who learned their profession from older, experienced women, helped pregnant women in the critical time just before and after childbirth.

Many Song emperors and officials realized the need for trained doctors with a better command of medical knowledge and experience in health matters, not only for their own class but for society as a whole. Thus academic education in these subjects received more official attention than before. In 1026 on order of Emperor Renzong, two life-sized human models with all the acupuncture points (354 holes for puncture) and channels on the surface were cast and placed in the Academy of Medicine and in a hall of Xiangguo Temple in Kaifeng. In the same year, Wang Weiyi wrote a monograph entitled *Illustrated Classic of the Bronze Man's Moxibustion and Acupuncture (Tongren yuxue zhenjiu tujing)* in three chapters. A good knowledge of anatomy and some experience was required for bone-setting and for placing needles that stimulate the release of endorphin, which we know today to be the brain's natural painkiller. Medical practitioners combined technical knowledge and experience with indispensable magic, cosmological considerations, and religious elements, and the result was a highly complex medical system.

Institutionalized medical education started in 1044 when the government established a Medical School Service. The total number of students may have amounted to 200 over a ten-year period.[54] After a wave of epidemics struck the empire between 1045 and 1060, a long overdue revision of medical texts took place under the government's supervision. In 1061 local medical schools with a curriculum similar to that of the Medical School Service were established for training physicians in their locality. Emperor Huizong aimed at improving the medical system by setting up a Medical School in 1103 comparable in its organization to the Imperial University. A new profession—literati physicians—opened up for elite families who otherwise might have sent their sons into the civil service. In 1115 local branches of the Medical School were established in the prefectures and counties, and after the migration to the south, the Medical School was resettled in Hangzhou, where four professors taught 250 students.[55]

By comparison with the number of people in the general population during the Northern Song, the services of hospitals and schools of medical education run by the government were almost nonexistent, but the basis was laid for a comparatively well-structured though still far from sufficient health care system for the poor and needy. At the beginning of the dynasty two hospitals in the eastern and western parts of Kaifeng called Hall of the Field of Good Fortune were opened to help abandoned old people and infants, along with the hungry and sick. Both halls were run by Buddhist monks and later became government institutions. In 1063 hospitals in the south and north of the city were added. Each of these institutions could take 300 patients, which meant that altogether 1,200 people could be accommodated in Kaifeng's hospital system.[56] During the last decades of the Northern Song, Halls to Remain to Be Cared For were established in the capital and in six regional towns.

Many people—not just doctors—considered themselves to be experts in drugs that could help restore or secure the physical well-being of patients. In the Northern Song, Chinese pharmacies, located near one another on certain streets and wards of the capital, prepared and sold medicine. The first government-run pharmacy in the history of medicine, the Imperial Pharmacy, was founded in 1076 in Kaifeng. Pharmacies gained even more importance to health and to the economy in Hangzhou. The number of officials ordered to dispense drugs to the needy and the number of drugstores specialized for illnesses and ailments increased during the Southern Song.[57]

Apart from governmental activities, the sick and destitute also benefited from private charity. In 1089 the official Su Shi donated fifty ounces of gold from his own purse to build the Peace and Happiness Hospital, which was open to all people in Hangzhou. Within three years the hospital had treated a thousand patients. By 1102 charity hospitals had been founded in all major cities. In 1132 two more charity hospitals, now called relief hospitals, were established for the poor, old, and destitute.[58] Pharmacists of the public Relief for the People drugstore dispensed drugs for free to the needy.

In the countryside, charity took the form of filial piety and was the responsibility of clan elders, who—if family assets allowed—set up charitable estates to support needy and impoverished kin. The eleventh-century reformer Fan Zhongyan founded the most famous charitable estate, though not the largest.[59] Income from the estates provided monthly allotments of cereals, aided orphaned children of relatives, secured their schooling, and helped to finance marriages, funerals, boy's capping ceremonies, and girl's hair-binding ceremonies. Very often the wife helped out by contributing from her own financial resources. But in many families, resources were insufficient to found a charitable estate, and very often a family was unable to maintain it, once established.

The charity of private households in the cities was not institutionalized, but it did help to ease the misery of the poor, sick, and destitute. The very rich living on Phoenix Hill supported whole families of poor or old people, who felt boundlessly indebted to their benefactors. Sometimes these elites gave quilted jackets to beggars or helped traders who had failed in their businesses. Occasionally they paid an impoverished family's expenses for a burial or a cremation. On winter nights when the streets were covered with snow, wealthy men would go to freezing shacks and put money into the cracks of the doors to relieve the suffering of those inside.[60]

When poor parents had no opportunity to place their infant with a well-to-do family and could not bring themselves to sell their son or daughter into slavery, they sometimes abandoned their child at the door of a residence or institution. During the mass immigration to the south, the number of foundlings increased dramatically. In 1138 responsible authorities prohibited the abandonment of children and opened orphanages in all counties of the empire to receive children whose parents could not raise them.[61] Still, the problem continued, and in 1248 another orphanage named Home of Compassion for Children was opened in the capital.

In modern terms, we could say that the Song people enjoyed an extraordinary degree of freedom of action in their private sphere, compared with other medieval societies. Yet they regarded themselves as obedient subjects of the Son of Heaven. Their daily activities followed well-established rules and regulations based on the prevalent Confucian norms of behavior that theoretically were binding on all members of society. However, the laissez-faire attitude that can be observed in economic matters pervaded all areas of private life, from preferences in house building and fashion to matters of hygiene, amusement, and charity. Only at the end of the thirteenth century, under Mongol rule, did the easiness of the self-determined Chinese lifestyle come to an end.

CONCLUSION

JUST over one thousand years ago the Song dynasty emerged as the most advanced civilization on earth. Its early emperors initiated a transformation of China based on rationality, efficiency, predictability, and economic dynamism—in short, the most pronounced features of enlightened modern capitalism. These innovative rulers relied heavily on an elite class of scholar-officials whom they recruited through a competitive civil service examination system. The education, experience, competence, and dedication of Song officials distinguished them not only from their aristocratic predecessors in the Tang dynasty but also from the elite of any other civilization on earth at that time. Chief councilors to the emperor in particular wielded political authority that was unprecedented in Chinese history. Yet Song China was neither despotic nor totalitarian. Administrative and economic efficiency was achieved not through control and surveillance of all societal activities, threat of punishment, or the terror of landlords but through an atmosphere of reliability, responsibility, and above all pragmatism. The low ratio of degree-holding administrators to people administered to, which stood at 1:7500 at the beginning of the thirteenth century, confirms the unequalled efficiency of the Song bureaucracy and the confidence people had in it.

The Three Doctrines—Confucianism, Buddhism, and Daoism—with their countless local folk-religious practices played a crucial role in everyday life. Buddhism was sanctioned by the court, and only Emperor Huizong preferred Daoism over all other creeds—a preference that contributed to his negligence of political affairs and was partly responsible for the collapse of the Northern Song. But regardless of the influence and practice of Daoist and Buddhist sects, which enriched the spiritual life of the masses, the Song dynasty was dominated by the ethical doctrine of Confucianism. This ancient creed formed the basis of education, examination, and both public and private rituals. It was effectively a Song state ideology. Confucian statecraft granted enough space for the transformative processes that distinguished the Song from all other dynasties in Chinese history. That Confucianism was ever-present at court is evident in the posthumous titles of the Emperor Renzong (Benevolent Ancestor), Xiaozong (Filial Ancestor), and Lizong (Principled Ancestor). *Ren* and *xiao* are key words in Confucian doctrine, while *li* refers to the Confucian Principle elucidated in Zhu Xi's School of Learning. These titles for emperors made their first appearance in Chinese history in Song times.

The distinctive qualities of Song statecraft formed part of a larger system of Confucian ethics that reached into every corner of Song society and influenced individuals from birth to burial. Yet Confucianism itself was reshaped and rationalized during this time, to open up new possibilities in the design of capital cities, in commerce and fashion, technology and science, painting, music, and literature. The revamped Confucian ideology that emerged from the philosophy of the Cheng brothers, Zhu, and other Song philosophers, its rationality and worldliness, permeated all levels of society and formed the bedrock of Chinese culture until the Communist Revolution. Nineteenth- and twentieth-century reformers excoriated Neo-Confucianism as a rigid system of thinking that prevented China from undertaking social and educational reforms and adopting technological advances. But as lively discussions in the Ming and Qing dynasties make clear, the "traditional" values inherited from the Song Neo-Confucians and handed down from generation to generation informed an understanding of chineseness and reinforced a sense of cultural identity that more than six centuries of political adversity could not shake. Though often attacked, the ethical system of "traditional China" helped to safeguard the nation from intellectual and cultural fragmentation or political disintegration.

A clear indication of the quality and stability of the Song government can be seen in a comparison of the tenure of Song emperors to those in other dynasties. From a total of 210 legitimate emperors in the 2,129 years of Chinese imperial history, the eighteen Song emperors ruled during roughly 15 percent of this entire period. While Chinese emperors overall ruled on average eight years, Song rulers ruled on average eighteen years. Only the Qing dynasty did better, and that was solely due to the sixty-year tenures of both the Kangxi and Qianlong emperors.

Of the three major early Chinese dynasties in the first millennium—the Han, the Tang, and the Song—it was the Song that invented a diplomatic strategy for establishing peaceful bilateral relations with its threatening neighbors. This new and pragmatic way of neutralizing the "barbaric" nomads on China's northern borders created long periods of peace that allowed standards of living to rise in cities and throughout the countryside. The eleventh-century philosopher and mathematician Shao Yong was justly proud of the unparalleled period of peace he enjoyed in his own lifetime: "I was born in a time of great peace, and I die in a time of great peace."

Agricultural technology and a functional system of land ownership laid the foundation for the Song's three centuries of prosperity. In many parts of the empire, the yields of Song farmers would not be surpassed until the twentieth century. Manuals written by experts popularized advances in agriculture and sericulture, and a state-funded investment and loan policy helped to protect farmers from ruinous debt. Self-managed farming households formed the backbone of the tax system, and a flourishing rural economy, with its millions of taxpayers contributing 10 percent or less of their yield, nourished economic growth and population increases that no region anywhere in the world could equal. Even in the thirteenth century, when the Mongol invasion caused the Song population to decline, almost half of humankind lived in China, and this mass of people enjoyed the highest per capita income in the world.

Chinese technological inventiveness can be seen in the various types of spindle-wheels, silk-reeling frames, water-powered silk, hemp, and ramie twisting frames, treadle-operated looms, and draw looms. This Song "industrial revolution," which took place between the eleventh and the thirteenth centuries, produced fashionable textile products in great quantity, which in turn spurred the creation of new markets and trade guilds. Song China surpassed medieval Europe in commercialization and consumption, in fiscal achievements, particularly its strong credit market and introduction of paper money, in advances in transportation (carts, passenger ships, and barges equipped with sternpost rudders and watertight compartments), in ceramic production, copper and iron mining, paper manufacture, high-quality printing and publishing, and in the standardization of machinery and technical terminology—all preconditions for profitable and efficient serial and mass production. Water mills drove trip-hammers, irrigated fields, ground grain, and crushed materials for industrial use. Communication networks and trade routes from China through Central Asia and the Islamic world—labeled the Silk Road, in the nineteenth century—allowed the diffusion of Chinese technologies to Europe, which copied, assimilated, and refined Eastern ideas during its own commercial and industrial revolutions centuries later.

The monetization of Song society, and in particular the use of paper money, helped to emancipate investors from their previous dependence on the agrarian sector and enhanced the growth of commerce in cities and towns. The Northern Song capital of Kaifeng—linked to the Great Canal by the Bian River—became a multifunctional urban center of a type that had never before existed in Chinese history. The emperor still ruled his empire from his palace, but his capital was no longer the materialized demonstration of imperial ideology and public order that the Tang capital, Chang'an, had been. As the ward walls inside Kaifeng came down and curfews were abandoned, the lifestyle of urban residents changed immediately and profoundly. The capital was on its way to becoming an almost liberal *laissez-faire* consumers' paradise. But it was in Hangzhou—the Southern Song capital on the Qian River, bordered by the West Lake and run through with canals—that the wealth and fashionable lifestyle of merchants and traders began to outpace that of officials. Contemporary authors praised the commercial hustle and bustle of this dynamic city and regarded it as the hub of the universe.

In both the north and the south, Song scholar-officials set the preconditions for an educational system and a civil service bureaucracy that would last for more than a millennium, until the end of imperial China in 1912. The activities of scholar-officials in science, technology, and art strongly support the claim that the Song elite functioned as catalysts for secularization, even as they complied with and supported Confucianism, and here in particular the Song Learning of the Way had a lasting effect on Chinese history. Trained in Neo-Confucian rationality as well as morality, this elite class investigated the natural world and painted what they saw with a new realism freed from the phantasmagorical subjects dominating Tang arts. A fresh understanding and interpretation of the secular world turned landscapes, plants, animals, street life, and domestic scenes into fit subjects for the fine arts.

These scholar-officials led elitist lives showered with privileges, benefits, political and intellectual influence, and family prestige unknown to contemporary commoners. But, true to their Confucian values, they never hesitated to pay the price asked of them by Chinese society. They endured decades of educational drill and grueling examinations, they spent their lives on official duty assignments far from their homes and separated from their families, and they subordinated their own wishes and desires to the interests of the emperor and the dynasty, even under sometimes desperate conditions. To citizens of the twenty-first century who value individuality, self-determination, and self-realization, this description of selfless Song scholar-officials may sound idealized or romanticized, but in fact it comes close to the way the Chinese practiced loyalty, discipline, and bravery.

DYNASTIC RULERS

MEASURES

PRONUNCIATION GUIDE

NOTES

BIBLIOGRAPHY

ACKNOWLEDGMENTS

INDEX

DYNASTIC RULERS

The Late Tang Emperor Succession

12 Xianzong, r. 805–820 (Li Chun, 778–820)
13 Muzong, r. 820–824 (Li Heng, 795–824)
14 Jingzong, r. 824–827 (Li Zhan, 809–827)
15 Wenzong, r. 827–840 (Li Ang, 809–840)
16 Wuzong, r. 840–846 (Li Yan, 814–846)
17 Xuanzong, r. 846–859 (Li Shen, 810–859)
18 Yizong, r. 859–873 (Li Cui, 833–873)
19 Xizong, r. 873–888 (Li Yan, 862–888)
20 Zhaozong, r. 888–904 (Li Ye, 867–904)
21 Jingzong, r. 904–907 (Li Zhu, 892–908)

The Five Dynasties Emperor Succession

LATER LIANG, 907–923

1 Taizu, r. 907–912 (Zhu Wen, 852–912)
2 Prince of Ying, r. 912–913 (Zhu Yougui)
3 Modi, r. 913–923 (Zhu Youzhen, 888–923)

LATER TANG, 923–936

1 Zhuangzong, r. 923–926 (Li Cunxu, 885–926)
2 Mingzong, r. 926–933 (Li Siyuan, 867–933)
3 Mindi, r. 933–934 (Li Conghou, 914–934)
4 Modi, r. 934–936 (Li Congke, 885–937)

LATER JIN, 936–947

1   Gaozu, r. 936–942 (Shi Jingtang, 892–942)
2   Chudi, r. 942–947 (Shi Chonggui, 914–954)

LATER HAN, 947–951

1   Gaozu, r. 947 (Liu Zhiyuan, 895–948)
2   Yindi, r. 948–951 (Liu Chengyou, 931–951)

LATER ZHOU, 951–960

1   Taizu, r. 951–954 (Guo Wei, 904–954)
2   Shizong, r. 954–959 (Chai Rong, 921–959)
3   Gongdi, r. 959–960 (Chai Zongxun, 953–973)

The Liao (Khitan) Emperor Succession

1   Taizu, r. 907–926 (Yelü Abaoji, 872–926)
2   Taizong, r. 926–947 (Yelü Deguang, 902–947)
3   Shizong, r. 947–951 (Yelü Ruan, 918–951)
4   Muzong, r. 951–969 (Yelü Jing, 931–969)
5   Jingzong, r. 969–982 (Yelü Xian, 948–982)
6   Shengzong, r. 982–1031 (Yelü Longxu, 971–1031)
7   Xingzong, r. 1031–1055 (Yelü Zongzhen, 1016–1055)
8   Daozong, r. 1055–1101 (Yelü Hongji, 1032–1101)
9   Tianzuodi, r. 1101–1125 (Yelü Yanxi, 1075–1128)

The Song Emperor Succession

NORTHERN SONG, 960–1127

1   Taizu, r. 960–976 (Zhao Kuangyin, 928–976)
2   Taizong, r. 976–997 (Zhao Kuangyi, 939–997)
3   Zhenzong, r. 997–1022 (Zhao Heng, 968–1022)
4   Renzong, r. 1022–1063 (Zhao Zhen, 1010–1063)
5   Yingzong, r. 1063–1067 (Zhao Shu, 1032–1067)
6   Shenzong, r.1067–1085 (Zhao Xu, 1048–1085)
7   Zhezong, r. 1085–1100 (Zhao Xu, 1076–1100)

8   Huizong, r. 1100–1126 (Zhao Ji, 1082–1135)
9   Qinzong, r. 1126–1127 (Zhao Huan, 1110–1160)

SOUTHERN SONG, 1127–1279

10   Gaozong, r. 1127–1162 (Zhao Gou, 1107–1187)
11   Xiaozong, r. 1162–1189 (Zhao Shen, 1127–1194)
12   Guangzong, r. 1189–1194 (Zhao Dun, 1147–1200)
13   Ningzong, r. 1194–1224 (Zhao Kuo, 1168–1224)
14   Lizong, r. 1224–1264 (Zhao Yun, 1205–1264)
15   Duzong, r. 1264–1274 (Zhao Qi, 1222–1274)
16   Gongdi, r. 1274–1276 (Zhao Xian, 1270–1323)
17   Duanzong, r. 1276–1278 (Zhao Shi, 1268–1278)
18   Dibing, r. 1278–1279 (Zhao Bing, 1271–1279)

The Xi Xia (Tangut) Emperor succession

1   Jingzong, r. 1032–1048 (Li Yuanhao)
2   Yizong, r. 1048–1067 (Li Liangzuo)
3   Huizong, r. 1067–1086 (Li Bingchang)
4   Chongzong, r. 1086–1139 (Li Qianshun)
5   Renzong, r. 1139–1193 (Li Renxiao)
6   Huanzong, r. 1193–1206 (Li Chunyou)
7   Xiangzong, r. 1206–1210 (Li Anguan)
8   Shenzong, r. 1210–1223 (Lin Zunxu)
9   Xianzong, r. 1223–1226 (Li Dewang)
10   Li Xian, r. 1226–1227

The Jin (Jurchen) Emperor Succession

1   Taizu, r. 1115–1123 (Wanyan Aguda, 1068–1123)
2   Taizong, r. 1123–1135 (Wanyan Wuqimai, 1075–1135)
3   Xizong, r. 1135–1149 (Wanyan Dan, 1119–1150)
4   Prince Liang of Hailing, r. 1149–1161 (Wanyan Liang, 1122–1161)
5   Shizong, r. 1161–1189 (Wanyan Yong (Wulu), 1123–1189)
6   Zhangzong, r. 1189–1208 (Wanyan Jing, 1168–1208)
7   Prince of Weishao, r. 1208–1213 (Wanyan Yongji, ?–213)
8   Xuanzong, r. 1213–1224 (Wanyan Xun, 1163–1224)
9   Aizong, r. 1224–1234 (Wanyan Shouxu, 1198–1234)

MEASURES

Length

    1   *chi* = 31.6 cm or 12.3 in

Area

    1   *mu* = 573 sq m or one seventh of an acre or the seventeenth part of a hectare (ha = 10.000 sq m)

    1   *qing* = 100 *mu* or 13.99 acres or 5.73 ha

Weight

    1   *liang* = 39.6 g or roughly 1.4 oz

    1   *jin* = 16 *liang* or 633 g or 1.3 lb

    1   *shi* or *dan* = 120 *jin* or 75,960 kg

Capacity

    1   *sheng* = 0.6641 liters

    1   *dou* = 10 *sheng* or 6.64 liters

    1   *hu* = 10 *dou* or 66.4 liters

    1   *shi* or *dan* = 94.88 liters

Counters

    1   *pi* = a bolt of tax silk approximately 13.29 m in length

    1   *guan* = a unit of account nominally worth 1.000 cash

PRONUNCIATION GUIDE

Pronunciation is as in English unless noted below.

c   as *ts* in *nets*
ch   as in *chat*
g   as in *girl*
j   as in *jingle*
q   as *ch* in *cheese*
x   as *sh* in *sheer*
y   as in *year*
z   as *dz* in *adze*
zh   as *j* in *John*
a   as *e* in *pen* for yan, jian, qian, xian; otherwise as *a* in *father*
ai   as in *aye*
ang   as *ong* in *wrong*
ao   as *ow* in *now*
e   as *e* in *yet* in the combinations ye, -ie, -ue; otherwise as *e* in *the*
ei   as in *neigh*
en   as *un* in *fun*
eng   as *ung* in *rung*
er   pronounced as *are*
i   as in the *i* of *sir* after c, s, z; as in the *ir* of *sir* after ch, sh, zh, r
ie   as *ye* in *yet*
iu   as *yo* in *yoyo*
ong   as *ung* in German Achtung
ou   as in *oh*
u   after j, q, x, and y as *ui* in *suit*; otherwise as *u* in *rule*
ua   after j, q, x, and y as *ue* in *duet*; otherwise as *wa* in *water*
uai   as in *why*
ue   as *ue* in *duet*
ui   as in *way*
uo   similar to *o* in *once*

NOTES

Introduction

1. Liu, *Chinese Classical Prose*, p. 55.
2. Standen, *Unbounded Loyalty*, p. 3.
3. Tillman, *Utilitarian Confucianism*, p. 175.

1. A Time of Turmoil

1. *XZZTJCB*, 357:8548.
2. *HCLQJ*, 3:7b.
3. *HCLQJ*, 1:7b–13a.
4. The translation is based on *Sources of Chinese Tradition*, p. 428.
5. Ch'en, "The Economic Background of the Hui-ch'ang Suppression of Buddhism," pp. 67–105; Weinstein, *Buddhism under the Tang*, p. 134.
6. *Ennin's Diary*, p. 388.
7. Pettersson, "Cannibalism in the Dynastic Histories," pp. 123–125; for details see Gernet, *Buddhism in Chinese Society*, pp. 65–66, 195–247, 254–255; Jan Yün-hua, "Buddhist Self-immolation in Medieval China," pp. 243–268.
8. *The Old Man Who Does as He Pleases*, p. 41.
9. See also Graff, *Medieval Chinese Warfare*, pp. 242–247.
10. Somers, "The End of the T'ang," pp. 695–700.
11. Yates, *Washing Silk*, p. 117.
12. Li Huarui, *Songshi lunji*, pp. 81–82.
13. Compare for the 880s Pettersson, "Cannibalism in the Dynastic Histories," pp. 143, 145–146; for the full story see *JTS*, 200 *xia*:5397; *JTS*, 19 *xia*:717; *XWDS*, 61:748; *JTS*, 20 *shang*:737; for the shortened quotation from the *CGL* see De Groot, *The Religious System of China*, Vol. 4, p. 385; for *xiangrou* and *liangjiao yang* compare *CGL*, 9:142–143.

14. Somers, "The End of the T'ang," p. 682.

15. The translation is based on Yates, *Washing Silk*, p. 116.

16. *BMSY*, 17:1a.

17. For biographic details see Wang, *The Structure of Power during the Five Dynasties*, pp. 102, 103, 149, 205–206.

18. Davis, *Historical Records of the Five Dynasties*, p. lxi.

19. Liu, *Chinese Classical Prose*, p. 191.

20. Standen, *Unbounded Loyalty*, p. 3.

21. Tao, "Barbarians or Northerners," p. 66.

22. Zhang Bozhong, "Qidan zaoqi wenhua tansuo," pp. 183–186.

23. Stein, "Leao-Tche," p. 28; Holmgren, "Marriage, Kinship and Succession under the Ch'i-tan Rulers," p. 44.

24. Kuhn, *How the Qidan Reshaped the Tradition*, p. 19.

25. Pelliot, *Notes on Marco Polo*, Vol. 1, pp. 216–229.

26. Twitchett and Tietze, "The Liao," p. 21.

27. *LS*, 32:373.

28. *LS*, 2:16.

29. *LS*, 64:967–968.

30. Kara, "Khitan and Jurchin," pp. 230–231; Franke, "The Forest Peoples of Manchuria: Khitans and Jurchens," p. 408; Di Cosmo, "Liao History and Society," p. 20.

31. Yu Yunguo, *Xishuo Songchao*, p. 13.

32. Wittfogel and Fêng, *Liao*, p. 435.

33. Twitchett and Tietze, "The Liao," pp. 87–88.

34. *LS*, 71:1202.

35. Twitchett and Tietze, "The Liao," p. 91.

36. On the variety of silk fabrics see *QDGZ*, 20:1a–4a.

37. *LS*, 12:133.

38. *LS*, 42:518.

39. For more details see Twitchett and Tietze, "The Liao," pp. 114–120.

40. Mote, *Imperial China*, p. 173–177.

41. Wu Tianzhi, *Xi Xia shigao*, p. 43.

42. Dunnell, "The Xi Xia," p. 156.

43. Dunnell, "The Xi Xia," pp. 168–172; Kycanov, "Les guerres entre les Sung du Nord et le Hsi-Hsia," p. 106.

44. *LS*, 105:1524–1525.

45. Wu Tianzhi, *Xi Xia shigao*, pp. 296, 49.

2. Model Rulers

1. *ZGDBK*, Vol. 2, p. 974.

2. *SS*, 436:12940.

3. De Bary, *Waiting for the Dawn*, p. 3.

4. Liu, *China Turning Inward*, p. 43.

5. Mote, *Imperial China*, p. 97.

6. *XZZTJ*, 1:2–3.

7. *SS*, 85:2093; for different figures see *WXTK*, 315:2470, 139 prefectures, 661 districts.

8. On Luoyang see Zhou Baozhu, "Bei Song shiqi de Xijing Luoyang," pp. 115–116.

9. *SS*, 439:12997.

10. Wyatt, *The Recluse of Luoyang*, p. 175.

11. *ZZYL*, p. 599.

12. Bol, *"This Culture of Ours,"* p. 148.

13. *Proclaiming Harmony*, p. 8.

14. *SS*, 3:51; *Songdai jiaoyu*, p. 263; Chen Rongzhao, *Fan Zhongyan yanjiu*, p. 5.

15. Lorge, "The Entrance and Exit of the Song Founders," p. 45; Fan Xuehui, "Guanyu 'bei jiu shi bingquan' ruogan wenti de zai tantao," pp. 38–48. Jia Haitao, *Bei Song 'rushu zhi guo' zhengzhi yanjiu*, pp. 8–10. The biographies of fifteen of the generals who helped him to power are in the *SS*, j. 273.

16. For full translation see Worthy, "The Founding of Sung China," pp. 174–175; Lorge, "The Entrance and Exit of the Song Founders," p. 43.

17. Mote, *Imperial China*, p. 103.

18. Li Huarui, *Songshi lunji*, p. 8.

19. *YH*, 139:4b; Worthy, "The Founding of Sung China," p. 181.

20. *DDSL*, j. 23 (zhuanlun).

21. The story is given in *XZZTJCB*, 9:204–205.

22. Xu Gui, Fang Rujin, "Ping Song Taizu 'xian nan hou bei' de tongyi zhanlue," pp. 517–534.

23. Yang Weisheng, "Lun Zhao Song zhi tongyi yu zhengzhi," p. 56.

24. Yu Yunguo, *Xishuo Songchao*, p. 82.

25. Li Huarui, *Songshi lunji*, p. 2; Chikusa Masaaki, *Sō no Taiso to Taisō*, pp. 134–147.

26. Chaffee, *Branches of Heaven*, pp. 26–29.

27. Davis, *Society and the Supernatural in Song*, p. 71.

28. *QSB*, p. 77.

29. Yu Yunguo, *Xishuo Songchao*, p. 56.

30. The translation is based on Liu, *Chinese Classical Prose*, p. 159.

31. Yang Shufan, "Songdai zaixiang zhidu," p. 1; *Zhongguo lishi. Sui Tang Liao Song Jin juan*, p. 202.

32. *WXTK*, 49:451.

33. *SS*, 161:3773, 3787.

34. *SS*, 162:3798.

35. *SHYJG*, ce 110, xuanju 7:4342.

36. *WXTK*, 32:304–305; He Zhongli, "Bei Song kuoda keju qushi de yuanyin," p. 88.

37. He Zhongli, "Bei Song kuoda keju qushi de yuanyin," p. 88.

38. See Giles, "Chinese Printing in the Tenth Century," pp. 513–515; Carter, *The Invention of Printing in China and Its Spread Westward*; Wu, "Chinese Printing under Four Alien Dynasties (916–1368)," pp. 447–523; Twitchett, *Printing and Publishing in Medieval China*; Kuhn, *Die Song-Dynastie*, pp. 56–64.

39. For a study on the subject see Kurz, *Das Kompilationsprojekt Song Taizongs*.

40. Cherniack, "Book Culture and Textual Transmission in Sung China," p. 5; De Weerdt, "Canon Formation and Examination Culture," p. 93.

41. Wang Gungwu, "Feng Tao: An Essay on Confucian Loyalty," p. 140.

42. Bol, *"This Culture of Ours,"* p. 192.

43. *A Sung Bibliography*, p. 48.

44. *Songdai wenhua shi*, pp. 169, 177. Ru Qihe, "Songdai guange zhi jiaokan jingbu shu," p. 90.

45. Tsien, *Science and Civilisation in China*, Vol. 5:1, p. 208.

46. Liu Jingzhen, "Bei Song qianqi huangquan fazhan zhi yanjiu," pp. 135–142.

47. *XZZTJCB*, 357:8540.

48. Kracke, *Civil Service in Early Sung China*, p. 137.

49. *ZZBZ* in *RSZBWJ*, 4:305.

50. Franke, "Historical Precedent or Accidental Repetition of Events?" pp. 200–201.

51. Hsieh, *The Life and Thought of Li Gou*, pp. 8–9; *QDGZ*, 20:2a–3a; *SS*, 7:124–127.

52. Ho, "Politics and Factionalism," pp. 184–185.

53. See *SHYJG*, ce 156, shihuo 64:6086–6093.

54. Tao, "Barbarians and Northerners," p. 68.

55. *LQJ*, 5:4b–5a.

56. *QDGZ*, 20:5a.

57. *ZYL*, 6:1a–4b.

58. *SS*, 3:51.

59. Cahill, "Taoism at the Song Court," p. 25.

60. See also *YH*, pp. 1779–1794; for the year 1008 see pp. 1792–1794.

61. *SS*, 104:2527–2528.

62. Bol, "Emperors Can Claim Antiquity Too," p. 176.

3. Reforming into Collapse

1. *ZZTJ*, 1:2.

2. Liu, "An Early Sung Reformer: Fan Chung-yen," pp. 105–131; Chen Rongzhao, *Fan Zhongyan yanjiu*.

3. Qian Mu, *Guoshi dagang*, pp. 379–382.

4. *SS*, 187:4576; see McGrath, "Military and Regional Administration in Northern Sung China," p. 148, tables 3–6.

5. Dunnell, "Tanguts and the Tangut State of Ta Hsia," p. 116.

6. Fischer, "Fan Chung-yen," pp. 39–85, 142–156; Buriks, "Fan Chung-yan's Versuch einer Reform," pp. 57–80, 153–184.

7. Dunnell, "The Xi Xia," pp. 158–159.

8. *SS*, 214:10273–10274; Bol, *"This Culture of Ours,"* pp. 171–172.

9. Elvin, *The Pattern of the Chinese Past*, p. 84.

10. *Sources of Chinese Tradition*, pp. 468–474.

11. *SDPQJ*, Vol. 1, p. 279.

12. *XZZTJCB*, 471:11256.

13. *Sources of Chinese Tradition*, pp. 490; on the reform see Williamson, *Wang An Shih*; Liu, *Reform in Sung China*; Deng Guangming, *Wang Anshi*; Qi Xia, *Wang Anshi bianfa*; Zhan Dahe, *Wang Anshi nianpu sanzhong*; Li Huarui, *Wang Anshi bianfa yanjiu shi*.

14. See for a chronological order Bol, *"This Culture of Ours,"* pp. 247–248.

15. See the memorials against the reform translated in *Sources of Chinese Tradition*, ch. 19, pp. 476–478, 480–489; Freeman, "Lo-yang and the Opposition to Wang An-shih."

16. On the militarization of the *baojia*-system in the early 1040s and in the 1070s in the Five Provinces along the northern border see Smith, *"Shuihu zhuan* and the Military Subculture," pp. 383–398, p. 391, table 2.

17. *WXTK*, 153:1335.

18. *XZZTJCB*, 218:5299.

19. *WXTK*, 153:1334; *XZZTJCB*, 218:5300; *XZZTJCB*, 235:5697.

20. *XZZTJCB*, 247:6033.

21. Williamson, *Wang An Shih*, Vol. 1, p. 285.

22. Tietze, "The Liao-Song Border Conflict of 1084–1076," pp. 143–144.

23. *SS*, 486:14012.

24. Kycanov, "Les guerres entre les Sung du Nord et le Hsi-Hsia," p. 112.

25. Ji, *Politics and Conservatism in Northern Song China*, pp. 165–180.

26. Williamson, *Wang An Shih*, Vol. 1, p. 381.

27. *ZZYL*, 24:599.

28. Twitchett and Tietze, "The Liao," p. 139.

29. *SMJW*, in *SF*, 8:170–171.

30. *LS*, 27:326; see Stein, "Leao-Tche," pp. 101–102.

31. *JS*, 24:550.

32. *SSJSBM*, 48:467.

33. Chaffee, "Huizong, Cai Jing, and the Politics of Reform," pp. 31–77.

34. *SS*, 19:367–69; Chien, *Salt and State*, pp. 13–14.

35. Smith, "Irredentism as Political Capital," pp. 78–79.

36. Hargett, "Huizong's Magic Marchmount," pp. 1–48.

37. See Franke, "Treaties between Sung and Chin," pp. 62–64; Franke, "The Chin," p. 225.

38. For details see *SCHB*, 30:13b–14a; *JSJSBM*, 6:116–117; He Zhongli, *Songdai zhengzhi shi*, pp. 269–270. Franke, "The Chin," p. 229, holds the opinion that the war indemnity amounted to not less than 180 years of annual payments.

39. *SS*, 455:13359–13362.

40. *DJGZ (jiaozheng)*, 4:64.

41. *JSJSBM*, 6:135; *XZZTJ*, 97:2557.

42. *JSJSBM*, 7:141, 8:172.

43. *DJGZ*, 32:3b; *JSJSBM*, 7:141–142; the figures given (without source) by He Zhongli, *Songdai zhengzhi shi*, p. 279, differ: for gold one million ingots, for silver ten million ingots, and ten million bolts of silk.

44. *XZZTJ*, 97:2567.

45. *SS*, 23:436; West, "Crossing Over," pp. 583–585.

46. Translation quoted from Ebrey, "Introduction," p. 16.

47. *SS*, 22:417, 28:520.

48. Compare Yu Yunguo. *Xishuo Songchao*, p. 323.

49. Wyatt, "The Invention of the Northern Song," pp. 220–224.

4. The Song in the South

1. Zhang Jiaju, *Liang Song jingji zhongxin de nanyi*, p. 31.

2. Li Jiannong, *Song Yuan Ming jingji shigao*, p. 185.

3. Liu Zhaomin, *Zhongguo lishi shang qihou de bianqian*, pp. 24–25, 28, 119.

4. *SS*, 61 and 62, pp. 1317–1374.

5. For change of climate and natural disasters see Liu Zhaomin, *Zhongguo lishi shang qihou de bianqian*, pp. 286–287, 117–118; for a detailed report on the Kaifeng climate see Zhang Quanming, "Lun Bei Song Kaifeng diqu de qihou bianqian ji qi tedian," pp. 98–108; Zhou Baozhu, *Songdai Dongjing yanjiu*, pp. 715–716; Cheng Suiying, *Tang Song Kaifeng shengtai huanjing yanjiu*, p. 23–25.

6. *SS*, 91:2255; on the changes of the Yellow River's course see Yoshioka,

Sōdai Kōga-shi kenkyū, pp. 423–425; compare Blunden and Elvin, *Cultural Atlas of China,* p. 16.

7. See Yao Hanyuan, *Zhongguo shuili shi gangyao,* pp. 162, 181–192, 184, 189; Lamouroux, "From the Yellow River to the Huai," p. 555, p. 547, map 15.1.

8. *SS,* 25:459. Yao Hanyuan, *Zhongguo shuili shi gangyao,* p. 290. In June 1938 Guomindang troops breached the dikes of the Yellow River as an ultimate recourse to halt the military advance of the Japanese troops; see Kuhn, *Der Zweite Weltkrieg in China,* pp. 126–129. Lamouroux, "From the Yellow River to the Huai," pp. 547–548.

9. Yao Hanyuan, *Zhongguo shuili shi gangyao,* p. 297, 299.

10. Deng, *The Premodern Chinese Economy,* p. 309.

11. *SS,* 86:2173, 89:2226, 95:2370; Zhang Jiaju, *Liang Song jingji zhongxin de nanyi,* p. 50.

12. Deng, *The Premodern Chinese Economy,* p. 313.

13. *SHYJG,* ce 127, 11:4992.

14. Franke, "The Chin," p. 278.

15. Robert P. Hymes quoted in Smith, "Problematizing the Song-Yuan-Ming Transition," p. 9.

16. The translation is based on Hu, *Li Ch'ing-chao,* p. 94; *Li Ch'ing-chao: Complete Poems,* p. 65.

17. Haeger, "Between North and South: The Lake Rebellion in Hunan, 1130–1135," pp. 469–488.

18. On the treaty activities between 1138 and 1142 see Teraji, *Nan Sō shoki seiji shi kenkyū,* pp. 160–259.

19. Mote, *Imperial China,* pp. 299–305; Wilhelm, "From Myth to Myth," pp. 146–161; Liu, "Yue Fei and China's Heritage of Loyalty," pp. 291–297; Kaplan, "Yue Fei and the Founding of the Southern Song."

20. Lorge, "Song Gaozong's Letters to Yue Fei," pp. 172–173.

21. He Zhongli, *Songdai zhengzhi shi,* pp. 376, 381, 384.

22. He Zhongli, *Songdai zhengzhi shi,* pp. 370–375; Chung, *Palace Women in the Northern Sung,* p. 31.

23. *JS,* j. 77:1755–1756; He Zhongli, *Songdai zhengzhi shi,* p. 371.

24. Quoted from Tillman, *Utilitarian Confucianism,* p. 173.

25. Tao, *The Jurchen in Twelfth-century China,* p. 42.

26. Tao, "Public Schools in the Chin Dynasty," p. 61.

27. *JS,* 83:1862–1863.

28. *JS,* 24:550.

29. *JS,* 89:1989.

30. *JS,* 46:1034.

31. Franke, "The Chin Dynasty," p. 281.

32. *JS*, 28:694.

33. Chan, *The Historiography of the Chin Dynasty,* pp. 148–163.

34. Davis, *Court and Family in Sung China, 900–1279,* p. 56; Wang Deyi, "Song Xiaozong jiqi shidai," p. 252.

35. Davis, *Court and Family in Sung China,* p. 85.

36. Han Tuozhou is categorized as "treacherous official"; *SS,* 474:13771–13776.

37. Schirokauer, "Neo-Confucians under Attack," p. 185.

38. *JS*, 12:278. Franke, *Studien und Texte zur Kriegsgeschichte der Südlichen Sungzeit,* pp. 158–213; Hana, *Bericht über die Verteidigung der Stadt Tê-an,* pp. 122–221.

39. *JS*, 98:2169–2170.

40. *JS*, 98:2172–2173.

41. Davis, *Court and Family in Sung China,* pp. 79–127; 198–224.

42. *XZZTJ,* 158:4288; Davis, *Court and Family in Sung China,* p. 92.

43. Chaffee, *Branches of Heaven,* pp. 202–203.

44. Martin, *The Rise of Chingis Khan,* pp. 170–171.

45. Ibid., p. 178.

46. Ratchnevsky, *Genghis Khan,* p. 151.

47. Hoang, *Genghis Khan,* pp. 286, 240–243.

48. Allsen, "The Rise of the Mongolian Empire," pp. 363–364.

49. *YS,* 3:54.

50. Allsen, *Mongol Imperialism,* pp. 84–85.

51. Franke, "Chia Ssu-tao," pp. 225–228.

52. Qi Xia, *Songdai jingji shi,* pp. 1082–1083.

53. He Zhongli, *Songdai zhengzhi shi,* pp. 545–546.

54. Franke, "Chia Ssu-tao," pp. 233.

55. Huan Kuan-chung, *Nan Song difang wuli,* pp. 299–304.

56. Rossabi, "The Reign of Khubilai Khan," pp. 427–428.

57. Soffel, *Ein Universalgelehrter verarbeitet das Ende seiner Dynastie,* pp. 16, 152.

58. Davis, *Wind against the Mountain,* pp. 29–30.

59. Ibid., p. 62.

60. Chen Shisong et al., *Song Yuan zhanzheng shi,* pp. 262–267.

61. Davis, *Wind against the Mountain,* p. 75.

62. *YS,* 9:176–177; *SS,* 47:937.

63. *SS,* 47:938; *Jianming Songshi,* p. 443.

64. *SS,* 446:13150; Jay, *A Change in Dynasties,* pp. 137, 137–194.

65. *SS,* 418:12540.

5. Three Doctrines

1. Yu, *Zhu Xi de lishi shijie*, Vol. 1:183; Hartman, "Zhu Xi and His World," p. 109.

2. Bol, "On the Problem of Contextualizing Ideas," p. 62.

3. See Fung, *A History of Chinese Philosophy*, Vol. II, pp. 407–413.

4. *HCLQJ*, 11:2a.

5. Chang, *The Development of Neo-Confucian Thought*, p. 43; Yao, *An Introduction to Confucianism*, p. 97.

6. See Birdwhistell, *Transition to Neo-Confucianism*; Wyatt, *The Recluse of Loyang*.

7. Chan, "Chou Tun-i," pp. 277–281.

8. Yao, *An Introduction to Confucianism*, pp. 98–99.

9. See Kasoff, *The Thought of Chang Tsai*.

10. Fung, *A History of Chinese Philosophy*, Vol. II, pp. 497, 478–484.

11. Yao, *An Introduction to Confucianism*, p. 103.

12. See Bruce, *Chu Hsi and His Masters*, pp. 17–55.

13. Bol, *"This Culture of Ours,"* pp. 302–303.

14. *SS*, 427:12720.

15. Fung, *A History of Chinese Philosophy*, Vol. II, p. 501.

16. Chan, *A Source Book in Chinese Philosophy*, pp. 544, 551.

17. *Reflections on Things at Hand*, p. xviii.

18. *SS*, 283:9565; van Ess, *Von Ch'eng I zu Chu Hsi*, p. 8.

19. *SS*, 429:12751–12770; Bruce, *Chu Hsi and His Masters*, pp. 56–96; see Chan, *Chu Hsi, Life and Thought; Chu Hsi and Neo-Confucianism*.

20. *Reflections on Things at Hand*, p. xvii.

21. Fung, *A History of Chinese Philosophy*, Vol. II, pp. 534–546.

22. *ZZYL*, 15:288; Tillman, "The Idea and the Reality of the 'Thing' during the Sung," p. 74.

23. For detailed information see Ebrey, *Chu Hsi's Family Rituals*, p. 3, and Ebrey, *Confucianism and Family Rituals in Imperial China*, p. 6.

24. Wilson, "Genealogy and History in Neo-Confucian Sectarian Uses of the Confucian Past," pp. 6–7; see also Makeham, *Transmitters and Creators*, pp. 176–177.

25. Li, *The Confucian Way*, pp. 3–4.

26. Schirokauer, "Chu Hsi's Political Career," p. 166.

27. For more details see Tillman, *Utilitarian Confucianism*, pp. 2–5.

28. For Chen Liang see Tillman, *Utilitarian Confucianism*; for Ye Shi see Lo, *Life and Thought of Yeh Shih*.

29. Tillman, *Utilitarian Confucianism*, p. 113.

30. *Neo-Confucian Terms Explained*, p. 105.

31. *XSQJ*, 11:10a.

32. *SS*, 429:12768; Schirokauer, "Chu Hsi's Political Career," p. 185; Schirokauer, "Neo-Confucians under Attack," pp. 163–196.

33. Lo, *The Life and Thought of Yeh Shih*, p. 149; Liu, "The Road to Neo-Confucian Orthodoxy," pp. 483–506.

34. Quoted from *Chinese Religion*, pp. 173–174.

35. *Neo-Confucian Terms Explained*, p. 168.

36. See Davis, *Society and the Supernatural in Song China*, pp. 69–74.

37. Ebrey, "Taoism and Art at the Court of Emperor Huizong," pp. 95–111.

38. Halperin, *Out of the Cloister*, pp. 113–114.

39. For regional statistical material see Liu, "Buddhist Institutions in the Lower Yangtze Region," pp. 39–41.

40. Karetzky, "The Representation of Women in China," pp. 242–243.

41. Yü, "Guanyin," pp. 151–160, 166–176.

42. Reed, "The Gender Symbolism of Kuan-yin Bodhisattva," pp. 159–180.

43. Ch'en, *Buddhism in China*, pp. 405–408.

44. Forke, *Geschichte der neueren chinesischen Philosophie*, pp. 9–10.

45. Yao, *An Introduction to Confucianism*, p. 227.

46. Rawski, "A Historian's Approach to Chinese Death Ritual," p. 29.

47. Nivison, Wright, *Confucianism in Action*, pp. 71–72.

48. Stuart and Rawski, *Worshipping the Ancestors*, p. 36

49. Luo Xinhui, "Zengzi yu Xiaojing," p. 6

50. Lai Yonghai, *Foxue yu ruxue*, p. 91; Ch'en, *Buddhism in China*, pp. 18, 49; Yao, *An Introduction to Confucianism*, p. 234.

51. Murray, "The Ladies' Canon of Filial Piety," p. 95.

52. Kuhn, *A Place for the Dead*, p. 49. An outstanding pictorial presentation of the filial piety programme comprising twenty-two scenes was completed by the painter Cui Qiong in the year 1158 of the Jin dynasty in Shanxi province.

53. *SYXA*, 39:2b.

54. For more details see the relevant chapters in Knapp, *Selfless Offspring*.

55. De Groot, *The Religious System of China*, Vol. 4, pp. 384–385.

56. Fu, "The Cultural Fashioning of Filial Piety," p. 74.

57. *LS*, 53:879–880.

58. *QLW*, pp. 125–128.

59. *LS*, 4:52; 11:123; 23:281.

60. Wittfogel and Fêng, *Liao*, p. 306, n. 45.

61. *LS*, 20:247.

62. Wittfogel and Fêng, *Liao*, p. 294.

63. Ibid., p. 296.

64. Steinhardt, *Liao Architecture*, p. 189, table 4; p. 59, table 2.

65. Ibid., p. 194.

66. Liang, *A Pictorial History of Chinese Architecture*, tables 34c–g, 29a–d;

Steinhardt, *Liao Architecture*, pp. 127–133; *Ancient Chinese Architecture*, pp. 89–91.

67. Liang, *A Pictorial History of Chinese Architecture*, tables 25a–g; Steinhardt, *Liao Architecture*, pp. 40–51; Ledderose, *Ten Thousand Things*, pp. 127–132. *Ancient Chinese Architecture*, p. 80.

68. Steinhardt, *Liao Architecture*, pp. 103–121.

69. See Franke, "The Chin," pp. 313–319; Yao, "Buddhism and Taoism under the Chin," pp. 145–180.

70. Mote, *Imperial China*, p. 144.

6. Education and Examination

1. Hymes, *Statesmen and Gentlemen*, p. 7.

2. Lo, *An Introduction to the Civil Service*, p. 24.

3. *XZZTJCB*, 221:5370.

4. Zhang Qifan, "'Huangdi yu shidafu gong zhi tianxia' shixi," pp. 114–115.

5. *WXTK*, 35:332.

6. Kuhn, *Status und Ritus*, p. 543.

7. *XZZTJCB*, 147:3564.

8. *SHYJG*, ce 113, xuanju 15:4496.

9. Chaffee, *The Thorny Gates of Learning*, p. 36.

10. *SHYJG*, ce 113, xuanju 14:4476.

11. *SHYJG*, ce 110, xuanju 7:4342; Miyazaki, *China's Examination Hell*, p. 116.

12. *XZZTJCB*, 51:1120; *SHYJG*, 1109: ce 110, xuanju 7:4357; Lee, *Government Education and Examination*, p. 148.

13. Chaffee, *The Thorny Gates of Learning*, pp. 196–202. *WXTK*, 32:304–307. The twelve *jinshi* examinations conducted until the end of the dynasty are not included. *SHYJG*, ce 107, xuanju 1:4217–4231; examinations from 960 until 1223. See Lee, *Government Education and Examination*, pp. 226, 279–285.

14. Chaffee, *The Thorny Gates of Learning*, p. 29. Sudō, *Sōdai kanryōsei to daitochi shoyū*, p. 66.

15. Sun Guotong, "Mendi zhi xiaorong," pp. 279, 283; Lee, *Government Education and Examination*, p. 212.

16. Kracke, "Family versus Merit," pp. 103–123.

17. Lee, *Government Education and Examination*, pp. 21, 221.

18. Hartwell, "Transformations of China," pp. 417–418; Hymes, "Prominence and Power," pp. 48–55.

19. Hartwell, "Transformations of China," p. 419.

20. The translation is based on Liu, *Chinese Classical Prose*, p. 175.

21. *Songdai wenhua shi*, pp. 94–95.

22. *Reflections on Things at Hand*, pp. 264–265.

23. *SS*, 11:217, 19:364.

24. Li, *The Ageless Chinese*, p. 243.

25. *SS*, 157:3657; *WXTK*, 42:395; *SS*, 157:3659.

26. See Chaffee, *The Thorny Gates of Learning*, p. 32, table 6.

27. Kracke, "The Expansion of Educational Opportunity," p. 11.

28. *SS*, 157:3657.

29. *Songdai jiaoyu*, p. 70

30. *XZZTJCB*, 67:1512, 1514.

31. *ZJLXSWJ*, 35:249. The translation is quoted from Lee, *Government Education and Examination*, p. 167.

32. Lee, *Government Education and Examination*, pp. 152–153; *XZZTJCB*, 147:3565.

33. *Songdai wenhua shi*, p. 101.

34. *XZZTJCB*, 143:3435.

35. *XZZTJCB*, 220:5334–5335.

36. *HCLQJ*, 12:1b–2a; based on the translation by Hartman, *Han Yü and the T'ang Search for Unity*, p. 163.

37. *HCLQJ*, 22:4ab.

38. Egan, *The Literary Works of Ou-yang Hsiu*, p. 17; Bol, "This Culture of Ours," p. 188.

39. *SDPQJ*, Vol. 1, p. 279.

40. *SDPQJ*, Vol. 1, p. 593.

41. *SYXA*, 1:27; see also *Sources of Chinese Tradition*, p. 439.

42. De Weerdt, "Canon Formation and Examination Culture," p. 123.

43. Lin Ruihan, "Songdai guanzhi tanwei," p. 199.

44. *SS*, 168:3996.

45. *WXTK*, 67:595–610.

46. *SS*, 168:3991–3996, 171:4109–4112, 169:4064–4069. Salaries for functional positions (*zhiqian*) on pp. 4112–4114.

47. Lo, *An Introduction to the Civil Service*, p. 160.

48. Deng, *The Premodern Chinese Economy*, p. 216.

49. *WXTK*, 65:592; Deng, *The Premodern Chinese Economy*, pp. 214–215; *THY*, 92:1669.

50. *SS*, 169:4052–4053; the list of military titles, *SS*, 169:4054–4059; the Tang list of prestige offices, *SS*, 169:4049–4051.

51. *SS*, 171:4110; *THY*, 91:1661.

52. *SXT*, 29:7b.

7. Life Cycle Rituals

1. De Pee, "The Ritual and Sexual Bodies," p. 59.

2. *Death Rituals in Late Imperial and Modern China*, p. ix; Kuhn, "Family Rituals," p. 370.

3. *SHYJG,* ce 14, 17090:555–556.

4. *LJZS,* 61:4b.

5. Ebrey, *The Inner Quarters,* pp. 47–50.

6. *SMSSY,* 3:29.

7. *SWJ,* 108:13.

8. *PZKT,* 1:16.

9. *ECJ,* 11:640–641; for a translation of the text see Ebrey, *The Inner Quarters,* p. 62.

10. See *DJMHL,* 5:151–155; *MLL,* 20:1a–6b.

11. See Ebrey, *Chu Hsi's Family Rituals,* p. 53, n. 17; for the "Six Rites" see De Pee, "The Ritual and Sexual Bodies," p. 60.

12. See *LJZS,* 61:4b; Chen Dongyuan, *Zhongguo funü shenghuo shi,* p. 30; *SMSSY,* 3:30–33; and *Chu Hsi's Family Rituals,* pp. 48–64.

13. See De Pee, "The Ritual and Sexual Bodies," pp. 86–89; *Chinese Civilization and Society,* pp. 84–94; Ebrey, *The Inner Quarters,* pp. 88–98.

14. *QTW,* 10:11a–12b; quoted from Ebrey, *The Inner Quarters,* p. 63.

15. Murray, "The Ladies' Classic of Filial Piety," pp. 98–99.

16. *The Old Man Who Does as He Pleases,* pp. 26–27.

17. *Songdai jiaoyu,* pp. 200–201.

18. See Su Zhecong, *Songdai nüxing wenxue;* see also Fong, "Engendering the Lyric."

19. Wu, "Childhood Remembered," pp. 141–142.

20. The translation is quoted from Wu, "Childhood Remembered," p. 144.

21. *SMSSY,* 4:41.

22. Birge, *Women, Property, and Confucian Reaction,* pp. 1–2.

23. Ibid., p. 37; *Family and Property in Sung China,* p. 117.

24. Birge, *Women, Property, and Confucian Reaction,* p. 197.

25. Ibid., p. 200.

26. *QDGZ,* 23:1a.

27. *QDGZ,* 23:3b.

28. *LS,* 4:49.

29. *LS,* 25:303; Wittfogel and Fêng, *Liao,* p. 266.

30. *JS,* 9:218.

31. Wittfogel and Fêng, *Liao,* p. 207, table 9.

32. *LS,* 71:1205.

33. *LS,* 52:864–865.

34. De Pee, "Material Ambiguity and the Hermetic Text," p. 85.

35. Kuhn, "Family Rituals," p. 371.

36. *Sources of Chinese Tradition,* p. 443.

37. Davis, *Society and the Supernatural in Song China,* pp. 171–172, 227–241.

38. See Ebner von Eschenbach, *Die Sorge der Lebenden um die Toten,* pp. 54–55.

39. *YZ*, 43:44a–49b; for a translation, see Ebner von Eschenbach, *Die Sorge der Lebenden um die Toten*, pp. 253–266.

40. *Bei Song Shaanzhou louzeyuan.*

41. Ebrey, "Cremation in Sung China," p. 417

42. *SMCJJ*, 27:381; Ebrey, *Chu Hsi's Family Ritual*, pp. 200, 103; Kuhn, *A Place for the Dead*, pp. 362–370.

43. *SMSSY*, 7:78–79; Kuhn, *A Place for the Dead*, p. 14.

44. For a slightly different translation, see Ebrey, *Confucianism and Family Rituals*, p. 91.

45. Ebrey, *Chu Hsi's Family Rituals*, p. 107.

46. See Asim, *Religiöse Landverträge aus der Song-Zeit*, pp. 32–44; Asim, "Status Symbol and Insurance Policy," p. 310.

47. *SS*, 124:2909.

48. Kuhn, "Decoding Tombs of the Song Elite," p. 11.

49. See Kuhn, *A Place for the Dead*, pp. 18–20, 27–33.

50. *JZYBGS*, p. 626; Ebner von Eschenbach, "Public Graveyards of the Song," p. 230.

51. *XWDS*, 72:888.

52. *LTSS*, 8:173.

53. Kuhn, *Die Kunst des Grabbaus*, pp. 207–215.

54. *Grand Exhibition of Silk Road Civilizations*, no. 158; nos. 150, 151.

55. *QDGZ*, 13:1b

56. *DJGZ*, 39:1b; Liu Xiaodong and Yang Zhijun, "Ruzhen guizu muzang de leixing ji yanbian," pp. 124–136.

8. Exploring the World Within and Without

1. Based on Fuller, *The Road to East Slope*, p. 39.

2. *Chinese Science*, p. xv.

3. Needham, *Science and Civilisation in China*, Vol. 1, p. 134.

4. Bacon, *Novum Organum*, p. 131.

5. Chaves, *Mei Yao-ch'en*, p. 51.

6. On Su Shi's poetry see Fuller, *The Road to East Slope*.

7. Hartman, "Poetry," p. 71.

8. Chaves, *Mei Yao-ch'en*, p. 115.

9. Leimbiegler, *Mei Yao-ch'en*, pp. 88–89; Chaves, *Mei Yao-ch'en*, p. 188.

10. Pease, "I Dreamed of Locusts," pp. 215–222.

11. *Su Dong-po*, p. 162.

12. Sargent, "Contexts of the Song Lyric in Sung Times," p. 226.

13. Lin, *The Transformation of the Chinese Lyrical Tradition*, p. 127.

14. Wagner, "Hua-chien chi," pp. 441–442.

15. Lam, "A Reconsideration of Liu Yong and His 'Vulgar' Lyrics."

16. Chang, "Liu Yung," p. 594.

17. The translation is based on Hoffmann, *Die Lieder des Li Yü*, pp. 129–130.

18. Liu, *An Introduction to Chinese Literature*, pp. 105.

19. Egan, *Word, Image and Deed in the Life of Su Shi*, p. 314.

20. Quoted from Hightower, "The Songwriter Liu Yong: Part I," pp. 350–351.

21. Egan, *The Literary Works of Ou-yang Hsiu*, pp. 168–177.

22. See Wixted, "The Poetry of Li Ch'ing-chao," pp. 145–168.

23. *Oeuvres poétiques complètes de Li Qingzhao*, p. 123.

24. Fong, "Engendering the Lyric," p. 119.

25. *Li Qingzhao shici wencun*, pp. 89–94.

26. Cheng Qianfan and Wu Xinlei, *Liang Song wenxue shi*, pp. 349–389.

27. Chan, *The Historiography of the Chin Dynasty*, pp. 67–119.

28. The translation is quoted from Yoshikawa, *Five Hundred Years of Chinese Poetry, 1150–1650*, p. 37.

29. West, "Chilly Seas and East-flowing Rivers," pp. 281–304; Wixted, "Yuan Haowen," pp. 953–955.

30. Kuhn, *A Place for the Dead*, p. 470.

31. See the discussion on Dong Yuan's *Riverbank* in *Issues of Authenticity in Chinese Painting*.

32. "Faku Yemaotai Liao mu jilue," pl. 1; Fong, *Images of the Mind*, p. 25.

33. Compare with Sullivan, *Chinese Landscape Painting*, pp. 44–45, 56–57, 74–75.

34. Fong, "Monumental Landscape Painting," p. 125.

35. Jang, "Realm of the Immortals," pp. 81–96.

36. Fong, *Images of the Mind*, p. 43.

37. Fung, *History of Chinese Philosophy*, Vol. II, p. 491.

38. *MQBT*, 17:173, no. 293.

39. Cahill, "The Imperial Painting Academy," p. 164.

40. *MQBT*, 17:173, no. 293.

41. Sturman, "Cranes above Kaifeng," pp. 33–68.

42. Bickford, "Huizong's Paintings," p. 463.

43. Ibid., pp. 454–455, 485–487.

44. See Weng, *Palastmuseum Peking*, pp. 159–161.

45. Compare "Jiangsu Ganjiang Caizhuang Wudai mu qingli jianbao," pl. 5:1–2.

46. Chen Zengbi, "Qiannian guta," S. 67.

47. *Gugong Song hua jinghua*, Vol. 1, pl. 4; Hay, "Along the River," pp. 294–302.

48. Kuhn, *Die Kunst des Grabbaus*, pp. 184–197; Little and Eichman, *Taoism and the Arts of China*, p. 137.

49. See Kuhn, *How the Qidan Reshaped the Tradition*, p. 15.

50. Tao Zongye, "Hebei Xuanhua Xiabali Liao Jin bihuamu," col. pl. 1:1.

51. *SMSSY*, 5:54.

52. Kuhn, *A Place for the Dead*, pp. 271, 289.

53. Tillman, "The Idea and Reality of the 'Thing' during the Sung," p. 75.

54. *MQBT*, 20:198, no. 340.

55. *MQBT*, 24:240, no. 437; p. 330, no. 588.

56. Needham, *Science and Civilisation in China*, Vol. 4.1, p. 246.

57. *The Washing away of Wrongs*.

58. Forage, "Science, Technology, and War in Song China," pp. 165–172; *MQBT*, 7:83, no. 130; full translation in Forage, "Science, Technology, and War in Song China," p. 194; Sivin, "Shen Gua," p. 374.

59. Needham, *Science and Civilisation in China*, Vol. 4:2, p. 465.

60. See Needham, Wang, and Price, *The Heavenly Clockwork*.

61. *JS*, 22:523–524.

62. Needham, *Science and Civilisation in China*, Vol. 4.2, pp. 495–497.

9. Transforming the Capitals

1. Sirén, *The Walls and Gates of Peking*, pp. 1–2.

2. The locus classicus for the layout of Chinese cities which served as the model for all city planning is to be found in the *Kaogong ji* (Records of the Investigation of Artisans) in the first century B.C.; *SKQSJH*, Vol. 3:768–769. Xu, *The Chinese City in Space and Time*, p. 34.

3. Al-Sirafi, Abu Zayd Hasan bin Yazid, *Ancient Accounts of India and China*, p. 59. See also Heng, *Cities of Aristocrats and Bureaucrats*, p. 1.

4. *XTS*, 49 *shang*: 1286. The translation is based on *Traité des fonctionnaires*, Vol.2, pp. 536–537.

5. *THY*, 86:1576.

6. *THY*, 86:1581.

7. *TLJCFK*, 1:30.

8. *YH*, 139:2587; Zhou Baozhu, *Songdai Dongjing yanjiu*, p. 74.

9. *WDHY*, 26:317–320.

10. *SDJK*, 1:2.

11. *SHYJG*, 7699:7305; *DJMHL*, 1:1, for differing numbers of gates and their names, see *DJMHL*, 1:26; compare Kracke, "Sung K'ai-feng," pp. 59; Zhou Baozhu, *Songdai Dongjing yanjiu*, pp. 61–63; Qiu Gang, "Beisong Dongjing sancheng de yingjian he fazhan," pp. 35–40; *SHYJG*, 7699:7313; Kuhn, *Die Song-Dynastie*, p. 225.

12. See Heng, *Cities of Aristocrats and Bureaucrats*, pp. 87–90.

13. Katō, Shigeshi, "Sōdai ni okeru toshi no hattatsu ni tsuite," pp. 93–140; see Skinner, "Introduction: Urban Development in Imperial China," pp. 23–24.

14. Hartwell, "A Cycle of Economic Change in Imperial China," p. 125; Elvin, *The Pattern of the Chinese Past*, p. 177.

15. *SDJK*, 24:339.

16. *SHYJG*, ce 158:6239.

17. Heng, *Cities of Aristocrats and Bureaucrats*, p. 101.

18. Zhou Baozhu, *Songdai Dongjing yanjiu*, p. 346. The figures are calculated on the basis of five individuals per household.

19. *SS*, 85:2097; Zhang Jin, "Kaifeng lidai huanggong yange yu Bei Song Dongjing huangcheng fanwei xinkao," pp. 87–94.

20. Kong Xianyi, "Bei Song Dongjing chengfang kaolue," p. 367.

21. See Kracke, "Sung K'ai-feng," pp. 65–67.

22. Ebrey, *The Inner Quarters*, pp. 114–151; Hansen, *Negotiating Daily Life in Traditional China*, p. 103.

23. Ebrey, *The Inner Quarters*, p. 24.

24. Tsao, "'Qingming shanghe tu'," p. 159, n. 7; Hansen notes: "Zhang . . . chose to create an ideal city." Valerie Hansen, *The Beijing Qingming Scroll*, p. 5; for differing views, see Johnson "The Place of Qingming Shanghe Tu," pp. 145–182.

25. *XZZTJCB*, 18:392–393.

26. Pang Dexin, *Songdai liangjing shimin shenghuo*, p. xxxvi.

27. *XZZTJCB*, 38:823.

28. Zhou Baozhu, *Songdai Dongjing yanjiu*, p. 72; *SHYJG*, 7699:7310; a helpful list is contained in Zhou Baozhu, *Songdai Dongjing yanjiu*, pp. 75–77.

29. *SHYJG*, ce 173:6788–6789; 7699:7311.

30. *SHYJG*, ce 173:6789.

31. Already in Tang times the Bian River had connected the Luo River to the Huai River; see *SS*, 7:2319–2320; Johnson, "The Place of Qingming Shanghe Tu," p. 166; see also *MQBT*, no. 457; Tsao, "'Qingming Shanghe Tu'," p. 176.

32. *DJMHL*, 2:52; Heng, *Cities of Aristocrats and Bureaucrats*, p. 123.

33. *DJMHL*, 1:26.

34. *DJMHL*, 6:180; see Idema and West, *Chinese Theater*, p. 35.

35. *DJMHL*, 2:60, 2:72.

36. *DJMHL*, 3:119; Kuhn, *Die Song-Dynastie*, p. 231.

37. *DJMHL*, 3:66.

38. *DJMHL*, 3:67; see also Idema and West, *Chinese Theater*, pp. 15–16.

39. *DJMHL*, 2:67–68.

40. *LS*, 32:737.

41. Steinhardt, *Chinese Imperial City Planning*, p. 124; compare the plans in Tamura, *Chūgoku seifuku*, Vol. 1, p. 320 (Shangjing), p. 336 (Zhongjing).

42. Tillman, *Utilitarian Confucianism*, pp. 173–174; see also Wright, "The Cosmology of the Chinese City," p. 63.

43. *MLL*, 10:9ab.

44. Heng, *Cities of Aristocrats and Bureaucrats*, p. 142.

45. Steinhardt, *Chinese Imperial City Planning*, p. 147.

46. Marco Polo, *The Description of the World*, Vol. 1, p. 326.

47. *MLL*, 13:1b, 13:3a.

48. The translation is based on Liu, *Chinese Classical Prose*, p. 141.

49. *The Old Man Who Does as He Pleases*, p. 33.

50. *MLL*, 13:3b–4b.

51. See the detailed map in Shiba, *Sōdai Kōnan keizai-shi no kenkyū*, pp. 324–325.

52. *MLL*, 16:14b.

53. Yang Dequan, "Tang Song hanghui zhidu," p. 220; *MLL*, 13:2a–3a.

54. *MLL*, 13:2b; see also *WLJS*, 6:14a–17a.

55. All the details given are quoted from the *MLL*, 13:3b–6b; *DCJS*, pp. 14–15; Kuhn, *Die Song-Dynastie*, pp. 256–257.

56. *MLL*, 13:6a.

10. A Changing World of Production

1. *Zhongguo lidai tongji*, p. 6.

2. Xing Tie, *Zhongguo jiating shi*, p. 90.

3. Golas, "Rural China in the Sung," pp. 300–305.

4. *SS*, 422:12605.

5. Based on Xing Tie, *Zhongguo jiating shi*, p. 28; Yanagida Setsuko, "Sōdai no katōko ni tsuite," p. 131.

6. *Zhongguo lidai tongji*, pp. 150–151; Kuhn, *Die Song-Dynastie*, pp. 196–197, 199; Xing Tie, *Zhongguo jiating shi*, p. 89.

7. See Deng, *The Premodern Chinese Economy*, p. 180.

8. See Bray, *Science and Civilisation in China*, Vol. 6:2, pp. 434–495, quotation on p. 478.

9. Ibid., p. 493.

10. *WXTK*, 4:59; Aoyama, "Le développement des transports fluviaux sous les Sung," pp. 283–284.

11. Bray, *Science and Civilisation in China*, Vol. 6:2, p. 514.

12. Zhang Jiaju, *Liang Song jingji zhongxin de nanyi*, pp. 11–12; Kuhn, *Die Song-Dynastie*, pp. 154–156; *JS*, 50:1114–1115; see also Franke, "The Chin," p. 299.

13. For more information see Zhu Zhongsheng, *Bei Song cha zhi shengchan yu jingying*; Saeki Tomi, *Sōdai chahō kenkyū shiryō*; Ukers, *All about Tea*.

14. See Kuhn, *Science and Civilisation in China*, Vol. 5:9, pp. 358–362.

15. *NS*, 26:6a–7b; 20:17ab; Kuhn, *Science and Civilisation in China*, Vol. 5:9, pp. 225–236.

16. Liu, "Painting and Commerce in Northern Song Dynasty China"; Liu, "The Water Mill and Northern Song Imperial Patronage," pp. 566–595; Kuhn, *Die Song-Dynastie*, pp. 179–180. For a mural painting, see Pan Jiezi, "Lingyan

caibi dongxin po," pl. 4; book illustrations are contained in the *NS*, 20:14, 30:6; see Kuhn, *Die Song-Dynastie*, pp. 177–180.

17. *SHYJG*, ce 147:5748.

18. From Southern Song times a great number of private travel diaries are still extant, but travel writing was marginal within the Chinese literary canon; see *LCJ*, 41:12a; Needham, *Science and Civilisation in China*, Vol. 3, p. 518; Aoyama Sadao, *Tō-Sō* jidai, p. 546; Brook, *Geographical Sources of Ming-Qing History*, p. 5.

19. *HHS*, 51:2328. *Zhonghua guwen mingda tuji*, Vol. 4, pp. 113–114, 123–124.

20. *Zhongguo gudai daolu jiaotong shi*, pp. 299–312, 336–339, 344–350.

21. So we read for example about the stone paved road measuring three meters wide leading from Luoyang to Taiyuan along the Taihang Mountains, built in 960 (*XZZTJ*, 1:20). Or we learn of the repeated road extension works starting from 962 between Gong county, Luoyang, and Shan county in present-day Henan province (*Zhongguo gudai daolu jiaotong shi*, pp. 308–309). For further information see Lewin, "Gewerbe und Handel im China der Song-Zeit. Teil I," p. 68; "Teil II," p. 152; *XZZTJCB*, 79:1806; *Zhonghua guwen mingda tuji*, Vol. 4, pp. 125 (Sichuanese courier route); *SHYJG*, ce 191, 14749:7462.

22. Quoted from Chaves, *Mei Yao-ch'en*, p. 61.

23. Fu Lehuan, "Songren shi Liao yulu xingcheng lao," pp. 725–753.

24. *LCJ*, 41:12a.

25. *LS*, 79:1271, 12:134, 17:201.

26. *Zhongguo gudai daolu jiaotong shi*, pp. 308–312.

27. *The Old Man Who Does as He Pleases*, p. 55, poem of 1202; for more information see Zhang, "The Culture of Travel in Song China."

28. *Zhonghua guwen mingda tuji*, Vol. 4, pp. 118–122.

29. *SS*, 93:2316; Kuhn, *Status und Ritus*, p. 499, map 22; Zhu Xie, *Zhongguo yunhe shiliao xuanji*, pp. 16–22.

30. Hargett, *On the Road in Twelfth Century China*, p. 26. See also Tsao, "Unraveling the Mystery of the Handscroll 'Qingming Shanghe Tu'," pp. 175–176.

31. Shiba Yoshinobu, *Sōdai shōgyō-shi kenkyū*, pp. 68–69.

32. *The Old Man Who Does as He Pleases*, p. 6.

33. Qi Xia, *Songdai jingji shi*, Vol. 2, p. 957; Hobson, *The Eastern Origin of Western Civilisation*, p. 58.

34. *Li Ch'ing-chao*, p. 67.

35. Shiba Yoshinobu, *Sōdai shōgyō-shi kenkyū*, pp. 72–73.

36. *SS*, 185:4525. Robert Hartwell estimated the annual taxed iron production of 1078 at somewhere in the region of 75,000 tons or even considerably more. The order of magnitude was doubted by Peter Golas, but recently confirmed by Donald Wagner. Qi Xia calculated that the farmers' households alone

consumed the annual iron production of 70,000 tons. See Robert Hartwell, "A Revolution in the Iron and Coal Industries during the Northern Sung, 960–1126," pp. 153–162; Hartwell, "Markets, Technology, and the Structure of Enterprise in the Development of the Eleventh-century Iron and Steel Industry," pp. 29–58; Peter Golas, *Science and Civilisation in China*, p. 170, n. 475; Donald Wagner, *Science and Civilisation in China*, pp. 279–280; Qi Xia, *Sondai jingji shi*, Vol. 2, pp. 552–553. Liu Sen, "Songdai de tieqian yu tie chanliang," p. 90.

37. Vogel and Theissen-Vogel, "Kupfererzeugung und -handel in China und Europa," pp. 14, 57; Golas, *Science and Civilisation in China*, pp. 90, 376–383; Qi Xia, *Songdai jingji shi*, Vol. 2, p. 573.

38. Golas, *Science and Civilisation in China*, p. 134, n. 352; Wang Wencheng, *Songdai baiyin huobihua yanjiu*, p. 21.

39. Waley, *The Life and Times of Po Chü-i*, pp. 61–62.

11. Money and Taxes

1. Von Glahn, *Fountain of Fortune*, p. 42.

2. *SHYJG*, 4676:4982; compare Qi Xia, *Songdai jingji shi*, Vol. 2, p. 602. Qi Xia, *Songdai jingji shi*, Vol. 2, pp. 602–603; see Hartwell, "The Evolution of the Early Northern Sung Monetary System," pp. 280–289. Xu Dongsheng, "Bei Song zhuqian zhu wenti kaobian," p. 92. *SS*, 180:4375. *WXTK*, 9:93.

3. *SS*, 180:4385.

4. Yuan Yitang, "Bei Song qianhuang," p. 131; Golas, *Science and Civilisation in China*, p. 380.

5. Von Glahn, "Re-examining the Authenticity of Song Paper Money," p. 80.

6. Quoted from *The Essence of Chinese Civilization*, p. 329.

7. *SS*, 180:4375–4376.

8. Xiao Qing, *Zhongguo gudai huobi shi*, pp. 222–224. Von Glahn, *Fountain of Fortune*, p. 52.

9. *SS*, 181:4403; Liu Sen, *Song Jin zhibi shi*, pp. 8, 10.

10. Von Glahn, "Re-examining the Authenticity of Song Paper Money," p. 90.

11. Peng Xinwei, *Zhongguo huobi shi*, fig. 58.

12. Ye Tan, "Songdai zhibi lilun kaocha," p. 134; *XZZTJCB*, 272:6663.

13. Liu Sen, *Song Jin zhibi shi*, pp. 24–26; *SS*, 181:4404.

14. Yang, *Money and Credit in China*, p. 53.

15. Miao Kunhe, *Songdai xinyong piaoju yanjiu*, pp. 131–135.

16. *SS*, 181:4403.

17. Peng Xinwei, *Zhongguo huobi shi*, fig. 58.

18. *KTLG*, 9:500.

19. Ibid.

20. Yan Jingping, "Baoji diqu faxian de Bei Song tieqian jiaocang," pp. 32–42.

21. *SS*, 415:12448. Liu Sen, *Song Jin zhibi shi,* pp. 80–81. *HCDQJ,* 51:10; *SS,* 415:12448.

22. *SS*, 430:12784.

23. Von Glahn, "Re-examining the Authenticity of Song Paper Money," p. 106. See Qi Xia, *Songdai jingji shi,* pp. 1082–1085.

24. Xiao Qing, *Zhongguo gudai huobi shi,* pp. 238–239; Von Glahn, *Fountain of Fortune,* p. 55.

25. Wang Wencheng, *Songdai baiyin huobihua yanjiu,* pp. 175–178, 198–201. See Golas, *Science and Civilisation in China,* pp. 123–124, 133–134.

26. Yang, *Money and Credit in China,* p. 95; Liu Qiugen, "Tang Song gaoli huoziben de fazhan," p. 37.

27. Twitchett, *Financial Administration,* p. 39; Chen Dengyuan, *Zhongguo tianfu shi,* pp. 99–108; *WXTK,* 3:45; Fu, "A Study of Governmental Accounting," p. 118.

28. *TS,* 145:4723–4733.

29. Liu, *Chinese Classical Prose,* p. 109.

30. Quoted from the translation of Giles, *Gems of Chinese Literature,* p. 156.

31. Peterson, "Court and Province in Mid- and Late T'ang," p. 498.

32. *SS,* 174:4202.

33. For diverging measures see also *SS,* 175:4231–4232; *Zhongguo chuantong gongyi quanji,* p. 542.

34. *Mei Yaochen ji biannian jiaozhu,* Vol. 3, p. 922; *Zhongguo lidai tongji,* p. 284; the calculation is based on *SHYJG,* ce 156, *shihuo* 64:6086–6093.

35. Wei Tian'an, "Songdai bubo shengchan gaiguan," p. 98; the figures of annual tax income are contained in Kuhn, "Songdai Sichuan de fangzhiye," pp. 253–254.

36. *SS,* 174:4202–4203; *Song Yuan jingji shi,* pp. 126–127; *SS,* 186:4541.

37. *The Old Man Who Does as He Pleases,* p. 56.

38. *SS,* 422:12605.

39. Lewin, "Gewerbe und Handel im China der Song-Zeit. Teil II," p. 135; Qi Xia, *Songdai jingji shi,* p. 1009; Bao Weimin, *Songdai difang caizheng shi yanjiu,* p. 319. Miao Kunhe, *Songdai xinyong piaoju yanjiu,* p. 42.

40. *SS,* 179:4349; Li Huarui, *Songdai jiu de shengchan he zhengque,* p. 367; for figures of salt from 996 to 1112 see Chien, *Salt and State,* p. 99; *SS,* 179:4353; Qian Mu, *Guoshi dagang,* p. 388. Gao Congming, *Songdai huobi yu huobi liutong yanjiu,* p. 18; Bao Weimin, *Songdai difang caizheng shi yanjiu,* pp. 316–318.

41. Von Glahn, *Fountain of Fortune,* p. 55.

42. Tao, *Two Sons of Heaven,* p. 32.

43. *DJGZ,* 32:3b.

44. Franke, "The Chin," pp. 302–303; *SSJSBM,* 72:755.

45. Von Glahn, *Fountain of Fortune*, p. 52.

46. See also Twitchett and Tietze, "The Liao," p. 95.

12. Private Lives in the Public Sphere

1. *SS*, 154:3600; see Ruitenbeek, *Carpentry and Building in Late Imperial China*, pp. 177–181.

2. Ebrey, *Chu Hsi's Family Rituals*, pp. 6–9.

3. Lamouroux, "'Old Models': Court Culture and Antiquity between 1070 and 1125 in Northern Song China."

4. *MQBT*, 24:236 (no. 425).

5. Lin, *The Transformation of the Chinese Lyrical Tradition*, p. 31.

6. Quoted from Shiba, *Commerce and Society in Sung China*, p. 204.

7. *HCLQJ*, 4:1b–2a. See for more information the erudite discussion of the shift in posture in Kieschnick, *The Impact of Buddhism on Chinese Material Culture*, p. 223.

8. Lin, *The Transformation of the Chinese Lyrical Tradition*, p. 216.

9. Zhang Jiaju, *Liang Song jingji*, p. 27.

10. Louis, *Die Goldschmiede der Tang- und Song-Zeit*, pp. 183–185. Qi Dongfang, *Tangdai jinyinqi yanjiu*; *SHYJG*, ce 44:1782; see Ch'ü, *Law and Society in Traditional China*, p. 144.

11. Hughes-Stanton and Kerr, *Kiln Sites of Ancient China*; Vainker, *Chinese Pottery and Porcelain*, pp. 88–133.

12. Zhang, "The Culture of Travel in Song China," p. 82.

13. *SHYJG*, ce 44:1782–1783.

14. *SMSSY*, 4:46. Wang Qingyu, *Liaodai fushi*, pp. 128–134.

15. Gernet, *Daily Life in China*, p. 126.

16. Chaves, *Mei Yao-chen*, p. 191.

17. *HCLQJ*, 4:11a–12b. Hartman, *Han Yu and the T'ang Search for Unity*, pp. 312–313, n. 223.

18. Su Bai, *Baisha Song mu*, col. pls. 6, 8:2, pl. 32.

19. *Gugong shuhua lu*, 7.22–23, 45. For Empress Liu's biography see Chaffee, "The Rise and Regency of Empress Liu."

20. *MLL*, 13:5a; *JLB*, in *SF*, 27:1272.

21. The translation is based on Liu, "Empress Liu's Icon," pp. 135–136; on the "pretty smile" see Zhou Xun and Gao Chunming, *Zhongguo chuantong fushi xingzhi shi*, p. 198, fig. 122.

22. *Li Ch'ing-chao*, p. 6.

23. Zhou Xun and Gao Chunming, *Zhongguo chuantong fushi xingzhi shi*, p. 204, fig. 281.

24. McKnight, *Law and Order in Sung China*, pp. 348–351; Pang Dexin, *Songdai liangjing shimin shenghuo*, p. 285.

25. *CGL,* 9:137; *JLB,* in *SF,* 6:118–127; quoted from Pang Dexin, *Songdai liangjing shimin shenghuo,* p. 286.

26. For various styles and a general description see Ko, *Every Step a Lotus.*

27. Ebrey, *The Inner Quarters,* pp. 37–43.

28. *CGL,* 10:158.

29. Yi Yongwen, *Songdai shimin shenghuo,* p. 34; Kuhn, *A Place for the Dead,* pp. 118, 123, fig. 2:3C; Wang Binling, *Zhongguo hunyin shi,* p. 228.

30. Quoted from Pang Dexin, *Songdai liangjing shimin shenghuo,* p. 291. See also Ebrey, *The Inner Quarters,* p. 40.

31. Ebrey, *The Inner Quarters,* pp. 40–43.

32. Wang, *Aching for Beauty,* p. 3; Hansen, *The Open Empire,* pp. 288–289.

33. *MQBT,* 1:23 (no. 8).

34. Li Yingqiang, *Zhongguo fuzhuang,* pp. 43–44. *SS,* 169:4051, 153:3561.

35. *MQBT,* 1:23–24 (no. 9). Kuhn, *Die Song-Dynastie,* pp. 328–329. *SS,* 153:3564, 3574; Chaves, *Mei Yao-ch'en,* pp. 144–145, 168.

36. *Su Dong-po,* p. 58. *Fuzhou Nan Song Huang Sheng mu,* pp. 30, 10, fig. 6; Kuhn, *A Place for the Dead,* pp. 144–145.

37. Egan, "Huizong's Palace Poems," p. 390.

38. *Fuzhou Nan Song Huang Sheng mu,* pp. 85–110; Kuhn, *Die Song-Dynastie,* pp. 356–365.

39. Zhu Tianshu, *Liaodai jinyin qi.*

40. *MQBT,* 1:24 (no. 9).

41. *LS,* 55:905–910, 22:264.

42. Leung, "Felt Yurts Neatly Arrayed, Large Tents Huddle Close," pp. 206–207. *LS,* 55:900, 56:906, 908.

43. Zhao Pingchun and Zhao Xianji, *Jindai sizhi yishu. LS,* 17:197.

44. *WLJS,* 3:1a–15b.

45. See the translation in Strassberg, *Inscribed Landscapes,* pp. 254–255.

46. Quoted from Lin, *The Transformation of the Chinese Lyrical Tradition,* p. 35.

47. Ibid., p. 27.

48. *MLL,* 16:2b–4a.

49. Gernet, *Daily Life in China,* pp. 133–140; Freeman, "Sung," pp. 143–176.

50. *MLL,* 16:8b–9a.

51. Blofeld, *The Chinese Art of Tea.*

52. *MLL,* 16:1ab.

53. *SMCJJ,* 62:753–755. Translation is quoted from Clart, "The Concept of Ritual in the Thought of Sima Guang (1019–1086)."

54. Goldschmidt, "The Transformations of Chinese Medicine," p. 209.

55. Ibid., p. 7; Goldschmidt, "Huizong's Impact on Medicine and on Public Health," p. 286; *MLL,* 15:4a.

56. Wang Weiping, "Tang Song shiqi cishan shiye gaishuo," p. 97.

57. *MLL*, 13:4a–5b.

58. *QBBZ*, 1:14; Moule, *Quinsai with Other Notes*, p. 44.

59. *Family and Property in Sung China*, p. 229; Wang Shanjun, *Songdai zongzu he zongzu zhidu yanjiu*, pp. 64–68.

60. Paraphrased on the basis of the text in *MLL*, 18:20b.

61. *SS*, 29:536; see Gernet, *Daily Life in China*, pp. 149–150.

BIBLIOGRAPHY

Primary Sources

BMSY. Beimeng suoyan (Connected Words, Compiled North of Yunmeng) by Sun Guangxian (d. 968).

CGL. Chuogeng lu (Talks While the Plough Is Resting) by Tao Zongyi (1366). Shijie shuju-ed.

DCJS. Ducheng jisheng (Record on the Splendours of the Capital) by Guanpu naideweng (1235). Beijing: Zhongguo shangye chubanshe, 1982.

DDSL. Dongdu shilüe (Historical Outline of the Eastern Capital) by Wang Cheng (1186).

DJGZ. Da Jinguo zhi (History of the Great Jin Kingdom) by Yuwen Maozhao (1234?). Hanyun zhai congshu-ed.

DJMHL. Dongjing menghua lu (Dreams of the Splendour of the Eastern Capital) by Meng Yuanlao (1147). Congshu jicheng-ed. *Dongjing menghua lu zhu* by Deng Zhicheng. Hong Kong: Shangwu yinshu guan, 1961.

ECJ. Er Cheng ji (Collected Works of the Two Cheng) by Cheng Hao (b. 1032, d. 1085) and Cheng Yi (b. 1033, d. 1107). Beijing: Zhonghua shuju, 1981.

HCDQJ. Houcun xiansheng daquanji (Complete Works of Mr. Houcun) by Liu Kezhuang (b. 1187, d. 1209). Sibu congkan-ed, Vol. 12.

HCLQJ. (Han) Changli (xiansheng) quanji (Complete Works of Han Yu). Sibu beiyao-ed.

HHS. Hou Han shu (Dynastic History of the Later Han), comp. Fan Ye (450). Beijing: Zhonghua shuju, 1965.

JLB. Jilei bian (Chicken Ribs) by Zhuang Chuo (1133). SF-ed.

JS. Jin shi (Dynastic History of the Jin), comp. Tuo Tuo (1344). Beijing: Zhonghua shuju, 1975.

JSJSBM. Jin shi jishi benmo (Record of Events of Jin History from the Beginning to the End) by Li Youtang (1903). Beijing: Zhonghua shuju, 1980.

JTS. Jiu Tang shu (Old Dynastic History of the Tang), comp. Liu Xu (945). Beijing: Zhonghua shuju, 1975.

JZYBGS. Ji zangyong baiguan shi (Report on Coffins Made of Cypress for Funerals) by Cheng Yi (b. 1033. d. 1107). *Er Cheng ji*, Beijing: Zhonghua shuju 1981.

KTLG. Keting leigao (Various Outlines from the Guest Pavilion) by Yang Guanqing (b. 1139). Siku quanshu, Vol. 1165.

LCJ. Luancheng ji (Collected Works of Su Che) by Su Che (b. 1039, d. 1112). Sibu beiyao-ed., Vol. 560.

LJZS. Liji zhushu (The Book of Rites with Commentaries). Siku quanshu-ed.

LS. Liao shi (Dynastic History of the Liao), comp. Tuo Tuo (1344). Beijing: Zhonghua shuju, 1974.

LTSS. Luting shishi (Facts from the Court of the Barbarians) by Wen Weijian (Song) in *SF*-ed.

MLL. Mengliang lu (Report of a Dream over a Bowl of Millet Gruel) by Wu Zimu (1334). Xuejin taoyuan-ed.

MQBT. Mengqi bitan (Notes Taken in Mengqi) by Shen Gua (1086–1093). Hong Kong: Zhonghua shuju, 1975.

NS. Nongshu (Book of Agriculture) by Wang Zhen (1313). Baibu congshu-ed. of 1530.

PZKT. Pingzhou ketan (Chats in Pingzhou) by Zhu Yu (1119). Congshu jicheng-ed.

QBBZ. Qingbo biezhi (Complementary Notes by One Who Lives Near the Gate of Qingbo) by Zhou Hui (1194). Congshu jicheng-ed.

QDGZ. Qidan guozhi (History of the Khitan) by Ye Longli (1247). Hanyun zhai congshu-ed.

QLW. Quan Liao wen (Complete Literature of the Liao Dynasty), ed. Chen Shu. Beijing: Zhonghua shuju, 1982.

QSB. Quesao bian (Notes Compiled in Seclusion) by Xu Du (ca. 1130). Congshu jicheng chubian, no. 2791.

QTW. Quan Tang wen (Complete Literature of the Tang Dynasty), ed. Dong Gao (b. 1740, d. 1818). Tainan: Qingwei shuju, 1965.

RZSBWJ. Rongzhai suibi wuji (Five Collections of Brush Notes from the Rongzhai Studio) by Hong Mai (1196), in *SKQSJH*.

SDJK. Song Dongjing kao (Investigation of the Eastern Capital of the Song Dynasty) by Zhou Cheng (1762). Beijing: Zhonghua shuju, 1988.

SDPQJ. Su Dongpo quanji (Complete Works of Su Shi). Taibei: Shijie shuju, 1964.

SF. Shuofu (Florilegium of [Unofficial] Literature), ed. Tao Zongyi (1368). Shanghai guji chubanshe-ed.

SHYJG. Song huiyao jigao (Drafts of Documents Pertaining to Matters of State in the Song Dynasty), comp. Xu Song (b. 1781, d. 1848). Taibei: Xin wenfeng chubanshe, 1976.

SKQSJH. Siku quanshu jinghua (Essential Parts of the Siku Quanshu), ed. Guo Wushi. Beijing: Guoji wenhua chuban gongsi, 1995.

SMSSY. Sima shi shuyi (Notes on the Yili by Master Sima) by Sima Guang. Congshu jicheng-ed.

SMCJJ. Sima wenzheng gong chuanjia ji (Collected Works of Sima Wenguo Wenzheng Gong) Sima Guang (1132). Guoxue jiben congshu-ed.

SMJW. Songmo jiwen (Records of Hearsay on the Pine-forests North of the Desert) by Hong Hao (b. 1088, d. 1155). SF-ed.

SS. Song shi (Dynastic History of the Song), comp. Tuo Tuo (1345). Beijing: Zhonghua shuju, 1977.

SSJSBM. Song shi jishi benmo (Record of Events of Song History from the Beginning to the End) by Chen Bangzhan (1604–1605). Beijing: Zhonghua shuju, 1977.

SWJ. Song wen jian (Mirror of Song Literature) by Lu Zuqian (ca. 1170). Taibei: Shijie shuju, 1960.

SXT. Song xingtong (Collected Penal Laws of the Song), comp. Dou Yi (b. 914, d. 966) et al. Beijing: Zhonghua shuju, 1984.

SYXA. Song Yuan xue'an (Historical Survey of the Philosophical Schools of the Song and Yuan) by Huang Zongxi (b. 1610, d. 1695). Taibei: Guangwen shuju, 1971.

THY. Tang huiyao (Important Documents of the Tang Period) by Wang Pu (b. 922, d. 982). Shanghai: Shanghai guji chubanshe, 1991.

TPHYJ. Taiping huanyu ji (Universal Geography of the Reign-period Taiping) by Yue Shi (ca. 980). Siku quanshu-ed.

TLJCFK. Tang liangjing chengfang kao (Study on the Walls and Wards of the Two Tang Capitals) by Xu Song (1848). Beijing: Zhonghua shuju, 1985.

WDHY. Wudai huiyao (Important Documents on the Five Dynasties Period) by Wang Pu (961). Congshu jicheng chupian-ed.

WXTK. Wenxian tongkao (General Investigation on Important Writings), comp. Ma Duanlin (1308). Beijing: Zhonghua shuju, 1986.

XSQJ. Xiangshan quanji (Complete Works of Master Lu Jiuyuan, 1521). Guoxue jiben congshu.

XTS. Xin Tang shu (New Dynastic History of the Tang), comp. Ouyang Xiu (b. 1007, d. 1072) and Song Qi (b. 998, d. 1061). Beijing: Zhonghua shuju, 1975.

XWDS. Xin Wudai shi (New Dynastic History of the Five Dynasties), by Ouyang Xiu (1072). Beijing: Zhonghua shuju, 1974.

XYXFY. Xin yixiang fayao (New Design for an Armillary Clock) by Su Song (1094).

XZZTJ. *Xu zizhi tongjian* (*Continuation of the Comprehensive Mirror to Aid in Government*) by Bi Yuan (1801). Beijing: Zhonghua shuju, 1957.

XZZTJCB. *Xu zizhi tongjian changbian* (*Long Draft of the Continuation of the Comprehensive Mirror to Aid in Government*) by Li Tao (1183). Beijing: Zhonghua shuju, 1979.

YH. *Yuhai* (*Sea of Jades*) by Wang Yinglin (b. 1223, d. 1296). Shanghai: Jiangsu guji chubanshe, 1990.

YQ. *Yiqian* (*Charity Gravepaths*) by Wang Yue (1237), in *Qinchuan zhi* (Monograph of Qinchuan, Jiangsu) by Lu Zhen (1365). Song Yuan difang zhi congshu-ed.

YS. *Yuan shi* (*Dynastic History of the Yuan*), comp. Song Lian (1370). Beijing: Zhonghua shuju, 1976.

YZ. *Yizhong* (*Charity Graveyards*), in *Jingding Jiangkang zhi* (*Description of Jiankang in the Jingding Reign-period, 1260 to 1264*) by Zhou Yinghe (1261). Song Yuan difang zhi congshu-ed.

ZGDBK. *Zhongguo dabaike quanshu. Zhongguo lishi* (*The Great Encyclopaedia of China: History of China*). Beijing, 1992.

ZJLXSWJ. *Zhijiang Li xiansheng wenji* (*Complete Writings of Li Gou*) by Li Gou (b. 1009, d. 1059). Sibu congkan-ed.

ZYL. *Zun Yao lu* (*Records Following Emperor Yao*), by Luo Congyan (1226). Luo Yuzhang xiansheng wenji in Zhengyi tang quanshu.

ZZBZ. *Zhenzong beizheng* (*The Northern Expedition of Emperor Zhenzong*) in *RZSBWJ*.

ZZTJ. *Zizhi tongjian* (*Comprehensive Mirror to Aid in Government*) by Sima Guang (1067–1084). Beijing: Zhonghua shuju, 1956.

ZZYL. *Zhuzi yulei* (*Topically Arranged Conversations of Master Zhu*) by Huang Shiyi (1219; published in 1270 by Li Jingde). Beijing: Zhonghua shuju, 1986.

Secondary Sources

Allsen, Thomas T. *Mongol Imperialism: The Policies of the Grand Qan Möngke in China, Russia, and the Islamic Lands, 1251–1259.* Berkeley: University of California Press, 1987.

———— "The Rise of the Mongolian Empire and the Mongolian Rule in North China." In *The Cambridge History of China.* Vol. 6: *Alien Regimes and Border States, 907–1368,* ed. Herbert Franke and Denis Twitchett, pp. 321–413. Cambridge: Cambridge University Press, 1994.

Al-Sirafi and Abu Zayd Hasan bin Yazid. *Ancient Accounts of India and China by Two Mohammedan Travellers Who Went to Those Parts in the 9th Century,* trans. from Arabic by Eusebius Renandot. London: S. Harding, 1733.

Ancient Chinese Architecture, ed. Chinese Academy of Architecture. Hong
  Kong: Joint Publishing, 1982.

Aoyama Sadao. "Le développement des transports fluviaux sous les Sung." In
  Études Song in memoriam of Étienne Balazs. Sung studies, serie I, ed.
  Françoise Aubin, pp. 281–296. Paris: Mouton, 1970.

—— *Tō-Sō jidai no kōtsū to chishi chizu no kenkyū (Studies of the Transportation Systems and the Gazetteers and Maps of the Tang and Song Periods).*
  Tokyo: Yoshikawa kōbunkan, 1963.

Asim, Ina. *Religiöse Landverträge aus der Song-Zeit.* Heidelberg: Edition Forum, 1993.

—— "Status Symbol and Insurance Policy: Song Land Deeds for the After-
  life." In *Burial in Song China,* ed. Dieter Kuhn, pp. 307–370. Heidelberg:
  Edition Forum, 1994.

Bacon, Francis. *Novum Organum,* trans. and ed. Peter Urbach and John Gibson.
  Chicago: Open Court Publishing, 1994.

Bao Weimin. *Songdai difang caizheng shi yanjiu (History of Regional Finances
  in Song Time).* Shanghai: Shanghai guji chubanshe, 2001.

*Bei Song Shaanzhou louzeyuan (The Louzeyuan of Shaanzhou Prefecture in the
  Northern Song Dynasty),* ed. Sanmenxia shi wenwu gongzuodui. Beijing:
  Wenwu, 1999.

Bickford, Maggie. "Huizong's Paintings: Art and the Art of Emperorship." In
  *Emperor Huizong and Late Northern Song China: The Politics of Culture
  and the Culture of Politics,* ed. Patricia Buckley Ebrey and Maggie Bickford,
  pp. 453–513. Cambridge: Harvard University Asia Center, 2006.

Bielenstein, Hans. *Diplomacy and Trade in the Chinese World, 589–1276.*
  Leiden: Brill, 2005.

Birdwhistell, Anne D. *Transition to Neo-Confucianism: Shao Yung on Knowledge and Symbols of Reality.* Stanford: Stanford University Press,
  1989.

Birge, Bettine. *Women, Property, and Confucian Reaction in Sung and Yüan
  China (960–1368).* Cambridge: Cambridge University Press, 2002.

Blofeld, John. *The Chinese Art of Tea.* London: Allen and Unwin, 1985.

Blunden, Caroline, and Mark Elvin. *Cultural Atlas of China.* Oxford: Phaidon,
  1983.

Bol, Peter K. "Emperors Can Claim Antiquity Too: Emperorship and Autocracy
  under the New Policies." In *Emperor Huizong and Late Northern Song
  China: The Politics of Culture and the Culture of Politics,* ed. Patricia
  Buckley Ebrey and Maggie Bickford, pp. 173–205. Cambridge: Harvard
  University Asia Center, 2006.

—— "On the Problem of Contextualizing Ideas: Reflections on Yü Yingshi's
  Approach to the Study of Song Daoxue." *Journal of Sung-Yuan Studies* 34
  (2004): 60–79.

———— "This Culture of Ours": Intellectual Transitions in T'ang and Sung
    China. Stanford: Stanford University Press, 1992.
Bossler, Beverly. "Shifting Identities: Courtesans and Concubines in Song
    China." Harvard Journal of Asiatic Studies 62, 1 (2002): 5–37.
Bray, Francesca. Science and Civilisation in China. Vol. 6.2: Agriculture. Cam-
    bridge: Cambridge University Press, 1984.
Brook, Timothy. Geographical Sources of Ming-Qing History. Ann Arbor: Cen-
    ter for Chinese Studies, University of Michigan, 1988.
Bruce, J. Percy. Chu Hsi and His Masters. London: Probsthain, 1923.
Buddhism in the Sung, ed. Peter N. Gregory and Daniel A. Getz, Jr. Honolulu:
    University of Hawai'i Press, 1999.
Buriks, P. "Fan Chung-yan's Versuch einer Reform des chinesischen
    Beamtenstaates in den Jahren 1043/44." Oriens extremus 3 (1956): 57–80,
    153–184.
Cahill, James. "The Imperial Painting Academy." In Possessing the Past, ed. Wen
    C. Fong, James C. Y. Watt, et al., pp. 159–199. New York: Metropolitan
    Museum of Art, 1996.
Cahill, Suzanne. "Taoism at the Song Court: The Heavenly Text Affair of
    1008." Bulletin of Sung-Yüan Studies 16 (1980): 23–44.
Carter, Thomas Francis. The Invention of Printing in China and Its Spread
    Westward, 2nd ed., rev. L. Carrington Goodrich. New York: Ronald, 1955.
Ch'en, Kenneth. Buddhism in China: A Historical Survey. Princeton: Princeton
    University Press, 1964.
———— "The Economic Background of the Hui-ch'ang Suppression of Bud-
    dhism." Harvard Journal of Asiatic Studies 19 (1956): 67–105.
Ch'ü, Tung-tsu. Law and Society in Traditional China. Paris: Mouton, 1961.
Chaffee, John W. Branches of Heaven: A History of the Imperial Clan of Sung
    China. Cambridge: Harvard University Asia Center, 1999.
———— "Education and Examination in Sung China." Ph.D. diss., University of
    Chicago, 1979.
———— "Huizong, Cai Jing, and the Politics of Reform." In Emperor Huizong
    and Late Northern Song China: The Politics of Culture and the Culture of
    Politics, ed. Patricia Buckley Ebrey and Maggie Bickford, pp. 31–77. Cam-
    bridge: Harvard University Asia Center, 2006.
———— "The Rise and Regency of the Empress Liu (969–1033)." Journal of
    Sung-Yuan Studies 31 (2001): 1–25.
———— The Thorny Gates of Learning in Sung China: A Social History of
    Examinations. Cambridge: Cambridge University Press, 1985.
Chan, Hok-lam. The Historiography of the Chin Dynasty: Three Studies.
    Wiesbaden: Franz Steiner, 1970.
Chan, Wing-tsit. "Chou Tun-I." In Sung Biographies, Vol. 1, ed. Herbert
    Franke, pp. 277–281. Wiesbaden: Steiner, 1976.
———— Chu Hsi, Life and Thought. New York: St. Martin's Press, 1987.

—— A Source Book in Chinese Philosophy. Princeton: Princeton University Press, 1963.

Chang, Carsun. The Development of Neo-Confucian Thought. London: Vision Press, 1958.

Chang, Kang-i Sun. "Liu Yung." In The Indiana Companion to Chinese Literature, Vol. 1, p. 594.

Chaves, Jonathan. Mei Yao-ch'en and the Development of Early Sung Poetry. New York: Columbia University Press, 1976.

Chen Dengyuan. Zhongguo tianfu shi (History of Land-tax in China). Shanghai: Shangwu shudian, 1938.

Chen Rongzhao. Fan Zhongyan yanjiu (Research on Fan Zhongyan). Hong Kong: Sanlian shudian, 1987.

Chen Shisong, et al. Song Yuan zhanzheng shi (History of the War between the Song and Yuan). Chengdu: Sichuansheng shehui kexueyuan chubanshe, 1988.

Chen Zengbi. "Qiannian guta" ("A One Thousand Years Old Bench"). Wenwu 1984.6:66–69.

Cheng Qianfan and Wu Xinlei. Liang Song wenxue shi (History of Song Literature). Shanghai: Shanghai guji chubanshe, 1991.

Cheng Suiying. Tang Song Kaifeng shengtai huanjing yanjiu (On the Ecological Conditions of Kaifeng in Tang and Song Times). Beijing: Zhongguo shehui kexue chubanshe, 2002.

Cherniack, Susan. "Book Culture and Textual Transmission in Sung China." Harvard Journal of Asiatic Studies 54 (1994): 5–125.

Chien, Cecilia Lee-fang. Salt and State: An Annotated Translation of the Song Shi Salt Monopoly Treatise. Ann Arbor: University of Michigan Center for Chinese Studies, 2004.

Chikusa Masaaki. Sō no Taiso to Taisō (The Emperors Taizu and Taizong of the Song). Tokyo: Shimizu shoin, 1975.

Chinese Religion: An Anthology of Sources, ed. Deborah Sommer. Oxford: Oxford University Press, 1995.

Chinese Science: Explorations of an Ancient Tradition, ed. Shigeru Nakayama and Nathan Sivin. Cambridge: MIT Press, 1973.

Chu Hsi and Neo-Confucianism, ed. Chan Wing-tsit. Honolulu: University of Hawai'i Press, 1986.

Chung, Priscilla Ching. Palace Women in the Northern Sung, 960–1126. Leiden: Brill, 1981.

Clart, Philip. "The Concept of Ritual in the Thought of Sima Guang (1019–1086)." In Perceptions of Antiquity in Chinese Civilization, ed. Dieter Kuhn and Helga Stahl, pp. 237–252. Heidelberg: Edition Forum, 2008.

Davis, Edward L. Society and the Supernatural in Song China. Honolulu: University of Hawai'i Press, 2001.

Davis, Richard L. Court and Family in Sung China, 900–1279: Bureaucratic

Success and Kinship Fortunes for the Shih of Ming-chou. Durham: Duke
   University Press, 1986.

———— *Wind against the Mountain: The Crisis of Politics and Culture in
   Thirteenth-Century China.* Cambridge: Harvard University Council on East
   Asian Studies, 1996.

Death Rituals in Late Imperial and Modern China, ed. James Watson and
   Evelyn Rawski. Berkeley: University of California Press, 1988.

De Bary, William Theodore. *Waiting for the Dawn: A Plan for the Prince;
   Huang Tsung-hsi's Ming-i-tai-fang lu.* New York: Columbia University
   Press, 1993.

De Groot, J. J. M. *The Religious System of China.* 5 vols. Leiden: Brill, 1892–
   1910; rpt. Taibei: Chengwen, 1972.

Deng, Gang. *The Premodern Chinese Economy: Structural Equilibrium and
   Capitalist Sterility.* London: Routledge, 1999.

Deng Guangming. *Wang Anshi.* Beijing: Renmin chubanshe, 1975.

De Pee, Christian. "Material Ambiguity and the Hermetic Text: Cities, Tombs,
   and Middle Period History." *Journal of Sung-Yuan Studies* 34 (2004):
   81–94.

———— "The Ritual and Sexual Bodies of the Groom and Bride in Ritual Manuals of the Sung Dynasty." In *Chinese Women in the Imperial Past,* ed. Har-
   riet Zurndorfer, pp. 53–100. Leiden: Brill, 1999.

De Weerdt, Hilde. "Canon Formation and Examination Culture: The Construction of Guwen and Daoxue Canons." *Journal of Sung-Yuan Studies* 29
   (1999): 92–134.

Di Cosmo, Nicola. "Liao History and Society." In *Gilded Splendour: Treasures
   of China's Liao Empire (907–1125),* ed. Hsueh-man Shen, pp. 15–23. New
   York: Asia Society, 2006.

Dunnell, Ruth Wilton. "Tanguts and the Tangut State of Ta Hsia." Ph.D. diss.,
   Princeton University, 1983.

———— "The Xi Xia." In *The Cambridge History of China.* Vol. 6: *Alien
   Regimes and Border States, 907–1368,* ed. Herbert Franke and Denis
   Twitchett, pp. 154–214. Cambridge: Cambridge University Press, 1994.

Ebner von Eschenbach, Freiin Silvia. "Public Graveyards of the Song." In *Burial
   in Song China,* ed. Dieter Kuhn, pp. 215–252. Heidelberg: Edition Forum,
   1994.

———— *Die Sorge der Lebenden um die Toten. Thanatopraxis und Thanatologie
   in der Song-Zeit (960–1279).* Heidelberg: Edition Forum, 1995.

Ebrey, Patricia B. *Chu Hsi's Family Ritual.* Princeton: Princeton University Press,
   1991.

———— *Confucianism and Family Rituals in Imperial China: A Social History of
   Writing about Rites.* Princeton: Princeton University Press, 1991.

———— "Cremation in Sung China." *American Historical Review* 95 (1990):
   406–428.

———— *The Inner Quarters: Marriage and the Lives of Chinese Women in the Sung Period*. Berkeley: University of California Press, 1993.

———— "Introduction." In *Emperor Huizong and Late Northern Song China: The Politics of Culture and the Culture of Politics,* ed. Patricia Buckley Ebrey and Maggie Bickford, pp. 1–27. Cambridge: Harvard University Asia Center, 2006.

———— "Taoism and Art at the Court of Emperor Huizong." In *Taoism and the Arts of China,* ed. Stephen Little with Shawn Eichman, pp. 95–111. Chicago: Art Institute of Chicago, 2000.

Egan, Ronald. "Huizong's Palace Poems." In *Emperor Huizong and Late Northern Song China: The Politics of Culture and the Culture of Politics,* ed. Patricia Buckley Ebrey and Maggie Bickford, pp. 361–394. Cambridge: Harvard University Asia Center, 2006.

———— *The Literary Works of Ou-yang Hsiu (1007–1072)*. Cambridge: Cambridge University Press, 1984.

———— *Word, Image, and Deed in the Life of Su Shi*. Cambridge: Harvard University Council on East Asian Studies, 1994.

Elvin, Mark. *The Pattern of the Chinese Past*. Stanford: Stanford University Press, 1973.

Ennin's Diary: The Record of a Pilgrimage to China in Search of the Law, trans. from the Chinese by Edwin O. Reischauer. New York: Ronald Press, 1955.

"Faku Yemaotai Liao mu jilue" ("Report on the Liao Tomb of Yemaotai, Faku District, Liaoning Province"). *Wenwu* 1975.12: 26–36.

Family and Property in Sung China: Yuan Ts'ai's "Precepts for Social Life," trans. Patricia B. Ebrey. Princeton: Princeton University Press, 1984.

Fan Xuehui. "Guanyu 'bei jiu shi bingquan' ruogan wenti de zai tantao" ("New Debates about 'The Removal of Warlords by Drinking'"). *Shixue yuekan* 2006.3: 38–48.

Fischer, J. "Fan Chung-yen, das Lebensbild eines chinesischen Staatsmannes." *Oriens extremus* 2 (1955): 39–85, 142–156.

Fong, Grace S., "Engendering the Lyric: Her Image and Voice in Song." In *Voices of the Song Lyric in China,* ed. Pauline Yu, pp. 107–144. Berkeley: University of California Press, 1994.

Fong, Wen C. "Monumental Landscape Painting." In *Possessing the Past,* ed. Wen C. Fong, James C. Y. Watt, et al., pp. 120–137. New York: Metropolitan Museum of Art, 1996.

Fong, Wen C., et al. *Images of the Mind*. Princeton: The Art Museum, Princeton University, 1984.

Forage, Paul Christopher. "Science, Technology, and War in Song China." Ph.D. diss., University of Toronto, 1991.

Forke, Alfred. *Geschichte der neueren chinesischen Philosophie*. Hamburg: Cram, de Gruyter, 1964.

Franke, Herbert. "Chia Ssu-tao (1213–1275): A 'Bad Last Minister'?" In *Confucian Personalities,* ed. Arthur F. Wright and Denis Twitchett, pp. 217–234. Stanford: Stanford University Press, 1962.

—— "The Chin." In *The Cambridge History of China.* Vol. 6: *Alien Regimes and Border States, 907–1368,* ed. Herbert Franke and Denis Twitchett, pp. 215–320. Cambridge: Cambridge University Press, 1994.

—— "The Forest Peoples of Manchuria: Khitans and Jurchens." In *The Cambridge History of Early Inner Asia,* ed. Denis Sinor, pp. 400–423. Cambridge: Cambridge University Press, 1990.

—— *Studien und Texte zur Kriegsgeschichte der Südlichen Sungzeit.* Wiesbaden: Otto Harrassowitz, 1987.

—— "Treaties between Sung and Chin." In *Études Song in memoriam of Étienne Balazs. Sung studies, serie I,* ed. Françoise Aubin, pp. 55–84. Paris: Mouton, 1970.

Franke, Wolfgang. "Historical Precedent or Accidental Repetition of Events? K'ou Chun in 1004 and Yu Ch'ien in 1449." In *Études Song in memoriam of Étienne Balazs. Sung studies, serie I, 3,* ed. Françoise Aubin, pp. 199–206. Paris: Mouton, 1976.

Freeman, Michael Dennis. "Lo-yang and the Opposition to Wang An-shih: The Rise of Confucian Conservatism (1068–1086)." Ph.D. diss., Yale University, 1973.

—— "Sung." In *Food in Chinese Culture: Anthropological and Historical Perspectives,* ed. Kwang-chih Chang, pp. 143–176. New Haven: Yale University Press, 1977.

Fu, Hongchu. "The Cultural Fashioning of Filial Piety: A Reading of 'Xiao Zhangtu' (Little Zhang the Butcher)." *Journal of Sung-Yuan Studies* 29 (1999): 63–89.

Fu Lehuan. "Songren shi Liao yulu xingcheng lao" ("An Investigation into the Travelling Routes of Song Embassies to the Liao as Seen from Their Records"). *Guoxue jikan* 5, 4 (1935): 725–753.

Fu, Philip Yuen-ko. "A Study of Governmental Accounting in China: With Special Reference to the Sung Dynasty (960–1279)." Ph.D. diss., University of Illinois, Urbana.

Fuller, Michael A. *The Road to East Slope: The Development of Su Shi's Poetic Voice.* Stanford: Stanford University Press, 1990.

Fung Yu-lan. *A History of Chinese Philosophy.* Vol. 2: *The Period of Classical Learning,* trans. Derk Bodde. Princeton: Princeton University Press, 1953.

Fuzhou Nan Song Huang Sheng mu (The Tomb of Huang Sheng of Southern Song Times in Fuzhou). Beijing: Wenwu chubanshe, 1982.

Gao Congming. *Songdai huobi yu huobi liutong yanjiu (Currency and Currency Circulation in Song Times).* Baoding: Hebei daxue chubanshe, 1999.

Gernet, Jacques. *Buddhism in Chinese Society.* New York: Columbia University Press, 1995.

—— *Daily Life in China on the Eve of the Mongol Invasion, 1250–1276.* Stanford: Stanford University Press, 1970.

Giles, Herbert. *Gems of Chinese Literature.* Shanghai, 1923; rpt. Taipei: Literature House, 1964.

Giles, Lionel. "Chinese Printing in the Tenth Century." *Journal of the Royal Asiatic Society of Great Britain and Ireland* 56 (1925): 513–515.

Golas, Peter J. "Rural China in the Song." *Journal of Asian Studies* 39, 2 (1980): 291–325.

—— *Science and Civilisation in China.* Vol. 5.13: *Mining.* Cambridge: Cambridge University Press, 1999.

Goldschmidt, Asaf. "Huizong's Impact on Medicine and on Public Health." In *Emperor Huizong and Late Northern Song China: The Politics of Culture and the Culture of Politics,* ed. Patricia Buckley Ebrey and Maggie Bickford, pp. 275–323. Cambridge: Harvard University Asia Center, 2006.

—— "The Transformations of Chinese Medicine during the Northern Song Dynasty (A.D. 960–1127)." Ph.D. diss., University of Pennsylvania.

Graff, David A. *Medieval Chinese Warfare, 300–900.* London: Routledge, 2002.

Grand Exhibition of Silk Road Civilizations, ed. Nara Prefectural Museum of Art. Nara, 1988.

Gugong shuhua lu (Catalog of Works of Calligraphy and Painting in the National Palace Museum). Taipei: National Palace Museum, 1965.

Gugong Song hua jinghua (Paintings from the Song Dynasty in the National Palace Museum). Taipei: Gakken, 1975.

Haeger, John W. "Between North and South: The Lake Rebellion in Hunan, 1130–1135." *Journal of Asian Studies* 28, 3 (1969): 469–488.

Halperin, Mark. *Out of the Cloister: Literati Perspectives on Buddhism in Sung China, 960–1279.* Cambridge: Harvard University Asia Center, 2006.

Hana, Corina. *Bericht über die Verteidigung der Stadt Tê-an während der Periode k'ai-hsi 1205–1208 (K'ai-hsi Tê-an shou-ch'eng lu) von Wang Chih-yüan.* Wiesbaden: Franz Steiner, 1970.

Hansen, Valerie. *The Beijing Qingming Scroll and Its Significance for the Study of Chinese History.* New Haven: Yale University Press, 1996.

—— *Negotiating Life in Daily China: How Ordinary People Used Contracts, 600–1400.* New Haven: Yale University Press, 1995.

—— *The Open Empire: A History of China to 1600.* New York: Norton, 2000.

Hargett, James M. "Huizong's Magic Marchmount: The Genyue Pleasure Park in Kaifeng." *Monumenta Serica* 38 (1988–89): 1–48.

—— *On the Road in Twelfth Century China: The Travel Diaries of Fan Chengda (1126–1193).* Stuttgart: Franz Steiner, 1989.

Hartman, Charles. *Han Yü and the T'ang Search for Unity.* Princeton: Princeton University Press, 1986.

———— "Poetry." In *The Indiana Companion to Traditional Chinese Literature,* Vol. 1, pp. 59–74.

———— "Zhu Xi and His World." *Journal of Song-Yuan Studies* 36 (2006): 107–131.

Hartwell, Robert M. "A Cycle of Economic Change in Imperial China: Coal and Iron in Northeast China, 750–1350." *Journal of the Economic and Social History of the Orient* 10 (1967): 102–159.

———— "Demographic, Political, and Social Transformations of China, 750–1550." *Harvard Journal of Asiatic Studies* 42 (1982): 365–442.

———— "The Evolution of the Early Northern Sung Monetary System." *Journal of the American Oriental Society* 87:3 (1967): 280–289.

———— "Markets, Technology, and the Structure of Enterprise in the Development of the Seventeenth-century Iron and Steel Industry." *Journal of Economic History* 26, 1 (1966): 29–58.

———— "A Revolution in the Iron and Coal Industries during the Northern Sung, 960–1126." *Journal of Asian Studies* 21 (1962): 153–162.

Hay, John. "Along the River during Winter's First Snow: A Tenth-century Handscroll and Early Chinese Narrative." *Burlington Magazine* 104:830 (1972): 294–302.

He Zhongli. "Bei Song kuoda keju qushi de yuanyin ji yu rongguan rongli de guanxi" ("The Extension of the Imperial Examinations in the Northern Song Dynasty: Its Causes and Relationships to the Emergence of Redundant Government Officials"). In *Song shi yanjiu jikan* (*Collection of Research Works on the Song Dynasty*), ed. Xu Gui, pp. 87–106. Hangzhou: Zhejiang guji chubanshe, 1986.

———— *Songdai zhengzhi shi* (*Political History of the Song Dynasty*). Hangzhou: Zhejiang daxue chubanshe, 2007.

Heng, Chye Kiang. *Cities of Aristocrats and Bureaucrats.* Singapore: Singapore University Press, 1999.

Hightower, James R. "The Songwriter Liu Yong: Part I." *Harvard Journal of Asiatic Studies* 41, 2 (1981): 323–376.

Historical Records of the Five Dynasties. Ouyang Xiu, trans. with introd. by Richard L. Davis. New York: Columbia University Press, 2004.

Ho, Koon-wan. "Politics and Factionalism: K'ou Chun (962–1023) and His T'ung-nien." Ph.D. diss., University of Arizona, 1990.

Ho, Ping-ti. "An Estimate of the Total Population of Sung-Chin China." In *Études Song in memoriam of Étienne Balazs. Sung studies, serie I,* ed. Françoise Aubin, pp. 3–53. Paris: Mouton, 1970.

Hoang, Michel. *Genghis Khan,* trans. Ingrid Cranfield. London: Saqi Books, 1990.

Hobson, John M. *The Eastern Origins of Western Civilisation.* Cambridge: Cambridge University Press, 2004.

Hoffmann, Alfred. *Die Lieder des Li Yü, 937–978, Herrscher der Südlichen T'ang Dynastie*. Cologne: Greven, 1950.

Holmgren, Jennifer. "Marriage, Kinship and Succession under the Ch'i-tan Rulers of the Liao Dynasty." *T'oung Pao* 72 (1986): 44–91.

Hsieh, Shan-yüan. *The Life and Thought of Li Kou, 1009–1059*. San Francisco: Chinese Materials Center, 1979.

Hu, Pin-ching. *Li Ch'ing-chao*. New York: Twayne Publishers, 1966.

Huan Kuan-chung. *Nan Song difang wuli. Difangjun yu minjian ziwei wuli de tantao* (*The Regional Military Forces in Southern Song China: Studies of Regional Armies and Local Militia*). Taipei: Dongda tushu gongsi, 2002.

Hughes-Stanton, Penelope, and Rose Kerr. *Kiln Sites of Ancient China*. London: Oriental Ceramic Society, 1980.

Hymes, Robert H. "Prominence and Power in Sung China." Ph.D. diss., University of Pennsylvania, 1979.

——— *Statesmen and Gentlemen: The Elite of Fu-chou, Chiang-hsi, in Northern and Southern Sung*. Cambridge: Cambridge University Press, 1986.

Idema, Wilt, and Stephen West. *Chinese Theater, 1100–1450: A Source Book*. Munich: Franz Steiner, 1982.

Indiana Companion to Traditional Chinese Literature, The, ed. William H. Nienhauser Jr. 2 vols. Bloomington: Indiana University Press, 1986, 1998.

Issues of Authenticity in Chinese Painting, ed. Judith G. Smith and Wen C. Fong. New York: Metropolitan Museum of Art, 1999.

Jan Yün-hua. "Buddhist Self-immolation in Medieval China." *History of Religions* 4, 2 (1965): 243–268.

Jang, Scarlett. "Realm of the Immortals: Paintings Decorating the Jade Hall of the Northern Song." *Ars Orientalis* 22 (1997): 81–96.

Jay, Jennifer W. *A Change in Dynasties: Loyalism in Thirteenth-Century China*. Bellingham: Western Washington University, 1991.

Ji, Xiao-bin. *Politics and Conservatism in Northern Song China: The Career and Thought of Sima Guang (A.D. 1019–1086)*. Hong Kong: Chinese University Press, 2005.

Jia Haitao. *Bei Song "rushu zhi guo" zhengzhi yanjiu* (*Political Research in the "Confucian Doctrine to Rule the State" in Northern Song*). Jinan: Qilu shushe, 2006.

Jianming Song shi (*Simplified History of the Song*), ed. Zhou Baozhu and Chen Zhen. Beijing: Renmin chubanshe, 1985.

Johnson, Linda Cooke. "The Place of Qingming Shanghe Tu in the Historical Geography of Song Dynasty Dongjing." *Journal of Sung-Yuan Studies* 26 (1996): 145–182.

Kaplan, Edward H. "Yue Fei and the Founding of the Southern Song." Ph.D. diss., University of Iowa, 1970.

Kara, György. "Kithan and Jurchin." In *The World's Writing Systems*, ed. Peter

D. Daniels and William Bright, pp. 230–238. New York: Oxford University Press, 1986.

Karetzky, Patricia E. "The Representation of Women in China: Recent Archaeological Evidence." *T'ang Studies* 12 (1999): 213–271.

Kasoff, Ira E. *The Thought of Chang Tsai*. Cambridge: Cambridge University Press, 1984.

Katō, Shigeshi. "Sōdai ni okeru toshi no hattatsu ni tsuite" ("The Development of Cities during the Song Dynasty"). In *Shina kezaī-shi kōshō (Studies in Chinese Economic History)*, pp. 93–140. Tokyo: Tōkyō bunko, 1952–1953.

Kieschnick, John. *The Impact of Buddhism on Chinese Material Culture*. Princeton: Princeton University Press, 2003.

Knapp, Keith Nathaniel. *Selfless Offspring: Filial Children and Social Order in Medieval China*. Honolulu: University of Hawai'i Press, 2005.

Ko, Dorothy. *Every Step a Lotus: Shoes for Bound Feet*. Berkeley: University of California Press, 2001.

Kong Xianyi. "Bei Song Dongjing chengfang kaolue" ("Study on the Streets of Dongjing"). In *Song shi yanjiu lunwen ji*, ed. Deng Guangming, pp. 346–369. Henan renmin chubanshe, 1984.

Kracke, E. A. Jr. *Civil Service in Early Sung China, 960–1067*. Cambridge: Harvard University Press, 1953.

——— "The Expansion of Educational Opportunity in the Reign of Hui-tsung of the Sung and Its Implications." *Sung Studies Newsletter* 13 (1977): 6–30.

——— "Family versus Merit in Chinese Civil Service Examinations under the Empire." In *Studies of Governmental Institutions in Chinese History*, ed. John L. Bishop, pp. 103–123. Cambridge: Harvard University Press, 1968.

——— "Sung K'ai-feng: Pragmatic Metropolis and Formalistic Capital." In *Crisis and Prosperity in Sung China*, ed. John Winthrop Haeger, pp. 49–77. Tucson: University of Arizona Press, 1975.

Kuhn, Dieter. "Decoding Tombs of the Song Elite." In *Burial in Song China*, ed. Dieter Kuhn, pp. 11–159. Heidelberg: Edition Forum, 1994.

——— "Family Rituals." *Monumenta Serica* 40 (1992): 369–385.

——— *How the Qidan Reshaped the Tradition of the Chinese Dome-shaped Tomb*. Heidelberg: Edition Forum, 1998.

——— "An Introduction to Chinese Archaeology of the Liao." In *Gilded Splendour: Treasures of China's Liao Empire (907–1125)*, ed. Hsueh-man Shen, pp. 25–39. New York: Asia Society, 2006.

——— *Die Kunst des Grabbaus. Kuppelgräber der Liao-Zeit (907–1125)*. Heidelberg: Edition Forum, 1997.

——— *A Place for the Dead: An Archaeological Documentary on Graves and Tombs of the Song Dynasty (960–1279)*. Heidelberg: Edition Forum, 1996.

——— *Science and Civilisation in China.* Vol. 5.9: *Textile Technology.* Cambridge: Cambridge University Press, 1988.

——— "Songdai Sichuan de fangzhiye: Das Textilgewerbe in Sichuan in der Song-Dynastie." In *Beiträge zur Geschichte der Song-Zeit/Contributions to the Study of Song History,* ed. Dieter Kuhn and Ina Asim, pp. 225–266. Heidelberg: Edition Forum, 2006.

——— *Die Song-Dynastie (960 bis 1279): Eine neue Gesellschaft im Spiegel ihrer Kultur.* Weinheim: Acta Humaniora VCH, 1987.

——— *Status und Ritus. Das China der Aristokraten von den Anfängen bis zum 10. Jahrhundert.* Heidelberg: Edition Forum, 1991.

——— *Der Zweite Weltkrieg in China.* Berlin: Duncker & Humblot, 1999.

Kurz, Johannes. *Das Kompilationsprojekt Song Taizongs (reg. 976–997).* Bern: Peter Lang, 2003.

Kycanov, E. I. "Les guerres entre les Sung du Nord et le Hsi-Hsia." In *Études Song in memoriam of Étienne Balazs. Sung studies, serie I, 2,* ed. Françoise Aubin, pp. 103–118. Paris: Mouton, 1971.

Lai Yonghai. *Foxue yu ruxue* (Buddhism and Confucianism). Taipei: Yangzhi wenhua, 1995.

Lam, Lap. "A Reconsideration of Liu Yong and His 'Vulgar' Lyrics." *Journal of Sung-Yuan Studies* 33 (2003): 1–47.

Lamouroux, Christian. *Fiscalité, comptes publics et politiques financières dans la Chine des Song. Le chapitre 179 du Songshi.* Paris: Collège de France, 2003.

——— "From the Yellow River to the Huai: New Representations of a River Network and the Hydraulic Crisis of 1128." In *Sediments of Time: Environment and Society in Chinese History,* ed. Mark Elvin and Liu Ts'ui-jung, pp. 545–584. Cambridge: Cambridge University Press, 1998.

——— "'Old Models': Court Culture and Antiquity between 1070 and 1125 in Northern Song China." In *Perceptions of Antiquity in Chinese Civilization,* ed. Dieter Kuhn and Helga Stahl, pp. 291–319. Heidelberg: Edition Forum, 2008.

Ledderose, Lothar. *Ten Thousand Things: Module and Mass Production in Chinese Art.* Princeton: Princeton University Press, 2000.

Lee, Thomas H. C. *Government Education and Examinations in Sung China.* Hong Kong: Chinese University Press, 1985.

Leimbiegler, Peter. *Mei Yao-ch'en (1002–1060). Versuch einer literarischen und politischen Deutung.* Wiesbaden: Harrassowitz, 1970.

Leung, Irene S. "Felt Yurts Neatly Arrayed, Large Tents Huddle Close: Visualizing the Frontier in the Northern Song Dynasty (960–1127)." In *Political Frontiers, Ethnic Boundaries, and Human Geographies in Chinese History,* ed. Nicola Di Cosmo and Don J. Wyatt, pp. 192–219. London: RoutledgeCurzon, 2003.

Levy, Howard S. *Biography of Huang Ch'ao* (trans. from *Hsin T'ang-shu*). Berkeley: University of California Press, 1955.

Lewin, Günter. *Die ersten fünfzig Jahre der Song-Dynastie in China.* Berlin: Akademie-Verlag, 1973.

Lewin, Marianne, and Günter Lewin. "Gewerbe und Handel im China der Song-Zeit. Teil I. Ein staatliches Verlagssystem im mittelalterlichen China?" *Jahrbuch des Museums für Völkerkunde zu Leipzig* 37 (1987): 13–75.

——— "Gewerbe und Handel im China der Song-Zeit. Teil II: Die chinesische Stadt." *Jahrbuch des Museums für Völkerkunde zu Leipzig* 38 (1989): 128–175.

Li Ch'ing-chao: Complete Poems, trans. and ed. Kenneth Rexroth and Ling Chung. New York: New Directions, 1979.

Li, Dun J. *The Ageless Chinese: A History.* London: J. M. Dent and Sons, 1968.

Li, Fu-chen. *The Confucian Way: A New and Systematic Study of the Four Books.* Taipei: Commercial Press, 1972.

Li Huarui. *Songdai jiu de shengchan he zhengque (The Production and Taxes of Alcohol in Song Times).* Baoding: Hebei daxue chubanshe, 2001.

——— *Song shi lunji (Collected Writings on the Song History).* Baoding: Hebei daxue chubanshe, 2001.

——— *Wang Anshi bianfa yanjiu shi (Research History of the Reform Policies of Wang Anshi).* Beijing: Renmin chubanshe, 2004.

Li Jiannong. *Song Yuan Ming jingji shigao (An Economic History of the Song, Yuan, and Ming Dynasties).* Beijing: Sanlian, 1957.

Li Qingzhao shici wencun (The Poems and Song Lyrics of Li Qingzhao), trans. Cao Shuming. Taipei: Taiwan Shangwu yinshuguan, 1992.

Li Yingqiang. *Zhongguo fuzhuang secai shilun (Historical Discussion on the Colours of Chinese Garments).* Taipei: Nantian shuju, 1993.

Liang Ssu-ch'eng. *A Pictorial History of Chinese Architecture,* ed. Wilma Fairbank. Cambridge: MIT Press, 1985.

Lin Ruihan. "Songdai guanzhi tanwei" ("Inquiry into the Officials' System of the Song Dynasty"). *Song shi yanjiu ji* 1977.9: 199–267.

Lin, Shuen-fu. *The Transformation of the Chinese Lyrical Tradition: Chiang K'uei and Southern Sung Tz'u Poetry.* Princeton: Princeton University Press, 1978.

Liu, Heping. "Empress Liu's Icon of Maitreya: Portraiture and Privacy at the Early Song Court." *Artibus Asiae* 62, 2 (2003): 129–190.

——— "Painting and Commerce in Northern Song Dynasty, 960–1126." Ph.D. diss., Yale University, 1997.

——— "The Water Mill and Northern Song Imperial Patronage of Art, Commerce, and Science." *Art Bulletin* 84, 4 (2002): 566–595.

Liu, James T. C. *China Turning Inward: Intellectual-Political Changes in the Early Twelfth Century.* Cambridge: Council on East Asian Studies, Harvard University, 1988.

———— "An Early Sung Reformer: Fan Chung-yen." In *Chinese Thought and Institutions,* ed. John K. Fairbank, pp. 105–131. Chicago: University of Chicago Press, 1967.

———— *Ou-yang Hsiu: An Eleventh-century Neo-Confucianist.* Stanford: Stanford University Press, 1967.

———— *Reform in Sung China: Wang An-shih and His New Policies.* Cambridge: Harvard University Press, 1959.

———— "The Road to Neo-Confucian Orthodoxy: An Interpretation." *Philosophies, East and West* 23, 4 (1973): 483–506.

———— "Yue Fei and China's Heritage of Loyalty." *Journal of Asian Studies* 31 (1972): 291–297.

Liu Jingzhen. *Bei Song qianqi: Huangdi he tamen de quanli (The Early Period of the Northern Song: The Emperors and Their Authority).* Taipei: Guoli bianyiguan, 1996.

———— "Bei Song qianqi huangquan fazhan zhi yanjiu" ("An Investigation of the Growth of Imperial Authority in Early Northern Song"). Ph.D. diss., National Taiwan University, 1987.

Liu Qiugen. "Tang Song gaoli huoziben de fazhan" ("On the Development of Usurers' Capital in Tang and Song Times"). *Shixue yuekan* 1992.4: 31–38.

Liu Sen. "Songdai de tieqian yu tie chanliang" ("Iron Coins and Iron Production in Song Times"). *Zhongguo jingjishi yanjiu* 1993.2: 86–90.

———— *Song Jin zhibi shi (Paper Currency in Song and Jin Times).* Beijing: Zhongguo jinrong chubanshe, 1993.

Liu, Shih Shun. *Chinese Classical Prose: The Eight Masters of the T'ang-Sung Period.* Hong Kong: Chinese University Press, 1979.

Liu, Wu-chi. *An Introduction to Chinese Literature.* Bloomington: Indiana University Press, 1966.

Liu Xiaodong, and Yang Zhijun. "Shilun Jindai Ruzhen guizu muzang de leixing ji yanbian." *Liaohai wenwu xuekan* 1991.1: 124–136.

Liu, Xinru. "Buddhist Institutions in the Lower Yangtze Region during the Song Dynasty." *Journal of Sung-Yuan Studies* 21 (1989): 31–51.

Liu Zhaomin. *Zhongguo lishi shang qihou de bianqian (Changes of Climate in Chinese History).* Taipei: Taiwan shangwu yinshuguan, 1992.

Lo, Winston Wan. *An Introduction to the Civil Service Examinations of Sung China, with Emphasis on the Personnel Administration.* Honolulu: University of Hawai'i Press, 1987.

———— *The Life and Thought of Yeh Shih.* Hong Kong: Chinese University of Hong Kong, 1974.

Lorge, Peter. "The Entrance and Exit of the Song Founders." *Journal of Sung-Yuan Studies* 29 (1999): 43–62.

———— "Song Gaozong's Letters to Yue Fei." *Journal of Sung-Yuan Studies* 30 (2000): 160–173.

Louis, Francois. *Die Goldschmiede der Tang- und Song-Zeit.* Bern: Peter Lang, 1999.

Luo Xinhui. "Zengzi yu Xiaojing" ("Master Zeng and the Classic of Filial Piety"). *Shixue yuekan* 1996.5: 6–11, 23.

Makeham, John. *Transmitters and Creators: Chinese Commentators and Commentaries on the Analects.* Cambridge: Harvard University Asia Center, 2003.

Martin, H. Desmond. *The Rise of Chingis Khan and His Conquest of North China.* Baltimore: Johns Hopkins University Press, 1950.

McGrath, Michael C. "Military and Regional Administration in Northern Sung China (960–1126)." Ph.D. diss., Princeton University, 1982.

McKnight, Brian E. *Law and Order in Sung China.* Cambridge: Cambridge University Press, 1992.

Mei Yaochen ji biannian jiaozhu (Chronologically-edited Collected Works of Mei Yaochen). 3 vols. Shanghai: Shanghai guji chubanshe, 1980.

Miao Kunhe. *Songdai xinyong piaoju yanjiu (Research on Credit Matters of Song Times).* Kunming: Yunnan daxue chubanshe, 2002.

Miyazaki, Ichisada. *China's Examination Hell: The Civil Service Examination of Imperial China,* trans. Conrad Schirokauer. New Haven: Yale University Press, 1981.

Mote, Frederick W. *Imperial China, 900–1800.* Cambridge: Harvard University Press, 1999.

Moule, A. C. *Quinsai with Other Notes on Marco Polo.* Cambridge: Cambridge University Press, 1957.

Murray, Julia K. "The Ladies' Classic of Filial Piety and Sung Textual Illustration: Problems of Reconstruction and Artistic Context." *Ars Orientalis* 18 (1988): 95–129.

Needham, Joseph. *Science and Civilisation in China.* Cambridge: Cambridge University Press, 1954–.

Needham, Joseph, Ling Wang, and Derek Price. *Heavenly Clockwork,* 2nd ed. Cambridge: Cambridge University Press, 1986.

Neo-Confucian Terms Explained (The Pei-hsi tzu-i) by Ch'en Ch'un, 1159–1223, trans. and ed., with introd. by Wing-tsit Chan. New York: Columbia University Press, 1986.

Nivison, David S., and Arthur F. Wright. *Confucianism in Action.* Stanford: Stanford University Press, 1959.

Oeuvres poétiques complètes de Li Qingchao, trans. Liang Paitchin. Paris: Gallimard, 1977.

Olsson, Karl F. "The Structure of Power under the Third Emperor of Sung China: The Shifting Balance after the Peace of Shanyuan." Ph.D. diss., University of Chicago, 1974.

Pan Jiezi. "Lingyan caibi dongxin po—Yanshansi Jindai bihua xiaoji" ("The

Motives of Mural Painting in the Lingyan Monastery"). *Wenwu* 1979.2: 3–10, pl. 4.

Pang Dexin (Pong Taksan). *Songdai liangjing shimin shenghuo* (*Daily Life in the Song Capitals*). Taipei: Longmen shudian, 1974.

Pease, Jonathan. "I Dreamed of Locusts." *Comparative Criticism* 15 (1993): 215–222.

Pelliot, Paul. *Notes on Marco Polo*. Paris: Imprimerie Nationale, 1959.

Peng Xinwei. *Zhongguo huobi shi* (*History of Chinese Currency*). Shanghai: Shanghai renmin chubanshe, 1958.

Peterson, Charles A. "Court and Province in Mid- and Late T'ang." In *The Cambridge History of China*. Vol. 3: *Sui and T'ang China*, ed. Denis Twitchett, pp. 464–560. Cambridge: Cambridge University Press, 1979.

Pettersson, Bengt. "Cannibalism in the Dynastic Histories." *Bulletin. The Museum of Far Eastern Antiquities* 71 (1999): 71–189.

Polo, Marco. *The Description of the World*, Vol. 1, ed. A. C. Moule and Paul Pelliot. London: G. Routledge, 1938.

Proclaiming Harmony, trans. O. Hennessey. Ann Arbor: Center for Chinese Studies, University of Michigan, 1981.

Qi Dongfang. *Tangdai jinyinqi yanjiu* (*Research on Tang Gold and Silver*). Beijing: Zhongguo shehui kexue chubanshe, 1999.

Qi Xia. *Songdai jingji shi* (*Economic History of the Song Dynasty*). Shanghai: Shanghai renmin chubanshe, 1988.

—— *Wang Anshi bianfa* (*Reform Policies of Wang Anshi*). Shanghai: Renmin chubanshe, 1959.

Qian Mu. *Guoshi dagang* (*An Outline of Chinese History*). Taipei: Shangwu yinshuguan, 1952.

Qiu Gang. "Beisong Dongjing sancheng de yingjian he fazhan" ("Construction and Development of the Three Walls of the Eastern Capital in Northern Song Times"). *Zhongyuan wenwu* 1990.4: 35–40.

Ratchnevsky, Paul. *Genghis Khan: His Life and Legacy.* Oxford: Blackwell, 1991.

Rawski, Evelyn S. "A Historian's Approach to Chinese Death Ritual." In *Death Ritual in Later Imperial and Modern China*, ed. James L. Watson and Evelyn S. Rawski, pp. 20–34. Berkeley: University of California Press, 1988.

Reed, Barbara E. "The Gender Symbolism of Kuan-yin Bodhisattva." In *Buddhism, Sexuality and Gender,* ed. José Ignacio Cabezón, pp. 159–180. Albany: State University of New York Press, 1992.

Reflections on Things at Hand: The Neo-Confucian Anthology Compiled by Chu Hsi and Lü Tsu-ch'ien, trans. Wing-tsit Chan. New York: Columbia University Press, 1967.

Rossabi, Morris. "The Reign of Khubilai Khan." In *The Cambridge History of*

China. Vol. 6: *Alien Regimes and Border States, 907–1368*, ed. Herbert Franke and Denis Twitchett, pp. 414–489. Cambridge: Cambridge University Press, 1994.

Ru Qihe. "Songdai guange zhi jiaokan jingbu shu" ("Classics Collated by the Academies and Institutes of the Central Government of the Song Dynasty"). *Zhongguo wenhua yanjiu* 2003.1: 82–91.

Ruitenbeek, Klaas. *Carpentry and Building in Late Imperial China*. Leiden: Brill, 1993.

Saeki Tomi. *Sōdai chahō kenkyū shiryō (Collected Materials on the Tea Taxes in Song China)*. Kyoto: Tōhō bunka kenkyūjo, 1941.

Sargent, Stuart H. "Contexts of the Song Lyric in Sung Times: Communication Technology, Social Change, Morality." In *Voices of the Song Lyric in China*, ed. Pauline Yu, pp. 226–256. Berkeley: University of California Press, 1994.

Schirokauer, Conrad M. "Chu Hsi's Political Career: A Study in Ambivalence." In *Confucian Personalities,* ed. Arthur F. Wright and Denis Twitchett, pp. 162–188. Stanford: Stanford University Press, 1962.

——— "Neo-Confucians under Attack: The Condemnation of the Wei-hsüeh." In *Crisis and Prosperity in Sung China*, ed. John W. Haeger, pp. 163–196. Tucson: University of Arizona Press, 1975.

Shiba, Yoshinobu. *Commerce and Society in Sung China*, trans. Mark Elvin. Ann Arbor: University of Michigan Center for Chinese Studies, 1970.

——— *Sōdai Kōnan keizai-shi no kenkyū (Studies in the Economy of the Lower Yangzi in the Song)*. Tokyo: Kyūko shoin, 1988.

——— *Sōdai shōgyō-shi kenkyū (Commerce and Society in Song China)*. Tokyo: Kazama shobō, 1968.

Sirén, Osvald. *The Walls and Gates of Peking*. London: John Lane, Bodley Head, 1924.

Sivin, Nathan. "Shen Gua." In *Dictionary of Scientific Biography*, ed. Charles C. Gillispie, Vol. 12, pp. 369–393. New York: Charles Scribner's, 1975. Rpt. in *Sung Studies Newsletter* 13 (1977): 13–55.

Skinner, G. William. "Introduction: Urban Development in Imperial China." In *The City in Late Imperial China*, ed. G. William Skinner, pp. 3–31. Stanford: Stanford University Press, 1977.

Smith, Paul Jakov. "Introduction: Problematizing the Song-Yuan-Ming Transition." In *The Song-Yuan-Ming Transition in Chinese History*, ed. Paul Jakov Smith and Richard von Glahn, pp. 1–34. Cambridge: Harvard University Asia Center, 2003.

——— "Irredentism as Political Capital." In *Emperor Huizong and Late Northern Song China: The Politics of Culture and the Culture of Politics,* ed. Patricia Buckley Ebrey and Maggie Bickford, pp. 78–130. Cambridge: Harvard University Asia Center, 2006.

——— "*Shuihu zhuan* and the Military Subculture of the Northern Song, 960–1127." *Harvard Journal of Asiatic Studies* 66, 2 (2006): 363–422.

Soffel, Christian. *Ein Universalgelehrter verarbeitet das Ende seiner Dynastie. Eine Analyse des Kunxue jiwen von Wang Yinglin.* Wiesbaden: Harrassowitz, 2004.

Somers, Robert M. "The End of the T'ang." In *The Cambridge History of China.* Vol. 3: *Sui and T'ang China,* ed. Denis Twitchett, pp. 682–789. Cambridge: Cambridge University Press, 1979.

Songdai jiaoyu (Education in the Song Dynasty), ed. Miao Chunde. Kaifeng: Henan daxue chubanshe, 1992.

Songdai wenhua shi (Cultural History of the Song Dynasty), ed. Yao Yingting. Kaifeng: Henan daxue chubanshe, 1992.

Song Yuan jingji shi (Economic History of Song and Yuan Times), ed. Wang Zhirui. Taipei: Shangwu yinshuguan, 1969.

Sources of Chinese Tradition, ed. William Theodore de Bary. New York: Columbia University Press, 1960.

Standen, Naomi. *Unbounded Loyalty: Frontier Crossings in Liao China.* Honolulu: University of Hawai'i Press, 2007.

Stein, Rolf. "Leao-Tche." *T'oung Pao* 35 (1939): 1–154.

Steinhardt, Nancy Shatzman. *Chinese Imperial City Planning.* Honolulu: University of Hawai'i Press, 1990.

—— *Liao Architecture.* Honolulu: University of Hawai'i Press, 1997.

Strassberg, Richard. *Inscribed Landscapes: Travel Writing from Imperial China.* Berkeley: University of California Press, 1994.

Stuart, Jan, and Evelyn S. Rawski. *Worshipping the Ancestors: Chinese Commemorative Portraits.* Washington, DC: Smithsonian Institution, 2001.

Sturman, Peter C. "Cranes above Kaifeng: The Auspicious Image at the Court of Kaifeng." *Ars Orientalis* 20 (1990): 33–68.

Su Bai. *Baisha Song mu (The Baisha Tombs of Song Times).* Beijing: Wenwu chubanshe, 1957.

Su Dong-po: A New Translation, trans. Xu Yuanzhong. Hong Kong: Commercial Press, 1982.

Su Zhecong. *Songdai nüxing wenxue (Female Literary Works in Song Times).* Wuhan: Wuhan daxue chubanshe, 1997.

Sudō Yoshiyuki. *Sōdai kanryōsei to daitochi shoyū (The Officials' System and Land Property in Song Times).* Tokyo: Nippon hyōronsha, 1950.

Sullivan, Michael. *Chinese Landscape Painting in the Sui and T'ang Dynasties.* Berkeley: University of California Press, 1980.

Sun Guotong. "Tang Song zhiji shehui mendi zhi xiaorong." In Sun Guotong, *Tang Song shi luncong,* pp. 201–308. Hong Kong: Longmen, 1980.

Sung Bibliography, A, ed. Yves Hervouet. Hong Kong: Chinese University Press, 1978.

Sung Biographies, ed. Herbert Franke. Wiesbaden: Steiner, 1976.

Tamura Jitsuzō. *Chūgoku seifuku ōchō no kenkyū (Research on the Chinese Conquest Dynasties).* 3 vols. Kyoto: Tōyōshi kenkyū kai, 1964–1986.

Tao Jing-shen. "Barbarians or Northerners: Northern Sung Images of the Khitans." In *China Among Equals: The Middle Kingdom and Its Neighbors, 10th to 14th Centuries,* ed. Morris Rossabi, pp. 66–86. Berkeley: University of California Press, 1983.

———— "The Influence of Jurchen Rule on Chinese Political Institutions." *Journal of Asian Studies* 340 (1970): 121–130.

———— *The Jurchen in Twelfth Century China: A Study in Sinicization.* Seattle: University of Washington Press, 1976.

———— "Public Schools in the Chin Dynasty." In *China under Jurchen Rule,* ed. Hoyt Cleveland Tillman and Stephen H. West, pp. 50–67. Albany: State University of New York Press, 1995.

———— *Two Sons of Heaven: Studies in Sung-Liao Relations.* Tucson: University of Arizona Press, 1988.

Tao Zongye, et al. "Hebei Xuanhua Xiabali Liao Jin bihuamu" ("Mural Painting of the Liao and Jin Dynasties in Tombs at Xiabali, Xuanhua, Hebei Province"). *Wenwu* 1990.10: 1–19, pls. 1–4.

Teng, Ssu-yü. *Family Instructions for the Yen Clan. Yen-shih chia-hsün by Yen Chih-tui.* Leiden: Brill, 1968.

Teraji Jun. *Nan Sō shoki seiji shi kenkyū (Political History in the Early Southern Song).* Hiroshima: Keishuisha, 1988.

The Essence of Chinese Civilization. ed. Dun J. Li. Toronto: Von Nostrand, 1967.

The Old Man Who Does as He Pleases: Poems and Prose by Lu Yu, trans. Burton Watson. New York: Columbia University Press, 1973.

The Song-Poetry of Wei Chuang (836–910 A.D.), trans. John Timothy Wixted. Tempe: Center for Asian Studies, Arizona State University, 1979.

The Washing away of Wrongs: Forensic Medicine in Thirteenth-century China, trans. Brian E. McKnight. Ann Arbor: Center for Chinese Studies, University of Michigan, 1981.

Tietze, Klaus. "The Liao-Song Border Conflict of 1084–1076." In *Studia mongolica: Festschrift für Herbert Franke,* pp. 127–151. Wiesbaden: Franz Steiner, 1979.

Tillman, Hoyt Cleveland. "The Idea and Reality of the 'Thing' during the Sung: Philosophical Attitudes toward *wu.*" *Bulletin of Sung Yüan Studies* 4 (1978): 68–82.

———— *Utilitarian Confucianism: Ch'en Liang's Challenge to Chu Hsi.* Cambridge: Council on East Asian Studies, Harvard University, 1982.

Traité des fonctionnaires et traité de l'armée. Traduite de nouvelle histoire des T'ang, trans. Robert des Rotours. Rpt. San Francisco: Chinese Materials Center, 1974.

Tsao, Xingyuan. "Unraveling the Mystery of the Handscroll 'Qingming shanghe tu.'" *Journal of Song-Yuan Studies* 33 (2003): 155–179.

Tsien, Tsuen-hsun. *Science and Civilisation in China.* Vol. 5.1: *Paper and Print-ing.* Cambridge: Cambridge University Press, 1985.

Twitchett, Denis. *Financial Administration under the T'ang Dynasty.* Cam-bridge: Cambridge University Press, 1970.

—— *Printing and Publishing in Medieval China.* London: Wynkyn de Worde Society, 1983.

Twitchett, Denis, and Klaus-Peter Tietze. "The Liao." In *The Cambridge History of China.* Vol. 6: *Alien Regimes and Border States, 907–1368,* ed. Herbert Franke and Denis Twitchett, pp. 43–153. Cambridge: Cambridge University Press, 1994.

Ukers, William. *All about Tea.* New York: Tea and Coffee Trade Journal, 1935.

Vainker, Shelagh J. *Chinese Pottery and Porcelain: From Prehistory to the Pres-ent.* London: British Museum Press, 1991.

Van Ess, Hans. *Von Ch'eng I zu Chu Hsi. Die Lehre vom Rechten Weg in der Überlieferung der Familie Hu.* Wiesbaden: Harrassowitz, 2003.

Vogel, Hans-Ulrich, and Elisabeth Theisen-Vogel. "Kupfererzeugung und -handel in China und Europa, Mitte des 8. bis Mitte des 19. Jahrhunderts: Eine vergleichende Studie." *Bochumer Jahrbuch zur Ostasienforschung* (1991): 1–57.

Voices of the Song Lyric in China, ed. Pauline Yu. Berkeley: University of Cali-fornia Press, 1994.

Von Glahn, Richard. *Fountain of Fortune: Money and Monetary Policy in China, 1000–1700.* Berkeley: University of California Press, 1996.

—— "Re-examining the Authenticity of Song Paper Money Specimens." *Jour-nal of Song-Yuan Studies* 36 (2006): 79–106.

—— "Imagining Pre-modern China." In *The Song-Yuan-Ming Transition in Chinese History,* ed. Paul Jakov Smith and Richard von Glahn, pp. 35–70. Cambridge: Harvard University Asia Center, 2003.

Wagner, Donald. *Science and Civilisation in China.* Vol. 5.11: *Ferrous Metal-lurgy.* Cambridge: Cambridge University Press, 2008.

Wagner, Marsha. "Hua-chien chi." In *The Indiana Companion to Traditional Chinese Literature,* Vol. 1, pp. 441–442.

Walton, Linda A. *Academies and Society in Southern Song China.* Honolulu: University of Hawai'i Press, 1999.

Waley, Arthur. *The Life and Times of Po Chü-i, 772–846 A.D.* London: George Allen and Unwin, 1949.

Wang Binling. *Zhongguo hunyin shi* (History of Marriage in China). Shanghai: Shanghai renmin chubanshe, 2001.

Wang Deyi. "Song Xiaozong jiqi shidai" ("Song Xiaozong and His Time"). *Song shi yanjiu ji* 1978.10: 245–302.

Wang Gungwu. "Feng Tao: An Essay on Confucian Loyalty." In *Confucian*

Personalities, ed. A. F. Wright and D. C. Twitchett, pp. 123–146. Stanford: Stanford University Press, 1962.

—— *The Structure of Power in North China during the Five Dynasties.* Stanford: Stanford University Press, 1967.

Wang, Ping. *Aching for Beauty: Footbinding in China.* Minneapolis: University of Minnesota Press, 2000.

Wang Qingyu. *Liaodai fushi (Garments and Adornments of the Liao Dynasty).* Shenyang: Liaoning huabao chubanshe, 2002.

Wang Shanjun. *Songdai zongzu he zongzu zhidu yanjiu (Research on the Clan and Clan System of the Song Dynasty).* Shijiazhuang: Hebei jiaoyu chubanshe, 1999.

Wang Weiping. "Tang Song shiqi cishan shiye gaishuo" ("A Brief Discussion on the Philanthropy during the Tang and Song Dynasties"). *Shixue yuekan* 2000.3: 95–102.

Wang Wencheng. *Songdai baiyin huobihua yanjiu (The Proliferation of the Silver Currency in Song Times).* Kunming: Yunnan daxue chubanshe, 2001.

Wei Tian'an. "Songdai bubo shengchan gaiguan" ("A Survey of Cloth Production in the Song Period"). In *Song shi yanjiu lun wenji,* ed. Deng Guangming, pp. 96–111. Henan renmin chubanshe, 1982.

Weinstein, Stanley. *Buddhism under the Tang.* Cambridge: Cambridge University Press, 1987.

Weng, Wan-go, and Po-ta Yang. *Palastmuseum Peking.* Munich: Prestel, 1982.

West, Stephen H. "Chilly Seas and East-flowing Rivers: Yüan Hao-wen's Poems of Death and Disorder, 1233–1235." In *China under Jurchen Rule,* ed. Hoyt Cleveland Tillman and Stephen H. West, pp. 281–304. Albany: State University of New York Press, 1995.

—— "Crossing Over: Huizong in the Afterglow, or the Deaths of a Troubling Emperor." In *Emperor Huizong and Late Northern Song China: The Politics of Culture and the Culture of Politics,* ed. Patricia Buckley Ebrey and Maggie Bickford, pp. 595–610. Cambridge: Harvard University Asia Center, 2006.

Wilhelm, Hellmut. "From Myth to Myth: The Case of Yue Fei's Biography." In *Confucian Personalities,* ed. D. C. Twitchett and A. F. Wright, pp. 146–161. Stanford: Stanford University Press, 1962.

Williamson, H. R. *Wang An Shih: A Chinese Statesman and Educationalist of the Sung Dynasty.* London: Probsthain, 1935.

Wilson, Thomas A. "Genealogy and History in Neo-Confucian Sectarian Uses of the Confucian Past." *Modern China* 20.1 (1994): 3–33.

Wittfogel, Karl A., and Chia-shêng Fêng. *History of Chinese Society: Liao (907–1125).* Philadelphia: American Philosophical Society, 1949.

Wixted, John Timothy. "The Poetry of Li Ch'ing-chao: A Woman Author and Women's Authority." In *Voices of the Song Lyric in China,* ed. Pauline Yu, pp. 145–168. Berkeley: University of California Press, 1994.

———— "Yuan Haowen." In *The Indiana Companion to Traditional Chinese Literature,* Vol. 1, pp. 953–955.

Worthy, Edmund Henry, Jr. "The Founding of Sung China, 950–1000: Integrative Changes in Military and Political Institutions." Ph.D. diss., Princeton University, 1975.

Wu, K. T. "Chinese Printing under Four Alien Dynasties (916–1368)." *Harvard Journal of Asiatic Studies* 13 (1950): 447–523.

Wu, Pei-yi. "Childhood Remembered: Parents and Children in China, 800 to 1700." In *Chinese Views of Childhood,* ed. Anne Behnke Kinney, pp. 129–156. Honolulu: University of Hawai'i Press, 1995.

Wu Songdi. *Zhongguo renkou shi, di san juan: Liao Song Jin Yuan shiqi (History of China's Population.* Vol. 3: *Liao, Song, Jin, and Yuan Periods).* Shanghai: Fudan daxue chubanshe, 2000.

Wu Tianzhi. *Xi Xia shigao (Draft of the History of the Xi Xia).* Chengdu: Sichuan renmin chubanshe, 1983.

Wu Xiaoping. *Songdai waijiao zhidu yanjiu (Research on the Foreign Affairs System of the Song).* Hefei: Anhui renmin chubanshe, 2006.

Wyatt, Don J. "The Invention of the Northern Song." In *Political Frontiers, Ethnic Boundaries, and Human Geographies in Chinese History,* ed. Nicola Di Cosmo and Don J. Wyatt, pp. 220–244. London: RoutledgeCurzon, 2003.

———— *The Recluse of Loyang: Shao Yung and the Moral Evolution of Early Sung Thought.* Honolulu: University of Hawai'i Press, 1996.

Xiao Qing. *Zhongguo gudai huobi shi (A History of Ancient Currency in China).* Beijing: Renmin chubanshe, 1984.

Xing Tie. *Zhongguo jiating shi. Di san juan. Song Liao Jin Yuan shiqi (A General History of the Chinese Family.* Vol. 3: *Song, Liao, Jin, and Yuan Dynasties),* ed. Zhang Guogang. Guangzhou: Guangdong renmin chubanshe, 2007.

Xu Dongsheng. "Bei Song chuqian zhu wenti kaobian" ("Study on the Money Casting in the Northern Song Dynasty"). *Zhongguoshi yanjiu* 2006.4: 91–100.

Xu Gui, and Fang Rujin. "Ping Song Taizu 'xian nan hou bei' de tongyi zhanlue" ("Commentary on the Unification Strategy 'The South First, The North Later' of the First Emperor of the Song"). In *Song shi yanjiu lunwen ji,* ed. Deng Guangming et al., pp. 517–534. Henan renmin chubanshe, 1984.

Xu, Yinong. *The Chinese City in Space and Time: The Development of Urban Form in Suzhou.* Honolulu: University of Hawai'i Press, 2000.

Yan Jingping. "Baoji diqu faxian de Bei Song tieqian jiaocang" ("Northern Song Hoards of Iron Coins Discovered in the Baoji Area"). *Zhongguo qianbi* 1988.1: 32–42.

Yanagida Setsuko. "Sōdai no katōko ni tsuite" ("Song Households of the Low Category"). *Tōyō gakuhō* 40:2 (1957): 131.

Yang Dequan. "Tang Song hanghui zhidu zhi yanjiu" ("Studies of the Guild System in Tang and Song Times"). In *Song shi yanjiu lunwen ji* (*Essays on Song Dynasty History*), ed. Deng Guangming, pp. 204–240. Shanghai: Shanghai guji chubanshe, 1982.

Yang, Lien-sheng. *Money and Credit in China*. Cambridge: Harvard University Press, 1952.

Yang Shufan. "Songdai zaixiang zhidu" ("The System of Chief Councilors of the Song Dynasty"). *Songdai yanjiu* 15 (1984): 1–34.

Yang Weisheng. "Lun Zhao Song zhi tongyi yu zhengzhi" ("Unification and Consolidation of the Song Dynasty"). *Hangzhou daxue xuebao* 1994.3: 54–65.

Yao Hanyuan. *Zhongguo shuili shi gangyao* (*An Historical Outline of Hydraulic Engineering in China*). Beijing: Shuili dianli chubanshe, 1987.

Yao, Tao-chung. "Buddhism and Taoism under the Chin." In *China under Jurchen Rule,* ed. Hoyt Cleveland Tillman and Stephen H. West, pp. 145–182. Albany: State University of New York Press, 1995.

Yao, Xinzhong. *An Introduction to Confucianism*. Cambridge: Cambridge University Press, 2000.

Yates, Robin D. S. *Washing Silk: The Life and Selected Poems of Wei Chuang (834?–910)*. Cambridge: Council on East Asian Studies, Harvard University, 1988.

Ye Tan. "Songdai zhibi lilun kaocha" ("Investigation on Paper Money Theory in Song Times"). *Zhongguo jingjishi yanjiu* 1990.4: 133–145.

Yi Yongwen. *Songdai shimin shenghuo* (*Daily Life of Song Urbanites*). Beijing: Zhongguo shehui chubanshe, 1999.

Yoshikawa, Kōjirō. *Five Hundred Years of Chinese Poetry, 1150–1650*, trans. John Timothy Wixted. Princeton: Princeton University Press, 1989.

Yoshioka, Yoshinobu. *Sōdai Kōga-shi kenkyū* (*Studies on the History of the Yellow River*). Tokyo: Ochanomizu shobō, 1983.

Yü, Chün-fang. "Guanyin: The Chinese Transformation of Avalokitesvara." In *Latter Day of the Law: Images of Chinese Buddhism, 859–1850*, ed. Marsha Weidner, pp. 151–181. Honolulu: University of Hawai'i Press, 1994.

Yu Yingshi. *Zhu Xi de lishi shijie: Songdai shidafu zhengzhi wenhua de yanjiu* (*Zhu Xi's Historical World: Researches on the Political Culture of the Song Shidafu*). Taipei: Yunchen wenhua gongsi, 2003.

Yu Yunguo. *Xishuo Songchao* (*Circumstantial Details: The Song Dynasty*). Shanghai: Shanghai renmin chubanshe, 2002.

Yuan Yitang. "Bei Song qianhuang: cong bizhi dao liutong tizhi de cha" ("Shortage of Coins in Northern Song Times: Investigation of Money Circulation on the Basis of the Money System"). *Lishi yanjiu* 1991.4: 129–140.

Zhang Bozhong. "Qidan zaoqi wenhua tansuo" ("On the Early Culture of the Khitan"). *Kaogu* 1984.2: 183–186.

Zhang, Cong. "The Culture of Travel in Song China (960–1276)." Ph.D. diss., University of Washington, Seattle, 2003.

Zhang Jiaju. *Liang Song jingji zhongxin de nanyi* (*The Shift of the Economic Centres to the South in the Northern and Southern Song*). Wuhan: Hebei renmin chubanshe, 1957.

Zhang Jin. "Kaifeng lidai huanggong yange yu Bei Song Dongjing huangcheng fanwei xinkao" ("Evolution of Kaifeng Palace through the Ages and New Analytic Research of Confines of the Northern Song Dynasty Dongjing Palace City"). *Shixue yuekan* 2002.7: 87–94.

Zhang Qifan. "'Huangdi yu shidafu gong zhi tianxia' shixi—Bei Song zhengzhi jiagou tanwei" ("Analysis of 'The Emperor Running the State Together with Scholar-Bureaucrats': Preliminary Study of the Political Framework of the Northern Song"). *Jinan xuebao: zheshe ban* (Guangzhou) 2001.6: 114–123.

Zhang Quanming. "Lun Bei Song Kaifeng diqu de qihou bianqian ji qi tedien" ("On the Vicissitudes and Features of Climate in Kaifeng District in the Northern Song Dynasty"). *Shixue yuekan* 2007.1: 98–108.

Zhao Pingchun, and Zhao Xianji. *Jindai sizhi yishu* (*The Silk Art in the Jin Dynasty*). Beijing: Kexue chubanshe, 2001.

Zhongguo chuantong gongyi quanji: Sichou zhiran (*Complete Works of Chinese Traditional Crafts: Silk Weaving and Dyeing*), ed. Lu Yongxiang. Zhengzhou: Daxiang chubanshe, 2005.

Zhongguo gudai daolu jiaotong shi (*History of the Road Communication System of Chinese Ancient Times*), ed. Li Lianxiang. Beijing: Renmin jiaotong chubanshe, 1994.

Zhongguo lidai hukou tiandi tianfu tongji (*China's Historical Population, Land, and Land-tax Statistics*), ed. Liang Fangzhong. Shanghai: Shanghai renmin chubanshe, 1980.

Zhongguo lishi. Song shi (*Chinese History: Song History*), ed. Zhou Baozhu and Chen Zhen. Beijing: Renmin chubanshe, 2006.

Zhongguo lishi. Sui Tang Liao Song Jin juan (*Chinese History: Sui, Tang, Liao, Song, Jin volume*), ed. Zhang Guogang and Yang Shusen. Beijing: Gaodeng jiaoyu chubanshe, 2001.

Zhonghua guwen mingda tuji, Vol. 4, ed. Liu Changle. Beijing: Renmin ribao chubanshe, 1992.

Zhou Baozhu. "Bei Song shiqi de Xijing Luoyang" ("Luoyang City in the Northern Song Dynasty"). *Shixue yuekan* 2001.4: 109–116.

——— *Songdai Dongjing yanjiu* (*Research on Dongjing of the Song Dynasty*).
     Kaifeng: Henan daxue chubanshe, 1992.
Zhou Xun, and Gao Chunming. *Zhongguo chuantong fushi xingzhi shi* (*History
     of Shape and Structure of Traditional Chinese Garment and Adornment*).
     Taipei: Nantian shuju, 1998.
Zhu Tianshu. *Liaodai jinyin qi* (*Gold and Silver Articles of the Liao Dynasty*).
     Beijing: Wenwu chubanshe, 1998.
Zhu Xie. *Zhongguo yunhe shiliao xuanji* (*Collection of Historical Materials on
     Chinese Canals*). Beijing: Zhonghua shuju, 1962.
Zhu Zhongsheng. *Bei Song cha zhi shengchan yu jingying* (*Tea Production and
     Management in the Northern Song Dynasty*). Taipei: Xuesheng shuju,
     1985.

ACKNOWLEDGMENTS

I would like to acknowledge my great debt to the community of Song, Liao, Jin, and Yuan scholars whose research and publications formed the basis for this history. Their names are contained in the notes and bibliography. Moreover, I wish to express my appreciation to Timothy Brook, General Editor of History of Imperial China, Kathleen McDermott, sponsoring editor at Harvard University Press and the originator of this series, a most helpful anonymous reviewer engaged by the Press, and in particular Susan Wallace Boehmer, also at HUP, for their numerous suggestions on how to improve this book. Without the patience of my wife, Ingrid Josefa, it would not have been possible to finish the manuscript on time. Any remaining errors and, unless otherwise quoted, all translations are my own.

INDEX

Abaoji, 20–23, 148, 156

Admonitions of Women (*Nüjie*), 142

Agriculture, 2, 21, 52, 55–57, 58, 80, 93, 126, 209, 213–220, 232, 246–247, 278; beans, 88, 219, 228; fruits and vegetables, 219; Green Sprouts program, 55–56; rice, 214, 217–219, 227. *See also* Farmers

Aguda (Jin Emperor Taizu), 63–64, 66–67, 69

Aizong, Jin Emperor (Wanyan Shouxu), 91

Alcohol, 209, 217, 246, 248, 270, 273; wine, 33, 34, 134, 141, 143, 148, 167, 177, 190, 197, 202–203, 208, 209, 242, 269–271

Among the Flowers (*Huajian ji*), 164

Analects, 51, 104, 129, 143

Ancestor worship, 30, 111–113, 138–139, 142, 146, 157, 187, 253

Ancestral halls, 138, 252–253

Ancient Prose Movement, 130–133

An Lushan, 11, 16

Anthology of Rhyme Prose (*Wenxuan*), 40, 41

Architecture, 3, 81, 127; ancestral hall as architecture, 252; architectural painters, 222; Buddhist, 117, 118; housing, 205; Liao, 117, 204; political significance, of 24; Tang, 118; tombs, 153, 157, 159, 177, 179–180; urban, 187–189, 200, 205; Zhou bridge as model, 200

Aristocracy, 1, 10, 14, 18, 19, 37, 56, 124, 125, 134, 214, 244, 265; alien regimes, 82, 115, 147, 155, 168, 178–179; Tang, 49, 120, 121, 152, 159, 189, 190, 276;

tombs, 152–154, 157, 159, 178–179; urban, 189, 190, 191, 199, 202, 211

Astronomical clock, 183–186

Astronomy, 182, 183, 186

Banditry, 14–17, 77

Bathing, 256–257

Beauty, 110, 139, 164, 166, 211, 254, 260, 262–263. *See also* Eroticism; Foot binding; Women

Beijing, 23, 24, 25, 35, 66, 81, 89, 98, 115, 117, 186, 212

Bian River, 199–200, 218–219, 228, 229, 230, 279

Bickford, Mary, 173

Biographies of Women (*Lienü zhuan*), 143

Bi Sheng, 183

Bo Juyi, 232, 257

Bol, Peter K., 1

Book of Agriculture (*Nongshu*), 220

Bronze, 14, 184, 235

Brothels, 63, 190, 202, 203, 271

Buddhism, 30, 41, 50, 107–119, 120, 121, 149, 199, 202, 208, 253, 270, 271; architecture, 117, 118; burial, 149–151; confiscation of Buddhist metal, 14–15; criticisms of, 108, 110–112, 117; impact on Confucianism, 99–101, 104, 109–112, 118–119, 130, 276–277; Indian Buddhism, 110–111; Liao and Jin dynasties, 22, 114–118; Meditation Buddhism, 109–110, 117, 118; monasteries, 108–109, 169, 189, 272, 274; persecution of, 13–15, 108, 109; Pure Land Buddhism, 109–110, 115; ritual and, 108, 111, 149;

Buddhism *(continued)*
  scholar-officials and, 106, 108, 110, 113,
  118; state support for, 108–109, 276;
  Three Doctrines, 99, 111, 276
Bureau of Astronomy, 183, 184
Bureau for Exchange Bills, 236
Bureau of Imperial Music, 202
Bureau of Military Affairs, 38, 44
Bureaucracy, 5, 19, 29, 32, 37–38, 52–53,
  80, 120–125, 130, 133–134, 137, 276,
  279; Chancellery, 38; Central Secretariat,
  38, 43; Department of State Affairs, 38;
  202; growth in, 124; protection appointments, 52, 124, 125, 134; provincial, 58;
  Tang, 133, 134, 135. *See also* Civil service examination; Scholar-officials

Cai Jing, 64, 68, 86, 127
Cai Xiang, 53, 140, 220, 271
Calendar, 25, 80, 184, 186, 268
Calligraphy, 53, 65, 108, 137, 144, 168, 173
Canals, 228–230
Canon of Filial Piety (Xiaojing), 113, 143
*Canon of the Way and Its Power (Daode
  jing)*, 107, 111
*Canon of Women's Filial Piety (Nü
  xiaojing)*, 113, 142
Capitalism, 251, 275, 276, 279
Cartography, 183, 186, 224
Centralization (of state authority), 2, 5,
  36–40, 56
Central Secretariat, 38, 43
Ceramics, 190, 209, 254–255, 265, 278;
  ceramic vs. metal housewares, 255, 265
Chai Rong (Later Zhou Emperor Shizong),
  19
Chairs: bamboo chairs, 255; in tombs, 179;
  sedan chairs, 142, 255; versus mats, 176,
  253; women and, 253
Chancellery, 38
Chang'an, 24, 164, 187–191, 194, 195,
  239, 279; as ideal Confucian capital,
  188, 204, 207; as model of urban development, 191; as Tang capital, 16–18,
  187, 191, 227; compared to other capitals, 195, 211–212; curfew, 191; decline
  of, 191; grandeur, 195; layout, 187–189;
  markets, 190; numerology and, 188–
  189; public executions, 191; ward system, 189–190. *See also* Cities
Changes, 100, 101, 129
Chen Chun, 107
Chen Dong, 67
Chengdu, 74, 171, 172, 227, 236, 237

Cheng Hao, 60, 100–103, 140, 277
Chengtian, Empress Dowager, 25
Cheng Yi, 100–104, 106, 111, 126, 140
Chen Liang, 29, 105; on foreign policy, 8,
  78–79, 167
Chen Yizhong, 96–97
Che Ruorui, 262
Chinggis (Genghis) Khan, 87–92; ferocity
  of, 89–90; succession, 92
Christianity, 30, 92, 243
Cities: architecture, 187–189, 200, 205;
  city expansion, 192–193; compared,
  211–212; Confucian ideals and, 188,
  204, 207; curfew, 190, 191, 194, 279;
  economic activity, 190, 197, 207–211;
  entertainment, 202, 203; layout, 187–
  189, 194, 199–203, 206–207; Liao and
  Jin, 204–205, 212; population, 191, 204,
  205, 207, 247; property rights, 192;
  public executions, 98, 191; suburbs,
  192–194, 197, 199, 212; taxes, 199; urban decline, 191; urban life of commoners, 189–190, 191, 196, 199, 200, 202,
  208; ward system, 189–190, 192. *See
  also specific cities*
Civil principle (*wen*), 29, 31, 32–33, 43–44
Civil service examination, 1, 3, 39, 42, 43,
  53–56, 61, 80–81, 100, 104, 120–124,
  127, 130–133, 141; Ancient Prose
  Movement, 130–133; effectiveness of,
  48, 137, 280; emperor role in, 123, 129;
  Jinshi degree, 25, 39, 53, 81, 82, 84, 98,
  101, 103, 121–124, 128–132, 140, 162,
  164; quotas, 122–123; social mobility
  and, 124–125. *See also* Bureaucracy; Education; Scholar-officials
Civil society, 2, 4, 9
Classics, Confucian, 3, 18, 29, 40, 42, 81,
  82, 125, 129, 130, 132, 149, 150
Clothing, 28, 81, 142, 179, 204, 263–266;
  alien regimes, 83, 268; "barbarian" influence, 264; commoners, 210, 220, 256,
  264, 265; precious metals in, 261, 262,
  264, 265–266, 268; regulations, 263–
  264; scholar-officials, 264; Tang, 264,
  265, 266, 268
Coexistence policy, 2, 28, 29, 45–48, 76–
  80, 278
Coins, 14, 66, 93, 230–243, 249, 250, 255
*Collected Commentaries on the Four
  Books (Sishu zhangju jizhu)*, 104
*Collected Writings of the Washing Away of
  Wrongs (Xiyuan jilu)*, 182
Commoners, 144, 255, 280; clothing, 210,

220, 256, 264, 265; education, 126, 127; Emperor Qinzong as, 68; foot binding, 263; forced labor and, 228; funerary practices, 149–150, 155; households, 211, 252; Jurchen, 82; Khitan, 147; marriage, 141, 147; money and, 236; taxes, 246–248; tea, 220; urban life, 189–190, 191, 196, 199, 200, 202, 208; working life, 256. *See also* Inequality, social

Compass, 161, 182

Complete Works of Ouyang Xiu (Jushi ji), 54

Comprehensive Mirror to Aid in Government (Zizhi tongjian), 59

Concubines, 139, 256, 263

Confucianism. *See* Neo-Confucianism

Confucius, 1, 5, 22, 47, 61, 80, 100, 103, 104, 106, 113, 120, 121, 167, 207, 264

Conservative Neo-Confucian thought, 50, 53, 54, 61, 186, 253

Conversations of Master Zhu (Zhuzi yulei), 103

Copper: funerary rites, 155, money, 231–236, 239–240, 243, 248, 250; mining, 278

Corruption, 4, 58, 64, 75, 134, 140, 162

Cosmetics, 197, 211, 257–261. *See also* Beauty; Eroticism; Women

Cosmology, 171, 183, 188, 194, 205, 211, 273

Cranes of Good Omen, 173, 174

Cremation, 151, 155, 157, 275

Cultural attitudes, 5, 8, 14, 20, 46–47, 65, 68, 79, 83, 87, 92–93, 151, 268. *See also* Han Chinese; Jurchens; Khitans; Tanguts

Cultural supremacy. *See* Cultural attitudes

Curfew, 190, 191, 194, 279

Daoism, 30, 36, 47, 65, 111, 112, 120, 121, 122, 149, 150, 173, 177, 258–259, 270; criticisms of, 111; influence on Confucianism, 99–101, 104, 106–108, 111, 118, 276–277; politics and, 107–108; Three Doctrines, 99, 111, 276

Dao (Way), 61, 100, 101, 107, 132, 207

Daozong, Liao Emperor (Yelü Hongji), 61–62, 115, 147

Da Qi buffer, 77

Department of State Affairs, 38, 202

Diplomacy. *See* Foreign policy (Song)

Discourse on Teachers (Shi shuo), 131

Divorce, 139, 143, 145, 148

Doctrine of the Mean (Zhongyong), 101–102, 129, 167

Dong Yuan, 169

Dou Jian, 69

Dowries, 145

Dreaming of Locusts (Meng huang), 162

Duanzong, Emperor (Zhao Shi), 97

Du Chong, 72

Du Fu, 161

Du You, 233

Duzong, Emperor (Zhao Qi), 94–95, 97

Dynastic History of the Jin (Jinshu), 168

Dynastic History of the Liao (Liao shi), 25

Dynastic History of the Song (Song shi), 31, 38, 46, 153

Education: commoners, 126, 127; Confucian, 3, 8, 9, 11, 30, 42, 104–105, 120, 124, 131, 137, 161, 273, 276, 277, 279–280; educational institutions, 125–128; legal, 56, 126, 127; Liao and Jin, 61, 80–81, 83; medical, 273; reform, 54, 56, 126–127, 129–130, 277; Tang, 120, 121, 124, 129, 130, 132, 160. *See also* Civil service examination; Scholar-officials; Women

Emperor: 10, 29, 30, 44, 47, 49, 123, 206; advice to, 36–38, 121; and civil principle, 2; as moral exemplar, 29–30, 44; as Son of Heaven, 10, 39, 46, 151; Buddhism and, 14, 15, 118; burial of, 151, 156; centralized authority and, 38; Confucianism and, 43, 118; eunuchs and, 12; Imperial Palace, 252–253; Liao, 115, 268; Mandate of Heaven, 31; property, 213, 214; relationship to aristocracy, 189; relationship to court officials, 39, 40, 121, 133, 255; relationship to military, 33; responsibility for dynastic decline, 10; ritual and, 10, 29, 30, 44, 47, 49, 123, 206; role in civil service examination, 123, 129; role in transformation of China, 276; tenure of, 277–278

Emperor Taizu Visits His Advisor Zhao Pu on a Snowy Winter Night (Xueye fang Pu tu), 34, 35

Entertainment, 268–270; urban life and, 202, 203

Eroticism, 106, 164, 166, 260, 263

Ethnicity, attitudes toward. *See* Cultural attitudes

Etiquette and Rites (Yili), 149

Eunuchs, 12–13, 14, 18, 19, 24, 58, 64, 68, 76, 97, 107, 128, 189

Europe, 22, 278, 279; ability to manage large-scale deaths, 150; Catholic Church,

Europe *(continued)*
37; compared to Song, 150, 186, 210, 230, 243, 278; Enlightenment, 183; funerary practices, 155–156; guilds, 210; money lending, 243; Mongols and, 91; population compared to Jin, 75; scientific advancements, 186; ships, 230; transmission of Chinese technology, 161, 182, 222, 279

Exchange bills, 236–239, 248

Executions, 13, 62, 63, 64, 86, 96; public, 98, 191

Explanation of the Diagram of the Great Ultimate (Taijitu shuo), 101

Extensive Records of the Grand Tranquility Reign (Taiping guangji), 41

Factionalism, 12, 37, 39, 49–53, 60, 62, 64, 77–78, 84–86, 105, 162; Old Policies vs. New Policies factions, 60

Family businesses, 210–211

Family Rituals (Jiali), 104, 149, 252

Fan Zhongyan, 126, 274; on Emperor Taizu, 32; reforms of, 49–54; Ten-Point Memorial, 52. *See also* Reform

Fan Zuyu, 54

Farmers: categories of farming households, 214–216; living conditions, 3, 15–16, 55, 56, 72, 74, 128, 227, 241–242, 244, 256; rice farmers, 218; self-managing farmers, 3, 213–216, 232, 246, 247, 278. *See also* Agriculture

Feng Dao, 40

Festivals, 136, 197, 256, 269; Buddhist, 112; Lantern, 173, 268; New Year's, 202, 268

Filial piety, 29, 98, 111, 112, 113–114, 142, 143, 148, 153, 155, 157, 179, 274

Finest Flowers of the Preserve of Letters (Wenyuan yinghua), 41

Finest of Ancient Prose (Guwen guanzhi), 133

Firearms, 161

Fiscal policy, 38, 54, 244, 245; alien regimes and, 249–250; fiscal reform, 93, 237–238, 241, 244. *See also* Money

Five Classics, 129

Five Dynasties, 4, 18–20, 31, 36, 191, 245, 261; problems of, 34, 41, 71

Five Virtues, 4, 55

Flower and Rock Network, 66

Foot binding, 196, 261–263; as ritual, 263; of commoners, 263. *See also* Beauty; Women

Foreign policy (Song), 2, 8, 50, 51, 54, 65, 85–87, 92, 99, 233, 235, 278; coexistence policy, 2, 28, 29, 45–48, 76–80, 278; Jin and, 8, 46, 65, 66–70, 76–80, 84, 86, 238; Liao and, 28, 32, 44–47, 52, 65; Mongols, and, 87–89, 92; Xi Xia and, 28, 51–53, 59. *See also* Treaties; Tributes; War

Forensics, 182, 183

Four Books, 104, 129

Four Scholars at Su Shi's Gate (*Su men si xueshi*), 163

Fu Bi, 53

Funerary practices, 111, 113, 138, 144, 148–157, 277; Buddhist influence, 149; burial as ritual, 138, 149, 157; commoners, 149–150, 275; cremation, 151, 155, 157, 275; Daoist influence, 149; human sacrifice, 156; Jin, 157, 159; large-scale burials, 150; Liao, 155–158, 177–178; mercy gardens, 150; timeliness of, 152; tomb art, 177–180, 258. *See also* Tombs

Gaozong, Emperor (Zhao Gou): abdication, 84; Hangzhou and, 205; Jin and, 69–70, 76–78; pragmatism of, 77; tenure of, 76

Gardens, 39, 65–66, 219, 252, 253, 269

Gender, 139, 146, 166

Genghis Khan. *See* Chinggis Khan

Gold, 14, 88, 89, 111, 202, 230, 232, 249, 261; as tribute, 67, 68; clothing, 262, 264, 265–266, 268; compared to silver, 231–232; dowry, 145; funerary rites, 153, 155, 157; in art, 173, 176; marriage and, 141, 143, 145; mines, 231, 232; money and, 232, 235, 243, 271, 274; taxes, 231, 247; value, 243; wares, 203, 210, 211, 254–255

Gongdi, Emperor (Zhao Xian), 97

Gonsu, 23, 27, 50, 227

Great families. *See* Aristocracy

Great Learning (Daxue), 101, 129

Great Liao dynasty. *See* Liao dynasty

Green Sprouts program, 55–56

Gresham's Law, 240

Guangzong, Emperor (Zhao Dun), 84

Gu Hongzhong, 173

Guilds, 58, 207, 209–10, 257, 268, 272, 278

Guo Wei (Later Zhou Emperor Taizu), 19

Guo Zhongshu, 222

Guwen style prose, 130–133

Hairstyles, 50, 257–258

Han Chinese, 4, 20, 21, 25, 26, 147, 155, 156, 157, 205, 267; cultural traditions, 42; identity, 1, 5, 9, 159; Mongols and, 89, 91, 94; population, 75, 80, 204

Han dynasty, 2, 5, 26, 41, 46, 70, 130, 153, 156, 177, 222, 233, 239

Hangzhou, 96–97, 128, 150, 205–212, 218, 255, 279; as Song capital, 65–66; 76, 79; as "temporary residence," 205–212; canal system, 228; compared to other capitals, 211–212; cosmology and, 205; economic activity, 209–211, 218; 237, 257, 265, 270, 274, 279; entertainment, 269–271; family businesses, 210–211; festivals, 268–269; homes in, 252–253; Imperial City, 206–207; Imperial University, 128; Medical School, 273; mercy gardens, 150; Mongols, 96–97; strategic location of, 205; urban life, 208, 209. See also Cities

Hanlin Academy, 169

Han Qi, 50, 53, 126, 129

Han River, 71, 74, 75, 227; Jurchen and, 85; Mongols and, 94, 95

Han Tuozhou, 84–86, 106

Han Xizai, 173, 175

Han Xizai's Night Revelry (Han Xizai yeyan tu), 173, 175, 176

Han Yu, 4, 5, 11, 106; Discourse on Teachers (Shi shuo), 131; literary style, 131–132; on Buddhism, 14; on hygiene, 257; on the Way (dao), 100

Hartman, Charles, 162

Hartwell, Robert M., 125, 193

Health care, 271–274

Heart Sutra, 111

History of the Great Jin Kingdom (Da Jinguo zhi), 157, 249

Homes, 251–255

Hong Mai, 44

Household registration, 74, 213, 215, 246. See also Taxes

Huai River, 14, 71, 72, 74, 81, 219; as border with Jin, 78, 86; canal, 199, 228

Huang Chao, 16–17, 19, 26

Huang Chouruo, 240

Huang Quan, 171–172

Huang Tingjian, 163

Huizi, 238–241. See also Money

Huizong, Emperor (Zhao Ji), 64–66, 68, 86, 126, 134, 195, 265; abdication, 67; as artist, 65, 173, 179; as poet, 69, 265; banishment of, 69–70; bureaucracy, 124;

collapse of Northern Song, 64–70; construction projects, 65; Daoism and, 65, 108, 276; death of, 77, 78; education and, 126; foreign policy, 65; health care and, 273; Jin and, 66, 69, 78; Kaifeng, 195; Liao and, 65; reform and, 64, 134; suppression of Buddhism, 108

Hu Yuan, 132

Hygiene, 256–257, 275

Idealist Neo-Confucian thought, 50, 102, 105, 132

Imperial Bodyguards, 19

Imperial City, 17, 67, 189, 191, 195, 202, 204, 206, 207

Imperially Reviewed Encyclopedia of the Grand Tranquility Reign (Taiping yulan), 41

Imperial Palace, 67, 173, 184, 195, 206, 207, 224, 252

Imperial University, 127–128

Industrial revolution: Song, 191; in Europe, 222, 279

Inequality, social, 4, 5, 30, 120, 125, 154, 189, 197, 211, 251–252; marriage and, 125, 141, 208

Inflation, 240, 241–243, 244

Iron, 2, 91, 182, 200, 208, 209, 231–232, 247; "iron cash," 234, 236, 240, 248; money and, 14, 66, 93, 230–243, 248–250, 255; mining, 278; value of, 231

Islam, 30, 90, 92, 94, 95, 279

Japan, 25, 95, 104, 191, 234

Jia Sidao, 86, 93–94, 96. See also Reforms

Jin dynasty, 2, 8, 46, 65, 66–70, 74–75, 76–91, 94, 95, 104, 111, 167–168, 186, 204, 205, 212, 219, 236, 238, 249; Aguda (Emperor Taizu), 63–64, 66–67, 69; Buddhism and, 114–118; capital cities, 204–205; Chinese influence on, 80–83; clothing, 268; commoners, 82; defeat by Mongols, 83, 87, 89, 93, 106, 186, 212; education, 80–81, 83; fiscal policy, 249–250; founding of, 61–70; funerary practices, 157, 159; Kaifeng, 86, 89, 204–205; marriage, 83, 146–148; poetry, 167; redistribution policies, 82; ritual and, 157; Song foreign policy toward, 8, 46, 65, 66–70, 76–80, 84, 86, 238; Song peace treaty (1142), 78, 81; war with Song, 66–68, 84–86, 238, 243; women, 146–148. See also under Jurchens

Jing Hao, 169

Jingzong, Liao Emperor (Yelü Xian), 148
Jingzong, Tangut Emperor (Li Yuanhao), 50
Jingzong, Tang Emperor (Li Zhan), 13
Jingzong, Tang Emperor (Li Zhu), 18
Jinshi degree, 25, 39, 53, 81, 82, 84, 98, 101, 103, 121–124, 128–132, 140, 162, 164
Jurchens, 8, 62–63, 75, 80, 82–83, 91, 94, 95, 117, 147, 157. *See also* Jin dynasty

Kaifeng, 44, 65, 70–79, 91, 107, 156, 207, 208, 211–212, 215, 226, 228, 242, 249, 252, 260, 270, 274, 279; administrative organization, 199; as Da Qi capital, 77; as new urban paradigm, 191–205; as Song capital, 8, 18, 31; astronomical clock in, 183–184; Bian River, 199–200; city expansion, 192–194; climate, 71–73; commercial activity, 194, 197; compared to other capitals, 211–212; fall of, 61, 67–68, 70, 74, 205; Jin and, 86, 89, 204–205; Later Jin capital, 23–24; layout, 199, 200, 202; migration and, 70–74; Mongols and, 91; population, 195, 196, 199; suburbs, 192, 193, 197; taxes, 199; ward system and, 192; Yellow River and, 191–192, 194, 199, 200, 212. *See also* Cities
Khitans, 20–24, 75, 82, 89, 94, 227, 249, 256; "Khitan" as ethnic designation, 22. *See also* Liao dynasty
Khubilai, 92, 94–95, 97
Khwarazm, Sultan Muhammad of, 90
Korea, 23, 62, 63, 91, 95, 104, 117, 234
Kou Zhun, 45–47
Kracke, E. A., 124, 125

Labor service, 3, 15, 210, 215, 216, 245, 249
Lament of the Lady of Qin (Qinfu yin), 17
Land ownership, 14, 16, 56, 71, 82, 93, 96, 154, 179, 192, 213–215, 252, 278. *See also* Agriculture; Aristocracy
Later Han dynasty, 18, 19. *See also* Five Dynasties
Later Jin dynasty, 18, 19, 23, 31, 65. *See also* Five Dynasties
Later Liang dynasty, 18, 20, 21, 31. *See also* Five Dynasties
Later Tang dynasty, 18, 19, 23, 192. *See also* Five Dynasties
Later Zhou dynasty, 15, 18, 19, 30, 31, 33, 57, 114. *See also* Five Dynasties
Law, 26, 50, 54, 80, 82, 92, 114, 188, 199;

alien regimes, 83, 146, 147, 157; Confucianism and, 3; cremation, 151; legal education, 56, 126, 127; marriage and, 139, 141; natural law, 103; patriarchy and, 138–139; property, 145–146, 192, 196; Public Field Law, 93, 96; scholar-officials, 136; sumptuary laws, 190, 191
Learning of the Way, 61, 85, 99–106, 133, 186, 279
Lending, 56, 233, 243. *See also* Money
Liao dynasty 19–28, 30, 34, 35, 44–46, 52, 54, 78, 80, 83, 168, 184, 236; architecture, 117, 204; Buddhism and, 114–118; capital cities, 204–205, 212; Chinese influence on, 22–23, 25–26, 61; clothing, 265–268; commoners, 147; Confucianism and, 22, 61; decline of, 61–66; education, 61; fiscal policy, 249–250; foreign policy, 23, 25, 62–64; funerary practices, 155–158, 177–178; marriage, 146–147; sacrifice and, 23, 115, 146, 156; Song foreign policy toward, 28, 32, 44–47, 52, 65; Song peace treaties, 25, 28, 45–47, 65, 78, 148; war with Song, 25, 26, 34, 45, 148. *See also* Khitans
Li (Principle), 87, 102–104, 105, 111, 180, 277
Li Ao, 228
Li Bai, 161
Li Cheng, 169
Li Cunxu (Later Tang Emperor Zhuangzong), 19
Li Fang, 41
Li Gou, 50, 51, 128
Li Jie, 127
Li Keyong, 17, 19
Li Qingzhao, 76, 143–144, 164, 166, 230
Li Siyuan (Later Tang Emperor Mingzong), 19
Literary Writings of Ouyang Xiu (Jushi ji), 132
Literature, 23, 40–42, 130, 140, 149, 160, 163, 182, 270, 277. *See also* Poetry
Liu Jin, 34, 35
Liu Yong, 164, 165
Liu Zongyuan, 244–245
Li Yu, 164
Lizong, Emperor (Zhao Yun), 87, 94, 98, 106, 277, 283
Lü Gongzhu, 58, 59; on emperor's behavior, 10, 44
Lu Jiuyuan, 102, 105
Luo Congyan, 46
Luoyang, 5, 16, 18, 19, 31, 56, 156, 191, 192, 253. *See also* Cities

Luo Ye, 5
Lü Yijian, 51, 53
Lu You, 143, 208, 229, 248, 253
Lü Zuqian, 103
Lyrics, song, 160; 163–166

Manchuria, 4, 23–25, 62, 69, 83, 89
Mandate of Heaven, 10, 31, 96, 97
Markets, 3, 25, 51, 211; technology and
    creation of new markets, 278; urban,
    189–191, 196, 203, 207–209; rice, 218
Marriage, 110, 111, 136, 138–148, 157,
    263, 274; age of, 139–140; class differ-
    ences, 125, 141, 208; divorce, 139, 143,
    145, 148; intermarriage, 83, 146–147,
    157; Khitan and Jurchen, 146–148, 157;
    Meaning of Marriage (Hunyi), 139;
    Mongol invasion and, 146; monogamy,
    139; Neo-Confucianism and, 143; re-
    marriage, 139, 145; social and economic
    functions, 125, 139–141, 157, 208;
    Tang, 140, 141, 143. See also Women
Material force (qi). See Qi
Mats, 34, 128, 252, 253–254; as measure
    of room size, 253, as organizing object
    for households, 253; shift to chairs, 176
Ma Yuan, 171
Medicine, 23, 65, 114, 182, 186, 203, 211,
    272–274; medical education, 273; On
    Medicine (Yishuo), 114
Meditation Buddhism, 109–110, 117, 118
Mei Yaochen, 162, 264
Mencius, 101, 102, 103
Merchants, 2, 3, 58, 120, 121, 122, 154,
    189, 190, 193, 197, 226, 236; agricul-
    tural, 218–219; in Hangzhou, 205–209;
    lifestyle, 251, 256, 271, 279; marriage
    and, 125, 140; merchant organizations,
    37; money and, 239–241; taxes on, 93,
    247–248; tea merchants, 219–220
Mercy gardens, 150
Metal. See Precious metal
Migration. See under Southern Song
Military (Song), 1, 2, 18, 26, 27, 32, 33–
    35, 45, 50, 126–127, 133, 134, 192,
    238, 245; as subordinate to civil, 2, 29,
    31, 33, 78, 80–81, 121; expenses, 45,
    49, 50, 54, 56, 95, 214, 247; military
    governors, 12, 18, 28, 31, 33, 62, 76–78,
    94, 191; Palace Army, 12, 16, 19, 30, 33;
    reform, 33, 49–51, 55–59, 130; size of,
    59; weakness of, 4, 8–9, 27, 28, 46, 55,
    57, 67, 68, 80, 85, 95, 96. See also For-
    eign policy (Song); War
Militia Act, 56–58

Mingzong, Later Tang Emperor (Li
    Siyuan), 19
Mining, 230–232, 278
Mobility, social, 124–125, 139–140, 208;
    family connections and, 39–40, 125
Monasteries, 108–109, 169, 189, 272, 274
Money, 233–244, 278; alien regimes and,
    81, 249–250; Bureau for Exchange Bills,
    236; confidence, 239; counterfeit, 241;
    exchange bills, 236–239, 248; foreign
    policy and, 235–236; inflation, 240,
    241–243, 244; lending, 56, 233, 243; li-
    quidity, 237; paper currency, 234–238;
    scholar's views of, 234, 235; Tang, 233,
    239, 243. See also Fiscal policy; Taxes;
    Tributes
Möngke, 92
Mongols, 22, 23, 28, 75, 87–98, 104, 227,
    275; as herders, 87, 88; Chinese influ-
    ence, 106; Chinggis (Genghis) Khan, 87–
    92; defeat of Jin, 83, 87, 89, 93, 106,
    186, 212; defeat of Song, 94–98, 146,
    242, 278; defeat of Xi Xia, 87, 89, 91;
    gender relations and, 146; human sacri-
    fice, 156; Khubilai, 92, 94–95, 97; mili-
    tary/tribal structure, 88–89; money and,
    234, 238, 241; Ögödei, 90–92; reputa-
    tion as monsters, 90; Song foreign policy
    toward, 87–89, 92
Mongol Yuan dynasty, 8, 104, 241
Monopoly commodities, 209, 220, 238,
    246, 248, 270; price of, 242
Movable-type printing, 43, 161; as predat-
    ing Gutenberg's invention, 183
Mukhali, 89
Music, 23, 137, 202; as elite pastime, 269–
    270; as urban entertainment, 191, 271;
    Bureau of Imperial Music, 202; court
    music, 65, 80; Neo-Confucianism and,
    132, 143, 277; song lyrics and, 163–164;
    women and, 143
Muzong, Tang Emperor (Li Heng), 13

Nanjing, 35, 45, 59, 96, 150, 171, 172,
    173, 218
Needham, Joseph, 161, 184
Neo-Confucianism, 30, 99–106, 154; an-
    cestor worship, 30, 111–113, 138–139,
    146, 157, 187, 253; as state ideology,
    119; Buddhism and, 99–101, 104, 109–
    112, 118–119, 130, 276–277; civil prin-
    ciple (wen), 29, 31, 32–33, 43–44; Con-
    fucian ideals, 29, 31, 32, 43, 54, 66, 104,
    110, 130, 144, 145, 149, 154, 164, 188,
    204, 207, 211, 215, 262, 263;

Neo-Confucianism *(continued)*
Confucianism and Neo-Confucianism compared, 29–30, 99–100; "Confucian state" defined, 29; conservative thought, 50, 53, 54, 61, 186, 253; criticisms of, 105, 277; Daoism and, 99–101, 104, 106–108, 111, 118, 276–277; denouncement of war, 8; education and, 3, 8, 9, 11, 30, 42, 104–105, 120, 124, 131, 137, 161, 273, 276, 277, 279–280; filial piety, 29, 98, 111, 112, 113–114, 142, 143, 148, 153, 155, 157, 179, 274; idealist thought, 50, 102, 105, 132; ideals regarding cities, 188, 204, 207; law and, 3; Learning of the Way, 61, 85, 99–106, 133, 186, 279; marriage and, 143; music and, 132, 143, 277; patrilineality and, 145; School of Mind, 102, 105; scientific achievements and, 43, 102, 183, 186; social elites and, 29, 99, 119; suicide and, 97; Systematic Confucianism, 102, 103–106; Taoism and, 99, 101; Three Doctrines, 99, 111, 276; women and, 113, 143, 144, 195, 196, 262–263. *See also* Ritual

New Design for an Armillary Clock (Xin yixiang fayao), 184

Ningzong, Emperor (Zhao Kuo), 84, 85, 87

North China, 24, 44, 49, 65, 69, 70, 75–76, 154, 191, 205, 221; agriculture, 217, 219; as site for capital, 194; climate, 71; Han Chinese in, 75; loss to Jin, 104; road network, 224–226, 227; shipyards, 230

Northern Han kingdom, 30, 34, 35

Northern Song, 94, 117, 122, 123–124, 134, 140, 156, 167, 193, 195, 209, 212, 214, 225, 231, 234, 252, 253, 263, 273–274, 279; collapse of, 61, 64–70, 71, 74–75, 80, 238, 242, 243, 247, 277; money in, 238, 239, 242–243; taxes in, 242–250

Notes on the Yili by Master Sima (Sima shi shuyi), 149

Notes Taken in Mengqi (Mengqi bitan), 183

Numerology, 100, 188–189

Ögödei, 90–92
On Factions (Pengdang lung), 53, 207
On the Difficulty of Being a Ruler (Wei jun nan lun), 36–37
Ouyang Jiong, 164

Ouyang Xiu, 53, 54, 55, 125, 165–166, 207; as poet, 162, 164; compared to Han Yu, 132; education and, 126; literary style and, 129, 132; on advising the emperor, 36–37; on Buddhism, 110; on burial rites, 149; on compulsory labor, 245; *On Factions (Pengdang lung)*, 53; *On the Difficulty of Being a Ruler (Wei jun nan lun)*, 36–37; on the Five Dynasties, 19–20; *On Factions (Pengdang lun)*, 53, 207; reputation as man of principle, 165; slander of, 165–166; Su Shi's works about, 54, 132

Palace Army, 12, 16, 19, 30, 33

Painting, 110, 137, 160, 164, 222, 264, 271, 277; architectural painters, 222; as communication, 168; Confucianism and Daoism, 177; landscapes, 169–171; murals, 168; new subjects, 173–177; realism in, 162, 171–172; Tang, 169, 171, 173, 176; tomb art, 177–180, 258

Parallel-prose style, 129, 130, 132

Patriarchy, 138, 148

Patrilineality, 145, 148

Peasants, 14, 16, 18, 51, 71, 232, 256. *See also* Commoners

Ploughing Ox (Gengniu), 162

Poetry, 4, 56, 137, 143, 160, 161–168, 271; gender and, 166; Jin dynasty, 167; patriotism and, 167; politics and, 165–166; regulated verse, 162–163; romantic, 166; Tang, 161, 162, 163, 164; Xikun-style, 162

Polo, Marco, 22, 207, 243

Population, 71, 74–75, 122, 125, 195, 204, 217, 273; Han Chinese, 75, 80, 204; increase in, 199, 278; north China, 228; overpopulation, 205; rural, 214–215, 251; Southern Song, 73–74; under-populated areas, 216; urban, 191, 204, 205, 207, 247; Xi Xia, 50

Pragmatism, 2, 8, 28, 30, 54, 56, 77, 119, 276, 278

Precious metal, 230–236, 249; as payment, 91, 249, 255; coins, 14, 230, 233; confiscation of Buddhist metal, 14–15; demand for, 234, 255; hoarding of, 255; housewares, 255, 265; in funerary rites, 155; metalist doctrine, 233; metallurgical technologies, 203; mines, 231; monetary policy and, 236; value of, 233, 235, 243. *See also specific metals*

Prices, 58, 238, 270; food, 93; impact of

printing technology on, 42, 43; iron, 231; monopoly commodities, 242; price fixing, 209; property, 192; rice, 218–219, 242–243; silk, 242–243, 247. *See also* Inflation

Prince Liang of Hailing (Wanyan Liang), 81

Principle (*li*). *See Li*

Printing, 278; as replacement for handwritten texts, 3, 42; impact on prices, 42, 43; money, 234, 237, 241; publications and, 40–43; technology of, 161, 183. *See also* Scientific achievements

Property: of emperor, 213, 214; marriage and, 140; prices, 192, 243; property rights, 145–146, 192, 196, 213; renting, 197; seizure of, 16, 41, 62, 127; taxation, 58, 247; urban, 192, 194, 197, 247; women, 145–146, 196. *See also* Land ownership

Prose: Ancient Prose Movement, 130–133; *Anthology of Rhyme Prose (Wenxuan)*, 40, 41; as part of civil service examination, 129–133; emotions in, 160; *guwen* style, 130–133; masters of, 132, 133; parallel-prose style, 129, 130, 132; popular, 118. *See also* Classics; Literature; Poetry

Prostitution, 63, 69, 190, 202, 203, 271

Protection appointments, 52, 124, 125, 134

Public Field Law, 93, 96

Pure Land Buddhism, 109–110, 115

Qi (material force), 101, 102, 103, 104, 111–112

Qin dynasty, 2, 224, 233

Qingli reforms, 52

Qin Gui, 78, 84, 86

Qinzong, Emperor (Zhao Huan): abdication and banishment, 68–69, 70; Jin and, 68, 69, 78, 249

Rationalism, 3, 99, 100, 102–103, 118, 187, 197, 276, 277, 279

Recorded Conversations of the Chan Masters (Yulu), 118

Record of Rites (Liji), 102, 139, 149

Record of the Blue Riff (Biyan lu), 118

Record of the World during the Grand Tranquility Reign (Taiping huanyu ji), 41

Records Following Emperor Yao (Zun Yao lu), 46

Reflections on Things at Hand (Jinsi lu), 103, 104, 171

Reform, 1, 2, 12, 36, 49–64, 68, 96, 130, 133–134, 136, 199, 231, 277; antireformers, 54, 58–61, 64, 163, 186; early "minor" reforms (Fan Zhongyan), 49–53; economic, 55–56, 58, 93, 96, 224, 237–238, 241, 244; education, 54, 56, 126–127, 129–130, 277; Green Sprouts program, 55–56; "major" reforms (Wang Anshi), 49, 53–61, 94, 121, 127, 130, 237; military, 33, 49–51, 55–59, 130; Militia Act, 56–58; monetary, 2, 93, 241; reforms of Jia Sidao (1263–1275), 86, 93–94, 96; Service Exemption Act, 56, 58; tax reform, 14, 58, 214, 232. *See also* Fan Zhongyan; Jia Sidao; Wang Anshi

Regionalism, 5

Reincarnation, 112

Renzong, Emperor (Zhao Zhen), 40, 49, 50–55, 121; as virtuous ruler, 54; medicine and, 273; posthumous title, 277

Reply to Wang Anshi, Former Chief Councilor, 162–163

Rice, 87, 94, 135, 205, 209, 214; 270; cultivation, 214, 217–219, 227; farmers, 218; price of, 218–219, 242–243; taxes, 230; trade, 228, 230–231

Ritual, 5, 8, 30 41, 79, 104, 138, 260, 277; ancestor worship, 30, 111–113, 138–139, 142, 146, 151, 155, 157, 187, 252, 253; Buddhism and Daoism, 108, 111, 149; burial as ritual, 138, 149, 157; court ritual, 65; emperors and, 10, 29, 30, 44, 47, 49, 123, 206; family rituals, 104, 149, 252; foot binding, 263; marriage as ritual, 138, 139, 141, 142, 147; ritual robes, 165; ritual vessels, 68; sacrifice, 30, 47, 112–115, 138, 142, 149, 156, 187, 202

Roads, 224–227

Russia, 62, 91, 92, 186, 234

Sacrifice, 187, 202; ancestor worship and, 54, 112–114, 142, 146, 252; Buddhism and, 15; burial and, 149; Court of Imperial Sacrifices, 202; *fengshan* sacrifices, 47; human sacrifice, 156; Khitan, 23, 115, 146, 156; sacrificial rites of the four seasons, 138; state sacrifices, 30, 47. *See also* Ritual

Sagacious Virtue of the Emperor of the Yuanhe Period (Yuanhe shengde shi), 11

Salt, 17, 183, 209, 219, 238, 247, 271; as payment, 134; burial practices, 155; monopoly, 238, 242, 246, 248; trade, 16, 51

Sargent, Stuart H., 163

Scholar-officials, 1–4, 9, 20, 36, 37–40, 52, 61, 82–83, 84, 120–121, 138, 140, 159, 186, 208, 227, 276, 279–280; artistic endeavors, 160; artistic representations of, 179; as elites, 40; attitudes toward alien regimes, 26, 68; Buddhism and, 106, 108, 110, 113, 118; career patterns, 133–134; clothing, 264; economic activities, 197; emergence of, 37, 39; family connections, 39–40, 125; healthcare and, 272; lifestyle, 254, 255, 261, 264; money, views of, 234–235, 237, 244; personal travel, 227; privileges of, 136; salaries, 134–136; tombs of, 152–155, 179. See also Education; Civil service examination

School of Mind, 102, 105

Scientific achievements, 102, 161, 180–186, 277, 279; astronomical clock, 183–186; astronomy, 182, 186; cartography, 183, 186, 224; compass, 161, 182; Confucianism and, 43, 102, 183, 186; diffusion of, 182, 279; firearms, 161; forensics, 182, 183; in Europe, 183, 186; movable-type printing, 43, 161, 183

Scrolls: books as replacement for, 3; depictions of production, 220–222; in teashops, 271; painting on, 35, 168–170, 172, 173, 176; production of, 210

Secret History of the Mongols, 88

Secularization, 186, 279

Self-managing farmers, 3, 213–216, 232, 246, 247, 278

Service Exemption Act, 56, 58

Seven Classics (Qijing), 42

Shaanxi, 51, 53, 72, 89, 91, 227, 231, 240

Shangjing, 22, 62, 81

Shanyuan Treaty. See under Foreign policy

Shao Yong, 5, 100–101, 160; on Song rule, 31, 278. See also Neo-Confucianism

Shen Gua, 43, 171, 182–183, 263

Shenzong, Emperor (Zhao Xu), 44, 64; Buddhism and, 108; death of, 59; military expenditures, 50; monetary policy, 237; reform and, 49, 50, 55–59, 121; Song calendar, 184; views of military, 57; Wang Anshi appointment, 55; war with Xi Xia, 59

Shi Jie, 111, 132

Shi Miyuan, 86–87, 106

Shipbuilding, 230

Shizong, Emperor (Later Zhou), 15, 30, 114, 192

Shizong, Jin Emperor (Wanyan Yong), 81–84

Shizong, Liao Emperor (Yelü Ruan), 147

Sichuan, 164, 227, 231, 235, 270; as safe area, 17, 45, 227; farm wages, 242; hygiene, 237; Jin and, 85–87, kingdoms in, 2; Later Shu, 34, 40; money in, 235, 236, 239; Mongols, 91, 92; political unification and, 34; precious metals, 231, 235, 235; printing, 40–41, 43; shipyards, 230; Tanguts and, 26; tombs, 152

Silk, 21, 25, 28, 144, 162, 202, 210, 228, 249, 257, 260; art and, 168, 170, 172, 174, 176, 179, 181; as dowry, 141, 145; as payment, 28, 45–46, 53, 66–68, 78, 86, 88, 89, 134, 136, 233, 234, 237, 245, 246–247, 249–250; clothing, 264–266, 268; foot binding, 261–262; home furnishings; 253–254; price of, 242–243, 247; production of, 52, 220–222, 278. See also Textiles; Silk Road

Silk Road, 90, 190, 232, 279

Silver, 14, 88, 115, 148, 183, 230, 254; as payment, 25–46, 53, 66–68, 78, 86; clothing, 261, 264, 266; compared to gold, 231–232; donations to Buddhist institutions, 115, 118; dowry, 145; in funerary rites, 155; mines, 231; money and, 233, 235, 243, 249–250; production, 231–232; taxes, 231, 246, 248; value of, 233, 235, 240, 243; wares, 203, 210, 211, 254, 255

Sima Guang, 59, 101, 253; as antireformer, 54, 56, 59–60; Notes on the Yili by Master Sima (Sima shi shuyi), 149; on burial, 149, 151; on Feng Dao, 41; on health, 272; on hygiene, 256; on ritual, 49, 104, 141, 149, 151, 152; on the emperor, 10; on women, 143, 144, 145, 196

Sivin, Nathan, 161, 183

Sketches of Precious Creatures (Xie sheng zhenqin), 172

Social elites, 3–4, 5, 15, 25, 30, 37, 40, 99, 127, 140, 189, 191, 255, 256, 276; aesthetic tastes, 254, 264–267; art, 168, 179; as catalysts for secularization, 186, 279; as civil servants, 3, 32, 122, 124, 136, 276; attitudes toward printing, 43; Buddhism and, 118; business activities, 197; charity, 275; clothing, 263–266;

Confucianism and, 29, 99, 119; criticism of, 162; definition of "elite," 120; entertainment, 269–270; family ties, 136; foot binding, 196, 261–263; funerary practices, 149, 153–154, 179; homes, 251–255; ideal man and woman, 168, 262, 263; intellectualism, 120; marriage, 125, 140; medicine and, 272–273; migration of elite families, 71; privileges of, 120, 134–136; ritual, 104, 252; Tang dynasty, 10, 15, 49, 69, 140; women, 140–146, 196, 255, 258, 262. *See also* Aristocracy; Land ownership; Scholar-officials

Song Ci, 182

Song dynasty: achievements, 1, 5, 8–9, 31, 278; as "Confucian state," 29–30; as meritocracy, 124, 135, 153; centralization of state authority, 2, 5, 36–40, 56; decline of, 84, 92–98; efficiency, 25, 32, 38, 51, 52, 56, 81, 137, 150, 199, 209, 213, 216, 228, 231, 245, 276, 279; founding, 20, 30–32; Han, compared, 2, 5, 46, 70, 130, 156, 222, 233, 239; stability of, 8, 277; unification of, 32–36. *See also* Foreign policy; Military; Neo-Confucianism; War

Southern Song, 8, 32, 38, 61, 66, 70, 128, 140, 141, 167, 171, 205–207, 209, 227, 255, 261, 262, 265, 269, 274, 279; bureaucracy in, 123–124, 134; decline of, 84, 92–98; establishment of, 70; migration patterns, 70–75; money and, 233, 234, 242, 248; Mongol defeat of, 94–98, 146, 242, 278; population, 73–74; relations with Jin, 76–80, 238. *See also* Northern Song; Song Dynasty

State Finance Commission, 38, 44

Suburbs, 192–194, 197, 199, 212. *See also* Cities

Su Che, 226

Sui dynasty, 2

Sumptuary laws, 190, 191

Sungari River, 62, 63

Su Shi, 252, 274; *Complete Works of Ouyang Xiu (Jushi ji)*, 54, 132; literary style and, 130, 132, 162, 163; on Kaifeng, 203; on printing, 42; on reform, 54; poetry, 162; *Reply to Wang Anshi, Former Chief Councilor*, 162–163

Su Song, 184, 186

Sutra of Parental Love (Fumu enzhong jing), 113

Systematic Confucianism, 102, 103–106

Taizong, Emperor (Zhao Kuangyi), 2, 27, 33–42, 44, 107–108, 224; as exemplary ruler, 2, 29; centralization of state authority, 36–40

Taizong, Jin Emperor (Wanyan Wuqimai), 64, 67

Taizong, Liao Emperor (Yelü Deguang), 23–24

Taizu, Emperor (Zhao Kuangyin), 2, 19, 36–37, 40, 41, 57, 64, 127, 133, 135, 194, 224, 252; as exemplary ruler, 2, 29, 30–36; Buddhism and, 108; military vs. civil rule, 32, 78, 87; Song unification, 32–36

Taizu, Jin Emperor (Wanyan Aguda), 63–64, 66–67, 69

Taizu, Liao Emperor (Yelü Abaoji), 20–23, 148, 156

Talks While the Plough is Resting (Chuogeng lu), 17, 261

Tang dynasty, 1–5, 28, 41, 57, 59, 71–72, 209, 214, 225, 227; architecture, 118; banditry, 15–18; Buddhism and Daoism, 13–15, 106, 107, 113, 117, 118; bureaucracy, 133, 134, 135; Chang'an as capital, 16–18, 187, 191, 227; clothing, 264, 265, 266, 268; compared to Song, 36–38, 39, 45, 46, 47, 49, 58, 65, 248, 254, 276, 279; cosmetics, 257, 260; decline of, 10–18, 26, 191; education and, 120, 121, 124, 129, 130, 132, 160; foot binding, 261, 262, 263; homes, 251, 254, 255; marriage, 140, 141, 143; money and, 233, 239, 243; painting, 169, 171, 173, 176; poetry, 161, 162, 163, 164; taxes, 244, 245, 246, 248, 249; tombs, 152, 153–154, 156, 159, 176, 177, 178, 179–180

Tanguts, 20, 23, 26–27, 50, 51, 249. *See also* Xi Xia dynasty

Tattooing, 260–261

Taxes, 2, 3, 4, 12, 14, 34, 48, 55–56, 58, 78, 93, 109, 115, 136, 213–220, 231, 233, 242–250, 265, 278; alien regimes and, 249–250; cities and, 189, 196, 199, 209, 248; evasion, 93, 248; in-cash vs. in-kind, 3, 218, 244, 245, 246–247; money and, 239, 240; reform, 14, 58, 214, 232; revenues, 45, 49, 50, 93, 245–246, 248; Tang, 244, 245, 246, 248, 249; tax burden, 15–16, 71, 246–249; trade, 247. *See also* Labor service

Tax households, 214–216, 232. *See also* Self-managing farmers; Taxes

Tea, 177, 228, 238, 242, 255, 271; as payment, 28, 53, commoners and, 220; monopoly, 209, 220, 238, 242, 246; taxes on, 209; teahouses, 203, 270, 271; tea merchants, 219–220
Technology. *See* Scientific achievements
Ten Kingdoms, 4, 18, 34
Ten Thousand Word Memorial (Wanyan shu), 54
Textiles, 2, 21, 179, 196, 209, 265; as payment, 244, 246; production, 2, 210, 213, 220–222, 278. *See also* Silk
Thirteen Classics (*Shisanjing*), 42
Three Doctrines, 99, 111, 276
Toiletries, 256–258
Tomb art, 177–180, 258
Tombs, 152–159, 169–169, 177–180, 258; as architecture, 157, 159, 177, 179–180; epitaphs, 149, 150, 152, 154, 180; scholar-officials and, 152–155, 179; Tang, 152, 153–154, 156, 159, 176, 177, 178, 179–180. *See also* Funerary practices
Tong Guan, 64, 68
Trade, 231, 238, 249, 251, 257, 275; 153 barter trade, 25, 232; economic reform and, 55; fruits and vegetables, 219; guilds, 58, 207, 209–210, 257, 268, 272, 278; rice, 218; salt, 16, 28; Silk Road, 90, 190, 232, 279; taxes, 247, trade centers, 28, 248; trade policy, 58; trade routes, 67, 279; urban, 191, 193, 205, 208–211
Transportation, personal, 196, 255–256
Travel, 65, 68, 69, 117, 123, 136, 150, 205, 218, 238; artistic representation of, 173, 176–177, 195, 197; as tomb painting theme, 177; conditions, 199, 224–230, 255–256; traveling merchants, 22, 218, 238, 241, 247
Travelers along the River in Early Snow, 176–177
Traveling up the River at Qingming Festival (*Qingming shanghe tu*), 195, 197, 198
Treaties: Jin peace treaty (1142), 78, 81; Liao peace treaty (1042), 28, 46; Shanyuan (Liao) treaty (1005), 25, 45–47, 65, 78, 148; Xi Xia peace treaty (1044), 28, 46, 53, 54. *See also* Foreign policy
Treatise on Architectural Methods (*Yingzao fashi*), 127

Tributes, 28, 47, 53, 66, 67, 78, 86, 236, 249, 250. *See also* Foreign policy; Treaties

Unification, political, 2, 31–37, 94, 233
Urban life. *See* Cities

Wages and earnings, 4, 20, 58, 82, 87, 135–136, 168, 176, 196, 204, 214, 215, 216, 242, 244, 270
Wang Anshi, 257; poetry, 162, 252; reforms, 49, 53–61, 94, 121, 127, 130, 237; Su Shi on, 162; Ten Thousand Word Memorial (Wanyan shu), 54
Wang Dan, 47
Wang Fu, 68
Wang Ling, 162
Wang Yinglin, 98
Wang Yucheng, 226
Wang Zhen, 43
Wanyan Kuang, 86
Wanyan Liang (Prince Liang of Hailing), 81
Wanyan Zongbi, 76, 78
War, 4, 54, 57, 108; Chinese unification and, 34; civil, 1, 8, 76, 92, 244; Confucian denouncement of, 8; economic impact, 240, 242–244; emperors' experience with, 43, 50; humane principles of, 33; impact on Chinese population, 75; Jin and, 66–68, 84–86, 238, 243; Liao and, 25, 26, 34, 45, 148; Mongols and, 88–98; Song preference for tributes over war, 8, 48, 66, 249; warlords, 11, 17–18, 31, 77, 94, 191; warriors, 23, 27, 80, 83, 179, 256; Xi Xia and, 27, 28, 58–59, 89, 242. *See also* Coexistence policy; Foreign policy
Ward system, 189–190, 192
Warlordism, 11, 17–18, 31, 77, 94, 191
Water mills, 222–224, 279
Way (*Dao*). *See* Dao
Wei Xian, 222
Wen Tianxiang, 96–98
Wen Tingyun, 164
Wenzong, Tang Emperor (Li Ang), 13
Wine, 33, 34, 134, 141, 143, 148, 167, 177, 208, 209, 242; wine shops, 190, 197, 202–203, 269–271
Women, 90, 97, 113, 118, 179, 253, 255, 256–260, 262; bathing habits, 257; chastity, 110, 146; clothing, 264–267; commodification of, 263; concubines,

139, 256, 263; education of, 125–126, 142–144; feminine ideal, 144, 262; hairstyles, 257–258; health care and, 272–273; Khitan and Jurchen, 146–148; marriage and, 138–142, 263; music and, 143; Neo-Confucianism and, 113, 143, 144, 195, 196, 262–263; property rights, 145–146; prostitution, 63, 69, 190, 202, 203, 271; sexual abuse, 63; toiletries, 257; urban life, 195–196, 271; widows, 112, 142, 145–146, 196. *See also* Beauty; Eroticism; Foot binding
Wuqimai, 64, 67
Wu Zetian, 39, 121
Wu Zhaoyi, 40–41
Wuzong, Tang Emperor (Li Yan), 13–15

Xenophobia, 5, 14, 20. *See also* Cultural attitudes
Xia Gui, 171
Xianzong, Tang Emperor (Li Chun), 11–14
Xiao clan, 24, 146, 156
Xiaozong, Emperor (Zhao Shen), 84, 105, 240, 277
Xikun-style poetry, 162
Xing Bing, 42
Xingzong, Liao Emperor (Yelü Zongzhen), 26, 61, 115
Xin Qiqi, 167
Xi Xia dynasty, 2, 20, 25, 26–29, 50–54, 64, 85, 236; defeat by Mongols, 87, 89, 91; economic situation, 249; founding, 50; Jin and, 68, 85; peace treaty with Song, 28, 46, 53, 54; populations, 50; Song foreign policy toward, 28, 51–53, 59; Song peace treaty, 28, 46, 53, 54; war with Song, 27, 28, 58–59, 89, 242. *See also* Tanguts
Xizong, Tang Emperor (Li Yan), 13, 16–18
Xuanzong, Jin Emperor (Wanyan Xun), 83, 89
Xuanzong, Tang Emperor (Li Shen), 13, 15, 47, 246
Xu Xi, 172

Yang Guanqing, 239
Yangzi River, 6, 16, 34, 76, 264, 270; agriculture near, 217; Battle of Caishi, 83; climate, 72; Jin and, 81, 85; Mongols, 92, 94–96; population, 74; travel conditions, 227–230
Yanjing, 81, 98
Yanshou, 109

Yan Yu, 162
Yellow River, 6, 50, 56; as strategic resource, 72–73; climate and, 72; Jin and, 67, 72–73, 83, Kaifeng and, 191–192, 194, 199, 200, 212; travel conditions, 226, 228–229
Yelü clan, 22, 24, 25, 26, 61–62, 146–147, 156
Ye Mengde, 42, 150
Ye Shi, 105, 235
Yingzong, Emperor (Zhao Shu), 55
Yizong, Tang Emperor (Li Cui), 13, 15
Yuan Menglao, 203
Yue Fei, 77–78, 84
Yue Shi, 41

Zhang Dun, 64, 186
Zhang Fangping, 121
Zhang Gao, 114
Zhang Shijie, 96–97
Zhang Zai, 100, 101, 106, 111–112
Zhang Zi, 252, 269
Zhangzong, Jin Emperor (Wanyan Jing), 83, 147, 176
Zhao Gan, 176
Zhao Pu, 33–35, 86, 252
Zhao Rugua, 136
Zhao Ruyu, 85
Zhaozong, Tang Emperor (Li Ye), 13, 18
Zheng Juzhong, 65
Zhenzong, Emperor (Zhao Heng), 28, 29, 34, 37, 40, 43–50, 108, 199, 202, 217, 226, 254, 254, 258; as exemplary ruler, 2, 29, 43; civil principle, 43–44; civil service examination, 39, 122; Daoism and, 173; foreign policy and, 2, 28, 44–46
Zhezong, Emperor (Zhao Xu), 59, 64, 184
Zhong Xiang, 77
Zhou, Madame, 257, 258, 262
Zhou Bridge, 200, 202
Zhou Dunyi, 100, 101, 106
Zhou dynasty, 18, 30, 36
Zhuangzong, Later Tang Emperor (Li Cunxu), 19
Zhu Mian, 66
Zhu Xi, 84–85, 87, 141; as creator of Systematic Confucianism, 102–106, 277; *Collected Commentaries on the Four Books* (*Sishu zhangju jizhu*), 104; compared to Confucius, 103; *Family Rituals* (*Jiali*), 104, 149, 252; on abolition of Buddhism and Daoism, 111; on burial, 151; on education, 126; on foreign

Zhu Xi *(continued)*
  policy, 8, 78; on printing, 42; on reform,
  55, 61; on rituals, 149, 151, 252; on
  Song rule, 31; on women, 145;
  Reflections on Things at Hand (Jinsi lu),
  103, 104, 171. *See also* Neo-Confucianism

Zhu Wen (Later Liang Emperor Taizu), 18–
  19, 191
Zhu Youzhen (Later Liang Emperor Modi),
  19